W9-CUU-963

incredible value

the official
hp guides

3 books in 1

- hp pavilion pcs made easy
- printing projects made fun & easy
- creating your own great dvds & cds

nancy stevenson • jan s. smith • mark l. chambers

PRENTICE HALL PTR

Prentice Hall PTR
Upper Saddle River, NJ 07458
www.phptr.com

ISBN 0-13-113296-2

92999

9 780131 132962

Acquisitions Editor: Jill Harry
Marketing Manager: Dan DePasquale
Buyer: Maura Zaldivar
Cover Design: Talar Boorujy
Cover Design Director: Jerry Votta
Art Director: Gail Cocker-Bogusz
Interior Design: Meg VanArsdale

© 2003 by Hewlett-Packard Company
Published by Pearson Education Inc.
Publishing as Prentice Hall PTR
Upper Saddle River, NJ 07458

PRENTICE
HALL
PTR

Prentice Hall books are widely used by corporations and government agencies for training, marketing, and resale.

For information regarding corporate and government bulk discounts, contact:

Corporate and Government Sales: (800) 382-3419 or corpsales@pearsontechgroup.com

All products mentioned herein are trademarks or registered trademarks of their respective owners.

Printed in the United States of America.

10 9 8 7 6 5 4 3 2

ISBN 0-13-113296-2

Pearson Education LTD.
Pearson Education Australia PTY, Limited
Pearson Education Singapore, Pte. Ltd.
Pearson Education North Asia Ltd.
Pearson Education Canada, Ltd.
Pearson Educación de Mexico, S.A. de C.V.
Pearson Education—Japan
Pearson Education Malaysia, Pte. Ltd.

Contents for
hp pavilion pcs
made easy

hp pavilion pcs

hp pavilion pcs

Contents for
printing projects
made fun & easy

printing projects

Contents for

creating your own great
dvds & cds

dvds & cds

dvds & cds

dvds & cds

dvds & cds

have fun with it!

hp pavilion pcs
made easy

the official hp guide

nancy stevenson

PRENTICE
HALL
PTR

Prentice Hall PTR
Upper Saddle River, NJ 07458
www.phptr.com

To my brother, Bill. Have a wonderful journey.

And to Liam Allard, who is just beginning.

Contents

Part 2

hp pavilion pcs

hp pavilion pcs

Preface

The world of computing today is a pretty magical one, filled with high-powered but easy to use hardware and software. Computers have broken out of offices and into homes in a big way, making possible all kinds of creative, fun, and productive activities, from designing multimedia greeting cards to managing your family's money.

All HP Pavilions come packed with the hardware and software any computer user needs, and most of it is pretty easy to use. But with so many features, a newer user just might need a guiding hand to get the most out of his or her computing experience. That's what this book is about: how to take full advantage of the tools your Pavilion has put at your fingertips.

How Is This Book Unique?

This book is like no other book on how to use a computer because it's written specifically for HP Pavilion users. You'll learn how to use HP's help system, as well as the software that comes preloaded on every Pavilion. You'll also get to know the basics of the Windows XP operating system which comes loaded on HP Pavilions, and learn how to get connected to the Internet.

Part 1 tells you how to get started setting up your Pavilion—connecting all the cables, turning the computer on, and getting an idea of what's on your computer.

Part 2 explores Windows™ XP, the operating system from Microsoft® that makes your Pavilion run. You'll learn how to get around the Windows desktop, manage the computer files you'll create as you work on your computer every day, and customize Windows and use Windows Accessories.

Part 3 is where you'll learn to use the software that comes with your Pavilion to write documents, create spreadsheets to calculate numbers, manage finances, and design presentations. You'll also learn to play games, and use multimedia software to generate greeting cards that talk, and compose songs.

Part 4 shows you how to get online, finding an Internet Service Provider to get an account if you don't already have one, and taking care of online security settings. Using the Internet Explorer browser you'll search for what you need online, and set up your home page. Finally, you will begin to e-mail all your friends, download file attachments, and organize your inbox.

Part 5 is where I cover some of the basics of upgrading your hardware, such as adding memory or replacing a disk drive. You shouldn't need to do this to your new computer for a long time, but when you do, refer to this section of the book.

Part 6 has only one chapter, and it covers the most up-to-date information on some new software that is included on the most recent Pavilion models.

Special Help

Along the way, I've included special elements to help you out:

 tip **Tips give you advice or tricks for getting things done faster and easier.**

caution **Cautions warn you about potential problems you might encounter as you go through a process or make changes to your computer.**

hp pavilion pcs

 note **Notes are little pieces of insight about a term or process or background information you may be interested in knowing.**

Projects are step-by-step procedures to accomplish something fun and useful with your Pavilion. When you finish a project, you'll have produced a document or set up something on your computer you can use right away.

1

Getting Started with Your HP Pavilion

The Box Is Open…Now What?

In this Chapter

✔ Understanding the parts of a computer

✔ Getting your computer, monitor, keyboard, speakers, and mouse hooked up

✔ Learning how surge protectors help keep your computer safe

✔ Getting help

When you get home with your new Hewlett-Packard (HP) Pavilion, you have a few things to do (although very few) to get up and running. You can get going so fast because HP has included tons of software you can start using right away, and because of something called plug and play.

Plug and play is a set of specifications that Microsoft and Intel came up with that automatically sets up your computer to work with peripherals. Do terms like peripherals make your head spin? Well, relax. You can consider this chapter your Personal Computer (PC) primer. You'll learn all about peripherals, plug and play, and what you need to get your new Pavilion going right out of the box.

PCs 101: The Parts of Your Computer

When you unpack your Pavilion you'll find several items, including hardware, software, and documentation to help you set up and use your computer. You'll find:

- *Central Processing Unit (CPU)*—This is the computer tower that holds the computer hard drive, which is where all the software and systems for the computer are stored.
- *Keyboard*—Hardware that attaches to your computer, such as a monitor, keyboard, or printer, is called a *peripheral*. A keyboard is an input device that allows you to enter text and move around software programs.
- *Mouse*—The mouse is a device that allows you to select and manipulate items in a software program.
- *Power cord*—The power cord connects the CPU to your power source.
- *Speakers*—Two speakers are provided to allow you to hear system sounds and audio files.
- *Modem/telephone cable*—In order to connect to the Internet or send faxes, you'll need to run this phone cord from your phone jack to your computer.

The Brains: The CPU

The computer tower that you'll find in your box is the brains of your computer. It's where software is installed and all the commands you give your computer through the keyboard or mouse are processed. The CPU is where you turn the computer on and off and where you insert floppy disks, CDs, and Digital Video Disks (DVDs) to run or make copies of computer files.

When you take the CPU out of the box and remove the packaging, find a good spot for it, either on your desk, some other computing surface, or on the floor by your desk. Keep in mind that a power source must be nearby. Unwrap the power cord, and plug the end without prongs into the back of your CPU (usually near the top of the tower).

Getting Stuff In: Keyboard and Mouse

Your keyboard and mouse are used to input data and to select and modify things in your operating system and in various software programs. Each has a cable coming out of it with a color-coded plug on the end. Hooking the keyboard and mouse up to your CPU is as simple as plugging the appropriate colored prong into the corresponding colored hole on the back of the CPU.

Seeing What You're Doing

You won't be able to do much on your computer if you don't have a monitor connected. You may have purchased a monitor as part of your HP Pavilion package, or you may be using a monitor from another manufacturer. It's easy to connect any monitor to your Pavilion.

tip **A Pavilion will work with just about any monitor, printer, mouse, and so on. However, HP consumer products are designed to work better together, so an HP monitor with an HP Pavilion CPU will be the most troublefree hardware combination for you.**

An HP monitor that comes with a Pavilion is color-coded to plug into a corresponding slot on your CPU. If you have a different monitor, don't worry. A little picture of a monitor is on the back of your computer so that you can easily spot the right place to plug it in. You must also connect your monitor to a power source using the power cord that comes with it.

Some monitors come with built-in speakers and sound controls. Most come with brightness and image controls. Check your manufacturer's documentation if you want to make any adjustments to your monitor, but most should work just fine out of the box.

Connecting to a Phone Line

If you're planning to connect to the Internet or to send faxes using a standard phone connection, you'll need to plug the phone cord that comes with your Pavilion into your phone jack. To be sure the jack is working properly, plug a standard phone into it first. If you get a dial tone, the jack is working. Plug one end of the phone cord into the wall jack and the other into the line connector on the back of your Pavilion. The line connector will either be labeled with the word "Line," or a jack symbol, or will be color-coded as red.

tip **If you are using a modem that offers a telephone line switch to access multiple phone lines, make sure the switch is set to 1.**

Starting and Turning Off Your Computer

Now that you've connected your mouse, keyboard, and monitor, go ahead and plug your computer into a power outlet. I recommend that you use a surge protector. Plug your computer into the surge protector and the surge protector into the wall. This protects your computer from damage in the event of a power surge. Now, you're ready to turn your computer on.

Turning Your Computer On

All HP Pavilions have a power button on the front of the CPU, although the exact location may differ somewhat. To start your computer, simply press the power button. It will take a few moments for the computer to start up.

The first time you use the computer you will be welcomed by an HP startup wizard, which will check to make sure the sound on your computer is working and that you are set up for the correct language, country, Internet connectivity, and time zone. When this wizard runs, you can even give your computer a name (which is helpful if you intend to have a few computers on a home network and need to refer to them in your network setup). When this routine is done, you'll click Finish, and Windows XP loads. This can take another few moments, during which time you'll hear your hard drive whirring. When Windows has loaded, you'll see the Windows desktop shown in Figure 1.1.

FIGURE 1.1   The Windows desktop is command central for your computer.

Breathing Life into Hardware: Windows XP

Windows XP is a kind of software program called an operating system. There are different kinds of operating systems, for example, the one that runs Macintosh computers and one called UNIX. Operating systems provide the tools for managing your computer systems and running other software. You can't really do anything with your computer without an operating system.

When you start your computer, after the computer loads all its system files (called booting up), which takes a few minutes, the Windows desktop shown in Figure 1.1 appears. This desktop holds shortcuts to software that is installed on your computer. HP has installed many software programs to get you going right out of the box, so you'll see several shortcuts the first time you turn your computer on. You can install other software programs, which you'll learn how to do in Chapter 6 of this book.

Besides the desktop, you'll use the commands on the Windows Start menu (see Figure 1.2) to get things done on your computer. You'll learn more about this menu and what the choices on it do in Chapter 4.

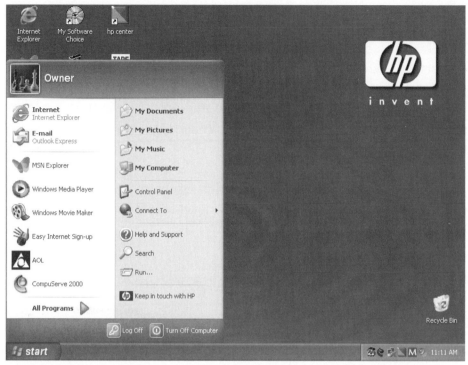

FIGURE 1.2   The Windows Start menu is the gateway to all the programs on your computer and features of Windows.

Get to Know Your Mouse and Keyboard

Your keyboard is what is called an input device. That means you use it to enter text into documents you create using a software program such as Corel WordPerfect. Your Pavilion keyboard is a sophisticated device, with several special function keys along the top. You'll read more about how these work in Chapter 3.

Your mouse is used to move around in documents and to select objects to move, copy, delete, or modify. Together your keyboard and mouse are the set of tools that you use to interact with your computer and documents.

Your mouse has three controls: the left button, right button, and scroll wheel button. The mouse also has a small roller ball on the bottom. When you place the mouse on a flat surface, you can move it around, rolling that ball and moving a corresponding icon called a *cursor* around your computer screen.

The left mouse button is used to select objects and to double-click on certain objects to initiate an action, such as opening up a dialog box to make formatting selections. The right mouse button is used to open shortcut menus. These menus have commands that initiate functions related to whatever you clicked on. When you use the right mouse button, it's called right-clicking, and, when you use the left mouse button, it's referred to simply as clicking.

The scroll wheel button in the middle of the mouse is used to scroll through a document, much as you drag a scrollbar in software programs to move a page or more at a time.

Adjust the Speaker Volume

The speakers that come with your HP Pavilion play sounds from your computer, including system sounds (sounds that occur when an event happens on your computer, such as closing a program), voice, and music.

You can control the volume of your speakers in a few ways:

- You can click the small icon of a speaker on your Windows taskbar, and a small volume control box opens up. Adjust the slider bar there up or down to raise or lower the volume, or click the Mute checkbox to temporarily stop sounds altogether.
- You can go to the Sounds and Audio Devices Properties dialog box from the Control Panel (Click Start, Control Panel, Sounds, Speech and Audio Devices) and adjust the Speaker Volume settings (see Figure 1.3).

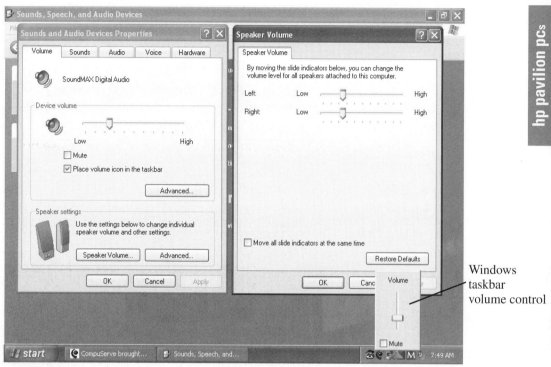

Windows taskbar volume control

FIGURE 1.3   You can control the left and right speakers with individual slide indicators in the Speaker Volume dialog box.

Finally, you can control the volume of specific devices, such as your music playback, with individual volume control settings from the same Control Panel dialog box (see Figure 1.4).

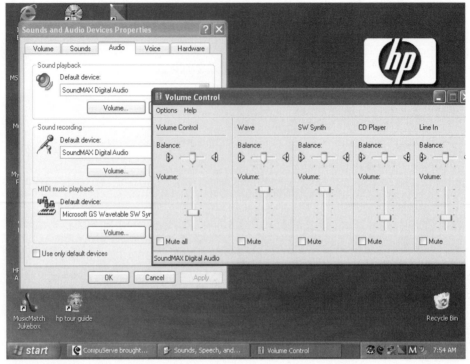

FIGURE 1.4   You can use these controls to make fine adjustments to individual playback devices.

Getting Help

As you begin to use your computer, there may be times when you'd like a little help. Well, you'll be glad to hear that HP provides a lot of help in its Help and Support Center, shown in Figure 1.5.

note The last chapter in this book, Troubleshooting, walks you through a problem-solving scenario using the Help and Support Center feature. Go there to appreciate the many ways you can find help using this invaluable tool.

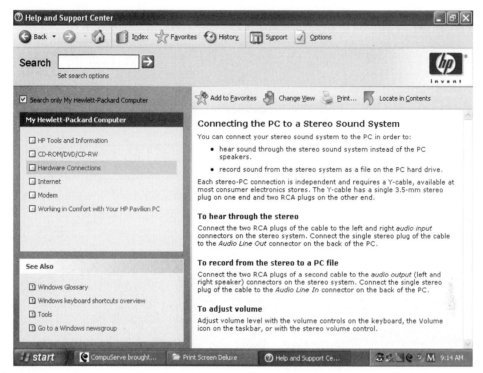

FIGURE 1.5   Access a treasure trove of help information and more from this center.

HP Help and Support Center

When you first start up your Pavilion, you might want to visit the My Hewlett Packard Computer section of the Help and Support Center. It provides information about the computer itself, as well as links to features such as a Windows Glossary of computer terminology and an overview of Windows keyboard shortcuts (combinations of keystrokes you can use to perform actions on your computer rather than using a menu or tool button).

✔ **Follow these steps to reach this and other topics:**

1. Select Start, Help and Support. The Help and Support Center shown in Figure 1.6 appears.

2. Click the My Hewlett Packard Computer link. The help feature for that category appears.

3. Click an item in the list on the left (see Figure 1.6). That topic opens in the pane on the right. If necessary, you can use the scrollbar in that pane to view more of the information.

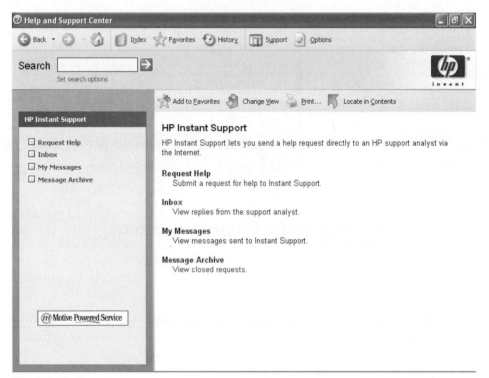

FIGURE 1.6   Each text item in blue on the left side links to additional information.

There are several other features of the Help system you can try:

- *Index*—Click the Index button to view a list of all Help topics (as shown in Figure 1.7). Type a word in the text box at the top of this list to locate an associated topic. As you type, the index narrows down to terms that match that text in the list.

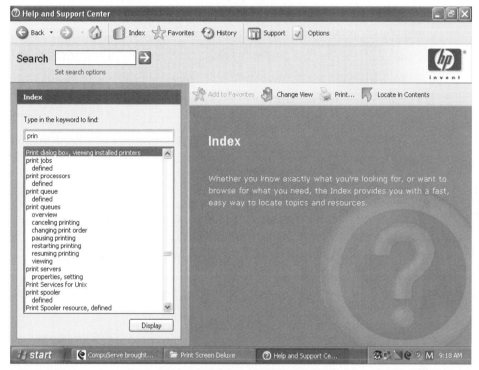

FIGURE 1.7   As you type a topic, a feature called QuickPick narrows down to words in the index that match.

- *Print*—Click the Print button to print the currently displayed topic.
- *Fixing a Problem*—This is a troubleshooting feature that walks you through possible fixes for the problem you're experiencing and sometimes runs tests of hardware settings.
- *Send Your Feedback to Microsoft*—Use this link to email Microsoft technical support about Windows-related problems.

- *Latest News*—This link appears when you are connected to the Internet. It offers links to online help resources.
- *Help and Support Resources*—If you are connected to the Internet, this link appears offering updates to the Windows XP software and tools, such as System Restore (a process that returns your computer to previous settings) and Remote Assistance to help with problems you haven't been able to solve in other ways.
- *Search*—Enter a topic or phrase in the Search box and click the arrow to find related help.
- *Support*—Click the Support button to see options for support, including asking a friend to help you by using the Internet, going to a Windows Web site and viewing information people have posted in a topic forum (an online bulletin board), or using HP Instant Support (more about that shortly).

note **The feature called Remote Assistance is explored in Chapter 19. Essentially, it is a way for somebody else to take charge of your computer remotely using the Internet. If you have a computer-savvy friend, this feature allows him or her to get onto your computer and fix a problem or make a setting for you using the Internet.**

HP Instant Support

One item in the Help and Support Center that's worth exploring is HP Instant Support. This feature allows you to access a live HP tech support person to help walk you through a procedure or to solve a problem. You communicate using instant messages you exchange across the Internet.

When you click HP Instant Support from the Help and Support Center, you'll see four possible actions, as shown in Figure 1.8.

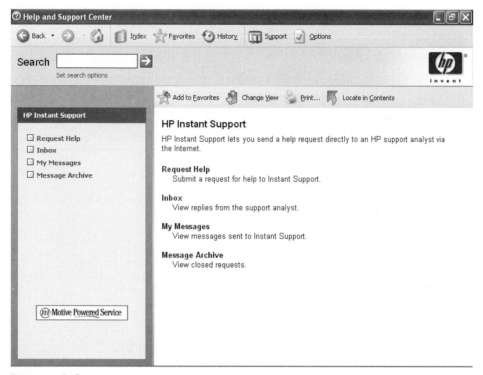

FIGURE 1.8 You can ask for help and track the various messages and responses here.

With the four items in the Instant Support area, you can do the following:

- Initiate a session with a tech support person by clicking Request Help.
- Open an inbox to see if you've received a response by clicking Inbox.
- Review the messages you've sent to Instant Support by clicking My Messages.
- View an archive of all messages and responses in the Message Archive.

When you request help, you'll soon be alerted that a response has been sent by a support person. Click your Inbox and then double-click the message to read it. If you want to respond, click Reply, enter your message, and then click Send. The discussion can go on for as many messages as it takes to get the help you need.

If you should leave Instant Support, for example, to try a procedure and reboot your computer and then need to get back in touch, just open your last message and add new comments. The tech support person who picks up your message will have information on your case available for review when you get in touch again.

When It's Time to Stop

When you've had enough fun playing around with your new Pavilion, you'll need to know how to turn the computer off. There are a couple of options here: placing the computer in a lower energy Standby mode or turning it off entirely.

Put Your Computer on Standby

If you intend to be away from your computer for a while, say to go to lunch, you have the option of putting the computer in Standby mode. Standby uses a lower energy setting, but, unlike when you turn your computer off, Standby keeps everything on your computer as you left it. Programs and documents stay open so that you can get right back to work when you return. You reactivate your computer by simply clicking your mouse button or striking a key on your keyboard.

✔ **To put your computer in Standby mode, follow these steps:**

1. Click Start, Turn Off Computer. The dialog box shown in Figure 1.9 appears.

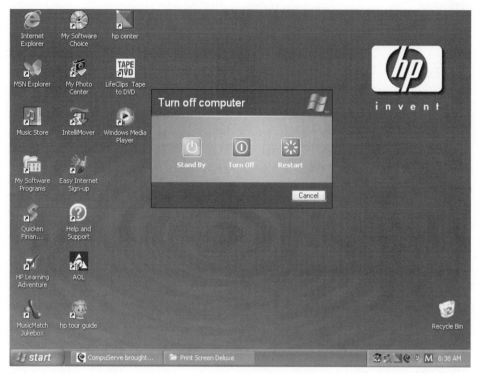

FIGURE 1.9   This is also the dialog box used to restart or turn off your computer.

2. Click the Stand By button. Your computer screen goes black.

3. To reactivate your computer, click your mouse button. A Windows screen appears.

4. Click Owner to log back into your computer.

Turning It Off

Turning your computer off shuts down all programs that are running. It's usually best for you to shut down programs yourself before turning the computer off so that you don't run the risk of losing any data.

You'll learn more about your choices when shutting down your computer in Chapter 3, but I don't want you to have to leave it on until you get there. Briefly, here's how you can turn your computer off:

1. Select Start, Turn Off Computer.

2. At the dialog box shown in Figure 1.9, click on Turn Off.

    That's it!

tip **If you crash, that is, if your computer freezes and won't accept mouse or keyboard commands anymore, you can try two things. Press Ctrl+Alt+Delete twice in succession. If nothing happens when you press Ctrl+Alt+Delete, you can turn your computer off by pressing and holding in the power button. You'll have to press the button again after it's shut down to start it up.**

Chapter Summary

In this chapter, you opened up the box and unpacked your Pavilion. You connected various peripherals and a phone line. You learned what the Windows XP operating system is and how you use it to control your computer settings.

You modified the speaker volume and learned to put your computer into Standby mode and to turn it off. Finally, you explored the HP Help and Support Center and learned how to initiate a live help session with HP Instant Support.

2

Setting Up Your Printer

In this Chapter

✔ Registering your Pavilion

✔ Connecting a printer to your Pavilion

✔ Setting your default printer

When you have finished connecting everything out of the box as you did in Chapter 1, your next step is to register your Pavilion as soon as possible. After that's done, you can get hooked up to a printer so that you can generate hard copies of documents, newsletters, emails, electronic tickets for airline reservations, and so forth.

Registering Your Pavilion and Windows XP

Registering your HP Pavilion is a very important step. After you're registered, HP can notify you of updates for your computer. Also, if you need to contact HP for support, the customer care person uses your registration information to assist you. HP can tell you about special offers if you're registered, and you can receive free newsletters with product information and tips.

note **HP respects your privacy. By registering with them, you do not run any risk that they will share your information with anybody else. They will share your information with HP partners to enable them to make special offers to you only if you give them permission. When you first use your computer, and periodically until you complete registration, a message appears asking you to register. You can register online if your modem is hooked up to a phone line and if you have an Internet account (if you don't, visit Part IV of this book to learn how to get one) by proceeding with the online registration when prompted or going to register.hp.com.**

note **Your Pavilion comes with a one-year warranty, but, when you register, you might also consider extending that warranty. You can pay to upgrade your warranty by calling 888-999-4747 or by visiting www.hp.com/go/hpsupportpack. An extended warranty protects your investment by covering you for three years and by providing toll-free technical support.**

Connecting a Printer

Guess what? The paperless office is a myth and so is the paperless home. Almost everybody needs a printer to go with their computer so that they can print out documents and emails and hand them on to others, stuff them in files, or tack them on a bulletin board.

Printers today come in various types, from expensive color Laser-Jets that print many copies a minute with very high quality, to less expensive black and white Deskjet or inkjet models. Some all-in-one machines even provide fax, scanner, copier, and printer capabilities in a single machine.

Whatever kind of printer you own, and whether it came with your HP Pavilion or was purchased separately, connecting it to your computer is done in the same way. However, first, you have to have a printer.

Which Is the Right Printer for You?

You may have a printer on hand, or you may have bought one with your HP Pavilion. However, if you haven't yet purchased a printer, here's some quick advice for how to pick the one that's right for you.

- **Price** is always a consideration. Printers range in price from less than $100 to more than $2,000.
- **Print quality** is important. If you need to print high-quality output, especially graphics, photos, and business documents, you want higher quality. On the high end are impact and laserjet technologies that produce smoother edges to text characters and crisp detail in graphics; on the lower end is dot matrix technology, which produces images and text made up of discernible dots of ink making output appear jagged. One of the great determining factors of image quality is the dots per inch (dpi) setting. The higher the dpi the better the quality. A typical dpi might be 1200 x 600 for higher quality or 600 x 300 for a lower quality resolution.
- **Speed** relates to how many pages a printer produces in a minute. Some printers describe this as characters per second (cps) and others as number of pages produced a minute. If you print a lot, speed can count.
- Do you want **color or black and white?** Color is fun and, for a family computing environment, is usually useful for graphics, greeting cards, posters, and so on. However, color printers of

any quality usually cost more, and you usually have to replace two ink cartridges, one color and one black and white.

- Consider **paper size.** Some printers (usually the pricier ones) can accommodate larger paper sizes, such as 13 x 19-inch poster stock. If you'll be printing odd-sized documents, make sure your printer can handle that or that it provides multiple paper trays for different sizes of paper.

The bottom line is that you have to decide how much you'll use your printer so that you buy one that is high enough quality to take the wear and tear. Then, consider the quality you want in the output and how much you can afford.

 caution   **Be sure your printer is Windows XP compatible before buying.**

Connecting and Installing the Print Driver

Your Pavilion CPU has a plug in the back with two rows of holes in a plastic casing. A little picture of a printer is displayed above this connection. To connect a printer, you have to use a parallel cable that comes with your printer. If you can't locate it, you can buy a parallel cable at any computer supply or office superstore. By default, Windows assumes new printers will be installed on your parallel port.

note   **Printers can also connect to computers using a serial cable. Because parallel cabling is more standardized (pretty much any printer can connect to any computer using this cable) and because the parallel transmits data at faster rates, most printers today do not use serial cabling.**

After you've connected the cable to both the CPU and printer, place the disk that came with your printer into your CD drive. An installation window such as the one shown in Figure 2.1 appears.

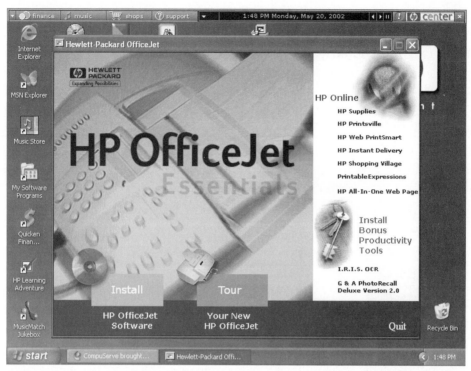

FIGURE 2.1   This HP OfficeJet installation routine offers a tour of the product to help you get acquainted with it.

Follow the directions in the installation program. During this process, you will probably be asked to confirm where to install the driver (in most cases, just accept the suggested location), and you may be asked if you want this printer to be set as the default. The default printer is the one that applications print to automatically, unless you make another setting. (If the installation doesn't make this setting for you, you can do it yourself. See Designating a Default Printer later in this chapter). You may also be asked to print a test page to make sure the connection is set up correctly.

Updating Printer Drivers

If you happen to have a slightly older printer, the drivers that come on the printer CD may not be compatible with Windows XP. In that case, you may get a message that says that the driver is not compatible, and you may have difficulty getting your printer to work. If you get such a message, you should go to the printer manufacturer's Web site (such as Compaq's, shown in Figure 2.2) and download an updated driver from there.

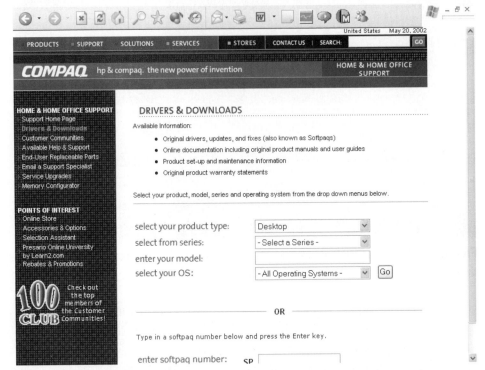

FIGURE 2.2   Look for an area for drivers and downloads on your printer manufacturer's Web site.

You can also download many hardware drivers from Microsoft's Web site, which includes a chart indicating that a product has been tested for Windows XP compatibility (see Figure 2.3).

hp pavilion pcs

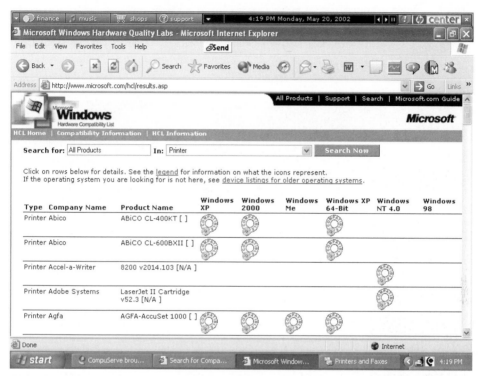

FIGURE 2.3 Microsoft works with hardware manufacturers to update their drivers for Windows XP compatibility and shows you which have been updated.

Designating a Default Printer

You may find that, over time, you will install a couple of printers to work with your computer or set up your computers so that they can access more than one computer through a network. You may also sometimes print to a fax printer.

Your Windows applications all use the printer you have set up as the default printer to print. If you just click a Print button or don't make any changes, that document is headed for the default printer. If you want to print to another printer, you can make that setting in a program's print dialog box.

This default usually saves time because you don't have to make any special setting to print to the printer that you use most of the time. However, if you do want to change the default, here's how it's done:

1. Select Start, Control Panel, Printers.

2. Click View Installed Printers or Fax Printers. The window shown in Figure 2.4 appears.

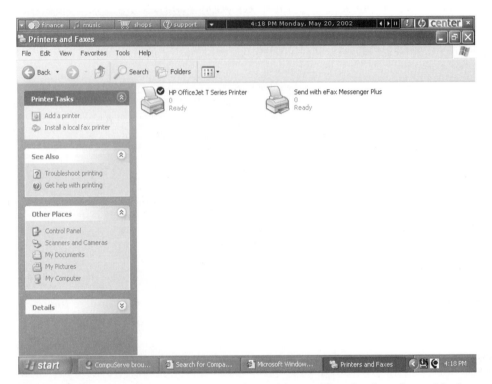

FIGURE 2.4   The default printer is indicated by a white checkmark in a black circle.

3. Click the printer you want to set as the default and select File, Set As Default Printer. (Note that this option will only be listed on the menu if you have selected a printer that is not currently the default).

4. Click the Close button to close the window.

Chapter Summary

In this chapter, you learned about registering your HP Pavilion so that you could get updates and support from HP. Then, you explored what's involved in connecting a printer to your computer, installing printer drivers, and setting the default printer. You also got advice about buying the printer that's right for you.

hp pavilion pcs

Turn on Your Pavilion: You're All Set to Go!

In this Chapter

✔ Taking a tour of your Pavilion with Victor

✔ Getting help

✔ Seeing what you can do with your keyboard

✔ Turning your Pavilion off

With your HP Pavilion home PC, after the plugs are plugged in and the power is switched on, you're good to go. However, because so much comes with your computer, it's worth taking a few minutes to explore before you get to work.

There's a wealth of preinstalled software, such as the Corel WordPerfect software suite, which includes a word processor, spreadsheet program, and more. You'll discover utilities such as McAfee VirusScan antivirus software and PC Doctor for Windows XP, which help to keep your computer in shape. Then, there are programs designed to help you find your way around and to provide help getting started, such as the HP Tour Guide. The list just goes on and on. Maybe its time to just take a look.

Don't forget the keyboard that comes with your Pavilion. It offers you far more than an alphabet soup of keys. With it, you can get instant access to your email, Internet shopping, and CD/DVD controls.

A Bounty of Computer Productivity

Starting up your HP Pavilion is like opening a treasure box filled with some very cool things. There are programs you can use to play music, write documents, calculate, and play games. You'll find media samples from music to video that you can get creative with. There are Web browsers and email programs and multimedia players. To help you discover all those programs, here's somebody you should know . . .

Meet the HP Tour Guide

When you first turn on your HP Pavilion, the Windows XP desktop appears. Windows XP is what drives all the programs on your computer, and the desktop is Windows' home base. Icons on the desktop (see Figure 3.1) represent shortcuts to often-used programs (and you can add more, which you'll learn about in the next chapter). There's a little Recycle Bin, which is where deleted files go. There's also a Start menu, which you can use to access computer controls, software programs, and documents you create.

FIGURE 3.1 The Windows XP desktop can use any picture you like as its background, bringing cheer to your computing day.

The first time you use your new Pavilion you are likely to be greeted by a little fellow who walks through a door on the desktop and greets you. This professorial-looking chap is Victor, the HP Tour Guide, and he provides an interesting introductory tour of all your HP Pavilion has to offer. The Tour Guide covers four main areas:

- How to use the Tour Guide
- What the Windows desktop is
- How to contact HP support
- How to use Internet and email

tip **You can also invite the Tour Guide to visit at any time by clicking the HP Tour Guide icon on the Windows desktop, or by selecting Start, All Programs, HP Tools, HP Tour Guide.**

You can interact with Victor at any time to tell him what to do (for example, run a specific tour or exit your desktop) through a menu of choices he displays. To move him around the screen, click anywhere on the guide with your left mouse button and drag him where you want him to go. To stop him in midcomment, just click him with your mouse. You can use the menu to start him up again at any time, switch to a different tutorial, or send him packing.

If you're new to Windows XP, it's a good idea to take the Tell Me About the Desktop tour when you first start up your Pavilion. The guide points out features of Windows XP on the desktop and shows you how to use the Start menu, Recycle Bin, and computer clock. When you're ready to connect to the Internet, the Tell Me About the Internet and E-mail tour is useful. Also, any time that you need help, the guide will be glad to provide support options in the Tell Me About Contacting HP Support tour.

Finding the Support You Need

Although the HP Tour Guide offers a nice overview of many features of Windows and your HP Pavilion, he's pretty much preprogrammed, so you can't ask him questions. For that, you should visit the Help and Support Center by clicking the Help and Support icon on the desktop or selecting Start, Help and Support. The Help and Support Center appears (Figure 3.2). From this area, you can find a Windows Glossary, Windows keyboard shortcuts, and information about customizing your computer.

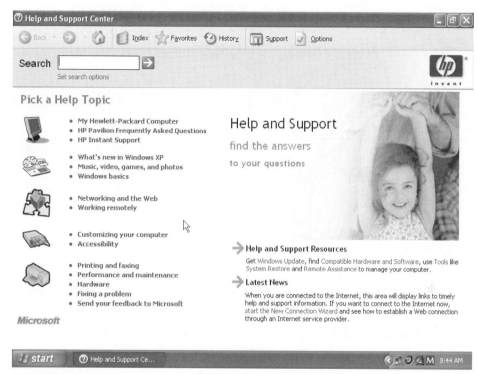

FIGURE 3.2   You can enter a word in the Search feature on any Help and Support window to find what you need.

Although this is based on a Microsoft help center, it also contains specific information about your HP Pavilion and a wealth of tools such as interactive tutorials. By using Instant Support with your Internet connection, you can send requests for help using email and keep an archive of help answers you receive.

✔ Here's how to use Help:

1. Click a topic in the Help and Support main window; you'll be taken to a window offering different items related to that topic.

2. Click one of the subtopics that's displayed; you'll be taken to more and more specific tasks. In Figure 3.3, for example, you'll see the third level of detail when you look for information on printing.

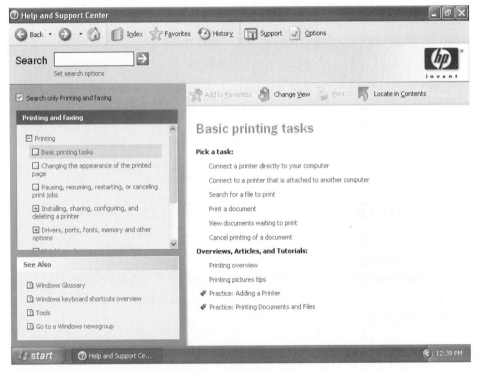

FIGURE 3.3   If you want an index of all topics, just click the Index button on any Help and Support window.

3. When you reach the task you want help with, click it; the system displays step-by-step directions for that task.

4. Click the X in the upper right-hand corner of the Help and Support window to close it when you're done. You return to the Windows desktop.

tip **Do you want to build your own help manual for features you use most often? If you like, you can save help topics you've found useful in your Favorites folder for future reference. Just click the**

Favorites button on the Help and Support Center toolbar with the page you want displayed.

Get a Friend to Help

Want help from a flesh-and-blood person? Try Remote Assistance (Start, All Programs, Remote Assistance). You can use this feature to send an invitation using the Internet and Windows Messenger asking for help. When your friend receives the message you can begin to hold an online conversation. He or she can even view your computer screen to help diagnose your problem and to take control of your computer remotely to make fixes from a distance. Learn more about this feature in Chapter 19.

Get Going Fast with Pre-installed Software

Software tells your computer how to perform certain sets of activities, such as drawing or entering text. Different kinds of software enable you to perform different types of activities. Software is also referred to as a program or an application.

In Part III of this book, you'll learn the basics of using some of the software that comes preloaded on your HP Pavilion. For now, let me introduce you to the kinds of software you'll find when you first turn on your computer.

✔ **Take a moment to look at what's available on your computer:**

1. Click the Start menu on the Windows desktop.

2. Click All Programs. A list of available programs pops up.

By scanning this list, you'll see that HP Pavilion computers come packed with software. Move your mouse around this list, and you'll see that some of these items contain submenus that list even more programs.

To give you an overview of the types of programs that are available, I've broken them into categories for you. Your Pavilion has the following:

- *Productivity software*—I call this productivity software because it's the kind of software you use to write and design documents, keep track of your finances, and manage data, in other words, to get work done. In this category of software your Pavilion has included Corel WordPerfect Productivity Pack, an integrated suite of applications that includes a word processor, calendar, presentation, and spreadsheet program. Another productivity application included is a program to manage your finances: Quicken from Intuit and Money from Microsoft. Note that if you have an older Pavilion model (prior to fall of 2002), you may have Microsoft Works (Figure 3.4) as your productivity suite and Microsoft Money as a second financial package.

FIGURE 3.4   Works is a great suite of products if you like to be led through the process of creating a new document.

- *Internet software and connections*—If you have an Internet account, you'll be glad to see that HP has already placed files for major Internet service providers on your Pavilion that are ready to install. Included are America Online (AOL), MSN Explorer, Earthlink, and CompuServe. If you don't have an Internet account, you can use the Easy Internet Sign Up item on the Programs menu, which helps you sign up for an account and get connected (you'll learn more about this in Chapter 13). An email program from Microsoft called Outlook Express also comes loaded on your Pavilion. Use it to retrieve, manage, and send out email and attached files. Finally, the popular Web browser, Internet Explorer, is all set up to help you find what you need online as soon as you connect.

- *Games*—Windows XP itself includes 11 games, from Hearts to Pinball, and even some Internet games that match you with an online player to play the game in real time through *Zone.com*.

- *Multimedia*—This is the category in which your Pavilion really takes center stage. What multimedia programs come with your HP computer? Well, depending on the model you purchased, there's InterVideo WinDVD, KazooStudio, Funhouse, My Movies, My Photo Center, Sonic Foundry, HP Record Now, Greeting Card Creator, MusicMatch Jukebox, Real Player, and Music Store. Some of these programs are media players (a player is a computer version of the equipment you'd use to play a CD or a video in your own home). Other programs help you organize multimedia into libraries or to download music or photos from the Internet. Still others allow you to edit or create multimedia files, such as Kazoo Studio (see Figure 3.5) for working with Three-Dimensional (3D) photo images. Note that several of these programs are trial or limited versions of the full programs. Typically, you can use them for about 30 days before you'll be asked to purchase the software. It's great to be able to play with these programs so that you can find the ones you like best before installing the full versions.

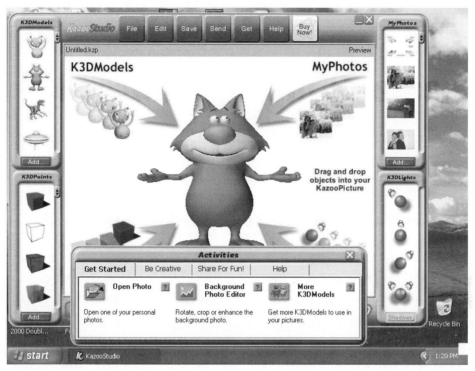

FIGURE 3.5   Kazoo Studio is a fun way to create 3D pictures with drag-and-drop ease.

- *Educational*—Many people today are buying home computers as a great tool for kids to do research and complete homework or other educational projects. You and your children will certainly get a lot out of the one year's subscription to Encarta Online Deluxe or Britannica that comes with various models of HP Pavilion. Encarta and Britannica are an online encyclopedias, but they're much more. There's a dictionary, atlas, and thesauras. Click the HP Learning Adventure icon on your desktop, and you'll have access to more than 500 software programs from The Learning Company. Their programs are already installed on your computer, ready for you to purchase and activate, and, as an HP Pavilion owner, you get one program for free.

- *Utilities*—Utilities are the handymen of the computing world. They root out computer viruses, make backup copies of files, protect your information, and restore your computer if you have a serious problem. Some utilities that come with your HP Pavilion are McAfee VirusScan for protection from computer viruses, Zero Knowledge Freedom security software, HP Application Recovery and PC System Recovery to help you if you have a serious problem with your software or hardware, and PC Doctor for Windows XP to diagnose problems with your computer operating system.

Getting to Know Your Pavilion Keyboard

Your keyboard is no longer just the thing you tap on to enter text and commands into your computer. It's a fully functional command central for your HP Pavilion, offering shortcut keys that let you instantly access Shopping, a DVD player, and more, as shown in Figure 3.6.

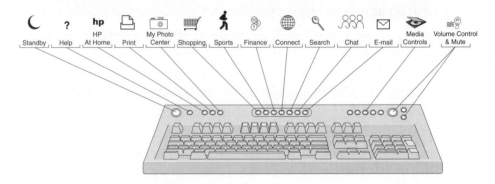

FIGURE 3.6   The Pavilion keyboard offers one-touch access to a wealth of features.

Here's what the special keys on your keyboard will do:

*   You'll find one-button access to HP, your printer, and My Photo Center on the left side of your keyboard. Using these, you can instantly log on to the My HP Club Web site, go to the Print dialog box to print the currently displayed document, or open the

My Photo Center program to edit or print photos or create photo slide shows.

- The middle section of the keyboard offers keys to instantly access the Internet: Shopping, Sports, Finance, Connect, Search, Chat, E-mail. Note that, if you are not connected to the Internet and press any of these keys, your HP Pavilion is smart enough to use your default connection to the Internet to log you on.
- The question mark button is the thing to hit if you want to go directly to the Help and Support Center.
- CD Player controls are on the right side at the top of your keyboard. You can press the button with a musical note on it to open the MusicMatch Jukebox program (see Figure 3.7) where you can create libraries of CDs or access favorite radio stations (note that you must be connected to the Internet to play radio stations). Then, use the keyboard controls to play, pause, stop, rewind, or fast forward music. You can also use the buttons with up and down arrow keys to adjust your computer's volume or press the Mute button (a button with a little speaker image on it) to temporarily turn off your computer's sound.

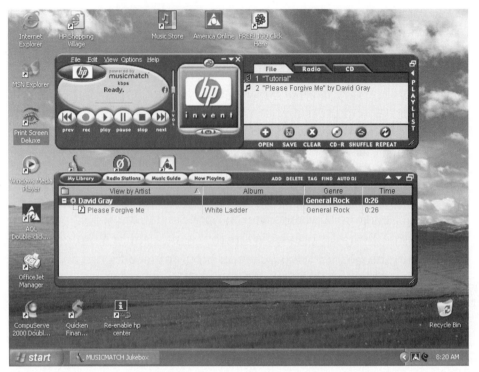

FIGURE 3.7　　MusicMatch lets you assemble libraries of music from CDs and the Internet.

- Want to put your computer to sleep? Reach for the snooze button. The Standby button on your keyboard, with the image of a half moon, puts your computer into Standby mode. In this mode, the screen turns black, and the computer uses a lower level of power. However, you will continue to receive any computer faxes or email messages. You can click your mouse to wake the computer up again. When you resume, whatever programs or documents were open will be available, just as they were when you hit the Standby button.

tip **You can reconfigure any of the Internet buttons to take you to any Web site or open any program you like. Click Start, Control Panel, Printers and Other Hardware, Keyboard. Use the Keyboard Properties window to change the function of buttons, but** remember that the little symbols printed there may no longer make sense to others if you change their functions.

Turning Your Pavilion Off

Now that you've mastered turning on your computer and have seen an overview of what comes with your HP Pavilion, it's time to learn how to turn the computer off. There are three simple choices to make here:

- *Stand by*—You can put your computer in Standby mode, which uses less power and turns your screen dark, as if the computer were off. Standby keeps everything that you had on your computer screen just the way it was at the point when you went into Standby mode; when you come out of Standby mode (which you can do by clicking your mouse or a key on your keyboard), any programs, documents, or dialog boxes you had open will still be open.
- *Restart*—You will sometimes be instructed to restart your computer, either because you have changed a setting or installed new software and the system needs to start again to implement the changes, or because a problem has occurred and the computer needs to reinitialize itself to solve it. When you choose Restart, your computer turns itself off and then on again.
- *Turn off*—Sayonara. Turn Off means just that. Your computer turns itself off completely, and you'll have to press the Power button on your Pavilion to start up again.

Note that, with the Restart and Turn Off mode, if you have programs running, Windows may ask you to close them, or it may close them itself. To use any of these three modes, follow these steps:

1. Click Start, Turn Off Computer. The Turn Off Computer window shown in Figure 3.8 appears.

2. Click any of the three buttons or, if you change your mind, click Cancel.

That's it, until you're ready to turn your Pavilion on and start computing again.

FIGURE 3.8   Your three options are laid out clearly here: Turn Off will actually turn your computer power off.

Chapter Summary

In this chapter, you got a tour of your HP Pavilion and Windows XP. You met Victor the HP Tour Guide and explored some other help features. You learned about some of the special features on your Pavilion keyboard. Then you discovered the few options available for turning off your computer.

part 2

Getting to Know
Windows XP

chapter

4

Getting Around Windows XP

In this Chapter

✔ Learning your way around the Windows desktop and Start menu

✔ Creating shortcuts

✔ Navigating around Windows and opening programs and folders

✔ Changing the appearance of things

All the wonderful software and tools that are packed into your HP Pavilion are like the parts of a car. They are wonderful to have, but, without an engine, they simply won't go. Windows XP is the engine for your computer. Windows is an operating system: It provides the functionality that enables you to use all that software and to give commands to your computer.

n this chapter you'll climb into Windows, take a look at its dashboard, and kick its tires, that is, you'll explore the Windows desktop and the commands on the Windows Start menu. Then, you'll take a look at where the files and folders that make up your computer programs and documents are kept and take a spin around your computer drives. You'll see a few ways to organize windows of information on your computer screen and explore how to open and close software programs and folders.

Just as you also like to look at different colors and upholstery fabrics when you buy a new car, you'll also enjoy looking at the different options Windows offers for changing colors and images that greet you on the Windows desktop.

Discovering the Desktop

In Chapter 3, you got your first look at Windows XP when you turned on your computer for the first time. After the few moments it takes your computer to start up (also called *booting*), you'll see the Windows XP *desktop*. The desktop serves the purpose of keeping the things you need to work on close at hand, just like your desktop at home. However, instead of books and pens and paper clips, what's on your Windows desktop is software, computer files, and menus of commands (see Figure 4.1).

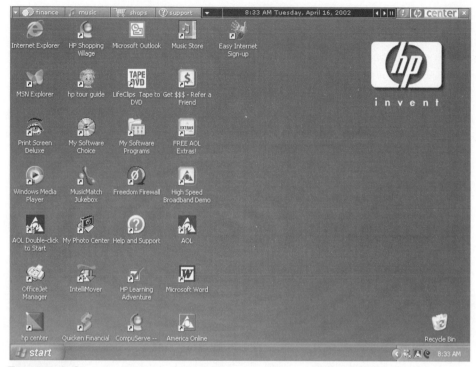

FIGURE 4.1 The Windows XP desktop contains icons that represent shortcuts to software programs, as well as the Start menu.

The icons you see on your desktop are *shortcuts* that you can double-click to open various software programs installed on your computer. HP has placed icons there for many of the most commonly used programs, but you can add or delete these shortcuts if you want (which you'll learn how to do later in this chapter). In addition to shortcuts, you'll notice a bright green button in the lower left hand corner of the desktop. This is the Start menu button.

Exploring the Start Menu

Menus are common elements of any Windows software. A *menu* holds lists of commands that you can click to do something, such as opening a program, going to a control panel where you can make changes to your computer settings, or launching an Internet connection.

The Windows Start menu is located on the *taskbar* that runs along the bottom of the Windows desktop. The Start menu is one of the largest menus you'll find, with a main panel and branches that display a menu of all the programs on your computer, and even some additional submenus (see Figure 4.2).

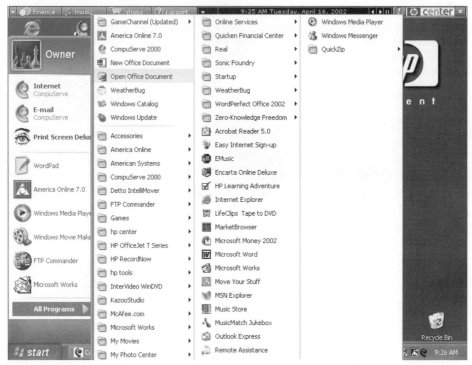

FIGURE 4.2 Working with this large menu can take a little practice, but you'll get the hang of it.

✔ **Take a moment to follow a branch of this menu to see how it works:**

1. Click the Start button. The Start menu main panel displays (see Figure 4.3).

FIGURE 4.3   This panel offers quick access to programs and documents you use all the time.

2. Click All Programs. The Programs menu appears.

3. Without moving your mouse up or down, slide the mouse or your trackball to the right so that your mouse is resting within the Programs menu. (Be sure to move only to the right. If you move your mouse up or down even slightly in the main Start panel, you may close the All Programs selection and highlight a different item. You may need to practice this motion a few times before it becomes comfortable).

4. Move your mouse around the Programs menu; note that some of the programs have a black arrow to their right (see Figure 4.4); this arrow indicates a submenu is available. The submenu appears when your mouse moves over that program name.

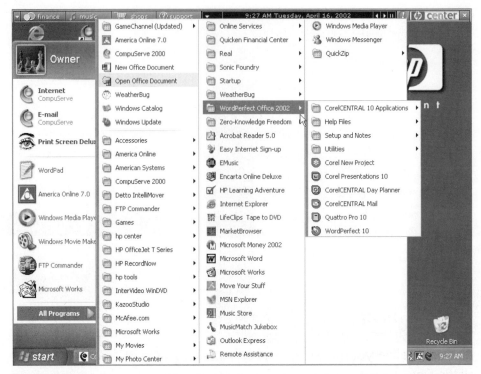

FIGURE 4.4   Programs without a black arrow launch immediately when you click them; those with a black arrow offer a submenu of choices.

5. Click the item named HP Tools. When the submenu appears, move your mouse to the right (again avoiding moving it up or down within the Programs menu) and drag your mouse to the HP Tour Guide option.

6. Click HP Tour Guide. The Start menu disappears, and the HP Tour Guide program is launched.

7. Click the Exit the HP Tour Guide choice on the menu the guide displays to close the program.

You can use the Start menu to open the folders where your documents or pictures are stored (the My Documents and My Pictures options on the Start menu main panel) or to open any software application stored on your computer. You can also use the Start menu to connect to the Internet and to access computer settings, as you'll learn as you proceed through this book.

Adding and Deleting Shortcuts

The shortcuts on your desktop are placed there for your convenience. However, the people who did that don't really know what programs you use most often in your work, so you might want to modify what's on your desktop at some point.

You can use the Start menu to place other shortcuts on your desktop. For example, if there's a program you use all the time, such as WordPad, you can get to it more quickly through a shortcut than you can by selecting Start, All Programs, Accessories, WordPad.

Project: **Add Shortcuts to Your Desktop**

To personalize your desktop, you should take a poll of those who'll be using your computer and find out what programs they'll use most often. You may have to compromise and leave some off the desktop because you don't want it to get too cluttered. You can then create shortcuts and organize them on the screen, perhaps with those used by each family member in their own corner of the desktop so they can be found easily.

✔ **Follow these steps to add a shortcut to a program:**

1. From the Start menu, click All Programs.

2. Right-click the software you want a shortcut for; a shortcut menu appears.

3. Click Create Shortcut. A copy of the item appears at the end of the Programs list (for example WordPad [2]).

4. Click the copy and drag it onto your desktop.

To delete a shortcut from the desktop, follow these steps:

1. Right-click the shortcut. A shortcut menu appears.

2. Click Delete. A verifying message appears.

3. Click Delete Shortcut to complete the operation.

tip **You can also create a desktop shortcut to documents you use frequently. Select Start, My Documents and then locate the document and follow the previous procedure to add a shortcut.**

Opening and Closing Software

In a Windows XP computer, such as the HP Pavilion, opening and closing software is done in the same way, no matter who created the software, because those functions are part of Windows.

When you open a program, it appears in a window (hence the name, Windows). You can have more than one program open at a time and can easily switch among the windows.

You have a couple of choices for starting software. You can do one of the following:

*   Click a shortcut icon on the Windows desktop.
*   Use the Start menu, click All Programs, and then click the software (or in some cases, click the software from a submenu, as you did to turn on the HP Tour Guide in the last section).
*   Locate a document you created in that software on your computer (saved by default in the My Documents folder) and double-click it. When you do, Windows opens the originating software along with the document automatically.

tip **There's also a My Software Programs icon on your desktop. You can double-click this to display all the programs loaded on your Pavilion instead of displaying the Start menu.**

✔ Try using a shortcut now to open a program:

1. Double-click the icon that says Windows Media Player. The program opens (see Figure 4.5).

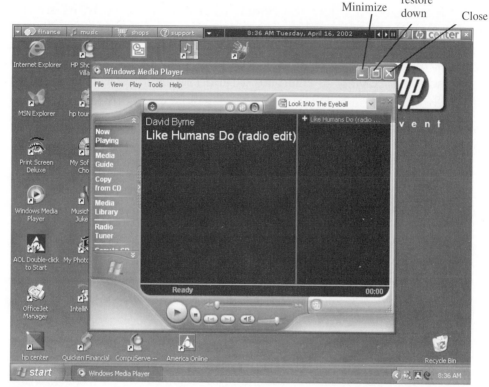

FIGURE 4.5 The Windows Media Player appears in its own window, floating on the desktop.

2. Click the title bar at the top of the window (in the blue bar that contains the words Windows Media Player) and drag the window around your desktop.

3. Click the Maximize button (the middle button in the group of three in the upper right-hand corner). The window enlarges.

4. Click the Minimize button. The program is reduced to a button on the taskbar (the taskbar runs along the bottom of the desktop).

5. Click the Windows Media Player item on the taskbar, and the program opens again.

6. Click the Restore Down button (it's the same button that you clicked on to maximize the program, but, now that the program is maximized, it offers the option to restore it down to its smaller size).

Now that you have a program window open and have played around with moving it, enlarging it, and reducing its size, it's time to learn how to close a program. There are a few options for how to do this as well. (You'll learn that there are usually several ways to do things in Windows programs.)

To close a program, you can do one of the following:

• Click the Close button in the upper right-hand corner.
• Click File, Exit.

Do one of these actions now to close the Windows Media Player program. Note that, if you had opened a file to work on and had not saved the changes you made, at this point, you'd be asked if you wanted to save the file before closing the application.

Doing Windows

Today people do something called multitasking. That means you've got several different things going at once, such as watching TV, memorizing a poem, and feeding the cat. In computer terms, multitasking means that you have more than one program or function of your computer open at the same time. As mentioned in the Opening and Closing Software section earlier in this chapter, you can have several programs open at the same time on your HP Pavilion and can easily switch between them.

Changing Windows

Try a little multitasking now by opening a couple of programs and moving among them on your desktop.

1. Select Start, All Programs, Accessories, WordPad. The WordPad window opens. If WordPad opens maximized (that is, if it fills your screen), click the Restore Down button.

2. Select Start, All Programs, Accessories, Paint. The Paint program appears. Again, if it opens maximized, click the Restore Down button. The two programs are now both on your desktop, as shown in Figure 4.6.

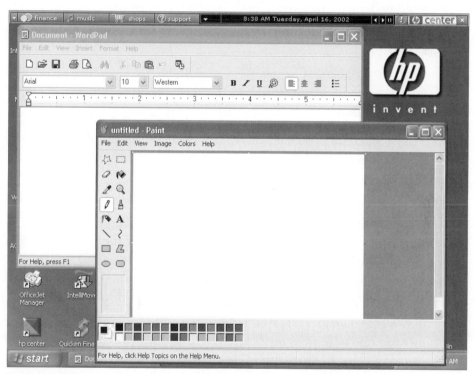

FIGURE 4.6 You can open as many windows as you like on your desktop, but remember that too many open windows can slow your computer down.

You can work in either window by clicking anywhere within it. The *active window*, that is, the window where any actions you take will take effect, will have a darkened title bar across the top. Only one window can be active at any time.

✔ **To switch between the windows, you can perform one of these actions:**

- Press Alt+Tab on your keyboard to toggle between the current active window and the last active window.
- Press Alt+Tab and keep holding the keys down; a box with all open programs appears. Press Tab to move to the one you want. When you release the Alt+Tab keys, that program will become active.
- Click any program name on the taskbar at the bottom of the desktop. If it is open, it will minimize; if it is minimized, its window will open.

Try these various methods now to switch between WordPad and Paint. Also try using the Minimize and Maximize buttons on each window to display or hide the program.

In addition to minimizing and maximizing windows, note that you can resize a window.

✔ **Follow these steps to resize a window manually:**

1. Place your mouse over any window corner until the cursor becomes a two-way arrow.

2. Click and drag to enlarge or reduce the window size.

3. When you release your mouse, the window is resized.

Arranging Windows

You can use the procedures for minimizing, maximizing, and resizing windows outlined in the previous section to help you view and work with several items on your desktop at once. However, Windows has provided a more automated method of arranging windows on your screen that can make organizing your desktop even easier.

You can even use a few different styles of arranging windows on the screen. Figure 4.7 shows windows arranged in what's called a cascading pattern. Figure 4.8 shows those same windows tiled on your screen.

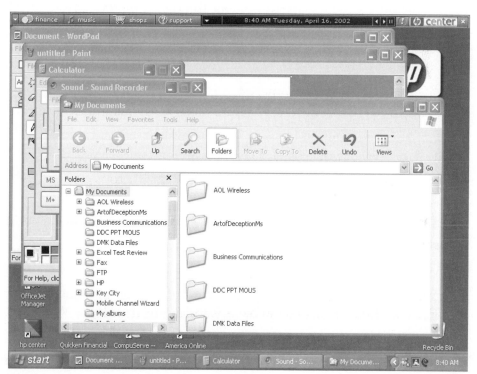

FIGURE 4.7   Cascaded windows arrange themselves like a deck of cards fanned out across your desktop.

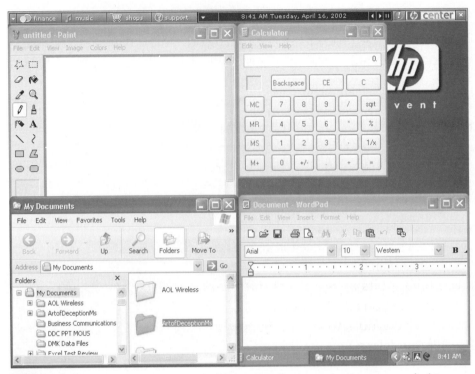

FIGURE 4.8   Windows can be tiled horizontally or vertically on your desktop.

✔ **To arrange windows on your desktop, follow these steps:**

1. With two or more program windows open, right-click (click the button on the right side of your mouse) on an area of the taskbar outside of the Start button or any minimized programs. A pop-up menu displays.

2. Click a selection from this pop-up menu: Cascade Windows, Tile Windows Horizontally, or Tile Windows Vertically. When you release your mouse button, the windows are arranged for you.

3. To undo a cascade effect, right-click the taskbar area again and choose Undo Cascade from the same pop-up menu.

Taking a Look at My Computer

Now its time to look at the contents of your computer a little more closely. Your HP Pavilion, like every other computer, stores computer programs and computer files, ready for you to open them up and get to work. The shortcuts on your desktop are just that: shortcuts to launch these programs. However, you can use the My Computer folder when you want to see the various items on your computer and to interact with other media, such as CDs and floppy disks.

Taking a Drive

There's a lot of stuff on your computer that lives on something called your *hard drive*. The hard drive is an actual metal disk inside your computer where bits and bytes of information about your programs, and the files that you create with those programs, are stored. In addition to a hard drive, you also have a floppy drive; a CD drive; and, on most Pavilion models, a Rewriteable CD (CD-RW) drive.

What's a Floppy?

Floppies are not floppy at all, but they once were. Back in the Dark Ages of computing (say 15 years ago), the disks that you could insert into your computer drive to make copies of your data were either 8-inch or 5-inch plastic film disks that you could literally bend in half, hence the name, floppy. After a while, 3.5-inch disks encased in hard plastic became the preferred storage media because of their size and durability. Though these smaller disks are not floppy at all, the industry continues to use the term "floppy" for this removable storage medium.

The folder on your hard drive called My Computer is where you can access the contents of the various drives on your computer so that you can see what's on them and move and copy items among them.

For example, you might have a file you took off another computer that you want to copy from a floppy disk to a folder on your Pavilion.

To view the My Computer folder, click Start, My Computer. The window shown in Figure 4.9 appears. If you've ever used the Internet, you'll recognize the browserlike interface of this window with buttons to move forward or backward to previously displayed windows, as well as a Search button and other tools for maneuvering around folders.

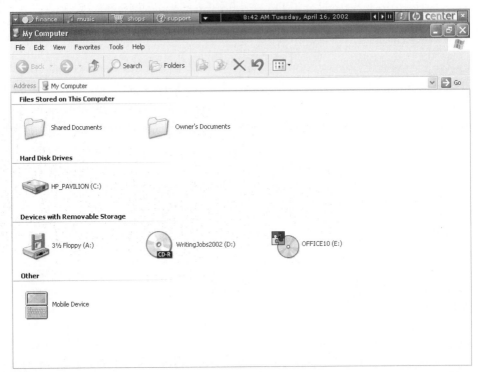

FIGURE 4.9 Your hard drive, documents stored on your hard drive, removable media, and even remote devices can be accessed through your My Computer folder.

The items listed in the Files Stored on This Computer area represent files stored on your hard drive in the Shared Documents and Owner's Documents folders (folders included with Windows for you to store documents in).

tip **You can easily create new folders, rename folders, move folders, or add files to folders. See Chapter 5 for more about file and folder management.**

The HP Pavilion (C:) item is your hard disk drive. Although a computer can have several drive letters representing different sections of your hard drive or media drives, C: is typically used for the main hard disk drive.

Devices in the Removable Storage area include floppy, CD, DVD, and CD-RW drives. If a disk is in any of these drives, the name of the disk appears here, rather than the drive name.

You may have an Other section in your My Computer folder if you have installed a remote computing device, such as a handheld computer.

Opening and Closing Folders

Double-click the HP Pavilion item in the My Computer folder to see all that your hard drive contains (see Figure 4.10). You can use the scrollbar on the side of this window to move up and down to view the list of files here. You'll notice that this window contains more folders, designated by little golden folder icons to their left (folders can be nested inside of other folders on your computer), as well as icons representing some individual files.

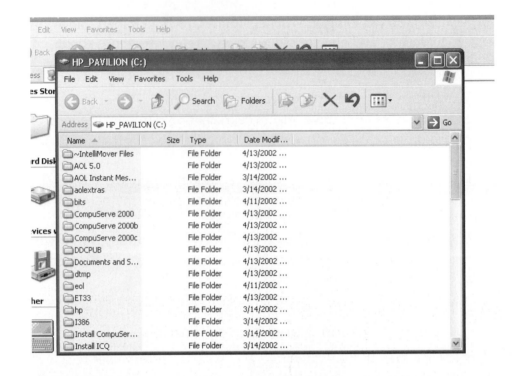

FIGURE 4.10 The My Computer folder contains everything that's stored on your computer hard disk drive—and that's a lot!

You can open a folder and see its contents by double-clicking on it or by clicking on it once and then choosing File, Open. If you double-click a file rather than a folder, a few things could happen. You could launch an application, run an installation program, or open a document in an application.

For now, after you've taken a look at the folders and files (best not to touch any of them at this point), go ahead and click Close to close the HP Pavilion window and then click Close on the My Computer window to close it. You'll see much more of both of these folders in Chapter 5.

Changing the Appearance of Things

When you are on the Windows desktop you'll notice that various colors are used for different elements, such as the taskbar, title bars on windows, and so on. There is also an image behind the desktop, probably a background put there by Hewlett-Packard like the one shown in Figure 4.11.

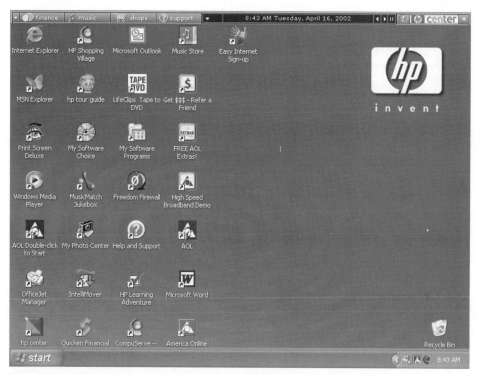

FIGURE 4.11 HP provides a nice blue background, but you'll be surprised at what you can do to change that, if you like.

If you'd like to make your Windows desktop reflect your personality, you'll be glad to hear that you can change colors, the background, and more.

Putting Up Wallpaper

The background image on your desktop is sometimes referred to as wallpaper. Just like wallpaper in a room, the wallpaper on your desktop provides a pleasing background to your computing activities.

However, no two Pavilion users are alike, so you'll be glad to hear that Windows XP provides dozens of backgrounds to choose from. You can even use a picture of your own (your kids, dog, garden, or whatever).

As with all the aspects of your desktop's appearance, the background is set from the Control Panel, which is operations central for modifying Windows settings.

Project: **Personalizing Your Computer Background**

Pick out a photo you'd like to include as your desktop background and scan or upload it into your computer (follow directions included with your scanner or digital camera).

✔   **To change the background on your computer, follow these steps:**

1.   Select Start, Control Panel. The Control Panel shown in Figure 4.12 opens.

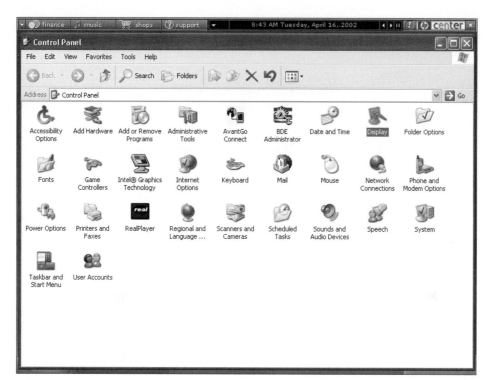

FIGURE 4.12 The Control Panel offers access to all Windows settings in one place.

2. Double-click the Display icon. The Display dialog box (a form used to enter information and make settings in Windows programs) appears.

3. Click the Desktop tab. The Desktop sheet appears, as shown in Figure 4.13.

FIGURE 4.13 The Display dialog box contains five tabs; click a tab to modify different settings.

4. To use any image file as your background, when you are on the Desktop tab of the Display dialog box (see Step 3), click the Browse button, then locate the file you want to use, and click OK twice to apply it.

5. At this point, you can click Apply to apply the new background, but not close the Display dialog box, or you can click OK to apply the background and close the dialog box.

note **If you want to use a provided background, you can click on any item in the Background list in Step 4, using the scrollbar to the right of the list to move up and down if you need to. The new background is previewed for you.**

Getting Just the Right Color Scheme

Computing with an HP Pavilion is a colorful experience, in more ways than one. You can pick the colors that most complement your style, changing the colors used on various elements of the Windows desktop and for folders, files, and certain elements in software programs, such as the title bar and dialog boxes.

There are two possibilities for changing the color scheme. One is to choose from a short list of color schemes on the Appearance tab of the

Display dialog box. The other is to apply a Theme from the Theme tab in the same dialog box. Themes apply not only a background and color scheme, but also variations on font styles and even sounds that play when certain computing events occur.

✔ **Follow these steps to apply a built-in theme to your computer:**

1. Click Start, Control Panel.

2. Double-click the Display icon.

3. Click the Themes tab to display it, if it's not already displayed.

4. Click the arrow to the right of the Theme list to display it.

5. Click a theme that interests you.

6. Click Apply to apply the theme without closing the dialog box (one advantage to this method is that, if you don't like the theme, you can simply choose another or click Cancel).

7. When you find a theme you like, click OK to close the dialog box.

Note that if you apply a different desktop background, it will replace any background included in the theme, although other settings of the theme will remain intact.

Chapter Summary

You've explored many areas of your computer and Windows in this chapter, including the Windows desktop and Start menu, which allow you to access programs and folders. You learned how to create short-cuts to programs, how to open and close software, and how to open folders on your computer. You used tools in Windows to modify how windows are arranged on your screen and to change the appearance of the elements you look at in Windows and other programs.

chapter

5

File Management Basics

In this Chapter

✓ Creating file folders

✓ Saving files to folders

✓ Moving, copying, and deleting files and folders

✓ Backing up files

✓ Searching for files

Anybody who has ever organized a home filing system or worked in an office knows that there's a place for everything and that it's important that you get all your documents in the right place or you'll be in chaos. The same is true of computer files. You have to know where to find the work you've done and how to avoid confusing multiple versions of the same document. Organizing your computer files involves two key steps: naming and storing files in a logical way.

73

Luckily, Windows already supplies a structure for filing computer documents, and it's essentially a variation on that old metal filing cabinet you're so familiar with. In this chapter, you'll open your virtual filing cabinet and see what's inside; you'll also learn about the importance of backing up computer files on a regular basis.

The Virtual Filing Cabinet

Computer files come in all types and sizes, from files containing photo images to the file where you saved your school play program or taxes. After you've been using your Pavilion for a while, you'll find that you have more files than you know what to do with. If you start out with a good filing system for your documents, you'll avoid a lot of pain down the road.

The filing system that Windows uses is one with folders. Just like the folders you use in a regular filing cabinet, you place related files in Windows folders. In addition, just as you place a manila folder inside a hanging folder, you can place folders within folders in Windows. You can even make copies of files and place them in other folders or move files between folders with ease.

tip **Your HP Pavilion home PC comes with many folders already created for you for common types of documents, such as My Albums, My Music, My Data Sources, My Webs, My Photos, and so on. All of these are located within the My Documents folder. You can delete these folders, move them around, or rename them as you like.**

How Files and Folders Are Organized

The location for top-level folders on your Pavilion is the My Computer area. You can add folders at this level or go into one of the existing folders, such as My Pictures, and add subfolders. For example, in the My

Pictures folder, you might find it convenient to have My Family and My Trip folders. You can also create new folders within My Computer.

Take a moment to look at the folder structure shown in Figure 5.1 (you get here by selecting Start, My Computer, HP Pavilion (C:), Program Files). The little manila colored folders are shown in a list.

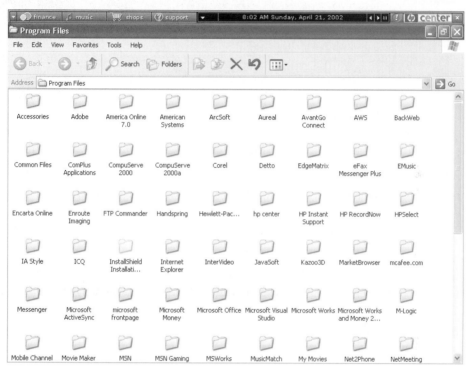

FIGURE 5.1   Windows XP contains many folders to organize the programs on your computer.

Creating Files and Folders

You create a file by saving a document in the software program where you generated the file contents. For example, you might create a letter in the word processor portion of Works and then save it to any folder you like. You can create folders either at the time that you save a file or by creating a new folder using the file menu in Windows Explorer (see Figure 5.2), which is the feature that displays contents of your computer drives (select Start, My Computer or My Documents, for example, to explore document folders).

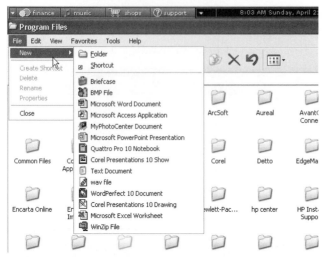

FIGURE 5.2   The File menu allows you to create a new folder wherever you are in Windows Explorer.

Project: **Create Your Projects Folder**

As you work on various projects throughout this book, you and your family may want a place to store them.

✔ **Follow these steps to create a new Family Projects folder in the My Documents folder:**

1. From the Windows desktop, select Start, My Documents. The My Documents folder appears.

2. Select File, New, Folder. A new folder appears at the bottom of the list. Note that the name of the folder is currently New Folder; this name is highlighted and ready for you to edit.

3. Type the folder name Family Projects. When you click anywhere outside of the folder, the new name is saved.

tip **To edit a folder name, just right-click the folder and select Rename from the shortcut menu that appears. Then type the new name. Click outside the folder and the new name is saved.**

Saving a File

Saving a file works the same way in most Windows programs. You use the File, Save command from within any software program and then use the Save dialog box (shown in Figure 5.3) to select a location to save your file. You can save a file into a folder on your hard drive, onto a floppy disk, or onto a writeable CD or DVD.

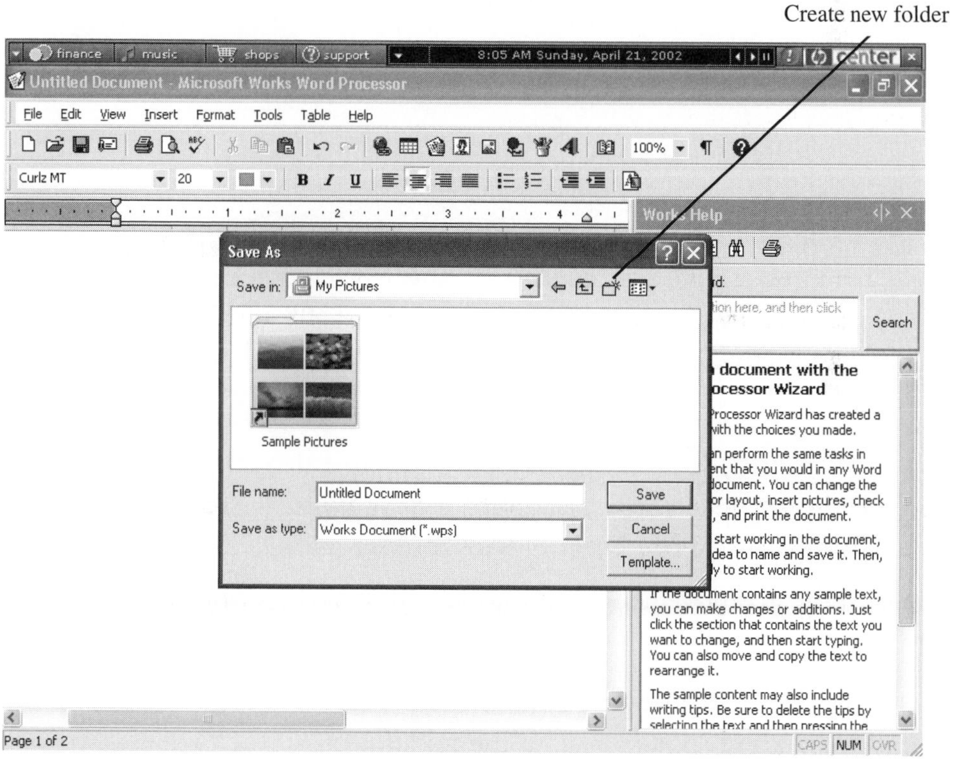

FIGURE 5.3 The Save dialog box contains a button for creating a new folder as you save a document.

✔ **Try saving a file now, creating a new folder as you do by using the Works word processor (if you have a later model Pavilion, use Corel WordPerfect for these steps).**

1. Select Start, All Programs, Microsoft Works.

2. Click Cover Letters and then Start this Task.

3. Click Finish to end the letter wizard and create the letter from a template (you'll learn more about this in Chapter 9).

4. Click to the left of the placeholder text, "Your Name Here", and drag to the right to select it.

5. Type your own name.

6. Select File, Save. The Save As dialog box appears.

7. Click the arrow to the right of the Look in box and select My Documents.

8. Type the file name, "My Letter", in the File Name box.

9. Click Save.

You've just saved a new file to the My Documents folder. If you close Works (click the X button in the top right corner), select Start, My Documents. You should now see a file named My Letter.

Moving, Copying, and Deleting Files and Folders

Not happy with where you saved your file? Want to move or make a copy of the file, or perhaps you don't need the file anymore? Time to learn how to move, copy, and delete files and folders on your computer.

Moving Files and Folders

Although you may have originally saved a file in one folder, you may decide at some point that the file should be moved. For example, you might save a letter in a folder called Writing in Progress while you're drafting it, but then move it to a folder named Personal Correspondence after the letter has been printed and sent.

✔ **You can move a file or folder by cutting and pasting it; you do this by following these steps:**

1. Locate the file by clicking Start, My Computer or My Documents (or another folder listed on the Start menu such as My Music, depending on the location of the file).

2. After you locate the file or folder, click it to select it.

3. Select Edit, Cut. (If you cut a folder, you also cut all the files and folders within it).

4. Go to the location where you want to move the file or folder. (You can click the Up arrow on the toolbar or click the arrow next to the Address box and choose a location of a folder).

5. When you have the folder open where you want to place the file or folder, select Edit, Paste.

Copying Files

You might want to make a copy of a file to store it in two places. For example, you might have a copy of important family contact information in your family finances folder and your babysitter folder. One option is to open the file and save it with a different name in another location on your hard drive. However, you can also use Windows Explorer to copy files and folders.

Copying a file or folder is simple. You can use a method very similar to cutting and pasting a file to move it. However, with copying you would choose Edit, Copy to copy the original file and Edit, Paste to paste it into the folder where you want the copy placed.

You can also use a shortcut menu if you want to copy a file or folder to a floppy disk, the Windows desktop, the My Documents folder, or a writeable CD or DVD.

✔ **Follow these steps to copy the My Letter file to a floppy disk:**

1. Insert a floppy disk into your floppy drive.

2. Select Start, My Documents.

3. Right-click the file name and select Send to, 3 1/2 Floppy (A:)(see Figure 5.4). The file is copied to the disk.

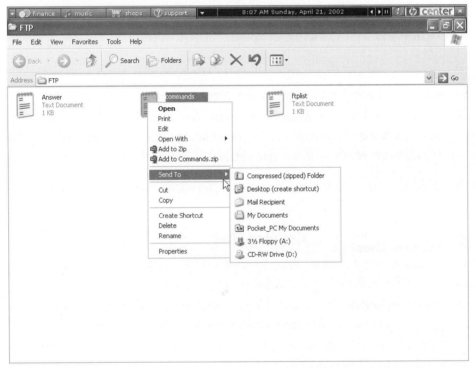

FIGURE 5.4   This shortcut menu offer commands you'll use often when managing files and folders.

4. Click the arrow to the right of the Address box in the My Documents window and then click on 3 1/2 Floppy (A:). The file should now be listed with the contents of your floppy disk.

 caution   **Be sure to insert a floppy disk that has enough room to store the file or folder you want to copy to it. If you don't, Windows will display a message that not enough space is on the disk to perform this action.**

tip   **You can also right-click the file and select the Copy command from the shortcut menu that appears.**

Deleting Files

Deleting files is an important part of file management. Because your computer memory gets filled up by all the files you save on your hard drive, it's a good idea to go through and delete files and folders you no longer need on a regular basis. If you like, you can archive old files on floppy disks or writeable CDs or DVDs before you delete them from your hard drive.

✔ **Follow these steps to delete a file or folder:**

1. Locate the file or folder with Windows Explorer.

2. Right-click the item and select Delete from the shortcut menu.

    That's it!

caution   **If you delete a folder, you delete all its contents as well. Make sure there isn't a file tucked away in a subfolder somewhere that you need before deleting.**

note **When you delete something, it is put in the Recycle Bin. This is a folder that keeps deleted files for a time in case you change your mind. To permanently delete a file, right-click the Recycle Bin on your desktop and select Empty Recycle Bin.**

Backing Up Your Files

One of the most important rules of file management is to back up your document files. Backing up means saving a copy of your files on some media, such as a floppy disk, writeable CD or DVD, or even on the Internet or a company network.

Why? Because all computer hard drives die eventually. If your computer is new, it should take many, many years, but it will happen. Even before that time comes, you will probably experience *crashes*, instances where the power to your computer suddenly cuts off, or two computer programs encounter a conflict that freezes your computer and causes it to shut down. When a crash happens, you can lose data from your hard drive or the file you were working on when the crash occurred. Having a backup file, even one that might be a version or so older, can save you a great deal of stress if you lose a file.

note **Most Windows software has an autorecover feature that saves copies of the document you are currently working on when you crash and that helps you recover it after you start your computer again. Open the program you were working in after recovering from a crash to see if such an option is offered.**

Backup up should be done daily (or even more frequently if you spend the day creating lengthy documents). You can back up each document you create or change when you're done working with it, or you can back up your entire set of documents at the end of your work day. If your Pavilion has a writeable CD/DVD drive, you can store a great many documents on a single CD/DVD by copying your My Documents folder to it.

note **You can follow the steps provided in the earlier section, Copying Files, to copy files from your hard drive to a CD/DVD or floppy to back up any new or recently changed documents.**

Finding What You Need

No matter how meticulous you are about setting up and using a logical filing system, there will be times when you will simply forget where you stored a file. Windows provides a powerful search tool to locate a file by a variety of criteria, such as a word that might be contained in the file name or in the file itself, the date it was last modified, or the size of the file (if you're looking for a very large file containing graphics, this last choice might narrow down the search).

✔ **Follow these steps to search for a file:**

1. Select Start, Search. The Search dialog box shown in Figure 5.5 appears.

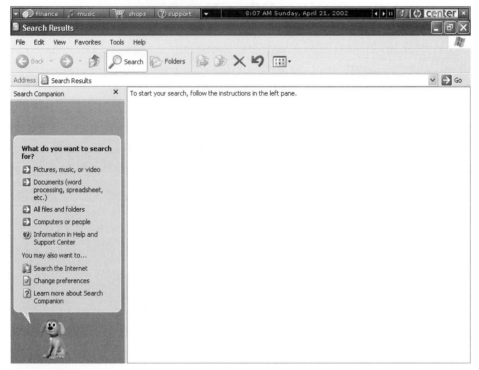

FIGURE 5.5   The little animated dog in this dialog box is your Search Companion.

2. Click the type of item you want to search for in the left pane of this box.

3. Select or enter criteria for your search, such as the date the file was last modified or a word used in the body of the document. If you want additional criteria, click the Use Advanced Search Items link at the bottom of this list.

4. Click Search. The items that match your criteria will be displayed on the right side of the dialog box.

tip After a search runs, some options will be offered in the left pane of this dialog box. Scroll down to review them. If the search wasn't successful, for example, an option is offered here to refine your search.

Chapter Summary

In this chapter, you learned about the importance of good file management, from storing files in logically named folders to backing up files and folders on a regular basis. You discovered how to search for a file you've saved on your computer and practiced moving, copying, and deleting files.

File management can make the difference between a well-organized computing experience and a frustrating one. Taking the time now to organize your computer will save you time and aggravation down the road.

hp pavilion pcs

Customizing Your Computing Experience

In this Chapter

✓ Installing software on your Pavilion

✓ Removing software

✓ Adding hardware

✓ Modifying the computer display

An HP Pavilion comes ready for action out of the box. However, there may be times when you'll want to add software or hardware or remove software you no longer need. In addition to setting up the software and hardware that match your computing needs, you might also want to take advantage of a wealth of graphics and colors that you can use to customize your Windows display.

This chapter walks you through what you have to do to get what's on your computer set up just the way you like.

Installing Software

Everybody needs different things out of a computer. Some use it for emailing and word processing, while others spend every computing minute playing the latest Lara Croft game or editing home videos. As you use your HP Pavilion, you'll discover additional software programs that you'd like to use. Luckily, installing software is a simple process.

What to Know Before You Install

There are a few things to keep in mind before you install software. First is computer memory. Your hard drive probably has a tremendous capacity compared to computers of only a few years ago, but everything has its limits. Your hard drive can get filled up with graphics and multimedia files, as well as the software you install. You have to be sure there's enough memory for the program you want to install. During most software installation routines, there will be a message concerning how much memory you need to install the software and how much is available on your hard drive. If those numbers are very close, consider deleting an unwanted program or two so that you're not at your memory limit.

Second, occasionally, programs aren't compatible with your operating system. You may encounter situations where they aren't compatible with Windows XP, especially when you're loading hardware drivers (programs used to run hardware such as printers). Check when you purchase software that you get a version that's compatible with Windows XP, or check with the software manufacturer's Web site to see if it provides an update to the software that you can download to make it compatible with XP.

Running the Installation

Software typically includes its own installation routine. With many programs, as soon as you put a software CD in your computer drive, it opens an installation window and you can simply follow its instructions to install the software. Installation usually involves the following steps:

- Designating where to install the software. (Typically, most software is installed in the Windows Programs folder.)

- Indicating whether the installation should be the typical installation, which installs the most often-used features, or a custom installation where you choose what to install.

- Entering information such as your name or phone or fax number. In some cases, such as with faxing software, this information is required to operate the software; in others, it is used to register the software.

- Choosing whether you want to register the software online now or later. Registering software ensures that you'll get technical support from the manufacturer.

- Restarting your computer to complete the installation.

Project: Install a Game on Your Computer

You can buy a game at most computer stores or office superstores. Pick a game that will appeal to everybody in your family. Some are quite inexpensive. When you find one you like, you can use the Windows Add or Remove Programs feature to walk you through the installation process.

✔ **To access the Add or Remove feature, follow these steps:**

1. Select Start, Control Panel.

2. Click Add or Remove Programs. The Add or Remove Programs dialog box shown in Figure 6.1 appears.

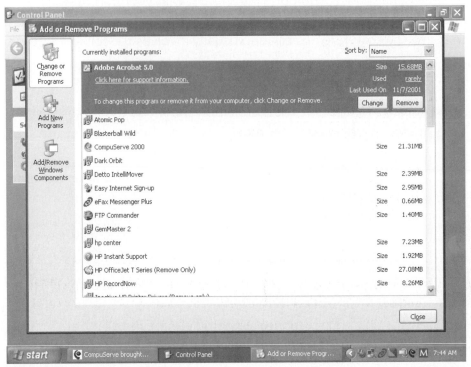

FIGURE 6.1 You can see all the programs you have installed and the amount of memory they are using in the Currently Installed Programs list.

3. Click Add New Programs.

4. Place the software disk or CD into the appropriate drive on your Pavilion.

5. Click the CD or Floppy button. The Install Program dialog box opens.

6. Click Next.

7. The Run Installation Program dialog box shown in Figure 6.2 appears, confirming the location and name of the setup file. If it's not correct, click Browse to locate the program you want to install.

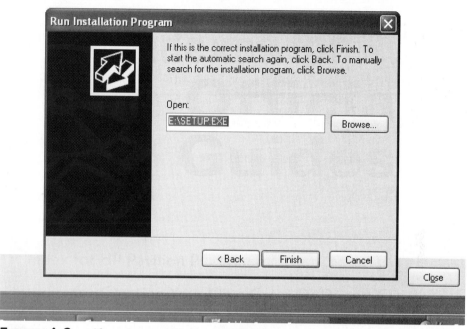

To add new Windows features, device drivers, and system updates over the Internet, click Windows Update

Windows Update

Run Installation Program

If this is the correct installation program, click Finish. To start the automatic search again, click Back. To manually search for the installation program, click Browse.

Open:

E:\SETUP.EXE

Browse...

< Back   Finish   Cancel

Close

hp pavilion pcs

FIGURE 6.2   If you have a CD inserted, Windows automatically identifies any executable installation file on it.

8. When the correct file is listed, click Finish. The installation program runs.

You will still have to make choices and enter information as requested by the individual program, but onscreen directions should walk you through that process.

tip **If you're not very familiar with the software you're installing, it's best to select the Typical Installation option. Custom installation requires that you make some more advanced choices.**

Time for a Change: Uninstalling Software

There's no need to leave software you'll never use cluttering up your computer. An overfull hard drive can actually slow down your computer's performance. Periodically, you should archive computer files you don't need and remove any software that isn't useful to you.

Uninstalling software can be tricky business. That's because software programs interact and share certain files. If you delete a folder containing one program's files, you could cause some problems with other programs. In fact, uninstalling programs used to be one of the main problems people encountered using their computers.

Many software products now include their own uninstall procedure, but the easiest way to remove programs is simply to use the Microsoft Windows Remove Programs feature. This step-by-step process notifies you when certain files should be kept.

✔ Follow these steps to remove a program:

1. Select Start, Control Panel. The Add or Remove Programs section of the dialog box should be displayed; if it's not, click that icon to display it.

2. Click the program you want to remove. A Change/Remove button becomes available.

3. Click Change/Remove. A Confirm Uninstall dialog box appears.

4. Click Yes to remove the program or No to stop the process.

With some programs that are made up of several pieces of software, such as the Corel WordPerfect Office suite or an operating system like Windows XP, when you click the Change/Remove button, you get the option to change the program, allowing you to remove only some elements.

Adding Hardware

Most computers aren't used on their own. They are connected to hardware devices, such as printers, scanners, cable modems, or fax machines, to produce printed output, load files into the computer, or communicate with others.

Most of these devices require a driver, that is, a software program that allows Windows to interact with and send commands to the device. Devices come with a disk that includes their driver. Place that disk in the appropriate drive and follow the steps displayed to install the driver and set up the hardware.

Occasionally, you might not have access to that disk. If that's the case, you can usually download the latest drivers from the manufacturer's site (see Figure 6.3).

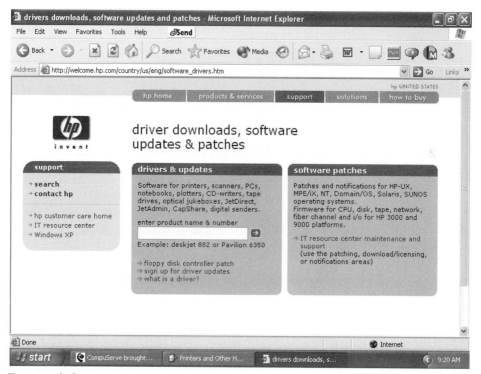

FIGURE 6.3 HP's download center offers the latest drivers for printers, monitors, and more.

What Is Plug and Play?

Plug and play is a set of specifications developed by Microsoft and Intel for how your computer automates the set up process when a new piece of hardware is detected. This involves a plug and play expansion card, which all recent HP Pavilions have.

The best procedure when you attach a piece of hardware to your computer is to insert the manufacturer's CD into your drive and then follow the installation instructions that should appear. If no installation program opens when you insert the CD, you can select Start, My Computer; locate the CD drive; and click the drive, which should begin the installation.

tip **If an installation window still doesn't appear, look at the CD contents; there should be a file with an .exe extension and possibly named Setup. Double-clicking that file runs the installation routine.**

Using the Add Hardware Wizard

The Add Hardware Wizard is provided by Windows to set up your hardware to work with Windows. It asks little of you, just that you provide a disk with a driver on it or designate the location of a driver on your computer (for example, if you downloaded the driver from the Internet).

✔ **Follow these steps to set up new hardware with the Add Hardware Wizard:**

1. If you have a disk for your hardware device, place it in your floppy or CD drive.

2. Plug the device into your computer. The New Hardware Wizard should appear (see Figure 6.4). If it doesn't, select Start, Control

Panel, Printers and Other Hardware, and click the Add Hardware link.

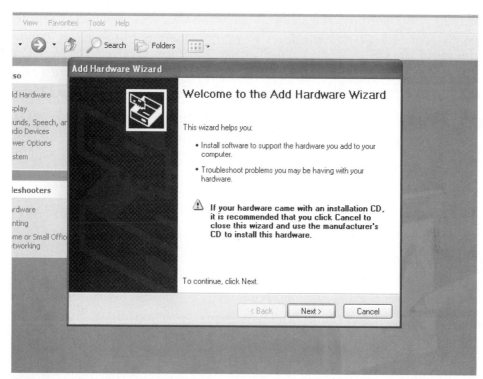

FIGURE 6.4   You can also use the Add Hardware Wizard if you're having problems with already installed hardware.

3. The wizard searches for new hardware you have attached to the computer. It then displays a dialog box asking you to confirm the location of the hardware driver. (Most times the wizard figures out that the driver is on the disk you've inserted, but, if it's somewhere on your hard drive, you may have to enter the path to get to it.)

4. Click Next and the wizard completes the setup.

Modifying Your Display

Because you'll probably spend a lot of time staring at your computer screen, you might as well enjoy the view. Windows allows you to modify the colors used on Windows elements, such as the desktop, dialog boxes, menu bars, and so on. Also, Windows offers themes, which are sets of sounds, backgrounds, colors, and special icons you can apply as a set. Finally, you can change the desktop background image, designate a screen saver to appear when your computer has remained inactive for a few minutes, and set the screen resolution and color quality levels.

Choosing Color, Background, and Themes

With Windows XP, Microsoft has changed the way you make the most of your computer display settings. In previous versions of Windows, several sets of color schemes and themes were included. Now you have a limited choice, and you have to buy a product called Windows XP Plus to get additional display choices. In some ways, that makes sense, both because all those graphics preinstalled on your system took up a chunk of memory and because today people have access to a great many scanned or downloaded graphics of their own that they can use as desktop backgrounds.

note **Note that if you apply a background, it replaces the background used in the current theme. If you apply a theme, it overrides your background and color scheme setting. If you change color schemes, that changes the theme color setting.**

Project: **Personalize Your Computer with Themes, Backgrounds, and Colors**

Your Pavilion should be a reflection of you, so sit down and brainstorm with your family to pick out colors and images that reflect your personalities. You can even use personal photos that you've scanned into your computer for a background.

✔ **Here's how you go about applying your choice of color scheme, background, or theme:**

1. Select Start, Control Panel.

2. Click the Change the Computer's Theme link. The Display Properties dialog box shown in Figure 6.5 appears.

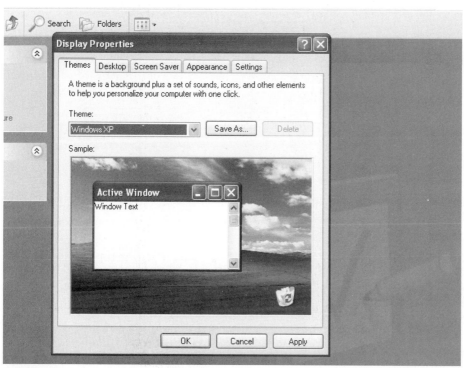

FIGURE 6.5   If you haven't changed anything since buying your computer, you should have the Windows XP theme set here.

3. Click the arrow at the end of the Theme box and select another theme in the list by clicking it. Windows Classic is the only installed

optional theme if you don't have Windows XP Plus installed, so click it.

4. Click Apply. The new theme background and colors appear on your computer.

5. Click the Desktop tab, shown in Figure 6.6; the background selected matches the one in the Windows Classic theme.

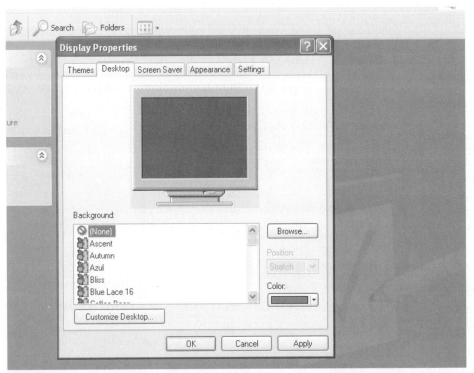

FIGURE 6.6   Microsoft has left you with quite a few background choices.

6. Click a background in the list. A preview of the graphic image displays.

7. Use the up and down arrow on your keyboard to move through the different backgrounds. When you find one you like, click Apply.

8. Click the Appearance tab.

9. Click the arrow on the Color Scheme box and then click a color scheme option. It is previewed for you. When you find one you're happy with, click Apply.

tip **If you want to use an image of your own for your desktop background, on the Desktop tab of the Display dialog box click Browse, locate the file in the Browse dialog box, and then click Open. It is added to your list of desktop backgrounds. Click it and then click Apply to use it.**

Modifying Display Settings

Certain settings in Windows XP will have an impact on the way things look on your monitor. Screen resolution deals with how fine an image you get, that is, how many dpi (dots per inch) are used to form those images on your screen. The lower the resolution, the grainier the picture.

caution **A higher resolution also causes all items to be smaller, which can make onscreen text difficult for some to read.**

Color quality controls how many bits of color information are used in each display dot. Windows XP allows 16-bit color and 24-bit color, with 24 bit being the higher color quality.

caution **Be aware that higher resolution and color quality can cause occasional problems with some software. If you experience problems because programs that display graphics keep crashing, consider lowering these settings a bit.**

tip **If you're using software that requires 256 colors (an older color setting), you can right-click the program name on the Start menu, click Properties, and, on the Compatibility tab, check the Run in 256 Colors option. When you close that program, the computer goes back to your regular color setting.**

✔ To modify the color quality settings, follow these steps:

1. Select Start, Control Panel.

2. Click on the Appearance and Themes link.

3. Click on the Change Screen Resolution option. The Display dialog box with the Settings tab displayed appears (see Figure 6.7).

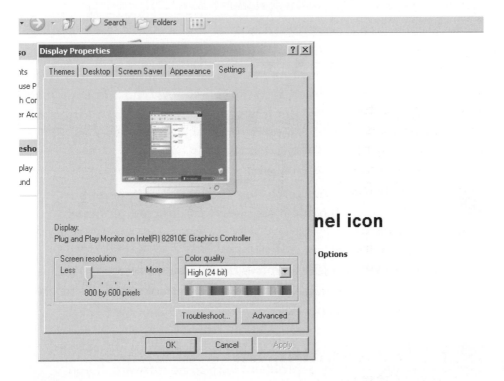

FIGURE 6.7 The little monitor previews how changed settings will affect your display.

4. Click the slider bar under Screen Resolution and drag it to the right or left to change the resolution. Note the changes in image size in the preview as you do.

5. Click the arrow next to the Color Quality box and select another color setting. When you do, the preview bar shows the effect. With the lower setting, the colors are a bit less crisp.

6. When you have the settings you want, click OK. If you want to save the default settings, click Cancel to close the dialog box without saving changes.

Choosing a Screen Saver

A screen saver is a utility program that automatically displays a random series of graphic images after your computer has remained idle for a period of time. Back in the early days of computing, screen savers were a necessity because having the same image on screen for long periods of time could actually etch an image onto your monitor display. That's no longer the case with more recent monitors. People just set screen savers to display because they produce intriguing graphic images. Also, having a screen saver come on when you're away from your computer keeps passersby from seeing what you're working on.

tip **There are many screen savers available for free download from the Internet, or you can purchase screen saver software that represents your interests, such as mountain climbing, sailing, or gardening.**

✔ **To set a Windows screen saver on your computer, follow these steps:**

1. From the Display Properties dialog box click on the Screen Saver tab to display the settings shown in Figure 6.8.

FIGURE 6.8   Microsoft provides several predesigned screen savers for you.

2. Click the arrow on the Screen Saver box and click a name on the list. The preview shows you what the screen saver will look like.

3. If you'd like a full screen preview of the screen saver, click the Preview button. Click your left mouse button when you want to return to the dialog box.

4. Click the spinner arrows in the Wait setting to specify when the screen saver comes on, for example, after 10 minutes of inactivity.

5. Click OK to apply the new settings and close the dialog box.

tip **If you want to prevent other people from seeing what's on your computer, you can check the On Resume, Password Protect checkbox in the Screen Saver settings. Then, only a password you select will turn off the screen saver and return to a normal view.**

Chapter Summary

In this chapter, you learned how to install new software and uninstall software you don't need anymore. You reviewed the process involved in installing new hardware, such as a fax machine or printer, and used the Add New Hardware wizard to set the hardware up with Windows. Finally, you made changes to your Windows XP display, including the theme, desktop background, color scheme, image settings, and screen saver.

chapter

7

Exploring Windows XP Accessories

In this Chapter

✓ Changing settings to accommodate disabilities

✓ Transferring files from your old computer to your Pavilion

✓ Faxing from your computer

✓ Saving contacts in Windows Address Book

✓ Using multimedia players and playing Windows games

Although every HP Pavilion home PC model comes packed with software (you'll learn all about those goodies in the next chapter), you should know that Windows XP itself offers several great programs you might want to take advantage of. Some of these are small utility programs that help you keep your system in shape, others are miniapplications for playing or editing multimedia files, and still others are applications to help you organize your life.

T hough there's not enough space here to take you through every accessory option in Windows XP, I've picked a few gems that you might want to check into as you learn your way around your new computing environment.

Set Yourself Up for Productivity

People come in all shapes and sizes: some with less-than-perfect hearing or vision and others who find typing or using a mouse to be a challenge. Therefore, shouldn't you be able to interact with your computer in the way that's most comfortable for you? You should. That's where Windows' Accessibility features come in. They help you to set up your computer in a way that provides optimum visual, sound, and input options.

Meet Accessibility Wizard

Wizards are what Windows uses to make your computing life easy. Accessibility Wizard helps you make all the right choices about how you'll interact with your computer. By walking you through a few step-by-step windows, this wizard helps you set up the text size that's best for you, the input mode that makes sense if you have difficulty using a keyboard or mouse, and other features that assist the vision and hearing challenged.

✔ **To run the wizard, follow these steps:**

1. Open the Start menu from the Windows XP desktop and then click All Programs, Accessories, Accessibility, Accessibility Wizard. The Welcome screen appears.

hp pavilion pcs

2. Click Next to move to the Text Size portion of the wizard, shown in Figure 7.1.

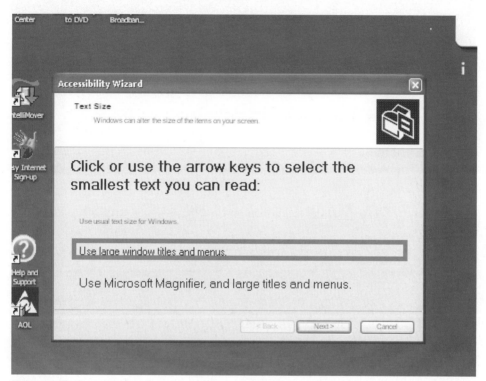

FIGURE 7.1 Pretend you're getting an eye test and pick out the line of text that's easiest to read from this window.

3. Click the size of text that you can read easily and then click Next. The Display Settings dialog box shown in Figure 7.2 appears.

FIGURE 7.2 These display settings include features to help those with vision challenges.

4. If you selected an increased font size in the previous window, the Change the Font Size option is already checked here. If you didn't make a previous choice and want a larger font size, click that option now.

5. To enlarge the display on your computer, click one or both of the next two options, Switch to a Lower Screen Resolution, or Use Microsoft Magnifier. A lower screen resolution makes items on your screen larger. (Microsoft Magnifier is a magnification program that you'll explore in more detail shortly.)

tip **Note that lowered screen resolution enlarges items, but it also makes for a less crisp screen image because of fewer dpi on your screen, so the tradeoff in readability may not be acceptable to some.**

6. You can click to disable personalized menus. This setting helps by keeping choices on menus in a consistent order, so you can depend on the location of each menu choice if you must make those choices without being able to read them easily.

7. Click Next to proceed. The Set Wizard Options dialog box appears.

8. Make choices here depending on whether you have vision, hearing, or input challenges. Based on what you select here, the rest of the wizard windows offer different options.

9. When you've made your selections in this window, click Next to proceed. You are then presented with various options, such as SoundSentry shown in Figure 7.3.

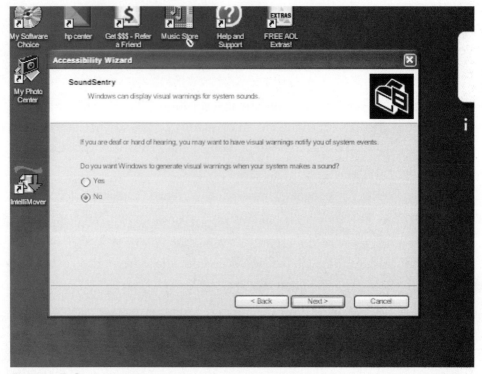

FIGURE 7.3   SoundSentry can generate visual signals whenever Windows plays an event sound; other sound options include ShowSounds, which provides captions for speech or sounds.

10. Work through each wizard window by making appropriate choices and clicking Next. When the wizard has run through all options, click Finish to save all your settings.

Expand Your Vision with Magnifier

Magnifier is a program that allows you to expand the images on your screen. If you've ever used a magnifying glass, you'll know the pros and cons of this feature. It can make elements on screen huge, but you can only see a small area at any one time.

Microsoft recommends that, if you have a serious visual disability, you consider obtaining a full magnification utility program. However if you have only a slight visual impairment and want to zoom in on things occasionally, this utility can be of help.

✔ **To use Magnifier, follow these steps:**

1. Open the Start menu from the Windows desktop and then click All Programs, Accessories, Accessibility, Magnifier. Your window is split in two with a smaller portion at the top showing a magnified view of your screen and the lower area showing the regular view. You'll also see a message about the limited usefulness of this program, with a link to an area of Microsoft's Web site that suggests more robust magnification utility programs.

2. Click OK to proceed. The Magnifier Settings dialog box shown in Figure 7.4 appears.

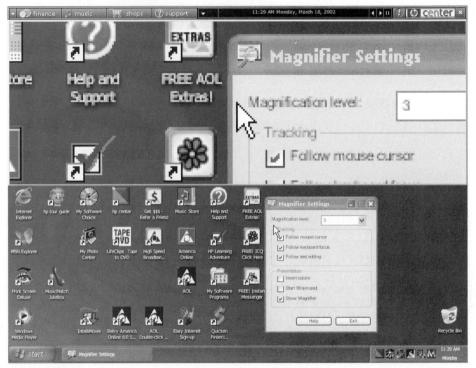

FIGURE 7.4 The enlarged mouse cursor in the upper window echoes the movements of your regular cursor in the lower window.

3. To see more of the magnified portion of your screen, place your mouse cursor over the bottom edge of the top window until it becomes a two-way arrow and drag down to enlarge it.

4. Move your cursor around the screen to see various portions of it enlarged.

5. If you want Magnifier to stop following your mouse cursor, deselect that option in the dialog box.

6. If you like, you can select a higher or lower magnification setting from the Magnification level drop-down list.

tip **You can also use the arrow or Page Up/Page Down keys on your keyboard to increase or decrease the magnification setting.**

7. When you're done using Magnifier, click Exit.

Note that Magnifier can be turned on from within any application to read documents or to view images that you might be having trouble seeing clearly.

Bring Your Old Computer with You

The Files and Settings Transfer Wizard is new to Windows XP and can save you time and frustration if you are moving from another computer to your HP Pavilion. The Files and Settings Transfer Wizard allows you to copy various files and settings from one computer to another. For example, you can download all the contacts from any address books and transfer settings for hardware or other features from another computer to your Pavilion.

The easiest way to run this wizard is to have a connection between your old and new computer. You can connect with a serial cable that plugs into the back of your computers or use a network connection. This gets a little technical, but the savings in time because you don't have to reenter information or redo settings can be worth it.

Do It the Old-Fashioned Way

You can also use the wizard without connecting your computers by copying the wizard to a disk (or having your Windows XP disk handy) and then using the wizard on your old computer to perform the process of transferring files and settings to a blank disk. Insert that disk into the new computer and transfer the contents to your new computer. The wizard transfers settings you've made as well as files.

You can use three types of cables for a direct connection, but you're likely to have to buy one, because this type of cable doesn't come with your HP or with any new computer. You can buy either a LapLink, or null modem serial cable, or a serial file transfer cable from your local computer store, or you can order one online through vendors such as CompUSA or an office supply superstore such as Staples. Each computer must also have a serial port with 25 or 9 pins. Any HP Pavilion has such a port, as will most newer computers, but some older computers may not. If you've got the right ports, when you plug a serial cable into each computer, Windows automatically detects the connection and runs the wizard.

If you have a home network set up, you can transfer files and settings between two PCs. Setting up a network involves installing additional hardware in each computer and connecting them with cables or a wireless hookup. Home networks allow you to access the same printers, fax machines, and Internet connections from more than one computer and to easily share files among the computers.

Start the wizard by selecting Start, All Programs, Accessories, System Tools, File and Settings Transfer Wizard. Depending on how you have been able to connect your two computers, follow the instructions to affect the transfer. If you don't have a direct connection, you may be asked to have your Windows XP CD available, or to copy the wizard onto a blank disk.

Connect with Others

Windows XP offers a nice little faxing program that allows you to fax documents saved as computer files. (If you have a scanner, this feature becomes even more convenient because you can scan any document, even a handwritten one, into a computer file and then fax it). In addition, there's an Address Book program that helps you keep all your email and phone addresses straight.

Fax It!

Here's good news. You may be able to throw away that clunky old fax machine forever. That's because Windows XP's little faxing program enables you to send and receive faxes from your computer. The program allows you to create cover sheets and then fax any file to which you have access.

caution **Don't throw away your fax machine if you don't have a scanner. Computer fax programs can only fax documents that exist as computer files. If you can't scan documents into a computer file format, you'll need that little machine to feed hard copy documents into the phone lines.**

Before you can use the faxing program, you have to set it up.

✔ **Follow these simple steps to configure your faxing program:**

1. Select Start, All Programs, Accessories, Communications, Fax, Fax Console. Assuming you've never used the program, the Fax Configuration Wizard shown in Figure 7.5 appears.

hp pavilion pcs

FIGURE 7.5   Some of the information you enter here automatically appears on fax cover sheets.

2. Complete any fields you want included on fax cover sheets; this allows the Fax program to automate the creation of cover sheets. Click Next.

3. At the second (and last) wizard window, click Finish. The Fax Console then appears.

4. Click Tools, Sender Information. All the information you entered in the configuration wizard should be included there. Edit the information if you like, and click OK when you're done.

5. To create a cover page, click Tools, Personal Cover Pages.

6. Click New to create a new cover page. The dialog box shown in Figure 7.6 is displayed.

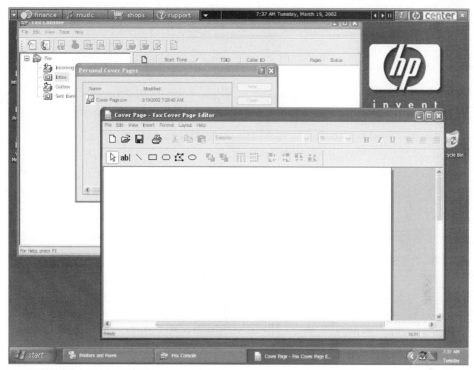

FIGURE 7.6 This simple editing program allows you to add text and drawing shapes to your cover sheets.

7. Click Text and drag on the page to create a text box.

8. Type any heading you want to use for your fax cover sheet, such as the addressee's contact information, your name, your company, phone number, fax number, and possibly the date and subject of the fax.

tip Instead of creating a text box, use the Insert menu as a shortcut to insert sender and recipient fields with placeholders for your specific information. After creating these fields, you can move them around the page as you like and format text within them.

9. If you want, you can use the drawing tools to draw rectangles, circles, and so on. There are also tools to align text and objects on the page.

10. Click File, Save to save the sheet. By default, Windows places the sheet in the Fax folder of the My Documents folder.

Project: **Send a Fax to a Friend**

Create an invitation to an upcoming event, such as a school play or party, and then fax it to a friend. If you don't know your friend's fax number, you'll have to call him or her to get it. Another possibility is to fax an invitation to the next holiday party from your office to your home fax.

To send a fax, you proceed as if you were going to print the document, but designate Fax as your printer.

✔ Follow these steps to fax a document:

1. Open the document in the application where it was created, such as Word or Works.

2. Select File, Print. The Print dialog box appears.

3. Select Fax from the Name drop-down list at the top of the dialog box.

4. Click Print. The Fax Wizard appears.

5. Click Next to begin the wizard. The Recipient Information dialog box shown in Figure 7.7 is displayed.

Ready

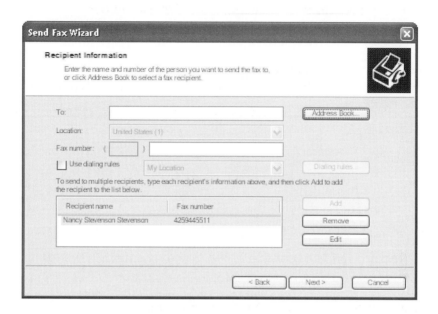

FIGURE 7.7   If you have contacts in an Outlook address book or the Windows Address Book, you can address your fax using the Address Book button in this dialog box.

6. Enter the recipient's name. If you want, you can click the Address Book icon and select a recipient from your stored contact information.

7. Click Use Dialog Rules. This makes the various fields for location and fax number available and tells Windows to use information about your location, phone, and modem settings to send the fax.

8. Enter a fax number. If the default location of the United States is acceptable, just leave that setting alone. If not, you can choose another location from that drop-down list.

9. Repeat steps 6 and 8 for any other recipients.

10. Click Next. The Preparing the Cover Page dialog box appears.

11. Select a cover page from the Cover page template drop-down list. If you created a personal cover page, it will be listed there.

12. Enter a subject in the Subject text box.

13. If you want, you can click Sender Information and fill in any information required by fields in your cover page. Note that, if you chose the recipient from the Address list, any information about them stored in your address book is already available to Windows Fax.

14. Click Next. The Schedule dialog box appears.

15. You can save a few pennies by selecting a time when discount long-distance rates apply in this dialog box. Click When discount rates apply, or click Specific time… to set a time to send the fax.

16. If you are sending multiple faxes, you might want to set the priority of this one by clicking High, Normal, or Low.

17. Click Next. The final wizard window appears displaying the information and settings you've entered.

18. Click Preview Fax. Both the cover page and document pages can be viewed here by using the Previous Image and Next Image buttons, and you can annotate the pages to add notes or drawing objects.

19. When you're ready to send your fax, click Close in the upper right corner to close the Preview, and click Finish to complete the Fax Wizard sequence. The Fax Monitor shown in Figure 7.8 appears, showing you the progress of your fax.

FIGURE 7.8 Make choices for when to send the fax and how to prioritize multiple faxes in this dialog box.

That's it. Your document and cover sheet are on their way to your recipient.

Address Book

We all have too many names, faces, email addresses, and fax numbers to remember these days. What to do? Take a look at Windows XP Address Book. Here's a central location where you can store all your contact information, and use it to easily address mail or even dial the phone for you.

You may have run into an address book feature in your email program. Programs such as Outlook and Outlook Express have an address book, which saves contact information in the Windows Address Book (.wab) format. If you don't have such a feature, or if you prefer to use an address book separate from a mail program, you can use the standalone Address Book feature in Windows.

tip **The good news is that you can import and export .wab files between Outlook and Address Book easily. Just open the program you want to copy an address book into and use the File, Import, Address Book (WAB) option. There is also an Other Address Book option on this menu to import Comma Separated Value (.csv) or Lightweight Directory Access Protocol (LDAP) Data Interchange Format (LDIF) files.**

✔ **To add contacts to your Windows Address Book, follow these steps:**

1. Select Start, All Programs, Accessories, Address Book. The Address Book appears.

2. Click New and select New Contact. The Properties dialog box shown in Figure 7.9 appears.

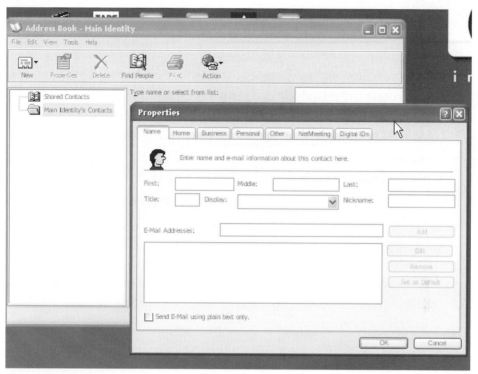

hp pavilion pcs

FIGURE 7.9 Seven—count 'em—seven tabs worth of information can be input in this little dialog box.

3. Enter information on the Name tab of this dialog box, including First, Middle, and Last names; Title; Display (the name that should be displayed in the list of contacts); and even a Nickname.

4. If you want to send email to people, record their E-mail Addresses. If there are multiple email addresses, enter one, click Add, then enter another, click Add, and so on until they are all entered.

tip Be sure to set the email address you use most often as the Default address by clicking it in the list and then clicking Set as Default. That's the address that will be used whenever you select this name from the contact list in your email program.

You can use other tabs in this dialog box to enter information, including the following:

- *Home tab*—Use this to enter home address information and even to have Windows display a map to the home address automatically.
- *Business tab*—Enter business information, such as address, job title, department, and company Web page.
- *Personal tab*—Here's where you can enter all that information that makes your next call or email more personal, such as the names of the contact's spouse and children, and special dates like birthday and anniversary. Sales people, take note.
- *NetMeeting tab*—If you're going to use Microsoft's online meeting feature, NetMeeting, you can enter connection information for conferences here.
- *Digital IDs tab*—If you practice secure emailing, you'll want to note any digital ID information for this contact's email address. Digital IDs allow you to identify and read protected information from this person.

When you've finished entering all the information for this contact, click OK. You can now click the contact in the Address Book list and use the Action button to send email or to dial the contact's phone number. In various programs, such as Microsoft Works, you can use commands, such as Insert, Address to open your Address Book and to select contact records to automate text entry.

Multimedia Madness

Now for the fun stuff! Without having to install fancy multimedia software, Windows allows you to work with sound, video, and photos with built-in, easy-to-use multimedia accessories. You can record and play voice and music files, edit video clips, and work with graphic images like a pro.

Windows Media Player

The Windows Media Player is an application that allows you to play back sound files, listen to the radio, and assemble play lists. You can copy music from a CD or the radio, or open any sound file on your computer or the Internet and play it back.

Sound files come in several formats, including Musical Instrument Digital Interface (MIDI), .wav, and so on, which Windows Media Player can handle with ease. Microsoft even provides several sample files you can use to learn your way around Windows Media Player.

✔ **Try opening and playing back a sample music file by following these steps:**

1. Select Start, All Programs, Accessories, Entertainment, Windows Media Player. The player window appears, looking like Figure 7.10.

hp pavilion pcs

FIGURE 7.10 Play a variety of media formats from the Windows Media Player.

2. Click the Media Library link on the list in the blue bar along the left side of the screen. If this is the first time you've used Windows Media Player, you may get a message at this point; just click OK.

3. In the Media Library list that appears, double-click the Album item in the Audio folder.

4. Click the file "Like Humans Do" (the file name with a blue dot next to it in the title list).

5. As the song plays, you can watch its progress as the Seek icon moves across the screen. To move through the song, drag the Seek button to the right to go forward or to the left to go back.

6. Use the Stop, Play, or Volume buttons to control the playback.

7. When the song has finished playing, you can continue to explore the Media Player window (check out the Radio Tuner or Media

Guide). Click Close in the upper right corner of the player when you're done.

Note that you must have a sound card and speakers to play and hear sound from your computer. Depending on your computer/monitor setup, speakers might be integrated with your monitor, or you can plug external speakers into your monitor and computer. Every HP Pavilion comes with your sound card and speakers either already set up for you, or they will set up automatically when Windows detects new devices you add on, such as speakers. Therefore, you should have no problem getting sound going.

There is one final cool feature. Try using different 'skins' for your playback controls by clicking the Skin Chooser option in Windows Media Player. These are artsy versions of the control buttons pointed out on Figure 7.10. Figure 7.11 shows a preview of the Canvas skin. Take a look and figure out which graphic elements match the Play, Stop, Previous, Seek, and other controls in this image.

hp pavilion pcs

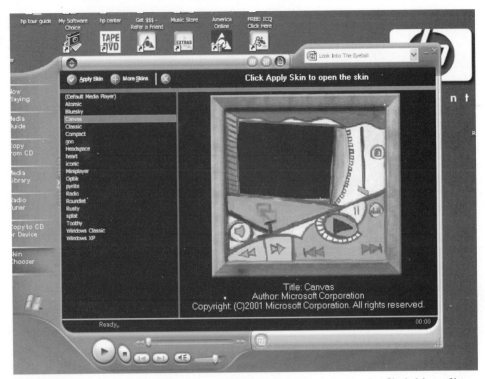

FIGURE 7.11   Several built-in skins offer cool playback controls. Click *More Skins* to access skins on the Net at WindowsMedia.com.

Windows Moviemaker

If you're a full motion kind of person, Windows Moviemaker is for you. This great little program lets you open video clips, edit them, organize them in collections, and even email them to friends.

caution   Keep in mind that video files can be memory hogs. You might consider using the writeable CD or DVD drive that comes with many Pavilion models to store video collections and free up space on your computer.

✔ **Take a look at Windows Moviemaker and play back a sample video by following these steps:**

1. Select Start, All Programs, Accessories, Windows MovieMaker.

2. Select File, Import.

3. If it's not already selected, locate the My Videos folder in the Look In drop-down list.

4. Click the Windows Movie Maker Sample File and click Open. The video sequence is opened in the Movie Maker window, as shown in Figure 7.12.

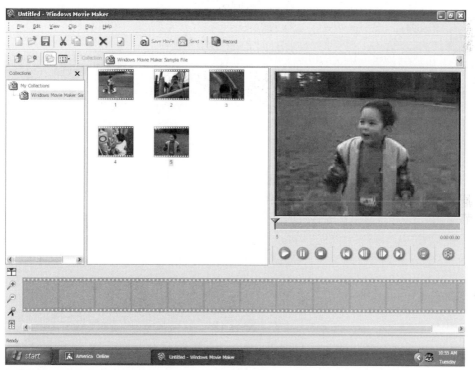

FIGURE 7.12 Use the controls here to stop or playback the video clip.

5. Click any one of the five segments displayed as a thumbnail and then click Play. That segment of the clip plays.

6. To play the entire segment, click the first segment and then, holding down Shift, click on the last one. Then click Play.

7. While the longer video is playing, if you want to have the video play back in a larger area, click Full Screen. When the video is done, press Esc to return to the Movie Maker.

8. You can string together several video clips in any sequence you like by using the Clip, Add to Storyboard/Timeline command. The selected images are added to the film strip area at the bottom of the screen. You can also cut individual segments using Edit tools.

9. If you create a movie you want to save, click File, Save and save it to your computer or a writeable CD.

10. If you want to email a video clip, select Send, E-mail and complete information about the video attachment in the Send Movie Via E-mail dialog box.

11. When you're done, select File, Exit to close Windows Movie Maker.

There are plenty of features in this product you can discover by playing with the sample file and exploring the Microsoft Movie Maker on the Web site (select Help, Microsoft Movie Maker on the Web to get there). If you have your own digital camcorder, upload your videos to your computer. You're in for hours of fun editing, storing, and playing back home videos.

Paint

Paint has been around a while, and, if you've used a Windows-based computer before, you have probably encountered it. It's an easy-to-use graphics program that lets you open graphics files in several formats, edit and annotate the images, and save them.

Using the tools in Paint, shown in Figure 7.13, you can crop an image, draw on it, fill objects with color, and add text. You can work with a variety of file formats, from a Joint Photographic Experts Group (JPEG) photograph file to a Windows bitmap file containing drawn objects, or even an animation file in Graphic Interchange Format (GIF).

FIGURE 7.13 Use text and drawing tools to modify any image in Paint.

Project: **Designing a Family Crest**

If your family were to have a family crest, as families did in olden days, what would it look like? Use Paint to draw shapes and add colors to design a new family crest. Think of one image that represents each person in your family and include it in a sort of collage. For example, if someone plays music, draw a musical note or, if another person plays basketball, draw a circle with lines on it to indicate that.

✔ **To design your crest in Paint, follow these steps:**

1. Select Start, All Programs, Accessories, Paint.

2. In the Paint program, select File, Open and locate the graphics file you want to work with.

3. Use the various tools to draw on the document.

4. Click objects to select them and use the Eraser, Fill with Color, or other tools to modify them.

5. Click the Text tool and then type text directly onto the image.

6. Use tools such as the Brush or Airbrush to paint on your image.

7. When you're done, save the file by selecting File, Save and choosing the best file format for your purposes in the Save dialog box, Save as Type list.

Fun and Games

Windows XP provides almost a dozen games you might want to know about to help you while away those long boring hours at work or home. The games on offer include the following:

- FreeCell
- Hearts
- Internet Backgammon
- Internet Checkers
- Internet Hearts
- Internet Reversi
- Internet Spades
- Minesweeper
- Pinball (shown in Figure 7.14)
- Solitaire
- Spider Solitaire

FIGURE 7.14 Pinball offers a virtual pinball game, complete with flashing lights and bouncing ball.

As the names suggest, several of these games are played on the Internet. When you select one of these, you will be set up by Zone.com to play a match with somebody else who is logged on at the same time that you access the game. Who knows, you might find yourself playing checkers with a sheep rancher in Australia or back-gammon with a rock star in London.

You access games by selecting Start, All Programs, Games. Internet games will direct you to an online site to find your partner. Other games simply open at this point ready for you to play. Check each game's menus to get a demo of the game, rules, or to launch a new game with one or more players. Many also allow you to control sounds, music, and player functions *tip* **Read more about playing games in Chapter 10.**

Chapter Summary

In this chapter, you explored some of the settings you can make to Windows XP to make your computer more accessible and easy to use. You learned about the Files and Settings Transfer Wizard and how it can save you effort by moving files from your old computer to your new one. Then you discovered what programs are built into Windows XP Accessories, from faxing software and an address book to multimedia players and games.

part 3

Taking Advantage of Pre-Installed Software

8

Working with Computer Utilities

In this Chapter

✔ Maintaining your hard drive with Disk Cleanup

✔ Running PC Doctor for Windows

✔ Saving yourself with System Restore

✔ Finding relief with HP Application Recovery and PC System Recovery

✔ Running McAfee.com VirusScan

A computer is something like the human brain. It takes in a lot of different kinds of information and input from a variety of sources, and all that information has to work together. Conflicting information can cause problems. In addition, sometimes both the brain and your computer have to deal with an invading virus.

Just as a stressed-out person can go on overload, your computer can come crashing down if it's being pulled in too many directions. There are programs that you use to maintain your computer's health, and they're called utilities. In this chapter, you'll learn about utility programs on your Pavilion that can help keep your computer going strong.

Keeping Your Hard Drive in Shape

Some utilities help to make your hard drive more efficient or test the setup of files for greatest efficiency. Disk Cleanup and PC Doctor for Windows are included with your Pavilion to organize and diagnose hard drive issues.

Using Disk Cleanup

Your hard drive is essentially a large storage medium, but it doesn't always store files in one piece. It can put some bits of data from a file in one sector and then throw a few others in a different location. As time goes by, your hard drive is like a checkerboard with bits of data spread everywhere. Many little bits of data become obsolete and are just sitting there cluttering things up.

Disk Cleanup is a utility that goes through your hard drive and identifies ways to make it more efficient. For example, it can consolidate some data into adjoining slots or delete things like temporary files that have been created while you were working, but that are not needed by any program anymore. By cleaning up how data is stored on your hard drive, you can improve your computer's performance.

To run Disk Cleanup, select Start, All Programs, Accessories, System Tools, Disk Cleanup. The dialog box in Figure 8.1 appears, indicating that the program is gathering data on your hard drive.

FIGURE 8.1   Disk Cleanup is taking a look at your hard drive.

When the program finishes checking your hard drive, the dialog box in Figure 8.2 appears. This shows how much total space Disk Cleanup can save you by deleting certain files. If you want to see the files the utility intends to delete, you can click View Files.

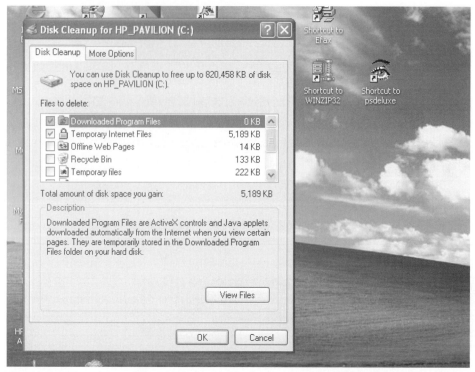

FIGURE 8.2   I had 820,458 kilobytes (kb) of junk on my computer to get rid of!

Click OK. You get a confirming dialog box, asking if you're sure you want to complete the cleanup and to delete the files. That's all there is to it.

You should run Disk Cleanup every few months to keep your hard drive in order.

note **The More Options tab of Disk Cleanup offers other ways of clearing space on your hard drive, including removing optional Windows components, uninstalling programs you don't use, or running a System Restore. You'll read more about System Restore later in this chapter.**

Getting a House Call from PC Doctor

One of the reasons computers can have problems is that the software and hardware you use were not created by one company. Companies have used different standards and even different computer languages to create your software and hardware drivers. When there are incompatibilities between two software products or between Windows' system settings and a piece of hardware, you run into situations where things don't work the way you expected them to. However, understanding what's causing the conflict is very difficult when you have hundreds of programs on your hard drive and possibly half a dozen hardware peripherals attached to your computer.

tip **If you buy hardware, such as your computer, monitor, printer, and fax machine from one manufacturer (such as HP or Compaq), you may cut down on some of these problems because that manufacturer typically uses common standards and designs its products to integrate smoothly.**

Before you can solve a problem with your computer, you have to diagnose it correctly. That's where PC Doctor comes in. This program, included with HP Tools on all Pavilion computers, runs tests on the hardware components of your system—for example, your modem, printer, scanner, or sound card—to see if they're working properly. PC Doctor doesn't solve the hardware problem, because that usually requires human intervention. However, it provides you or a technical support or service person with the information required to identify the problem.

✔ **Take a moment to run a test on one element of your system to see what kind of information PC Doctor can provide.**

1. Select Start, All Programs, HP Tools, PC Doctor for Windows XP. The window shown in Figure 8.3 appears.

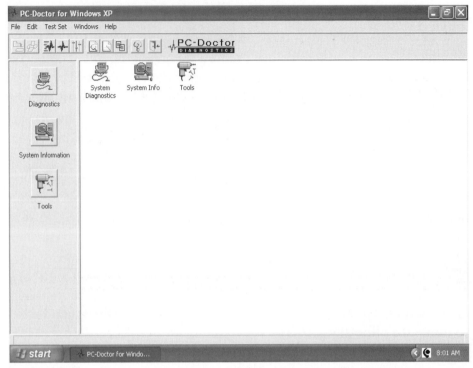

FIGURE 8.3   There are three areas of PC Doctor: System Diagnostics, System Info, and Tools.

2. Double-click System Diagnostics. A list of tests appears.

3. Double-click Audio Test. The dialog box shown in Figure 8.4 appears.

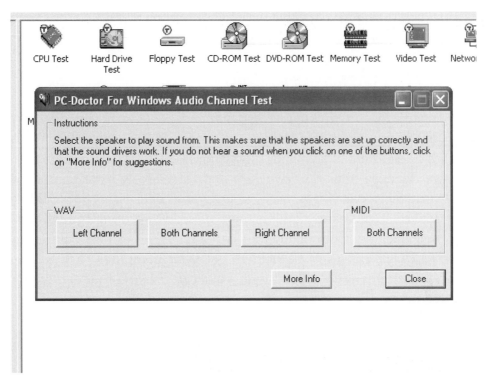

FIGURE 8.4 Some tests, such as this one, require your input; others simply run on their own.

4. Click Left Channel. Music should play from your left speaker.

5. Click Right Channel. Music should play from your right speaker.

6. Click MIDI Both Channels. Music should play from both speakers.

7. If you don't hear sound when you perform any of these steps, click More Info. This opens a dialog box suggesting some steps you could take to solve the problem.

8. Click OK to close the More Info dialog box and then Close to finish the test.

Go ahead and try any other test included here. They can't hurt anything on your system. You'll see that some simply run on their own producing a test result, and others, such as the Keyboard or Audio test, require that you take certain actions to test your hardware.

Next time you have trouble with hardware, go to PC Doctor to see if it can help isolate the problem.

Recovering from Disaster

Most of the time your computing experience will be just great, with no crashes or disasters of any kind. However, I won't kid you; disasters do happen. Because of all the hardware and software on your computer, files you download from here, there, and everywhere (including destructive viruses) and new versions of software bringing new settings and files, conflicts occur that can cause you to lose data or, in extreme cases, not even be able to get your computer to function. Several programs are included with your HP Pavilion that give you a disaster safety net.

Going Back in Time with System Restore

One utility that is part of Windows XP is called System Restore. You can use this program to restore your computer to some time in the past, for example, one hour ago or last Tuesday. System Restore creates automatic restore points, and you can select which one will suit your purposes or create your own. Then, you can go back to those computer settings to undo some change you may have made that resulted in a problem.

System Restore doesn't affect your documents or email, but it will change Windows XP settings for your system and hardware back to what they were before you started having trouble. In many cases, that solves the problem.

System Restore can also be a useful preventive method if you are considering making a change to your computer and you're concerned that action could cause a problem. You can create a restore point yourself just before making the change and restore to that point if you encounter a problem.

hp pavilion pcs

✔ **To restore to an automatically saved restore point, follow these steps:**

1. Select Start, All Programs, Accessories, System Tools, System Restore. The Welcome screen shown in Figure 8.5 appears.

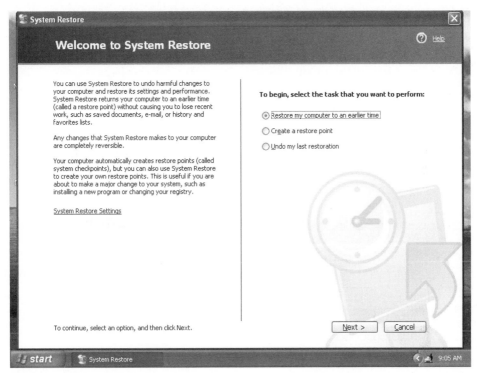

FIGURE 8.5   You have the option of using an automatically saved restore point or creating one of your own.

2. Make sure the Restore My Computer to an Earlier Time option is selected and then click Next. The Select a Restore Point dialog box appears.

3. Click a date with a bold number on it; these are the restoration points available to you. You'll see a listing of actions performed on each date that created a restore point, as in Figure 8.6.

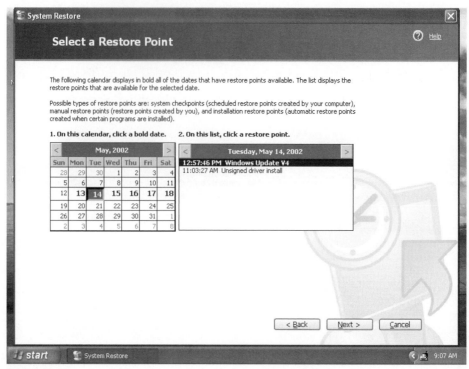

FIGURE 8.6   Find the action you want undone in this list.

4. Click a restore point and then Next. The Confirm dialog box shown in Figure 8.7 appears, explaining what will happen should you click Next to proceed.

FIGURE 8.7 Warnings are in red in this descriptive dialog box.

5. Click Next. The System Restore runs, shutting down Windows and restarting. A Restoration Complete window appears, allowing you to view any files that were renamed.

6. Click OK to close System Restore.

caution **If you run a System Restore to a point before you installed a piece of software, it doesn't uninstall the software; it just reverts any changes made to your system at the time of installation. You should still go to the Control Panel and run the Add or Remove Programs sequence to remove the program entirely.**

How HP Application and System Recovery Work

HP Application Recovery and System Recovery are programs that restore factory settings to your computer. Application Recovery reinstalls any software applications that came with your Pavilion when you first opened the box. System Recovery restores system settings. You can do a nondestructive recovery. This does not delete your documents and other files and does reinstall Windows and restore settings. You can also do a destructive recovery that gets rid of anything you've added to your computer since you first booted up. Destructive recoveries are used in case of severe computer problems.

Each program can be accessed through the HP Tools item on your Start, All Programs menu. When you select HP Application Recovery from the HP Tools menu, you'll go through a series of windows, such as the one shown in Figure 8.8, to select the applications to recover.

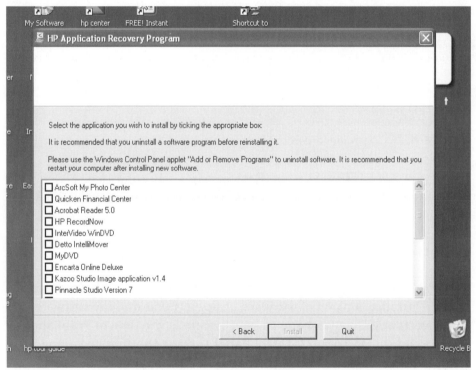

FIGURE 8.8   Click the checkbox for any application you want the feature to recover.

When you access System Recovery through the HP Tools menu, you see a message (see Figure 8.9) asking you if you're sure you want to run the recovery. Simply click Yes to proceed.

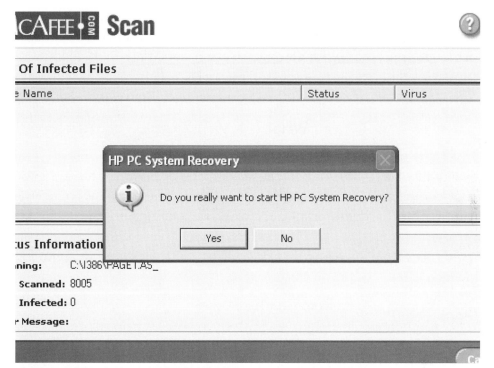

FIGURE 8.9   Because System Recovery makes changes to your computer, you are asked to confirm your choice to run it.

If you have experienced serious damage and your computer cannot load Windows, you can access System Recovery by turning off your computer. When you next turn it on and the HP Invent blue screen appears, press F10 repeatedly to open the System Recovery program.

caution   **It is strongly recommended that you try using Windows XP's System Restore before using System Recovery to solve any problem because System Recovery can cause a more drastic change to your computer systems.**

Get Protected with McAfee Online VirusScan

With so much time spent on the Internet today, people and their computers are at risk. Because it's often difficult to tell where downloaded files and email attachments originated, it's hard to keep potentially harmful material off your hard drive. That's where antivirus software comes in. It protects your computer settings and data from changes or damage.

What Is a Virus?

A virus is a small computer program, typically taking the form of an executable file, that runs and causes damage or performs an action on your computer. Viruses are created and spread by people who run the gamut from harmless pranksters to those wanting to cause serious damage.

Viruses have appeared that do a variety of things, including the following:

- Wiping all data from your hard drive
- Generating an email to everybody in your e-mail address book to spread the virus to their systems
- Causing a message or graphic to appear on your screen
- Making your CD drawer open and close continuously
- Causing files to be saved in a different format than you think you're saving to, for example, saving a word processing document as a template rather than a document

You get the idea. These things can be jokes, or they can ruin your whole day. Luckily, a good antivirus program can spot many viruses and stop them in their tracks.

What Options Does McAfee Offer?

McAfee antivirus software is one of several popular antivirus programs, and it's included on your Pavilion as a 90-day free trial. McAfee, like other antivirus programs, depends on you updating a list of virus definitions from their Web site frequently and scanning your hard drive to spot viruses included on that list. The definitions must be updated regularly because new viruses appear all the time. If you haven't updated your software and a new virus appears, you're not protected at all, no matter how many times you scan your computer.

When you've installed McAfee and signed up for its online service, it sends you notices when new viruses have been added so that you can keep up to date.

McAfee VirusScan Online provides protection through the Internet through a one- or two-year subscription. During that time, you get all updates to virus definitions and even upgraded McAfee software for the subscription fee.

Scanning for Viruses

To run a scan for viruses using McAfee, you have to open an account. As you use your Pavilion, you'll be shown a message about activating your 90-day free trial. Follow the directions in that message to open your McAfee account and to update to the latest virus definitions.

✔ **After you have, follow these steps to run a virus scan:**

1. Select Start, All Programs, McAfee.com, McAfee.com VirusScan Online, Scan. The window shown in Figure 8.10 appears.

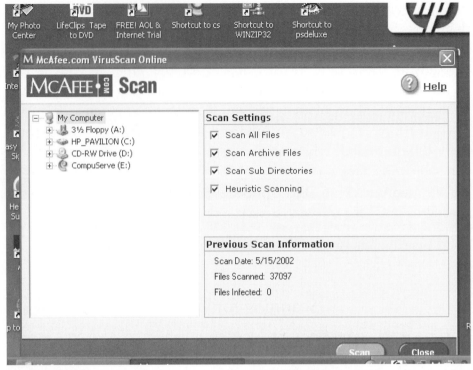

FIGURE 8.10   Choose where you want to scan from this window.

2. Click a drive, such as HPPavilion (C:), to scan your hard drive or 3 1/2 Floppy (A:) to scan a floppy disk.

3. If you want, you can change the Scan Settings to select what specific files and directories should be scanned.

4. When you're done with the settings, click Scan to run the program. The dialog box shown in Figure 8.11 appears, showing the scanning in progress and any infected files that McAfee locates.

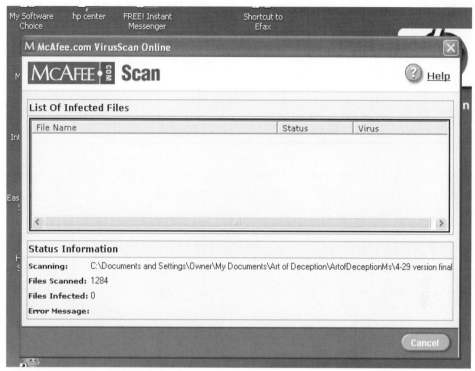

FIGURE 8.11 The scan may take a few minutes, but you can continue to use your computer while it does.

5. When the scan is complete, close the dialog box by clicking Close in the top right-hand corner.

note Heuristic scanning, an option in the Scan Settings, scans files not only for known viruses, but for anything that seems viruslike by identifying certain traits.

Chapter Summary

In this chapter, you saw some of the utilities included on your HP Pavilion that help you diagnose problems and keep your hard drive in shape. You learned about restoration utilities you can use in the event of disastrous system problems or data loss. Finally, you tried out McAfee antivirus software to scan your computer for potentially harmful viruses.

chapter

9

Words and Numbers

In this Chapter

✓ Creating documents in Works

✓ Trying out WordPerfect Office 2002

✓ Organizing your finances with Quicken

✓ Finding (Microsoft) Money

If you have work to do, you'll be happy to hear that HP has included on your Pavilion just what you need to write documents, design presentations, keep track of appointments, and run the numbers.

Depending on when you purchased your computer, you'll have some of these productivity tools:

- Suites of office software that allow you to design common documents, Microsoft Works and Corel WordPerfect Office
- Financial planning software packages, Quicken and Microsoft Money

note **If you purchased your Pavilion prior to September 2002, you have Works installed and a trial version of the WordPerfect Suite. If you purchased after that date, you will have a fully functional version of WordPerfect instead of Works. Quicken will be available on all models, but Microsoft Money is only available on earlier models.**

Working with Office Suites

Various software packages include several commonly used tools, such as word processing, spreadsheet, and presentation programs. These are called office suites because the programs they include are useful for getting your work done. Two such programs may already be installed on your HP Pavilion: Microsoft Works and Corel WordPerfect Office 2002.

One nice thing about these programs is that they integrate the features and functionality of the various programs they contain. You can easily work with similar tools and menus, move information between documents created in the different programs, and find help.

 tip **You can also relatively seamlessly convert Works documents into WordPerfect documents and vice versa, because each recognizes several other program formats.**

Getting to Work with Microsoft Works

Works from Microsoft has several good things going for it. It contains word processor, spreadsheet (to work with numbers), database (to

hp pavilion PCs

manage data), calendar, and address book components. In addition, it works with other Microsoft programs, such as Microsoft Money, MSN Photos, and Outlook Express.

One neat thing about Works is that it's designed to use wizards to easily generate commonly created documents. This makes it easy to use for people who have little experience using different types of software. Figure 9.1 shows the types of templates available in the Works Word Processor program.

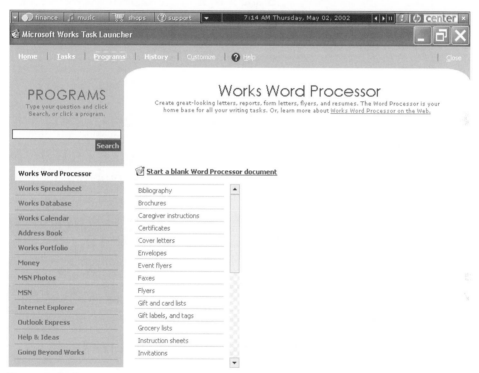

FIGURE 9.1   From brochures and event flyers to grocery lists, Works Word Processor makes designing polished-looking documents easy.

Working with Wizards

You get things done in Works by using simple-to-follow wizards. A wizard is a step-by-step walkthrough of the process involved in creating a document. Typically, with a wizard you will be asked to enter information or make choices from lists. Based on your responses, Works builds the document you've chosen. Figure 9.2 shows the choices of themes that are offered by the Event Flyers Wizard from the Works Word Processor, for example.

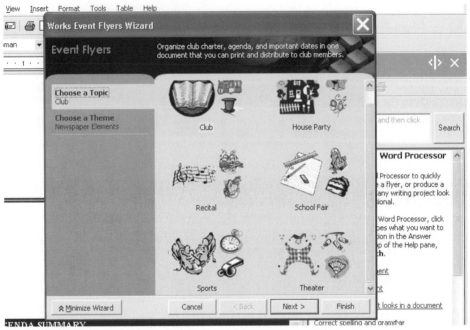

FIGURE 9.2   Microsoft has built in various common themes for your event flyer; all you have to do is choose one.

Project: **Designing an Event Flyer**

Using a Works Wizard, design a flyer for an upcoming theatrical event. Include a graphic image for the event that you find in Clip Art or download from the Internet, as well as information about where and when the event will be held.

✔ **Follow these steps to create your flyer:**

1. From the Windows desktop, select Start, All Programs, Microsoft Works, Microsoft Works Task Launcher.

2. Click the Programs tab.

3. If the Word Processor option isn't showing, click Works Word Processor in the list of programs along the left side of the Works window.

4. Click Event Flyers in the list of Word Processor documents and then the Start This Task link that appears. The wizard window shown in Figure 9.2 appears.

 tip **You can see additional types of documents by dragging the scrollbar along the right side of the list of document types.**

5. Click the Theater topic and then on Next. The Choose a Theme wizard box appears, as shown in Figure 9.3.

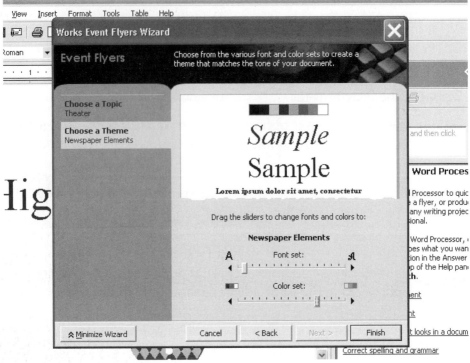

FIGURE 9.3   Easy-to-use sliders help you choose among preset fonts and color schemes.

6. Click the slider bar for either the Font set or Color set elements and drag it to a new position. You can also click any tick mark along the slider line to preview a sample of another format set.

7. When you're happy with your choices, click Finish. The event flyer shown in Figure 9.4 appears, using placeholder text and the font and color set you selected.

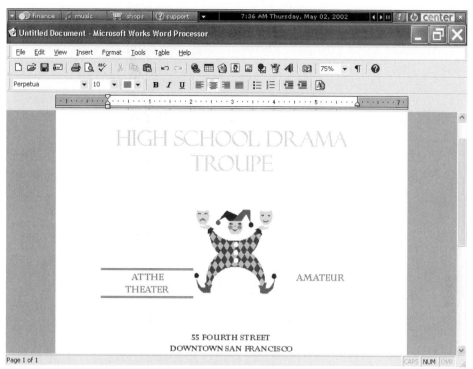

FIGURE 9.4   All the graphics and colors have been preset for you by the Works Wizard.

You can now edit the flyer as you like, entering the text you want included. You can also use any of the tools and menus of Works to modify the document in a variety of ways and then save it or print it.

Editing Works Documents

After you've generated a document in Works, you need to make it serve your specific purposes. Works has provided only placeholder text. You have to enter the specific information or data for your particular project. You can also move elements around on the page, delete or add graphics and text, or change the style of elements, such as making text bold or surrounding a graphic with a border.

✔ **Follow these steps to make some changes to the theater flyer you just generated to see how this works:**

1. Click your mouse to the left of the title "High School Drama Troupe" and drag to the right and down to highlight the entire phrase.

2. Type "Barnes Community Theater".

3. Click just above the address 55 Fourth Street and type "Presents TWELFTH NIGHT".

4. Click to the left of the line you just entered and drag to the right to select it.

5. Click the arrow next to the Font Size box on the Formatting toolbar (shown in Figure 9.5) and click 20 to enlarge the type size.

6. With the text still selected, click the Underline button.

Font   Font Size   Font color   Bold   Italic   Underline

Alignment
(4 buttons)

FIGURE 9.5   Use these tools to change the format of document text in a variety of ways.

7. Click just below the address and select Insert, Picture, Clip Art.

8. Click a piece of art, for example, one with two drama masks, and then click Insert to insert it into your document.

9. When the clip art appears, you may have to click a corner of the image and drag inward to make it small enough for all the flyer text to appear on a single page.

10. Click the Print Preview tool on the standard toolbar. The flyer should look something like the one shown in Figure 9.6.

hp pavilion pcs

FIGURE 9.6   A few simple changes have produced a professional-looking flyer or poster for your event.

11. You can save the file by selecting File, Save. Locate a folder to save it to using the Save In feature and enter a file name. Click OK to save it.

 tip **You can see the names of various tool buttons on toolbars in Works by holding your mouse pointer over each tool.**

Performing Tasks in Works

Works has several other programs available, and most are as easy to use to generate documents as the Word Processor module you just worked with to create a flyer. However, Works also allows you to approach your work a little differently, by using a task wizard instead of a document wizard.

Where the Programs listing in Works gives you lists of common documents, such as invoices and flyers, the Tasks listing lets you choose from a list of common tasks, such as checking email messages or making hotel reservations on the Internet. Figure 9.7 shows the types of tasks listed in the Household Management category to give you an idea of what's offered. Some of these tasks lead you through a wizard to produce a document, much like the event flyer wizard you used earlier. Others lead you onto the Internet to display relevant sections of MSN.com.

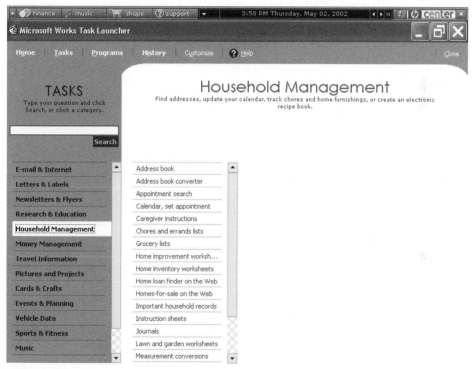

FIGURE 9.7 From home improvement to finding a home loan, these tasks help you to create documents or browse the Web.

To perform a task, you click the Tasks tab on the page that appears when you first start Works. If you select an option that involves a Web-based activity, such as Car Rental on the Web or Currency Converter on the Web, Works automatically opens your default Internet connection and takes you to the relevant Web site. If you click a task that involves producing a document, such as Caregiver Instructions or Party Planner, you'll be taken through a wizard to produce that document.

 tip **Use the History tab of the opening window of Works to look for documents you created in Works organized by Name, Date, and the Task or Program you used to create them.**

Trying out Corel WordPerfect Office

Corel WordPerfect Office 2002 is included on older HP Pavilions with a 30-day trial edition and on more recent models in a full version called Corel WordPerfect Productivity Pack. WordPerfect Office is a more robust office suite, providing more functionality than Works. WordPerfect Office includes a word processor, spreadsheet program, presentation software, day planner, email program, address book, calendar, card file, and alarm reminder feature.

✔ **To activate the trial version, follow these steps:**

1. Select Start, All Programs, WordPerfect 2002; clicking on any program listed here, such as WordPerfect 10, displays a dialog box allowing you to Buy, Relicense, or Try the program.

2. Click Try. Whatever application you had clicked opens.

note **If you have both programs available, which is better for you to use, Works or WordPerfect Office? If you are running a home business, WordPerfect Office offers stronger features, especially in the spreadsheet and presentation areas. If you're creating simple documents, spreadsheets, and databases, Works will do just fine and has the advantage of the easy-to-use wizard design.**

✔ **To Open the WordPerfect Productivity Pack, follow these steps:**

1. Double-click on the WordPerfect Task Manager icon on your desktop.

2. Click on the WordPerfect choice in the WordPerfect Task Manager to open the word processor, then on Start This Task.

Processing Words

Word processing software allows you to create documents that are largely word based, although modern word processors also make graphics and even animation available to you for Web-based documents. However, the real forte of word processors is the way they let you design with text and modify text to use various fonts and effects.

WordPerfect Tools

Take a look at the toolbars in the WordPerfect 10 word processor program, shown in Figure 9.8. They'll give you a good idea of some of the extra features you can use to design the most elaborate documents. Though you have to do more of the work yourself than you do with Works wizards, you have greater control and more tools at your disposal.

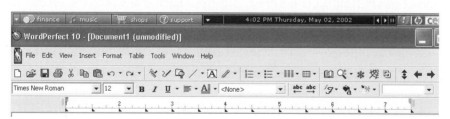

FIGURE 9.8 WordPerfect offers a great many tools that help you create documents with tables, columns, drawing objects, and more.

Project: **Creating an Invitation**

Try using WordPerfect to create a simple invitation to a reception for a family member who is visiting from far away. Pick a location for the reception and a date and time to include.

✔ **To create an invitation, follow these steps:**

1. If you need to, select Start, All Programs, WordPerfect 2002, WordPerfect 10 to open the program. If you're using the Productivity Pack, select Start, All Programs, WordPerfect Productivity Pack, WordPerfect 10.

2. In the new blank document that appears, type the following (replacing this text with your own family member and time and location information), and press Enter to start each new line:

   Please join us
   at a reception for
   Dr. Alvin Tuttle
   Monday, June 3rd at 4 p.m.
   2020 River Road
   Savannah
   RSVP 555-6699

3. Select all the text you entered and then click the Font box arrow to display possible font styles.

4. Move your mouse down the list. Font previews appear, and the selected text displays in each font as you move over that choice in the font list.

5. Click the font named Papyrus.

6. With the text still selected, click the Justification button and then click the Center choice.

7. Place your mouse at the end of the line "at a reception for" and press Enter twice.

8. Select the text "Dr. Alvin Tuttle" and change the font size to 16 (use the Font Size list on the toolbar) and make the text bold (use the Bold button on the toolbar).

9. Click at the end of the line you just formatted and press Enter.

10. Click Insert Symbol. The Symbols dialog box appears, as shown in Figure 9.9.

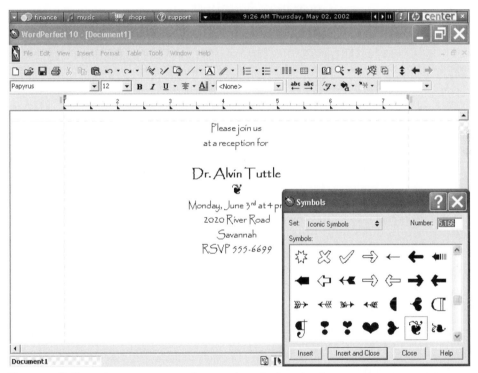

FIGURE 9.9 An elegant typeface and symbol make for an attractive invitation.

11. Click a grape leaf symbol and then click Insert and Close.

With just a few steps, you've created an elegant-looking invitation. You'll find that the rich feature set for formatting text in WordPerfect make it a word processor of choice for many professionals.

tip **If you have the trial version of WordPerfect, you can use the Buy Now button that appears on the opening window each time you start up a WordPerfect Office 2002 application during your trial period to buy the full product. This takes you to the Corel Store on the Internet. At this writing, you can extend the product installed on your computer for unlimited access for only $99 or purchase a boxed version with full documentation and CD for $119.**

Crunching Numbers

WordPerfect Office 2002 also contains a spreadsheet program called QuattroPro 10. This program allows you to create complex financial documents, performing calculations and building formulas for anything from a simple household budget to a corporate profit and loss statement.

When you open QuattroPro, you're faced with a blank spreadsheet. You can enter numbers and words in the various cells formed by intersecting columns and rows. You can then perform calculations on the numbers and format the columns and rows to make polished-looking documents. You can even include ranges of numbers contained on one sheet in a calculation performed on another sheet. For example, if you create a table of employee salaries on one sheet, you can then use them to calculate payroll taxes on another by referencing them in a formula.

Teaching you how to work with functions and formulas in a sophisticated spreadsheet program such as QuattroPro is beyond the scope of this book, but a look at Figure 9.10 shows you the type of document you can produce.

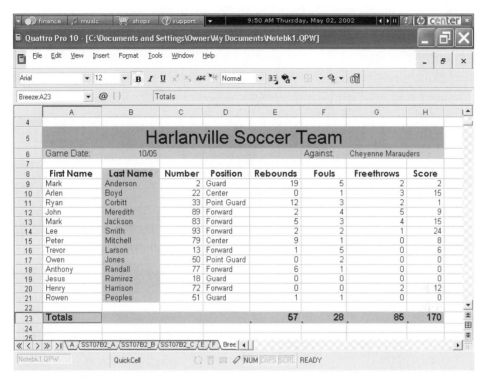

FIGURE 9.10 The totals of the columns in this team report are created as a simple Sum calculation.

 tip Use the Publish to the Web feature in WordPerfect Office 2002 to post Web browser-friendly versions of your documents online.

Presentations

One of the programs included with WordPerfect Office (included with the full version and trial version but not the Productivity Pack) is Corel Presentations 10. With this program, you can create sophisticated slide or Web presentations. Presentations 10 includes many features to make this easy, such as predesigned slide backgrounds and color schemes.

Presentations can be shown on a computer screen (for example at a science fair kiosk), projected with an Liquid Crystal Display (LCD) screen, generated as 35 mm slides, or published to the Web. You can also print presentation contents as audience handouts or to use as speaker's notes when giving a presentation.

note **If you print a presentation to the Web, it will include controls so that those viewing it with a browser can move through the slide show on their own.**

✔ **Try using the tools of Presentations 10 in the trial version of WordPerfect Office to create a simple presentation about a book you've read by following these steps:**

1. Select Start, All Programs, WordPerfect Office 2002, Corel Presentations 10.

2. When the trial version opening window appears, click Try to continue. The PerfectExpert dialog box appears. Click Corel Presentations Slide Show and then Create. The Startup Master Gallery shown in Figure 9.11 appears.

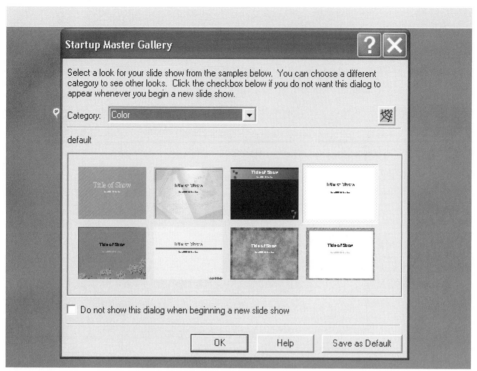

FIGURE 9.11 The gallery offers a selection of slide backgrounds for your presentation.

3. Click the second background from the left in the top row; this background contains an image of a book.

4. Click OK. The main Presentations window appears, displaying the background you selected.

5. Double-click the Title placeholder. It opens for editing as shown in Figure 9.12.

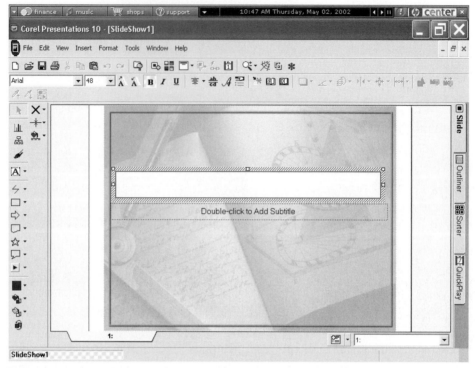

FIGURE 9.12 *Slides in Presentation have layouts applied that include various placeholders for entering text.*

6. Enter the text "Oliver Twist".

7. Double-click the Sub-title placeholder and type "By Charles Dickens".

8. Select Insert, New Slide. The New Slide dialog box appears.

9. Click the Bullet List layout (note the title of a selected layout appears above the layout previews) and click OK.

10. Double-click the Title placeholder and enter "Oliver's Adventure".

11. Double-click the Text placeholder and type these items, pressing Enter to begin each new bullet point:
    Oliver becomes an orphan and is mistreated.
    Oliver escapes and is taken in by Fagin.
    Fagin uses boys to steal money for him.

12. Click the Slide Sorter tab along the right side of the Presentations window to switch to that view.

13. Click the first of the two slides.

14. Click the QuickPlay tab to play the show from the first slide.

15. Press the right arrow key on your keyboard to advance to slide two and display the text of the slide one bullet point at a time.

16. Press Esc to end the slide show.

By creating new slides and entering text for each of the points you want to make, you can build effective presentations. You can even add special effects, such as sound and animation, or insert graphics into your show.

Profiting from Financial Software

A popular type of application for home businesses and families is financial software. Financial software helps you organize your spending, track tax information, and even print out checks while keeping a record of every expense. Two programs are leaders in this field: Quicken from Intuit and Microsoft Money.

 tip **You can access Microsoft Money from within Microsoft Works or by clicking Microsoft Money 2002 on your All Programs menu.**

A Quick Tour of Quicken

Quicken is one of the most popular financial management packages around, and you'll soon see why. With Quicken, you can manage banking, investments, family and business budgets, and loans. The beauty of the program is that you can enter all your financial information—from school loans to stock market investments and monthly household expenses—in one place and then use and track that information in a wide variety of ways.

note **The version of Quicken on your Pavilion is the New User Edition, which does not have all the features of the full program. If you like, you can install the Quicken Deluxe version for $29.95. Do this by selecting Start, All Programs, Quicken, Unlock Quicken Deluxe and following the instructions there.**

✔ **You have to run an installation program to be able to use Quicken. To do this, follow these steps:**

1. Select Start, All Programs, Quicken New User Edition Setup.

2. Click Next.

3. On the next window, click Yes to accept the license agreement.

4. On the final screen, make sure the Express installation is selected and click Install Now.

After it's installed, you can open Quicken by selecting Start, All Programs, Quicken, Quicken 2002 New User Edition. The first time you open the program you are asked to go through a New User Setup wizard. Complete this wizard by checking options that apply (such as whether you're married or own your own home) so that Quicken can build a basic financial profile of you. You'll then be presented with the main window shown in Figure 9.13.

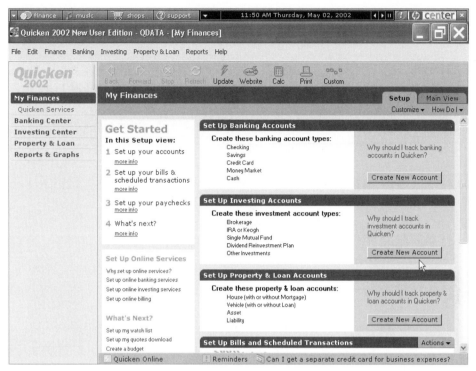

FIGURE 9.13 Quicken offers setup options for your various financial accounts.

To use Quicken effectively, you have to enter information about your various accounts, such as bank accounts, investments, loans, and regular expenses (see Figure 9.14). For example, you can enter information about your bank accounts by following these steps:

1. Click Create New Account in the Set Up Banking Accounts section of the Setup window.

2. Select a type of account, such as checking or savings.

3. Enter the last statement date and balance.

That's it. You can now connect with any institution that offers online access to your account and your online account information can be interfaced with Quicken. You can continue to create accounts and then use Quicken to write checks or to generate tax information.

FIGURE 9.14 This sample account list from the Quicken 2002 Tour shows the kind of information you can obtain after you've entered data into Quicken.

caution **It can take time to enter all your financial information into Quicken, but after you do, financial management will be much easier. However, do set aside a few hours to set Quicken up the first time you use it.**

After all your information is up to date in Quicken, you can use a variety of reports to review your financial status, such as your net worth or investment trends. Quicken can also generate charts and graphs that help you visualize your financial information.

Getting Familiar with Money

Microsoft Money is similar to Quicken, but does not offer quite as many features for more serious financial management, such as running a small business. If your goal is to keep track of personal finances and to keep the family accounts in order, Money may be just fine. It offers an easy-to-use interface (see Figure 9.15) and the ability to interface with online account information.

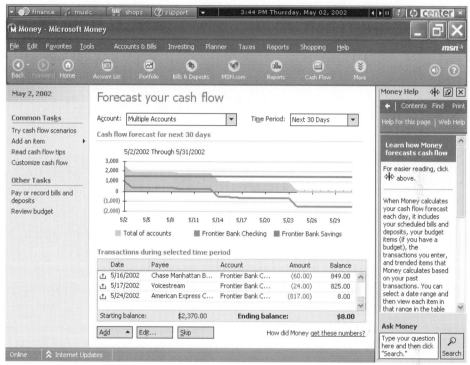

FIGURE 9.15 Money offers details on all your accounts and an overview of your projected cash flow.

Being a product of Microsoft, Money has great connections with Microsoft online resources, including MSN's business and finance channels. You can get updates to your stock prices instantly and track your overall portfolio performance. As with Quicken, you need to input your account data and build a financial profile to start using Money. (Note that Money is not included in HP Pavilions purchased later than the fall of 2002.)

Chapter Summary

In this chapter, you focused on software you can use to get your work done, from designing attractive documents to calculating numbers. You learned how to generate documents with easy-to-use wizards in Microsoft Works. You got a glimpse of the word processor, spreadsheet, and presentation programs included in Corel WordPerfect Office 2002, and you toured the money management features of Intuit's Quicken and Microsoft Money.

10

Fun and Games

In this Chapter

✔ **Playing games with Windows**

✔ **Listening to the radio**

✔ **Playing music**

✔ **Building a music library**

A computer should do more than help you work; it should also help you play. Your Pavilion does just that by making almost a dozen Windows XP games available for you to play. In addition, your Pavilion includes MusicMatch Radio to listen to your favorite radio stations, build a playlist of your favorite tunes, and listen to them all on your computer.

Playing Windows Games

Windows XP comes with several games built in, from card games such as Solitaire and Hearts, to more strategy-oriented games such as Pinball and Minesweeper. In addition, you can access Internet versions to play games, such as Checkers and Reversi, with real opponents through Microsoft Network's (MSN's) *zone.com*.

Playing Cards

If your idea of heaven is sitting down with a deck of 52 cards and counting on the luck of the draw, you'll find Windows XP's card games to be right up your alley. You can play four card games: Hearts, Solitaire, Freecell, and Spider Solitaire. Each is played with a virtual deck of cards. In some cases, you click and drag cards to play. In others, you click the card you want to move and then click the location to move it to. In Hearts, the computer acts as the other player; in other games, such as Solitaire, you play against yourself.

Try a hand of Spider Solitaire to see how these games work. Spider Solitaire is played with 2 decks of cards and 10 stacks of cards, similar to regular solitaire. You can deal additional cards by clicking on the card decks in the bottom right-hand corner of the game area. In Spider Solitaire, you can move a card from the bottom of a stack to an empty stack. You can also move a card from the bottom of a stack to place it on a card with the next highest value. Color or suit don't matter. You can move a set of cards onto a blank stack. Keep in mind that, if a blank stack is on the screen, you can't deal more cards until you've placed something there.

✔ **Let's get started playing cards:**

1. Select Start, All Programs, Games, Spider Solitaire. A blank game appears with a Difficulty dialog box open.

2. Accept the Easy: One Suite difficulty level by clicking OK. The computer deals a set of cards, as shown in Figure 10.1.

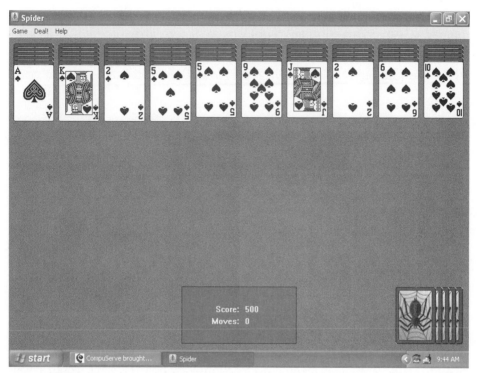

FIGURE 10.1 Note the spider design on the cards.

3. Click any card and drag it to rest on another card that is one higher than it. For example, place the 9 in the figure on the 10. As you move the card from a stack, the computer flips the next card in that stack face.

4. Continue to move cards to stacks with the next highest card on them. Be aware that you can't move sets of cards that aren't consecutive. Therefore, for example, if you have a stack with 10, 9, 8, 3, 2, 1, you can't move the 10 and all the cards under it to another stack. You would have to move the 3, 2, 1 to another stack first and then move the 10, 9, 8.

When you have created a set of cards from King to Ace, the set folds up and moves off to the side. The goal is to make every possible set from the two decks of cards.

Before you finish the game, note some of the options for controlling the game, which are similar to options in other card games in Windows XP.

In the Game menu, shown in Figure 10.2, you have several commands:

FIGURE 10.2 The Game menu provides controls for how the game works, as well as statistics about the number of games you've won (or lost).

- There are controls to start or restart a game.
- You can undo a move, deal the next set of cards (you can also do this by simply clicking the deck of cards on the screen), or get a hint (Show An Available Move).
- Use the Difficulty command to change the difficulty level.
- Click statistics (see Figure 10.3) to see how many wins or losses you have racked up.

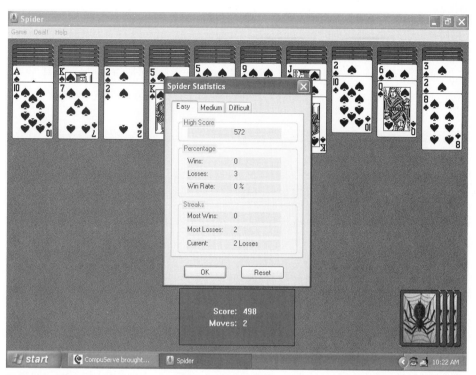

FIGURE 10.3 Don't worry. If you lose a lot like me, you can reset the statistics and get a clean slate.

- Open Options to control how sound, animation, and automatic dealing works.
- If you have a game going and have to leave, you can save it (Game, Save This Game) and finish it later, or you can exit (Game, Exit) without saving.

caution **Don't be fooled. The Deal button on the menu bar doesn't open a menu containing commands; it just deals the next row of cards.**

Clicking to Score

Minesweeper and Pinball rely more on your dexterity or ability to strategize than on the luck of the draw.

Minesweeper has you click on squares trying to avoid uncovering any mines, which ends your game (see Figure 10.4). The numbers that appear on clicked squares indicate how many mines are located within eight squares. If you think a square has a mine underneath, mark it by right-clicking it.

FIGURE 10.4 Use your noodle to figure out likely hiding spots for mines.

Pinball is a virtual pinball game with flashing lights and dinging bells. You can play pinball with up to four players. You control play with simple keyboard commands (see Figure 10.5). Using these commands, you can bump the table from different sides and swing flippers to stop the ball.

FIGURE 10.5 It won't take you long to memorize these keyboard controls.

caution **If you bump the virtual pinball table too hard (usually a matter of initiating the bump command too frequently), you can tilt.**

Project: Challenge Your Friend to a Pinball Match

Time to play some pinball. Get a few friends to come over for a pinball tournament. Remember, you can have up to four players with Windows Pinball. Decide the order of play and determine a prize for the winning player.

✔ **Follow these steps to play a game:**

1. Select Start, All Programs, Games, Pinball. A welcome screen appears while the game loads. Then, you'll see the pinball game shown in Figure 10.6.

FIGURE 10.6 Looking for all the world like an arcade game, this pinball machine even tilts.

2. Select Game, Launch Ball. After a few seconds, the ball is in play.

3. Use <Z> and </> to move the left and right flipper, respectively.

4. Use <X>, <.>, and <Up> to bump the table from various sides.

5. If you want to pause the game at any time, press <F3> and then press <F3> again to resume.

When the game ends, your score is displayed. You can explore the menu of the 3D Pinball game to set it up to play sounds and music, to select the number of players, and to review high scores.

Playing Online

Stuck for a playing partner? Through *zone.com*, you can be matched with another player to play a game such as Backgammon on the Internet. The game takes place in real time, that is, the other person is logged on at the same time you are and you have consecutive turns at play. Internet games included with Windows XP include Backgammon, Checkers, Hearts, Reversi, and Spades.

note **You need to get a .NET Passport, which is free. A .NET Passport allows you to log in with a single click to any Web site that displays the .NET Sign In button. Go to www.passport.com to get yours.**

✔ **To initiate a game of Internet Checkers, follow these steps:**

1. Select Start, All Programs, Games, Internet Checkers. The *zone.com* opening screen shown in Figure 10.7 appears.

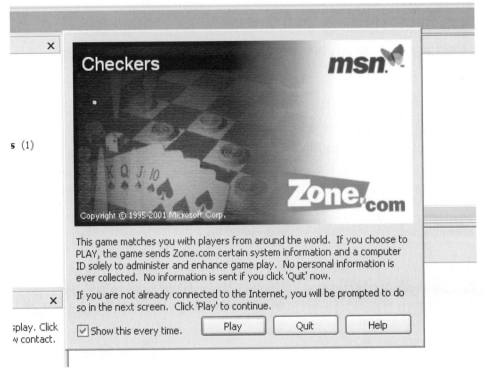

FIGURE 10.7 This screen explains how online games work.

2. Click Play. You are connected to another user on the gameboard.

3. If you want to chat with preset phrases while playing, leave the Chat on setting and click the arrow in the Select a Message to Send field (for example, "It's your turn" or "Good move").

4. When the display says Your Turn (see Figure 10.8), you can click a checker and then click the square you want to move it to.

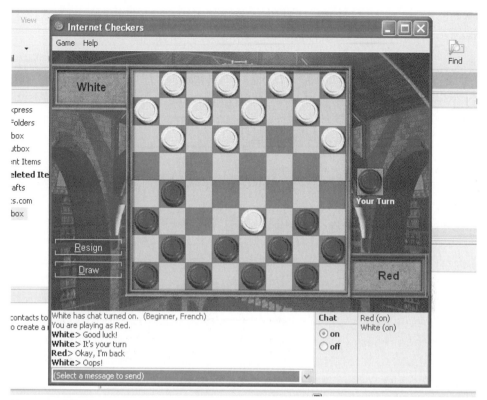

FIGURE 10.8 I lost this game, but had a lot of fun.

5. To jump a checker, click your piece and then on the square on the other side of the piece you want to jump.

6. When the game is over, if you don't want to play anymore, it's a good idea to send the message that you have to go now and then click Close to close the game.

Because you can only communicate with preset phrases, you don't have to worry about encountering anybody who will speak to you inappropriately. Also, there is no way the other player can contact you directly. Play as much as you like and enjoy.

Music to Your Ears

If you're like me, you love to sit at your computer working or playing while listening to music. Well, now you can forget the DVD player or FM radio set. You've got both built into your Pavilion. With Music-Match Jukebox, you can tune into radio, play CDs, and even build music libraries that match your tastes.

Tuning Into Radio Stations

From country to jazz, you can pick and choose radio stations that match your musical interests. You can mix and match different categories of music to create a personal radio station. The Music Matching feature allows MusicMatch Jukebox to observe your listening habits and to provide a personalized radio experience based on your preferences. You can also view a list of broadcast stations and tune into any one of them at any time. To listen to radio stations, you must first be connected to the Internet (see Chapter 12 of this book if you need help getting connected).

✔ **To tune into a broadcast station, follow these steps:**

1. Double-click the MusicMatch Jukebox shortcut on your desktop or select Start, All Programs, MusicMatch Jukebox.

2. Click the Radio tab in the top pane of the jukebox. The program takes a moment to connect to the MusicMatch Jukebox site, and then the information shown in Figure 10.9 appears.

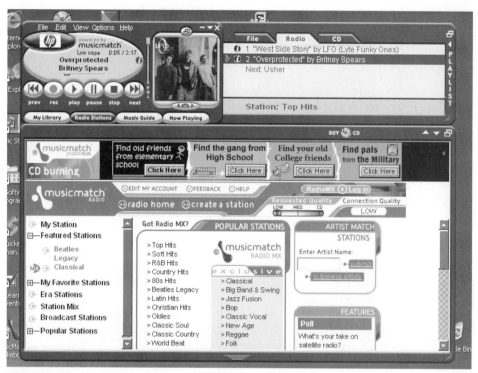

FIGURE 10.9 A wide variety of broadcast radio stations is accessible through the Jukebox.

3. Click the Broadcast Stations link in the left-hand pane. A list of categories appears.

4. Click a category name and then click a station. A listing of that station's Web address is shown.

5. Click the link to go to the station. You may have to click a listen button when the station Web page appears.

Project: **Create Your Own Radio Station Mix**

Next time you have a party coming up, you can create your own station with a mix of music that matches your friends' tastes. You might even create a logo for your own "audio station" and put it on your party invitations (see Chapter 9 for more about designing invitations).

✔ **Identify at least four stations that play the type of music you and your friends like and then follow these steps:**

1. From the Radio window in Figure 10.9, click Create a Station.

2. When prompted to save the station in the mixer window, click the mixer window link. The window in Figure 10.10 appears.

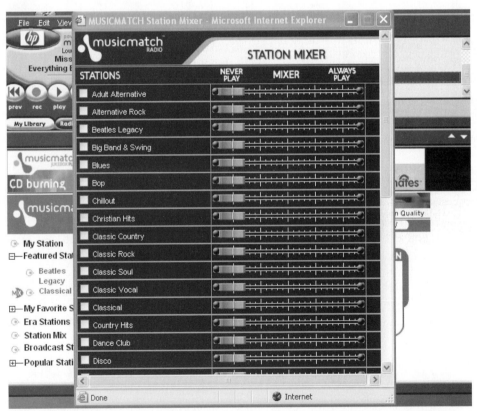

FIGURE 10.10 You can mix and match various kinds of music using the tools on this screen.

3. Select the categories of music you'd like to hear by clicking the appropriate boxes and moving the slider to the right to represent how much of that type of music you'd like your music mix to include.

4. Scroll to the bottom of the list, enter a name for your personal station, and then click Save & Exit.

tip **Try the Era Radio feature. With this, you specify a date range, say 1950 to 1960, and MusicMatch plays only music from that era.**

Playing CDs

Man does not live by radio alone, so I'm sure you'll want to be able to play your own CDs now and then. You can do that with MusicMatch Jukebox, which provides controls for playing, pausing, and jumping easily to any song on the CD. You don't even have to have a CD player cluttering up your computer workstation.

✔ **To play a CD, follow these steps:**

1. Double-click the MusicMatch Jukebox shortcut to open the program.

2. Place a CD in your CD/DVD drive.

3. Click the CD tab in the top pane of the Jukebox. The CD begins playing, and you see the title list, such as the one shown in Figure 10.11.

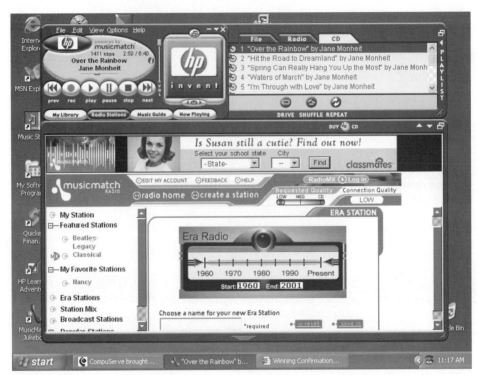

FIGURE 10.11 Click another title in this list at any time and click the Play button to play it.

You can use the playback controls to the left of the title list to play, pause, stop, or move to the previous or next title on the CD.

 tip **You can switch among your radio stations, audio files, and CD by just clicking on the appropriate tab at any time.**

Adding to a Music Library

A music library is a customized list of audio files you build in Music-Match Jukebox. You may find music to include in these libraries any place, for example, downloaded from the Internet or from a CD. You can mix and match titles from different sources and play them in any order.

✔ **To create a music library playlist, follow these steps:**

1. Click My Library. A list of any existing music libraries appears, as in Figure 10.12.

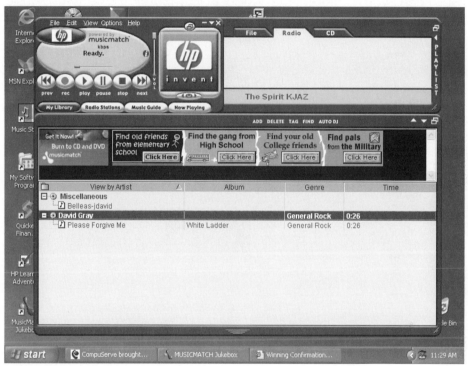

FIGURE 10.12 You can build multiple music libraries.

2. Select Options, Music Library, Search and Add Tracks from All Drives. The Search for Music dialog box appears.

3. Locate an audio file that you have stored on your computer by selecting a drive to search in the Look in drop-down list or using the Browse feature. For these steps, you should find a few music samples that are included with Windows XP (such as the Windows welcome music) by searching all drives.

4. All the audio files that were found are listed in your playlist.

5. Double-click a file, and it plays.

Chapter Summary

In this chapter, you got to have some fun playing games both offline and online. You practiced a card game, played a virtual pinball machine, and got online to play a game of checkers with another game enthusiast. Then, you explored the world of computer music with Music-Match Jukebox using radio, CDs, and personalized playlists.

chapter
11

Getting Creative

In this Chapter

✓ Designing a multimedia e-postcard with Multimedia Email

✓ Creating fun photo effects with PhotoFantasy

✓ Playing around with 3D animation in Kazoo Studio

✓ Making Music with Super Duper Music Looper from Sonic Foundry

If you have the urge to get creative, you'll have a lot of fun with several programs that come with your HP Pavilion home PC. My Photo Center from ArcSoft offers some easy-to-use photo manipulation tools. Kazoo Studio lets you play with 3D animation effects, and Sonic Foundry's Super Duper Music Looper brings out the musician in you. All of these programs can be used by kids and adults alike, although their colorful graphic interfaces will definitely appeal to the young at heart.

199

note **The programs discussed in this chapter were available on Pavilion models purchased before the fall of 2002. If you have a newer model, check out Chapter 20 for some of the newer creativity tools on your computer.**

Using My Photo Center

My Photo Center has four programs that you'll find creative uses for: Multimedia Email, My Photo Center, PhotoFantasy 2000, and Photo-Studio 2000 SE. All of these programs let you work with photographic images. Sample photo images are included to get you going, but you can also work with any photo you've uploaded to your computer from a digital camera, downloaded from the Internet, or scanned into a graphics file format. Here's what you can do with My Photo Center:

- Multimedia Email lets you design e-mail postcards for a variety of occasions.
- My Photo Center provides simple photo manipulation tools for modifying photo contrast and brightness and rotating your photo image.
- PhotoFantasy 2000 contains fantasy images with cut-out faces. You can take a photo of a friend or pet and stick it on the face of some character, such as a sheik riding a camel (see Figure 11.1) or a British beefeater.

hp pavilion pcs

FIGURE 11.1 My dog makes a great desert sheik.

- PhotoStudio 2000 is a more robust photo imaging program. With it you can manipulate and modify photos in a wide variety of ways.

tip ArcSoft, which manufacturers these products, offers a Web site called PhotoIsland where you can get great ideas and can even download photos to use with the My Photo Center software. Visit it at atlantic.photoisland.com.

Try using a couple of these programs, just for fun.

Greetings from Multimedia Email

Multimedia Email uses a simple six-step process to design, write, and send postcard e-mail. You select a design, add a photo, write a message, add audio, address the message, and then send it. Designs are provided to give you a head start (see Figure 11.2).

FIGURE 11.2 Whether you want to send a birthday or get-well greeting, you'll find fun designs in Multimedia Email.

Project: **Creating a Birthday Card**

Think of the next person in your family who has a birthday coming up and design a multimedia card you can send to him or her through email. As you go through this project, feel free to pick a design or greeting that best matches that person and his or her interests. For example, if your sister loves animals, pick a design with a cat or dog.

✔   **To create a birthday email postcard, follow these steps:**

1. Select Start, All Programs, My Photo Center, Multimedia Email.

2. Click step 1, Select Design. The design window shown in Figure 11.2 appears.

3. Click the arrow to the right of the design box and click Birthday Wishes in the drop-down list that appears.

4. Click one of the designs, which then appears as the postcard background.

5. Click OK. You return to the main window.

6. Click Get Photo/Video.

7. Click a photo image. Your window will look something like Figure 11.3.

FIGURE 11.3 After you have a background design, select a photo to place on it.

8. If the photo is too large, click Edit. Use the Rotate, Flip, Reduce, or Enlarge tools to modify the image or adjust the Brightness or Contrast of the photo by adjusting those sliders. Click OK to save any changes.

9. Click the Write Message icon (step 3). The Write Message dialog box, shown in Figure 11.4, appears.

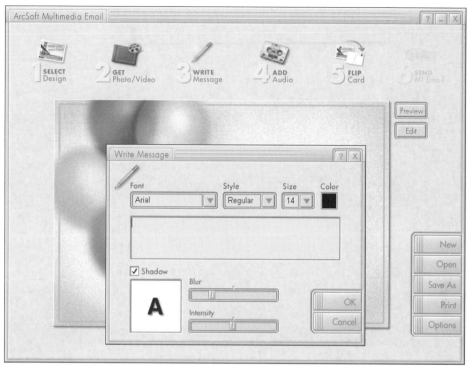

FIGURE 11.4 Use simple text formatting tools in this dialog.

10. Type this message (or one appropriate to whoever will receive the card): "Happy birthday to my favorite brother!"

11. Click the Color block and then click a bright blue color in the palette that appears.

12. Click OK to save the message. (If you need to move the message to fit on the postcard, click the text and drag it to a new position).

13. Click step 4, Add Audio.

14. Click the Record New Message button. The Record Audio dialog box appears.

15. Click the Record button (the red one) and record a birthday greeting. When you're done, click the stop button (the one with a square on it).

16. Click Save, then enter a file name in the Save As dialog box, and click Save.

17. Click the Flip Card option (step 5). The back of the postcard appears, as shown in Figure 11.5

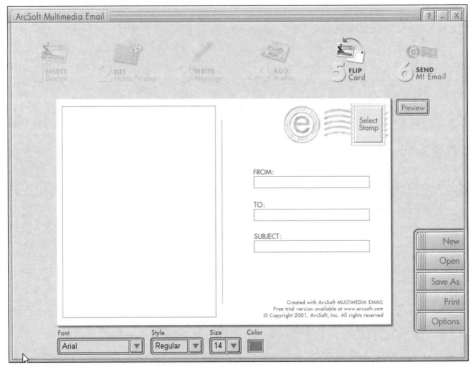

FIGURE 11.5 This e-postcard template sports a familiar interface.

18. Type a message in the box on the left and then type your email address and a recipient's email address, as well as a Subject, into the appropriate boxes on the right.

19. Click Select Stamp.

20. Click a stamp design.

21. Click the Preview button to see the card you've created.

If you want to send the email now, you can click on Send Email, select a file format (Windows or QuickTime for Macintosh), and then click OK. Click Close to close the program when you're done.

caution   **You must have a default email client, and some email clients will not accept these postcards. If you use Microsoft Outlook for your email, you should have no problem.**

Playing Around with PhotoFantasy

PhotoFantasy is the online equivalent to the cutout figures at old-time amusement parks. You'd stand behind them with your face filling the cutout part, and friends would take pictures of you appearing as a farmer, astronaut, or policeman. With PhotoFantasy, you can take a predesigned background image; stick a picture of anybody or anything where the face should be; and save it, email it, or print it out.

✔ **Use some sample photos provided with PhotoFantasy to try this out:**

1. Select Start, All Programs, My Photo Center, PhotoFantasy.

2. Click the Get Fantasy icon. The Get Fantasy window appears, as shown in Figure 11.6.

FIGURE 11.6 Each fantasy background has a cutout for a face where you can place your photo.

3. Use the filmstrip of pictures along the left side to view different fantasy pictures. When you find one you like, click it, and it appears in the preview.

4. Click OK.

5. Click Get Photo. The Sample Photos window appears. To get a photo of your own, you click Add, then locate the file, and open it. For now, click any sample photo to select it and then click OK.

Now you can play around with the image, clicking and dragging the photo to fit in the cutout space and using the icon tools to enlarge or reduce the image or rotate it at an angle. You can also use the brightness, contrast, and color sliders at the bottom of the window to modify the image. When you're done, you'll have an image something like the one in Figure 11.7, which you can save, print, or send in an email.

FIGURE 11.7 This modern day lady has stepped into a medieval fantasy.

tip Can't resist commenting on your silly PhotoFantasy? You can even add text to the photo by clicking the text tool (the one with an "abc" and the image of a pencil), selecting font formats, and typing the message.

Getting Animated with Kazoo Studio

Kazoo Studio is a simple program with a lot of fun packed into it. KazooPictures are supplied, along with various characters, such as a dinosaur, and images like a spaceship. You can place the characters or

objects on the photo, play with 3D creating shadow effects, and move
the objects in 3D space.

 note   Kazoo Studio is included as a free 30-day trial. Try it out. If you've
enjoyed it, you can buy the product, which is priced at only $19.99 as of this
writing.

✔ **Follow these steps to check out Kazoo Studio's capabilities:**

1. Select Start, All Programs, Kazoo Studio, Kazoo Studio.

2. On the window that appears, click Start to begin using your 30-day
   trial. The Kazoo Studio window shown in Figure 11.8 appears.

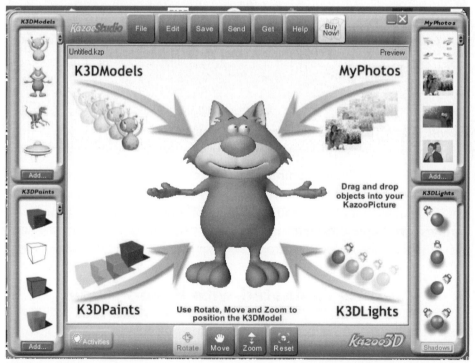

FIGURE 11.8 *Use models, paints, lights, and photos in 3D with Kazoo Studio.*

3. Click any photo in the My Photos section and drag it into the center of Kazoo Studio.

4. Click a K3D Model and drag it onto the picture. You'll have an image something like the one shown in Figure 11.9.

FIGURE 11.9 The juxtaposition of the 3D figure and the sample photos can make for some weird images!

5. Click a K3DLight effect and drag it onto the picture. This provides shadows from various directions that give the model more of a 3D feel.

6. Click a 3-DPaint item and drag it onto the 3D model to fill it with various colors and patterns.

7. Now click the 3D model and maneuver it. Just drag it and spin it around in 3D space.

8. If you want to use more tools to modify the image, click the Activities button. In the Activities dialog box that appears (see Figure 11.10), you can click various tabs to get more models, add text, edit the background photo, print, or send your photo by email.

FIGURE 11.10 You can use the Erase tool on the Be Creative tab to erase portions of the model to make it appear as if it's behind an object in the photo.

9. When you're done with the image, click the close button to close the program.

caution   **If you use the Eraser tool to remove parts of the 3D model, you won't be able to move the model around in 3D space anymore.**

Working in the Sonic Foundry

With an improbable name like Super Duper Music Looper, you might think this software is just for kids. However, whether you're young or not so young, you should try it. It's a fun way to edit and add effects to music.

How Music Looper Works

Sonic Foundry is the maker of the Super Duper Music Looper, a great program that makes writing your own music as easy as dragging a slider left or right on your screen. Music Looper lets you add any combination of nine musical effects, from Latin rhythms to piano or horns. You use a paint tool to paint segments of different effects on your screen. You can vary your music by switching from one sound to another, or you can play several in combination.

When you're done, you've created a loop, that is, a piece of music that will play from beginning to end and, then go back to the beginning and play again. You can save songs in the Windows Media Audio format. Then, you can use those files to provide musical backgrounds. For example, you could use a music file to play along with a WordPerfect Office Presentations slide show.

Project: **Writing Music**

Write a song that uses all the available musical effects and then play it back at different speeds and in different keys. Save the song and email it to a friend.

✔ **Compose your own music now by following these steps:**

1. Select Start, All Programs, Sonic Foundry, Super Duper Music Looper XPress, Super Duper Music Looper XPress. The window shown in Figure 11.11 appears.

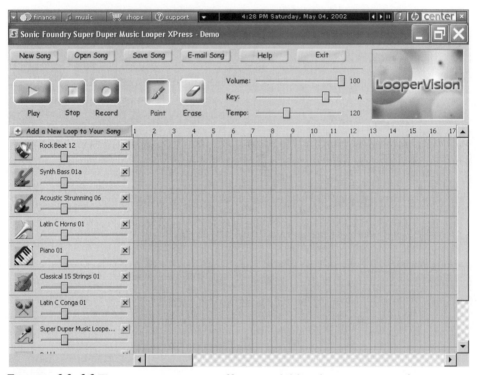

FIGURE 11.11 There are nine music effects available when you open the program.

2. Click any of the icons to the left to hear a sample of that musical effect.

3. To add an effect to your music loop, click and drag the blue area under the numbers 1 through 120 along the top. You can click a single band or drag to have that music effect play for a longer period of time.

4. Continue painting other music effects. If you add something you don't want, click Erase and drag over it to erase it. Click Paint to paint more sounds.

5. When you've finished adding musical effects, click Play to hear what you've composed; your finished song might look something like the one shown in Figure 11.12.

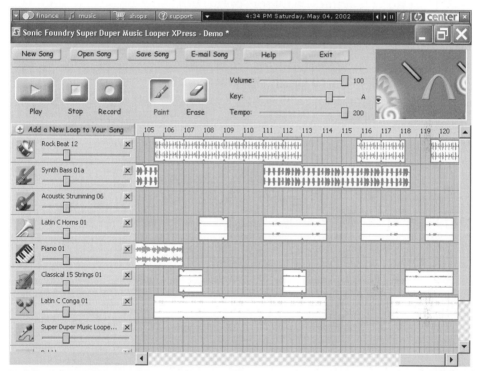

FIGURE 11.12 All of these effects will play in combination just as you've painted them.

note Note that you can change the key, volume, or tempo of your song by dragging the sliders at the top of the screen to the left or right. If your volume isn't loud enough, you can also click the volume control on the Windows taskbar to raise the system volume.

tip You can save a song or email a song to a friend.

Chapter Summary

In this chapter, you learned about several software products included on your HP that help you get creative with visual and musical works.

The Photo Center has four photo imaging products, and you explored two: Multimedia Email and PhotoFantasy. All of the Photo Center products enable you to modify and add effects to photographs.

Kazoo Studio offers fun with 3D images by working with predesigned background photos and pasting in 3D objects that you can manipulate in various ways.

The Super Duper Music Looper provides tools to edit musical compositions and then save them, use them with other programs, or email them to a friend.

Connecting to the Internet

chapter

12

Get Online Today!

In this Chapter

✓ How the Internet works

✓ What you need to get connected

✓ Signing up for an Internet account

✓ Choosing a browser

For many people, it's hard to imagine life without the Internet. It's a wonderful research tool for students and professionals, and it's a fast and easy way to communicate with people around the world. You can find the nearest location of a retail store, read restaurant reviews, build the ideal price and feature set for your car before you go to the dealer, and buy almost anything. You can chat with people from Calcutta to Rio who have common interests and interesting stories to tell. In short, if you're not online now, you should be. This chapter tells you how.

219

What You Need to Get Online

Getting connected to the Internet is a pretty easy process after you know what you need in the way of hardware and what service you want to use to get online. For an HP Pavilion user, most of that is taken care of. You have an internal modem built in, you have installation files for several major Internet service providers, and you have a wizard to take you through the process step by step. About the only thing you need to supply is a credit card.

What's an Internet Service Provider (ISP)?

ISPs are companies, such as America Online (AOL) or Earthlink, that maintain servers (computers) that you use to access the Internet and to exchange email with others using the Internet. You usually pay a monthly fee for unlimited access to these services.

Most ISPs offer an email account and a Web site with informational services such as weather reports or news, as well as links to other sites. You can use your ISP site as your home page (the page that appears when you first log on to the Internet), or you can set another page as your home page (see Chapter 14 for more about setting your home page).

All About Modems

If you've recently purchased your HP Pavilion, you'll be glad to hear it comes with an internal modem built right in (probably a 56 kilobits per second [kbps] modem or faster). A modem is the hardware that allows your computer to connect to a server using a standard phone line to transmit data. If you want to connect by a standard phone line, you've got everything you need already set up when you unpack your Pavilion.

tip Although most people are able to get online with their Pavilion with no problem, modems are one of the most common problems encountered by people contacting HP Technical Support. To make sure your experience with your modem is smooth, check Chapter 2 for information about setting up your computer, Chapter 17 for information about updating drivers, and Chapter 19 for more about getting Help from HP.

note You can also get a cable modem, which enables your computer to transmit data across a cable television line. If you want to use a cable connection, you'll have to contact your local phone, cable television company, or ISP to sign up for their service and to purchase a cable modem.

Phone Lines and High-Speed Access

There are several options for connecting to the Internet today, from your regular phone line to high-speed phone and cable connections, and even completely wireless connections using a laptop or handheld computer. Speed is the name of the game here because connecting to the Internet at slower speeds can be a very frustrating experience. With a slow connection, files take forever to download, and you could go make a sandwich while waiting for a Web page with graphics to appear.

In the world of high-speed Internet access, here are some of the technologies and terms you'll encounter:

- *Broadband* refers to any connection that allows data to be transmitted at higher speeds than a standard phone connection (sometimes called narrowband).
- *Cable* access transmits data using a cable modem and uses the same type of cable across which you get your cable television signal. A cable connection means you don't tie up a phone line when you're on the Internet, and you don't have to log on to get online. Turn your computer on, and you're there.

- The *Digital Subscriber Line (DSL)* has several variations, such as Asynchronous Digital Subscriber Line (ADSL), and probably others by the time you read this book. Both DSL and cable modems use broadband technology, which means they can handle a lot of data faster than a standard phone line. However, DSL works using a telephone line, and cable modems run across cable. DSL is generally faster than cable, but it may or may not be available in your area. Check with your phone company or ISP to find out.

- *Integrated Services Digital Network (ISDN)* is a technology that provides data and voice transmission across the same line. The technology is most often sold to businesses that integrate network features with it or that connect to telecommuting employees in their home offices. However, you might use ISDN if you're interested in setting up a home network. Your house must be wired to use ISDN lines.

What Will It Cost You?

Connecting to the Internet through your standard phone line will cost you a monthly fee to an ISP, averaging around $20. You'll use a local access phone number to log on, so you shouldn't incur any toll call charges.

caution **If you have limited local message units on your present calling plan, you may incur additional costs on your phone bill. If you're going to use the Internet at all, it's worth upgrading to unlimited local calls.**

If you want high-speed phone or cable access, you'll have to pay for service installation and will probably pay a higher monthly fee to your phone or cable company. What kind of service you need and what you want to pay for it should relate to how often you use the Internet. If you're a casual user and not a home business owner, you can probably tap into the cheaper alternative of a simple phone-line connection.

Signing Up

The first step to getting online is to select an ISP. Hundreds of them are out there. Some, such as AOL and MSN, are online services with special member benefits, shopping malls, and research tools. Others, such as Earthlink and Leapfrog, focus on Internet access, Web hosting, and support. Your phone company and cable TV company probably offer Internet access as well.

HP has made it easy for those who don't care to go hunting for an ISP by building in an Easy Internet Sign-Up wizard (see Figure 12.1) and by providing what you'll need to connect to several of the major Internet service providers.

tip **If you'd rather find an ISP on your own, visit *thelist.internet.com* to see listings of hundreds of ISP providers across the United States and Canada to compare their offerings.**

Welcome to easy Internet sign-up!

Get connected to the Internet quickly and easily.

Sign-up for Internet access from a full selection of hp recommended service providers.

Come back often to see the latest service options and offers in your area.

©2000-2001 Hewlett-Packard company

FIGURE 12.1 This easy-to-follow process gets you online quickly.

Project: **Getting Online with HP's Easy Internet Sign-Up**

If your family doesn't have an online account yet, it's time to get one. First, go the library or a friend's house and use their connection to visit the Web sites for AOL, CompuServe, MSN, and Earthlink, four of the services offered by the HP Internet Sign-up. (Tip: use a search engine to locate each service's publicly accessible Web page, or enter the addresses as *aol.com, msn.com,* and so forth). Make a list of the features you like about each and then vote on which service you'd like to use. Consider price, ease of use, interface (what the Web site looks like), and features offered to members.

✔ **Then, use the Easy Internet Sign-Up feature to set up your account on your new computer:**

1. Make sure your computer is connected to a phone line.

2. Select Start, All Programs, Easy Internet Sign-Up. A Welcome screen appears.

3. Click Next, and the startup screen in Figure 12.2 appears.

 easy Internet sign-up

To download the latest service options and offers for your area, please complete the information below, and press the connect button:

Country   USA ▾

Zip/Postal Code   98368

*Telephone
   area code   prefix
   (360   ) - 555 - XXXX

Purchase   where latest hp product purchased.
Location   Circuit City ▾

Press connect when done.

*Enter your area code and the first 3 digits of your phone number.

All information remains strictly private. All fields are required.

privacy   clear form   skip form   connect   exit

FIGURE 12.2 Start working with the wizard by entering details about your location.

4. Enter your phone number and zip code.

5. Click Connect. The wizard searches for and downloads service options and offers for your area. The Sign-Up Options window appears (see Figure 12.3).

 easy Internet sign-up
sign-up options

Choose the option that fits your needs:

○ Help me sign-up for a new account or transfer my existing account.

○ Help me learn the different ways to connect to the Internet.

○ I will set up my own Internet account.

HP provides a variety of Internet Service Providers and connection options for you to choose from. Visit the easy Internet sign-up often for the latest service options and offers in your area.

privacy back next exit

FIGURE 12.3 If you want more information about how to connect to the Internet, you can click the second option.

6. Click Help me sign up for a new account or transfer my existing account. The Select Service window shown in Figure 12.4 appears.

FIGURE 12.4 What's offered here depends on service and options available in your location.

7. Assuming you're using a standard phone line, click Dial-Up. (If you're using a DSL connection, click DSL). Providers such as AOL, MSN, Earthlink, GoAmerica, or DirectTV will be shown, depending on what's available where you live.

8. Click a logo to find out what the terms and cost of each plan are.

9. If you are ready to order one, click Setup on the plan terms window.

Depending on which plan you choose, you will be taken through a series of windows to run the installation procedure for that service's software and then to sign on and provide payment information (a credit card and billing address). During this process, you will have to select an email account name.

note **An email account name is important because it should be easy for you and others to remember. However, it's not always easy to get the name you want. Your own name (depending on how unique it is) is probably taken by somebody else. Your first name and last initial are also probably in use. Names like BestMom or SmartCookie are likely to have been used before. My advice is try to get your favorite name, but, just in case, have some backup names in mind or be willing to add a number or two to your name to make it unique.**

After you've finished the installation, you can log on by selecting Start, All Programs. Click the ISP's name in the list of programs, and, when the software opens (for example AOL's opening screen shown in Figure 12.5), enter your user name and password. Click Connect, and you'll be connected in moments.

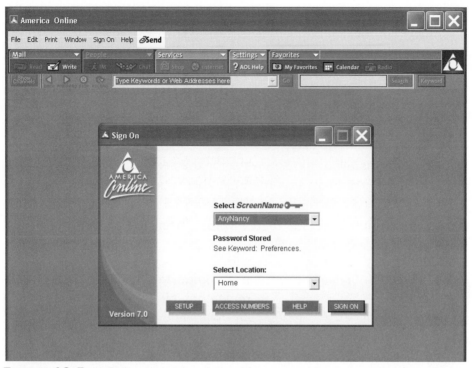

FIGURE 12.5 AOL's opening window asks you to enter your name, password, and then click the Sign On button.

tip Most ISPs allow you to save your password so that you don't have to enter it each time you log on (which is the case for the account shown in Figure 12.5). This can save time, but be aware that anybody who can get to your computer can log on to your ISP and access your email.

What Providers Are Already on Your Pavilion?

If you already have an account with AOL, CompuServe, Earthlink, or MSN, you'll be glad to hear that the files for installing those applications are already on your computer.

✔ Here's all you have to do to install them:

1. Select Start, All Programs, Online Services.

2. Click the ISP with whom you have an account. The installation program runs.

3. Click any confirmation windows that come up to proceed.

After it is installed, the software for the service should be available on your Start, All Programs menu. When you run that software for the first time, you will probably be asked to log on to retrieve local phone access numbers (see Figure 12.6). After you've selected a local number to dial in on, you're all set.

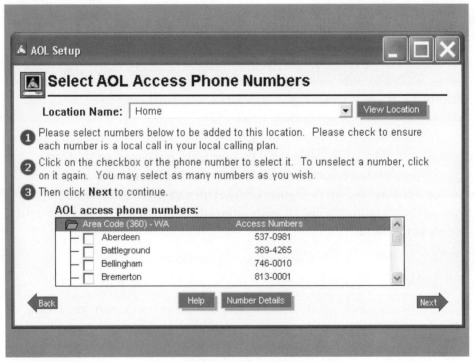

FIGURE 12.6 Your service will suggest several phone numbers in your area to use for dial-up.

tip **It's recommended that you set up a couple of access numbers. If there's a problem with one or it's busy, the other number is used as an option automatically. Try to pick two that fall within your area code that are not toll calls, if available. Also note that some access numbers only allow slower modem access speeds.**

Choosing a Browser

Browsers are software programs that enable you to move around the documents on the Internet and keep a record of your browsing activity and favorite sites.

Internet Explorer from Microsoft comes preinstalled with Windows XP on your HP Pavilion (see Chapter 14 for how to get around using a browser). There are other browsers, including Netscape Navigator and the browser functionality that probably comes with your Internet service.

Browsers all offer similar features, but with a slightly different look and feel, so try out your ISP's browser and Internet Explorer to see if either of those will fit the bill. You will have to be logged onto the Internet through your service provider first; then, when you open your browser, it will go through your connection to access the Internet.

 note **See Chapter 14 for more about using a browser.**

Chapter Summary

In this chapter, you were introduced to the Internet and what you need to get connected to it. You walked through HP's Easy Internet Sign-Up process and considered the options available in browsing software.

chapter
13

Security and You

In this Chapter

✓ Setting passwords

✓ Making security settings in your browser

✓ Protecting yourself against viruses

✓ Keeping kids safe online

✓ Avoiding spams and scams

The Internet can be a wonderful place, but, when you set foot online, you are opening yourself and your computer up to millions of people. Some of these people are nice, and some are...well...not so nice. Some transmit viruses, commit credit card fraud, pelt you with junk mail, or sell your name and contact information to other people who may or may not be nice themselves. There are abuses of your privacy and several sites out there that you would probably prefer your kids not see.

The good news is that there are protections built into Windows and your browser software that you can use to keep safe. You can also use McAfee VirusScan (you get a free 90-day trial of this software with your Pavilion purchase) to stop damaging viruses from doing your computer any harm.

Passwords

The system that has been developed to identify people as they roam around the faceless Internet is password based. When you create an account with an online retailer, you pick a user name and password. If you sign up to use a research site, there's another password to enter. You can even use a password to protect your computer when you're away, ensuring that nobody can access the information stored there if they should happen to have physical access to your machine.

How you come up with passwords and make settings for using them can make them useful, or, if you do it wrong, not so useful.

A note about encryption, digital certificates, and signatures

Today many sites are going beyond simple passwords, which are a somewhat flimsy form of security because they depend on the human element to protect them. Digital certificates are used to authenticate software that you download and ensure that the source is reputable. Digital signatures can be used in sending messages from one place to another on the Internet. A digital signature consists of two keys: one that encrypts (or codes) the message before sending and one that decrypts (or decodes) it on the other end. Because only the recipient has the decrypting code, this should ensure some level of security for the message. Visit the PC Security and Performance area at *www.myhpclub.com* for more about keeping your computer and information safe.

hp pavilion PCs

Choosing Passwords Wisely

Most people know that you should avoid using passwords that would be easily guessed, for example, your last name, your street address, or your birthdate. If you choose such a password and your wallet is lost, all a clever computer hacker would have to do is run through a few bits of personal information until he discovered the right password.

Therefore, what makes a good password? Pick a password that is:

- The most random one you can think of (words you can look up in the dictionary are not good choices)
- One that uses a combination of letters and numbers
- Changed periodically
- Not used for every account and site you sign up for

A good password would be 56UN880PW5. However, that would be really hard to remember, and, if you had a unique password for every account and Web site similar to this hodgepodge of numbers and letters, you'd need to carry a book around to remember them all. So what's the solution? Try to find a middle ground between the completely obvious personal word or name and random gibberish that's impossible to remember. Simply adding a number to the beginning and end of a word can make the password more secure, for example.

Most important of all, never give your passwords to anybody else or leave a record of them lying around near your computer.

caution   **Nobody from any Web site or Web store has any business asking you for your password to their site, so, if they do, don't give it to them. Immediately email the company about the incident. It's very easy for people to assume the role of somebody else online, even pretending to be an employee of a company with which you regularly do business.**

Setting Passwords

You can set passwords to online stores and other sites by simply following the registration process on each site. Some sites have strict requirements for passwords, for example, that they have at least six characters and use a combination of numbers and letters. Most require at least four characters. When you enter your password, you'll be asked to confirm it. That's in case you've introduced a typo when you first typed it.

 tip **If you forget your password, most sites have a feature that allows you to enter your email address, and they will email you your password.**

✔ **To set a password for Windows XP to protect your Pavilion from being accessed by others, follow these steps:**

1. Select Start, Control Panel. The Control Panel appears.

2. Click User Accounts. The User Accounts dialog box opens.

3. Click Change an Account.

4. Click the account you want to change (probably Owner if you haven't set up other accounts).

5. Click Create a Password. The dialog box shown in Figure 13.1 appears.

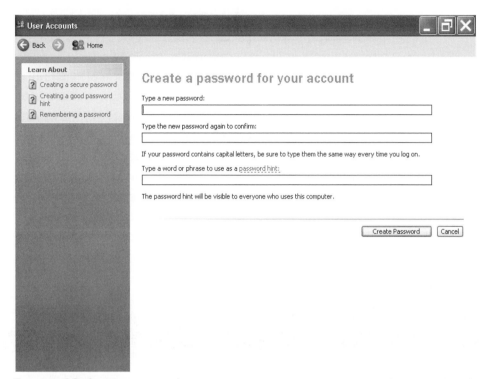

FIGURE 13.1 The password you enter is case sensitive, meaning that capital and lowercase letters must be entered the same way each time.

6. Enter your new password in the Type a New Password box.

7. Press tab.

8. Enter the password again in the second box.

9. If you like, you can enter a password hint. If you forget your password, you can use this hint to remember it.

10. Click Create Password and close the User Accounts dialog box.

caution People can log on to your computer as a guest. Don't leave the Guest account unprotected if you're really concerned about security. Be sure to set a password for it as well.

Cookies, Hold the Milk

Cookies may be good with milk, but computer cookies are not always so good for your privacy. A cookie in computer terms is a small bit of data that's sent to your computer whenever you visit a Web site. Cookies are used to identify you. For example, if you log onto a site such as *Amazon.com* and you're greeted with a cheery, "Hi, Joe! Here are our recommendations for you," that's made possible because your computer has provided data to that site about you. This can be very convenient because it can save you from having to reenter information about yourself, such as your billing address, each time you visit a site or place an order. However, it also means that information about you is being pulled from your hard drive whenever you're online.

note The term "cookie" comes from the original name for this feature, fortune cookie. This name was a result of a program for UNIX computers that sent out a unique message every time it ran, just as you get a unique message every time you open a fortune cookie.

You can set up how cookies are handled in your browser. With most browsers, if you have set your browser for high security, cookies are not allowed to be stored on your computer. That's more private, but it means you may not be allowed to use features of some sites, such as being able to download software. Most people are okay with a medium security setting

In Internet Explorer 6.0, which is probably the version on your Pavilion, you can actually control cookie settings separately from your security setting, which means you can keep your security levels strong and still allow cookies so you can access site features.

✔ **Follow these steps to set your security level and make settings for cookies:**

1. Open Internet Explorer.

2. Select Tools, Internet Options.

3. Click the Privacy tab (see Figure 13.2).

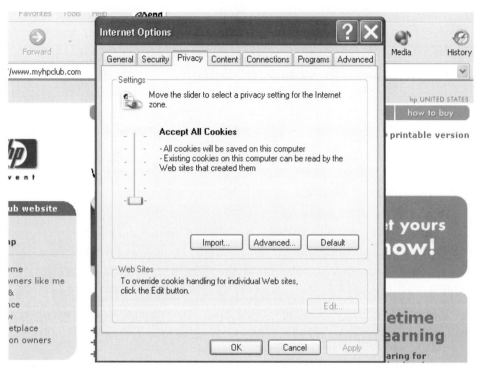

FIGURE 13.2 The Privacy tab is devoted to cookies.

4. Click the slider bar and move it up to higher levels of security (which allow less and less cookies to be saved to your computer).

5. Click Apply when you find a setting description you feel comfortable with.

6. Click the Security tab and then the Custom Level button (see Figure 13.3).

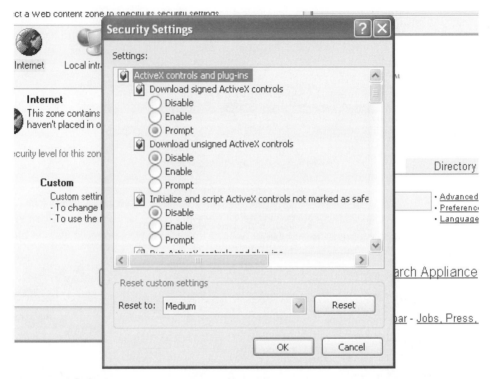

FIGURE 13.3 You can modify individual settings, but the simplest way to use this is to set a level of security you feel comfortable about.

7. Click the arrow on the Reset to field and select a setting from the drop-down list that appears.

8. Click Reset. A message appears confirming that you want to change security settings.

9. Click OK twice to close all dialog boxes.

tip **If you want higher security, you can keep a higher setting for security and cookies. If you come across a site that requires that you accept cookies to perform a certain function, change the setting. When you're done, just be sure to change the setting back to higher security.**

Avoiding Viruses Like the Plague

Computer viruses are the snake in the computing garden of Eden. Why people create them is beyond the understanding of most of us, but they do. A virus can play havoc with your computer's performance, making software crash or weird messages appear. The bottom line is that you don't want to catch this kind of virus.

How Viruses Work

Viruses are little programs called *executable* files that are set to run on your computer and perform some activity. Computer viruses can do a number of things. They can destroy data on your computer hard drive. They can generate an email to everybody in your Address Book and send the virus to their computer to do similar damage. Some initiate immediately when you open the file, and others are set to run on a particular date or when you perform some specific action.

You can do a couple of things to avoid viruses. First, don't open attachments to email messages from people you don't know or if you consider it odd that a particular person you do know sent you this attachment. Second, you can adjust the macro security level of many software programs on your computer, such as Word for Windows (see Figure 13.4). Macros are often the carriers of viruses. Finally, you can run an antivirus software on a regular basis.

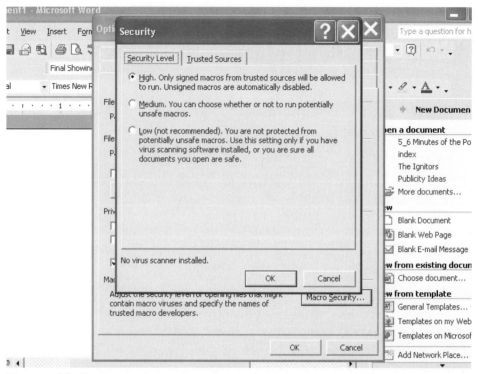

FIGURE 13.4 Most software programs in which you open documents can be set to warn you if a macro is attached to a document you're trying to open.

Using McAfee VirusScan

McAfee.com VirusScanOnline (see Figure 13.5) is one of the most popular antivirus software products. Your Pavilion comes with a free 90-day subscription to McAfee. When you run the program for the first time (Start, All Programs, McAfee.com, McAfee.com VirusScan Online, Scan for Viruses), you are asked to sign up and install the VirusScan software. When you install antivirus software, the latest virus definitions are downloaded; simply run a scan from the dialog box in Figure 13.5 to check your computer for viruses.

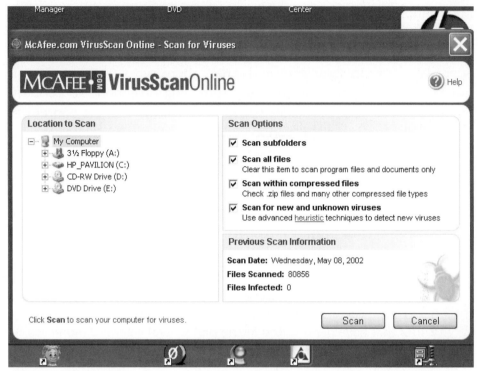

FIGURE 13.5 McAfee lets you scan a floppy, CD/DVD drive, or hard drive.

However, because new viruses come out all the time, you must update your definitions on a regular basis. After you've installed McAfee, you'll get regular prompts to update whenever new definitions become available.

note Another product comes loaded on your Pavilion to help with viruses and security: Freedom Firewall from Zero Knowledge. This software blocks unwanted traffic to your computer when you're online and helps you manage cookies.

Protecting Your Kids Online

One of the wonders of the Internet is the sheer amount of information, software, and graphics that are available. You can research, exchange information, read articles, get pictures, chat with others in real time, and more. However, one of the dangers of the Internet is the type of information you can encounter. Although some organizations offer approval ratings to some sites and refuse approval to others, nobody is out there policing the Internet and removing objectionable content. That's because nobody has legislated a right to censor the content of the Internet. As parents, it's up to you to proactively control what your children can and can't access online.

You can do a few things to help keep your kids safe, and the first thing is to educate them. Rules that you lay down offline, such as not talking to strangers, should pertain online as well. Kids should not respond to email or instant messages from people they don't know. If they see something offensive or somebody continues to attempt to contact them, encourage them to report it to you right away.

tip You can use the history listing on your browser to review the sites that have been visited in the past several weeks to monitor where your kids are going online.

Another thing you can do is to look for rating systems that approve the type of content you want your kids to see and then only allow them to visit sites that display that approval symbol. Finally, you can use your browser settings or third-party software to create lists of approved sites.

Project: **Creating a Family Online Safety Pact**

Every family is different, with kids of different ages and interests. Sit down with your family and create a Family Online Safety Pact. Agree on what types of sites the family wants to avoid and make sure everybody understands why certain sites can be dangerous or disturbing.

✔ **Then, set up Internet Explorer Content Advisor for your family, following these steps:**

1. Select Tools, Internet Options and then click the Content tab.

2. Click Settings for the Content Advisor and be sure the Ratings tab is displayed. The dialog box shown in Figure 13.6 appears.

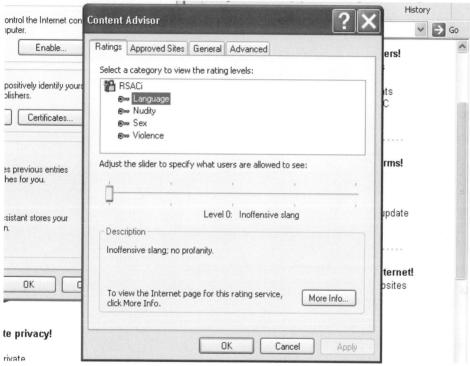

FIGURE 13.6 Although different things offend different people, one of the settings here is probably a match for your standards.

3. Click a category such as Language or Violence and then adjust the slider bar to a setting that you prefer. The further to the right you move means the more explicit the content that is allowed.

4. Click Apply.

5. Click the Approved Sites tab to create a list of sites you approve or disapprove of (see Figure 13.7).

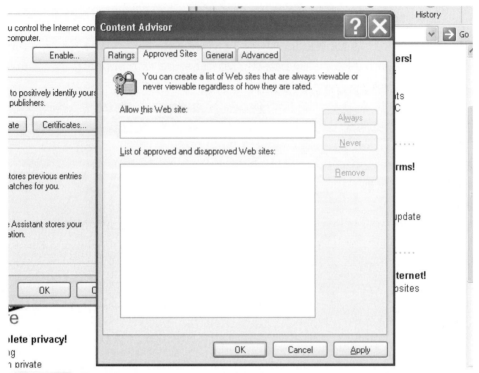

FIGURE 13.7 If there are sites you never want your kids to see, add them to the list of not viewable sites here.

6. Enter the address of a Web site in the Allow this Web site box.

7. Click Always to allow it to be viewed or Never to never allow it to be viewed.

8. Click Apply.

9. Click OK twice to close the Content Advisor and then the Internet Options dialog box.

note **If you want to specify that a rating system from some organization must be present to view sites, you can use the General tab of the Content Advisor.**

tip Zero Knowledge, the manufacturers of Freedom Firewall, which is installed on your Pavilion, also offers a product called Freedom Parental Control that helps you set filtering levels and block access to certain sites. Learn more about this product and a discount for HP Pavilion users at *www.freedom.net/partners/store/hp/buy_package.html.*

Steering Clear of Spams and Scams

Another assault on your privacy and security comes from the realm of email. One form of abuse of your privacy is spamming. This is when a company or individual sends you frequent emails promoting a product, site, or service when you haven't requested such email. Some of this email can be offensive in nature.

The other worry about email is that you'll get an offer for something—a free gift or lucrative career opportunity, for example—that is really just a come-on from a shady business or individual. The variations on how these people trick you, from getting you to give them your credit card number, which they then use for their own purposes, to selling you something that is not as they represented it, are many.

Avoiding Spam

Spam can proliferate and fill up your email inbox faster than weeds in spring. Your time is too valuable to waste deleting these, let alone worrying that the messages might introduce viruses to your computer.

Use these methods to avoid spam:

- When you register for anything on a Web site, from simple access to the site to membership to a retail account, look for any option that allows that site to share your information with others. Often, the selection to allow sharing is the default, and you have to uncheck that option.
- If you get mail you didn't ask for, DON'T send a reply asking to be taken off their list unless you know that it's a very reputable business. Most disreputable spammers use your reply as confir-

mation that your email account is indeed active, and they spam you even more.

- If you're being harassed repeatedly, you might try reporting the sender to an organization such as *bbbonline.org*, an online better business bureau.

tip Many email programs, such as Outlook Express, allow you set up rules on what kinds of email you accept. For example, you can set up a rule that email from a particular sender should always be moved directly to your Deleted folder.

Staying Out of Trouble Online

Avoiding online con artists can be tricky because their methods and approaches are so various. Some good rules of thumb, however, would be these:

- Don't buy anything from anybody you don't know. Stick with companies you trust and that you know are likely to be around tomorrow to deal with if you have some problem with their service or product.
- If somebody's trying to sell you something online, they should have a business Web site you can visit. When you do, review their policies relative to returns, guarantees, and customer privacy. Look for seals of approval from organizations such as *bbbonline.org*.
- Never give out your passwords, credit card numbers, or contact information to anybody you don't know.
- Don't believe anybody who tells you you'll get rich quick, get something for nothing, or look 10 years younger. It doesn't happen, and it's a red flag that you're dealing with a less-than-reputable person.
- If somebody tells you someone you know provided your contact information, confirm with your friend that that's so before dealing with anyone online.

If you follow some common sense rules of conduct online, the Internet can be a safe and fun place to be.

Chapter Summary

In this chapter, you've seen ways to protect your privacy and security when you go online. You've learned about how to use passwords and how to avoid viruses. You've discovered some browser settings that keep you safe from objectionable material and that help you control how cookies can be stored on your computer. Finally, you got some advice about keeping safe online and protecting your privacy by minimizing spam.

hp pavilion pcs

14

Exploring the Internet

In this Chapter

✔ Using Internet Explorer to get around

✔ Keeping track of favorite places

✔ Setting your home page

✔ Visiting My HP Club and HP Help and Support Online

✔ Take a shopping trip

✔ Learning online with Encarta and Next Generation Learning

The Internet, which began in the 1960s as a way for government and academic researchers to share information among themselves, has today become a venue for shopping, learning, investing, playing games, listening to music, getting the news, and communicating with others.

In this chapter, you get to explore the Internet and the World Wide Web. The Internet is a large network of computers, while the Web is a set of documents stored on those networks in the form of Web sites and Web pages.

note **People use terms like riding the Internet highway and surfing the Web somewhat interchangeably. For the most part, most of what you'll see online consists of Web documents stored on the Internet.**

Using the Internet Explorer Browser

Internet Explorer is a browser program from Microsoft that is included on your HP Pavilion home PC as part of Windows XP. A browser is a program used to navigate around the Internet, taking you to various Internet addresses called Uniform Resource Locators (URLs) or following hyperlinks you click with your mouse to go from one Web document to another.

Browsers also have features that allow you to go quickly to sites you visit often, to review the history of sites you've visited recently, and to help to ensure your online privacy. In this chapter, you'll use Internet Explorer to browse the Internet. If you end up using a different browser, for example, one provided by your ISP, you'll find that most browsers offer features similar to the ones you'll see here.

Getting Places

One of the main functions of a browser is to get you from here to there on the Internet. It allows you to do that in several different ways. Take a look at Internet Explorer in Figure 14.1 and note the following features:

- The address line allows you to enter an Internet address, such as *www.myhpclub.com*; you then press <Enter> or click Go to go to that site.
- The Favorites feature lets you save favorite sites and return to them anytime by picking them from the Favorites list.
- The History button displays a list of sites you've visited during the past several weeks.
- The Search button opens a Search window where you can enter keywords and search for sites.

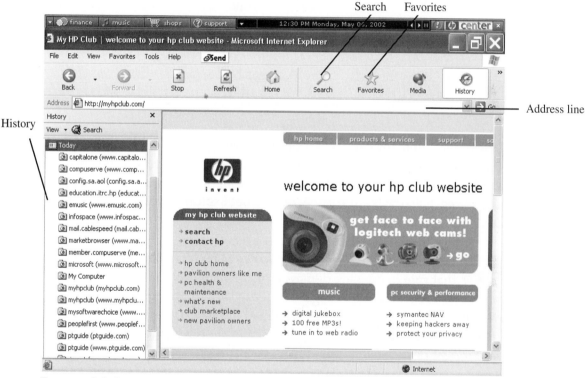

FIGURE 14.1 This simple set of tools makes browsing the Internet easy.

You'll also see hyperlinks on many Web pages; these provide another method of navigation. A hyperlink is a feature of a programming language called Hypertext Markup Language (HTML), which is used to design Web pages. Text coded as a hyperlink is usually a different color from regular text on a Web page. When you click a hyperlink (also referred to as "following a link"), your browser takes you to the linked Web document. This document might be on the same Web site or might be on another Web site entirely.

✔ To go to a specific Web address, follow these steps:

1. Click in the Address box of the browser; this highlights the address of the currently displayed site.

2. Type the address you want to go to, for example, *www.ama-zon.com*.

3. Click Go to the right of the Address box or press <Enter>.

   It may take a few moments, but the page should display shortly.

tip In many cases, you don't have to type a full URL (which normally takes the form *http://www.myhpclub.com*). You can simply type the site name and .com and press <Enter>. If the site name isn't recognized, a search feature opens in Internet Explorer to help you find the site.

caution You may have difficulty going to some addresses. In that case, a message displays that the site is unavailable. This could mean that the Web site no longer exists, the URL for it has changed, or the Web server that it runs on is busy. You may also have typed the address incorrectly. If you get this message, enter the address again to be sure you have it right or try again later.

Navigating Around

Browsing is mostly about moving from one Web page to another. You can do that by entering URL addresses as you did in the previous section, or you can use the Back and Forward buttons on your browser to move backward or forward through pages you've recently viewed, one page at a time.

Here's how this works. If you open *MyHPClub.com*, then go to *Amazon.com*, and then you move on to *Microsoft.com*, clicking Back moves you back to *Amazon.com*; then clicking Forward moves you forward to *Microsoft.com*.

You can also use the Address list and History features to go to a previously viewed page. The Address list is a drop-down list of addresses you've visited in your current Internet session. The History feature keeps track of all the Web sites you've visited for the last four weeks.

✔ Follow these steps to use the Address list:

1. Click the downward-pointing arrow on the right end of the Address box. Recently visited sites like the ones shown in Figure 14.2 are displayed.

2. Click on any one of these site names to return to that site.

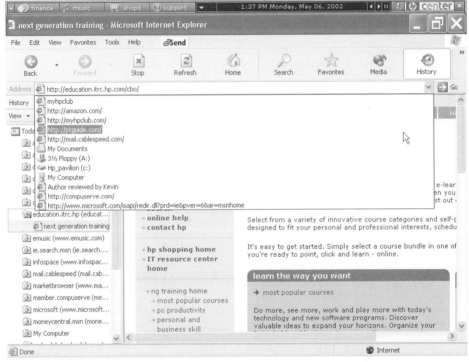

FIGURE 14.2 All the sites you've visited during your current Internet session are displayed here.

✔ **To locate a site from the History listing, follow these steps:**

1. Click History. You'll see the History window shown in Figure 14.3. This displays all sites visited today, as well as sites visited during the past several weeks.

2. Click a week to display all the sites from that week.

3. Click any site to return to it.

FIGURE 14.3 Having trouble remembering the site you visited last Tuesday? Check out your browsing History.

Saving Favorites

In addition to the record of sites that you've visited that are kept automatically by Internet Explorer, you can save your own record of favorite sites so that you can jump back to them at any time. The Favorites feature is found on most browsers.

✔ **You can save a Web page to your Favorites collection and visit it again by following these steps:**

1. Select Favorites, Add to Favorites. The dialog box in Figure 14.4 appears.

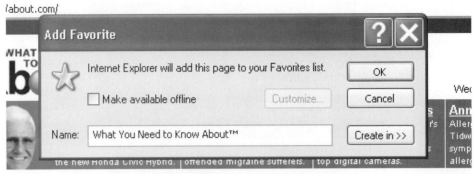

FIGURE 14.4 Adding a favorite is as easy as naming it.

2. Enter a Name if you want to locate the page by a name other than its URL (for example, if you wanted to name the Hewlett-Packard site HP or Pavilion).

3. Click OK to save it.

4. To go to a Favorite page, click Favorites.

5. From the list that appears in the Favorites window, shown in Figure 14.5, click the site you want to visit.

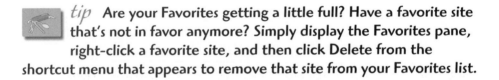 *tip* **Are your Favorites getting a little full? Have a favorite site that's not in favor anymore? Simply display the Favorites pane, right-click a favorite site, and then click Delete from the shortcut menu that appears to remove that site from your Favorites list.**

Setting Your Home Page

You may have heard the term "home page" before. There are actually two varieties of home pages. There are Web site home pages, and then there's your browser home page.

Web sites, which are typically made up of several individual Web pages, will have a single home page, which is their command central. You can typically get an overview of site contents and move to any page on the site from the home page.

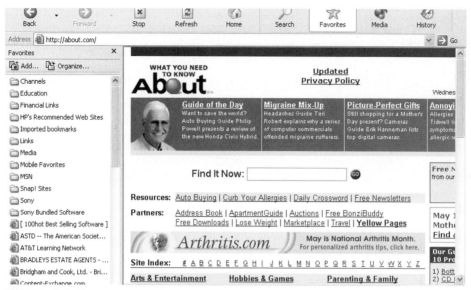

FIGURE 14.5 Click any folder to display sites within them or any site to go directly to it.

On the other hand, your home page is like your home base for browsing the Internet. It's the first page that your browser displays whenever you go online, and you can return to it at any time by clicking the Home button on your browser.

Project: **Picking Your Perfect Home Page**

By default, Microsoft has set *MSN.com* as your Internet Explorer home page, but you might want to set your favorite search engine, such as Google or Ask, or your school Web site or a news channel as your home page.

✔ **First locate a Web page that you think you'd like to use as a home page. Then, just follow these steps:**

1. Select Tools, Options. The Internet Options dialog box shown in Figure 14.6 appears.

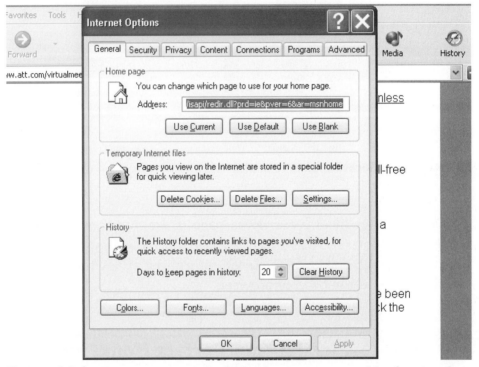

FIGURE 14.6 The seven tabs on this dialog box contain a wealth of settings for how Internet Explorer takes you around the Internet.

2. If you have the page you want to use currently displayed, click Use Current to set it as your home page. If you don't have the page you want to use displayed, type its URL in the Address box, and click Apply.

3. Click OK to close the dialog box.

    Now whenever you log on, your home page will be displayed.

Roaming Around with HP Center

HP Center is a feature included with all HP Pavilions shipped with Windows XP. When you turn on HP Center, a menu bar appears at the top of your screen (see Figure 14.7). From here, you can click various modules including finance, music, and shopping sites. These modules consist of windows that include links to access Web sites. Some of the links in modules provide special offers to Pavilion users.

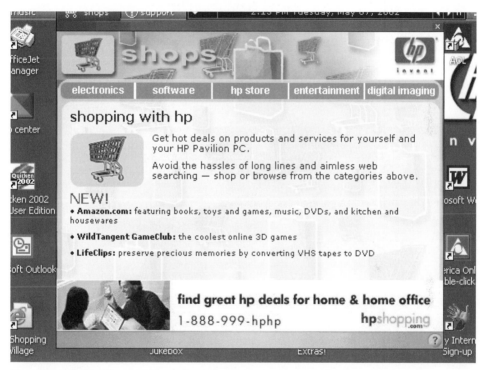

FIGURE 14.7 The items on the HP Center menu bar display windows with links to various Web sites.

There's also a clock and date reminder on this bar, and a tool you can click that looks like an exclamation point and that displays a list of alerts you have received. Alerts notify you of events that one of the linked resources sends or that you've signed up to receive.

Customizing HP Center

You can customize the HP Center by setting which modules appear on the menu bar and in what order. Therefore, if you love to shop and get entertainment software and CDs, but aren't so crazy about finance, remove the Finance module and put Shops and Entertainment on the menu bar. However, beware. When you remove a module, it's gone forever.

✔ **Here's how to customize HP Center:**

1. Click the button labeled HP Center and select Customize. The Customize hp center dialog box shown in Figure 14.8 appears.

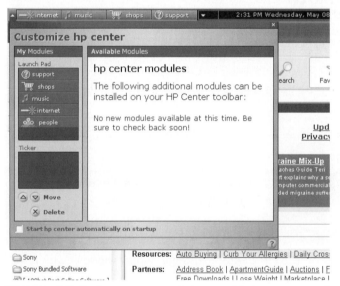

FIGURE 14.8   Rearrange modules or add them to your Launch Pad with this dialog box.

2. Click an item on the HP Launch Pad list. You can then click the up Move arrow to move it toward the left side of the HP center menu

bar, the down Move arrow to move it to the right, or Delete to remove it from the bar entirely.

caution **If you delete a module, it isn't just hidden. It's gone for good.**

Visiting My HP Club and HP Support Center

The Support module of HP Center is a gateway to three helpful Web sites: My HP Club, Help and Support, and the HP Support Web site. To access these sites, open the Support module on the HP Center menu bar, click the appropriate tab and click the link to a site contained there.

Here's what you'll find there:

- My HP Club (see Figure 14.9) provides helpful tips and information about your computer, free downloads of music, and information on PC maintenance and security. Look for special offers on other HP products, useful software on this site, and feature articles on topics such as digital photography and e-books.

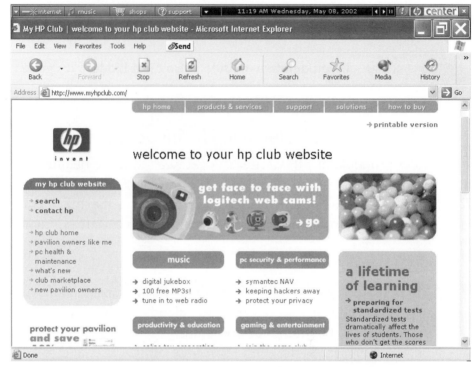

FIGURE 14.9 My HP Club keeps you up to date on new ways to use technology.

- HP Support (see Figure 14.10) offers updated drivers for HP hardware, a search engine, and HP product information.

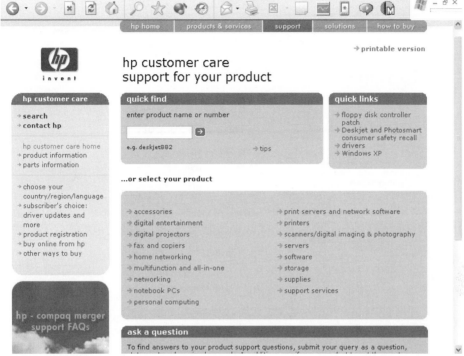

FIGURE 14.10 If you want up-to-date product information, the HP Support site is the place to go.

- The HP Help and Support Center (see Figure 14.11), which you can also access by pressing the special key on your keyboard that has a question mark symbol on it, is like no help system you've ever seen. It contains troubleshooting advice, information about every aspect of using your computer, tools to help you make Windows XP most efficient and maintain your computer system, and more.

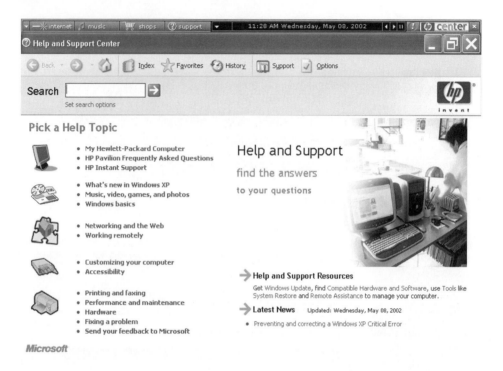

FIGURE 14.11 Follow links here to get answers about various features of your Pavilion.

 note See Chapter 19 to get a step-by-step walkthrough of how the Help and Support Center works.

You can go to these sites by clicking the Support module on the HP Center menu bar and then clicking either the MyHPClub or HP Support tabs. Click the link for the site you want to visit.

Going Shopping

Several of the modules on HP Center take you to online sites where you can purchase things. The Finance module has links to products such as financial software. The People module provides access to services like Ofoto, which is an online photo service from Kodak that you

hp pavilion pcs

can access from the Photo Sharing tab. However, if you're a serious shopper, the Shops module (see Figure 14.12) is definitely worth a look.

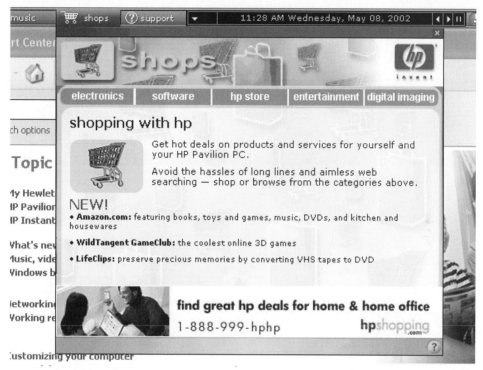

FIGURE 14.12 Each tab in this window offers links to online shopping.

The Shops module opens in a main window listing current partners and deals. Click any of the five tabs to find shopping links. The links are listed along the left side of the window, as on the Entertainment tab shown in Figure 14.13. Note that these links may change periodically.

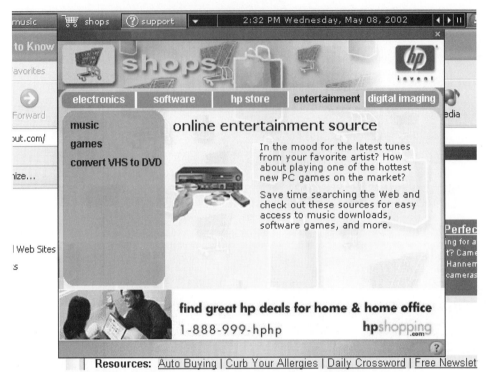

FIGURE 14.13 Music, games, and VHS conversion are available on the Entertainment tab of the Shops module.

The HP Store tab takes you to HP sites where you can buy HP products, such as printers and digital cameras, and where you can access online photo services. If you click the *hpshopping.com* link, you'll go to the HP online shopping site (see Figure 14.14).

FIGURE 14.14 *HP Shopping.com* gathers several HP products together in one location for your online shopping convenience.

Shopping Online Safely

Shopping online is generally a safe way to do business, but here are a few things to check for. There should be a privacy statement on store sites that ensures that your name and contact information will not be given out to any other business. Also, a security statement should include the use of Secure Sockets Layer (SSL) software, which protects information that you send online. Finally, look for a little icon of a padlock in your browser window. If the padlock is closed, the site is secure; if it's open, think twice about purchasing anything on that site.

Shopping online requires a credit card and sometimes involves shipping charges. Have your credit card and shipping information ready before you go shopping. Most sites use the metaphor of a shopping cart or shopping bag where you place items, and you then go through a checkout process where you provide your credit card and shipping information.

Check out return policies before you buy. If what you get isn't what you wanted, it can be a hassle to make returns if the site doesn't make the process easy for you.

Learning Online

Whether you call it distance learning, online learning, or e-learning, learning over the Internet is becoming very popular. People are taking computer training, and earning college degrees and studying everything from genealogy to astrology, all from their computers.

HP helps get you started in online learning in a couple of ways. It maintains a training Web site called Next Generation Training where you can take courses, and HP provides a free one-year subscription to Encarta Online, a virtual encyclopedia and learning resource.

note **If you purchased your Pavilion before the fall of 2002, you'll get Encarta. If you purchased your computer more recently, you have Britannica available to you. Check out Chapter 20 to learn more about the features of Britannica.**

Exploring Encarta Online Deluxe

Your HP Pavilion includes a one-year subscription to Encarta, Microsoft's online encyclopedia. The first time you select Start, All Programs, Encarta Online, you will be asked to sign on with a .NET Passport. If you don't have a .NET Passport, follow the on screen instructions to obtain one. When you've activated Encarta, you'll see the opening window shown in Figure 14.15.

hp pavilion pcs

FIGURE 14.15 Encarta Online Deluxe includes a dictionary, atlas, and more.

Here's what Encarta includes:

- A searchable English dictionary that includes an audio feature so you can hear words pronounced correctly.
- A challenge trivia game. Note that you have to install Macromedia Shockwave Player to run the game, but don't worry. A window pops up when you open the game offering to download the player automatically and for free.
- An online atlas you can use to search for maps of any country and can zoom in to view details of different regions.
- A comprehensive encyclopedia that covers a wide variety of topics with articles, activities, and Web links.
- Terraserver, which contains views of the Earth from a satellite out in space.

- Schoolhouse provides a page that contains lesson plans that students and teachers can use for free.

Getting around Encarta essentially involves clicking a link, then entering a search term to retrieve an article or definition (see Figure 14.16), or making choices from lists, such as the region for which you want to retrieve maps in the atlas.

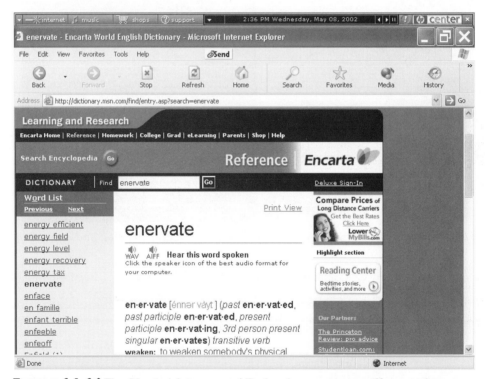

FIGURE 14.16 The Physical Science and Technology category offers articles on several scientific disciplines.

Visiting HP's Next Generation Training

Although you don't have to own a Pavilion to take advantage of HP's Next Generation Training site (see Figure 14.17), you can get there through the HP Center. Open the Internet module and then click the training item to go there. You can also get there by entering the address *education.itrc.hp.com/cbo/*.

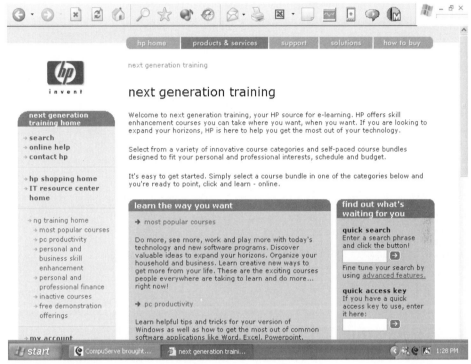

FIGURE 14.17 Search for courses that match your needs or explore free course demonstrations.

This site includes free demonstrations, as well as fee-based courses. The courses are self-paced learning (meaning you review material and practice skills by yourself with no instructor around) and cost about $30. Courses run the gamut from career development and personal finances to PC productivity.

tip **Most courses offer a preflight test to establish your level of knowledge before the course and a postflight test to show your improvement. You don't have to take these tests if you don't want to, but they're a good way to note your own progress.**

hp pavilion pcs

Chapter Summary

In this chapter, you learned the basics of browsing the Internet using Internet Explorer. You learned to navigate using your browser, set up a home page, and save favorite Web sites. You explored HP Center and its links to online sites providing education, shopping, and support opportunities.

15

Getting in Touch with Email

In this Chapter

✔ Selecting an email program

✔ Using Outlook Express to send and receive email

✔ Downloading attachments

✔ Organizing email folders

✔ Using email etiquette

It's hard to believe that email wasn't around a dozen or so years ago. Many of us check our email several times a day, sending and receiving hundreds of messages a year to family, friends, business associates, and online businesses. Email is also used to send files around the world, helping us to do business and to communicate in the blink of an eye.

I n this chapter, you'll use Outlook Express, which comes installed on your Pavilion, to learn about the basics of email.

Choosing an Email Program

There are many email software programs out there, including the one that's typically provided by your ISP when you get an online account. They all do things somewhat alike, but some are more feature rich than others. Before you can decide which program is for you, you need to understand a few basics about email itself.

How Does Email Work?

Email is simply the sending and receiving of text messages, Web content in HTML format, and sometimes computer file attachments in an electronic form from one computer to another. Email can be sent across a home or office network or can be sent to others across the Internet.

You must have an email address, such as anyusername@aol.com, for people to send email to you. You must know a person's email addresses to address email to him. You need an email client, that is, a service that sends and receives your email and that is usually provided by your ISP, but that is also available through services such as Hotmail. You will also use some form of email software to receive, read, send, and manage your email.

Selecting an Email Program

ISPs, such as AOL or Earthlink, provide an email account with your Internet connection. You can use their email program from their home page, or you can set up another program, such as Outlook Express, to access those email accounts.

Not everybody needs all the same features in their email program, but, in deciding which e-mail program to use, consider whether the program you think you'd like to use has these features:

- When you save copies of sent and received messages is it easy to manage the stored messages? Can you create and rename folders to store them in, and can you find stored messages easily? Can you set up the program to save sent messages for a certain length of time automatically?
- Can you modify the appearance of emails by changing fonts or adding graphics. (See Figure 15.1 to see how Outlook Express allows you to do this.)

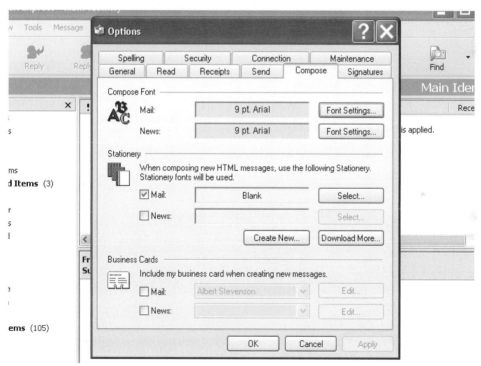

FIGURE 15.1 You can even create a stationery design for your email messages using these settings.

- Does the program include a good download management feature that lets you control where files are downloaded to and whether they open after download?
- If you go out of town, does the program offer a feature to send a reply automatically letting people who email you know you're away?
- Can you set up the software to forward email to another address in case you have two accounts and want to redirect messages temporarily?
- Does the software provide tools to block email from certain sources to help you avoid spamming or harassing email?
- Will the software allow you to download email and read it offline?
- Can you easily sort messages by sender name, date, or subject?
- Does the program offer ease of use in addressing, forwarding, and copying people on messages?
- Can you add a signature (for example your name, address, and phone number) to be attached to every outgoing email automatically?

Using Outlook Express

Outlook Express is an email program from Microsoft that is included on your HP Pavilion. It is a slightly less robust version of Microsoft Outlook, which you may have used at work or on a previous computer.

tip Although Outlook Express lacks a few features of Outlook, it takes up less memory when it's running than Outlook. This can help alleviate some problems with computer memory when you have to send or receive very large files.

Setting Up Your Email Account in Outlook Express

To allow Outlook Express to retrieve your mail, you have to tell it something about your email account. You can get that information from your ISP, so contact them first and tell them what you want to do. They'll provide you with a protocol to use for your incoming email server (such as Internet Message Access Protocol [IMAP] or Post Office Protocol [POP]), along with incoming and outgoing mail server addresses.

✔ **To set up the account, follow these steps:**

1. Select Tools, Accounts.

2. Click Add, Mail.

3. On the Internet Connection Wizard that appears, enter the name you want to appear on messages when you send email and click Next.

4. In the dialog box that appears, enter your email address and then click Next. The E-mail Server Names dialog box shown in Figure 15.2 appears.

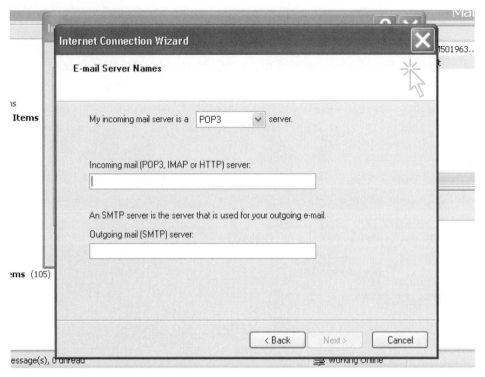

FIGURE 15.2 This is where the information from your provider comes into play.

5. Click the arrow to display a choice of server types and select the correct one for your provider.

6. Enter an incoming mail server address and an outgoing mail server address.

7. Click Next.

8. Enter your Account Name and your Password in the appropriate field.

9. Click Next, and you've finished the wizard. Click Finish to return to the Internet Accounts dialog box.

10. If you want this account to be your default email account, click Set as Default and then click Close.

If you have set this account as your default account, when you are connected to the Internet through your ISP and you click the Send/Recv button, Outlook Express goes out and retrieves your mail from that account.

Setting Up the Address Book

You can send messages by simply entering an email address for a recipient in a new message form. However, emailing becomes much easier when you've stored addresses of people you frequently contact in Outlook Express's Address Book.

Project: Building Your Online Address Book

Create a form and make enough copies of it for everybody in your family. Include on this form a column for First Name, Last Name, Email Address, and Home Phone. Have each person in the family fill out a sheet for people they want included in your online Address Book. Designate somebody to create the contacts in Outlook, and somebody else to assemble the sheets in a binder to keep in case something damages your computer and you lose your email addresses someday.

Then, you can address messages by choosing a contact from a list. You can also simply begin typing a name, and Outlook will recognize it and enter the full email address for you.

✔ **Follow these steps to add contacts to your Address Book:**

1. Click Addresses. The Address Book dialog box opens, as shown in Figure 15.3.

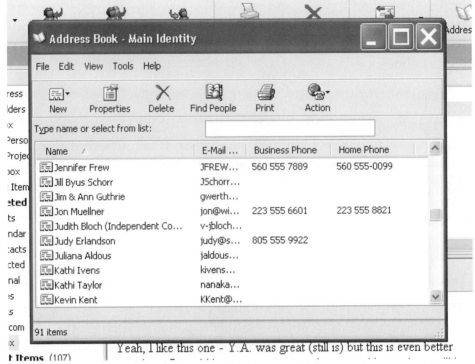

FIGURE 15.3 You can address a message to somebody from this dialog box or even initiate a phone call to them using choices on the Action button.

2. Click New and then New Contact. The Properties dialog box shown in Figure 15.4 appears.

FIGURE 15.4 You can enter a wealth of information about your contacts on the seven tabs in this dialog box.

3. Enter the contact's first, middle, and last name, a title such as Mr. or Dr., and an email address.

4. Click Add to add the e-mail address. If you want to add a second e-mail address, type it in the now blank E-Mail Addresses box and click Add again.

5. Click the Home or Business tab and enter contact information, such as address, phone, fax, Web page, or mobile phone number.

6. If you want to enter personal information, such as the contact's spouse's name or birthday, go to the Personal tab.

7. When you're done entering information, click OK to add the contact to the Address Book.

tip You can use the New, New Group command in the Address Book to create a group of email addresses so you can send messages to everybody in the group with a single action. This becomes useful to communicate with everybody on a project team at work or the neighborhood carpool, for example.

Creating and Sending Messages

Creating an email message is a simple matter of entering a recipient's address, a subject, and the text of your message. You can address an email to as many people as you like and can also copy or blind copy people. A blind copy involves sending a copy of the message to somebody without letting the recipient know that that person has been copied.

note As an email courtesy, try to create a subject line that makes it clear what the message is about. People who get lots of email will find it much easier to prioritize and deal with each message that way and won't have to read a message to discover its topic.

✔ **Follow these steps to create a new message in Outlook Express:**

1. Click Create Mail. The blank New Message form shown in Figure 15.5 appears.

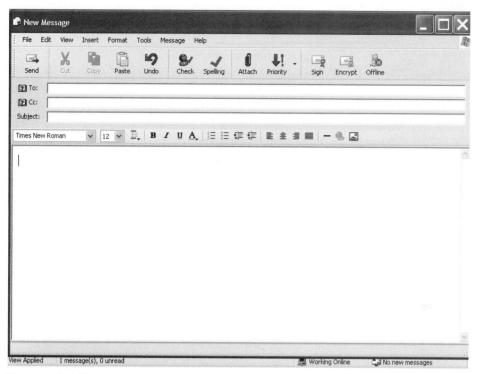

FIGURE 15.5 The formatting tools in this form don't become available to you until you've clicked in the message area.

2. In the To: field, you can enter an email address (such as Smith@aol.com).

3. If you have stored contact information, you can click the To: button to display the contact list, shown in Figure 15.6. If you have created contacts for your address book, they are listed here. You can then click a name in the list and click the To:, Cc:, or Bcc: buttons to address the message to as many people as you like. Click OK to close the dialog box and return to the message.

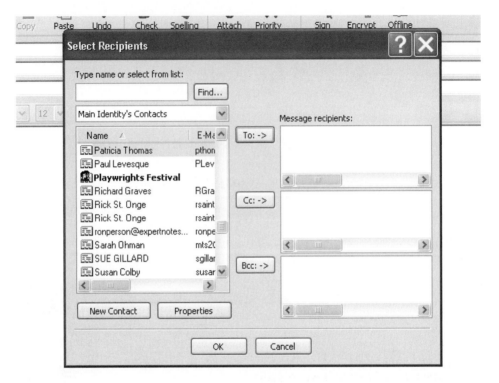

FIGURE 15.6 Address your message to as many people as you like from this dialog box.

4. Enter a topic for the message in the Subject box.

5. Click in the message area and type your message.

6. When the message is ready to go, you just click Send to send it on its way.

note **You can control whether emails are sent immediately (which can slow down your work a bit while you wait for each one to go) or sent all at once when you exit Outlook Express. You make this setting by selecting Tools, Options, and displaying the Send tab. Select or remove the checkmark from the Send Messages Immediately checkbox to control this.**

Controlling the Look and Feel of Your Email

You can format your email in a variety of ways. You can use predesigned stationery to add an attractive background to your message, or you can use the text formatting tools available to you in a New Message form.

Project: Pick a Stationery for Family Email

Stationery can make your emails look special, adding color or graphics to every message you send out. Have your family review the stationery available in Outlook Express and pick one that appeals to you all. Consider changing the stationery you use with each season of the year.

✔ **To specify stationery to be used on all your email messages, follow these steps:**

1. With no new message open, select Tools, Options and then click the Compose tab, shown in Figure 15.7.

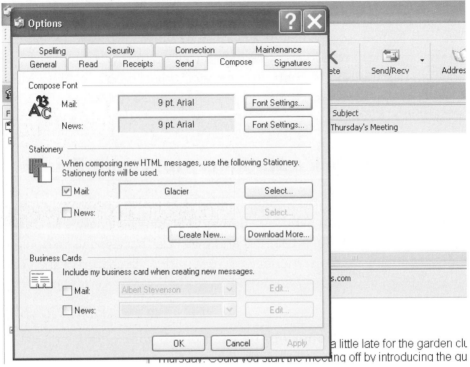

FIGURE 15.7 Set defaults for font and stationery here.

2. Click Select in the Stationery section of this dialog box. The Select Stationery dialog box opens.

3. Click any stationery listed here and then click OK.

4. Click Apply and then OK again to close the Options dialog box.

note **You can also change the stationery you're using as you create an email message. With a new message open, click Format, Apply Stationery, More Stationery to make a different choice for that message only.**

You can use the formatting tools in a new message to format selected message text, or you can use the Compose tab of the Options dialog box to set default formatting for all message text. Settings you can apply include which font to use, font style (bold, italic, and so on), font size, color, and effects, such as underlining.

caution   **Not all email programs can read background graphics and font styling. Be aware of this if you use formatting for emphasis in your message, such as making a phrase bold or underlining it. Some people might not get it.**

Receiving and Forwarding Messages

When you receive emails—and you will—they appear in your Inbox. Double-click the Inbox to open it. Messages are listed in the order they were received by default, with the most recent on top of the list.

Double-click any message to read it. It will open, looking like the message in Figure 15.8.

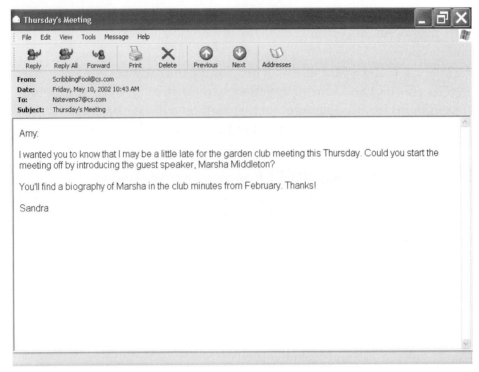

FIGURE 15.8 Information about who sent the message and when will appear at the top of each message.

At this point, you have a few options:

- You can reply to the sender of the message or reply to the sender and all other recipients (if any). If you use the Reply or Reply All options, your response is automatically addressed for you with a subject line that starts Re: and includes the original subject line text. All you have to do is enter your return message and click Send.

- You can forward the message to somebody else. If you click Forward, you'll have to enter an address or addresses to forward to and add a comment, if you like. Note that the recipient of a forwarded message will see notations of the original sender's name in their copy.

- You can print the message, using the standard Windows print dialog box.
- You can delete the message. If you make this choice, the message is moved to your Deleted folder, where you can retrieve it (but only for a short period of time) if you change your mind.
- If you want to store the message, you can select File, Move to Folder, or Copy to Folder. (You'll learn more about managing message folders shortly).

If you don't want to take any of these steps, you can either click the close button in the upper right hand corner, or click Previous or Next to view another message in the Inbox. The message you were viewing remains in your Inbox.

Working with Attachments

Attachments are computer files that you include with an email. The two processes that you need to learn about related to attachments are how to attach a message to your emails and how to view and download messages others attach when they email you.

caution   **Email attachments may slow down the transmission of your email, especially if they are large files, such as graphics. Some email programs may actually block receipt of very large files.**

✔ **When you create a message, you can attach a file by following these steps:**

1. In the new message form, click Attach. The Insert Attachment dialog box shown in Figure 15.9 appears.

FIGURE 15.9 Locate the document you want to attach on your computer or a floppy disk.

2. Use the Look in drop-down list to locate the folder where you've stored the file.

3. Click the file name and then Attach.

That's it. When you send the message, the attachment will go along with it.

When you receive a message with an attachment, the symbol of a little disk will appear on the message icon in your Inbox.

✔ **To open an attachment you receive with an email, follow these steps:**

1. Double-click the message in your Inbox to open it. The Attach line under the Subject lists the name of the document that's attached and its size.

2. Double-click the attached file. The Open Attachment Warning dialog box opens (see Figure 15.10).

FIGURE 15.10 Note the warning about files containing viruses and consider the source before opening any attachment.

3. If you want to open the attachment in the program it was created in, such as Works, click the Open it option. If you want to save the file to a folder on your hard drive or a floppy disk, select the Save it to disk option.

4. Click OK.

Depending on your choice in Step 3, the document will open for you to read it, or the Save As dialog box appears so that you can select a place in which to save the file.

> *note* **If the program that the file was created in is not installed on your computer, you won't be able to open the file. There are programs such as Adobe Acrobat (which is included on your Pavilion) that can open files created in any format, as long as the files were saved in Adobe Acrobat and you have Adobe Acrobat on your system to open them.**

Organizing Email Folders

Outlook Express is organized with folders. Your Inbox is a folder and so are your Sent Items, Contacts, and Deleted Items. When you send a message, a copy is automatically filed in your Sent Items folder. When you delete a message, it is moved into the Deleted Items folder. However, you can also create folders of your own and move messages into them at any time. For example, you might create a folder for each person in your family or folders for Family Finances or School Projects.

✔ **To create a new folder, follow these steps:**

1. Click the folder where you want the new folder to appear. For example, if you want to create a subfolder in your Inbox, click the Inbox folder.

2. Select File, New, Folder. The New Folder dialog box shown in Figure 15.11 appears.

3. Enter a name in the Folder Name field.

4. Click OK to create the folder. It now appears in the list of folders along the left side of the Outlook Express window.

hp pavilion pcs

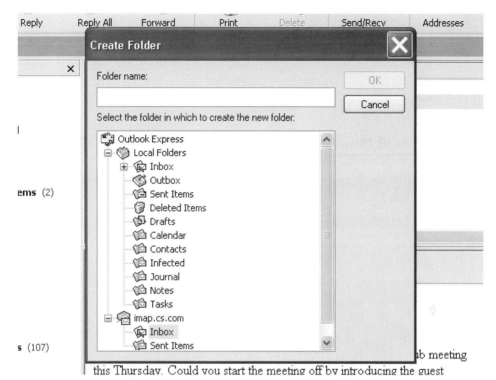

| Reply | Reply All | Forward | Print | Delete | Send/Recv | Addresses |

Create Folder

Folder name:

[   ]   OK

                                         Cancel

Select the folder in which to create the new folder:

- Outlook Express
  - Local Folders
    - Inbox
    - Outbox
    - Sent Items
    - Deleted Items
    - Drafts
    - Calendar
    - Contacts
    - Infected
    - Journal
    - Notes
    - Tasks
  - imap.cs.com
    - Inbox
    - Sent Items

ems (2)

s (107)

this Thursday. Could you start the meeting off by introducing the guest

FIGURE 15.11 Enter a folder name that's descriptive of the contents you intend to place there.

To move a file into a folder, you click the message in your Inbox and drag it to the folder. Alternately, you can select Edit, Move to Folder, or Copy to Folder and specify the folder in which you want to place the file.

Email Etiquette

Just as it's polite to end business letters with "sincerely" and to answer phone calls with "hello," email communication has its own newly minted rules of conduct called netiquette. Paying attention to netiquette will help you not only come off as a polite emailer, but also make sure your communication or the feeling behind it isn't misunderstood.

Here are a few rules of netiquette to live by:

- When you use all capital letters in your message, it's called shouting because it gives a sense of larger-than-life urgency that fairly shouts at the reader. Capitalize all the letters in a word occasionally for emphasis, but never leave your Caps Lock on for the duration of a message.

- If you have email, you should check it regularly and reply promptly. People who send you a message and then wait a week for a reply will be frustrated. Even if you can't deal with typing a lengthy response right away, send a quick reply acknowledging that you got the message and will be replying in a day, a week, or whenever you think you can get to it.

- Repeat portions of the original email you reply to so the person receiving your message will remember what the original comment is that you're referencing. Many email programs will format the original text differently from your reply text automatically, but, if not, you can use the << and >> symbols to set off original lines of text in your reply.

- Double-check who each message is addressed to before sending and be sure that you want all those people to read what you have to say, especially if you're replying to all the original addressees of a message. Email is so instant that, after you've clicked Send, there's no turning back.

- Keep your head. If you are angry or upset, take time before sending an email. Remember, your anger will be frozen in text forever and can be forwarded to anybody. If you think you might regret what you're saying later, wait until you calm down to review and then send the message.

Chapter Summary

In this chapter, you've learned all about email and how to create, send, forward, and reply to messages. You've explored the features of Outlook Express and walked through the process of setting up an email account and formatting email messages. Finally, you learned about email netiquette so you can be a good citizen of the Internet.

5

Upgrading Your Pavilion

Managing Computer Memory

In this Chapter

✔ **Understanding how computer memory works**

✔ **Checking your available memory**

✔ **Freeing up hard disk space**

✔ **Adding memory**

Computer memory has come a long way in recent years. It wasn't that long ago that your computer came with 4 megabytes (Mb) of memory. Today, 256 Mb is pretty average. However, somehow we humans use up what we've got, whether it's our paycheck or our computer memory. When you're feeling the pinch of a full hard drive, you'll be glad to know your Pavilion is easy to upgrade. Before you do, though, you should understand what memory is.

What Is Computer Memory?

The type of memory called Random Access Memory (RAM) is essentially the available space on your computer that can be used to run programs. Windows can also use your hard drive space to create temporary memory called *virtual memory* that serves the same purpose as RAM. In addition to the program you are working in at the moment, your computer will try to keep recently used programs available in RAM memory so you can access them quickly as you work. Unlike the files stored permanently on your hard drive, when you turn your computer off, whatever was in RAM and virtual memory is lost.

Sometimes you can solve a temporary RAM memory issue by simply closing some programs on your computer if you have too many running at one time. However, if you have to do this all the time, you probably don't have enough RAM. In that case, you may find that your programs run slowly, or you may experience computer crashes on a regular basis. That's when it's time to upgrade.

RAM memory comes in modules that you can buy and install in your CPU by opening it up and slotting the modules into place. Those memory modules come as different types. In fact, today, you need a good memory just to remember all the different types of memory. There are options such as Single Inline Memory Modules (SIMMs) that are generally found on older computers, Rambus Dynamic RAM (RDRAM), Rambus Inline Memory Module (RIMMs), Dual Inline Memory Modules (DIMMs), and Double Data Rate Synchronous Dynamic RAM (DDR SDRAM). These are different types of memory based on the chip set (such as a Pentium or Celeron chip) in your computer. HP Pavilion models differ somewhat in the type of memory modules they use (see Figure 16.1) .

In addition to RAM, there is a certain amount of storage space on your hard drive where you save all your software programs and files. Where RAM can be upgraded by adding memory modules, if you don't have enough hard disk space to store all the files and software you want on your computer, you will either have to remove some files or

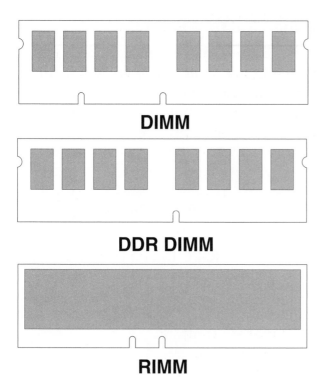

DIMM

DDR DIMM

RIMM

FIGURE 16.1 Memory modules fit into sockets inside your Pavilion computer.

programs or replace the hard drive. (Replacing the hard drive is covered in Chapter 17).

Check Your Available Memory

Before you can determine the best way to manage your memory needs, you need to know how your system is using your current memory. First, you can check on how much RAM you have in use when you're running the programs you typically work in. Then, you can check the space on your hard drive and take some steps to clean it up to free up some storage memory.

Checking Out Your RAM

Adding to RAM is easy, but it does mean spending the money to buy memory modules. Before you do that, you should know how much RAM memory you have and how much of it is being used. The best way to do this is to use some of the system information reports in PC Doctor for Windows XP, which comes installed on every Pavilion.

✔ **Follow these steps to review system information in PC Doctor:**

1. Select Start, All Programs, HP Tools, PC Doctor for Windows XP.

2. Click System Information.

3. Double-click the System Information test. The information shown in Figure 16.2 appears.

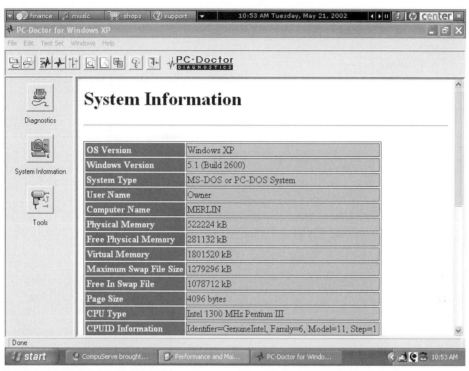

FIGURE 16.2 You can learn all about your computer's specifications here.

According to this system information listing, I have 522,224kb (or about 512Mb) of physical memory, that is, RAM. Of that, I have 281,132 kb free, or almost half. Any problems I might have shouldn't relate to available RAM. However, if you notice that these two numbers are very close on your system, it may be time to upgrade.

Freeing Up Hard Disk Space

If you need hard disk space because you don't have enough available to install a new piece of software, for example, you can use the Drive information from PC Doctor. If there's not enough disk space, you can then run the Disk Cleanup feature to maximize your hard drive.

✔ **Follow these steps to see how much space you have on your hard drive:**

1. From the PC Doctor main window, click System Information.

2. Double-click Drive Info. The report shown in Figure 16.3 appears.

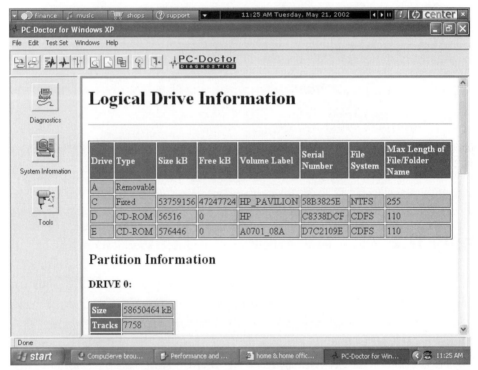

FIGURE 16.3 The hard drive is drive C:, the Fixed drive.

Notice in this figure that I have a hard drive with 53,759,156 kb, and, of that, 47,248,520, or about 85 percent, is free. I should have no problem installing a legion of programs, but, if you find your free kb number is tiny, you may need more disk space.

Before you run out to buy a new hard drive, try these two things to free up more disk space:

- First, remove any programs you don't need and archive any files you don't use on a regular basis. See Chapter 6 to learn about uninstalling software.
- Second, run a utility called Disk Cleanup, which suggests deletion of files no longer used by your system and which optimizes the storage of other data on your hard drive. Chapter 8 tells you how to run the Disk Cleanup utility.

Adding Memory Modules to Your Pavilion

If you've decided that what you need is more RAM, it's time to go shopping and buy your memory modules and then install them. First, check the HP At Home Web site (*www.hp-at-home.com*) and search for your system to view its technical specifications, like those shown in Figure 16.4 for the Pavilion 520N.

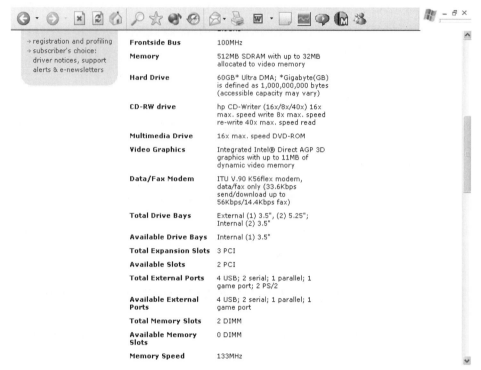

→ registration and profiling	
→ subscriber's choice: driver notices, support alerts & e-newsletters	
Frontside Bus	100MHz
Memory	512MB SDRAM with up to 32MB allocated to video memory
Hard Drive	60GB* Ultra DMA; *Gigabyte(GB) is defined as 1,000,000,000 bytes (accessible capacity may vary)
CD-RW drive	hp CD-Writer (16x/8x/40x) 16x max. speed write 8x max. speed re-write 40x max. speed read
Multimedia Drive	16x max. speed DVD-ROM
Video Graphics	Integrated Intel® Direct AGP 3D graphics with up to 11MB of dynamic video memory
Data/Fax Modem	ITU V.90 K56flex modem, data/fax only (33.6Kbps send/download up to 56Kbps/14.4Kbps fax)
Total Drive Bays	External (1) 3.5", (2) 5.25"; Internal (2) 3.5"
Available Drive Bays	Internal (1) 3.5"
Total Expansion Slots	3 PCI
Available Slots	2 PCI
Total External Ports	4 USB; 2 serial; 1 parallel; 1 game port; 2 PS/2
Available External Ports	4 USB; 2 serial; 1 parallel; 1 game port
Total Memory Slots	2 DIMM
Available Memory Slots	0 DIMM
Memory Speed	133MHz

FIGURE 16.4 My system has two DIMM slots.

Your HP documentation will tell you what kind of memory module you must use for your Pavilion. From the information on this site, I know my system uses DIMM slots, and my documentation tells me that DIMM modules have to be 168-pin unbuffered SDRAM compliant with Intel PC SDRAM Unbuffered DIMM Specification and that I can install 64Mb, 128Mb, or 256Mb modules. Now don't be intimidated by this string of technobabble! It's just information you have to take with you when you go shopping for memory. The store where you buy the memory should be able to provide the right type of module to fit these specifications.

caution **Putting the wrong kind of memory module into your Pavilion could cause damage to the computer, so check carefully for the proper specifications.**

tip **You can add memory modules, but you can also replace the memory modules that come with the computer with higher capacity modules.**

Safety First

To install memory, you have to open up your computer. Before you go digging around your CPU with a screwdriver, remember that you're dealing with expensive equipment that has many small parts and that can hold an electrical charge even when it's turned off.

There are several safety procedures you should know about:

- Disconnect everything from the system, including phone lines, network connections, and power connections.
- It's a good idea to wear an antistatic wrist strap when working with electronic equipment and to use a foam pad of some sort to conduct any electricity away from you.
- Beware of sharp metal edges when removing the cover to your computer.
- If you don't feel comfortable working with electronic equipment, consider having a service technician do it for you.

Opening Your Computer Up

If you have your new module in hand, it's time to open up your computer. This is really a very simple process, so, if you've followed the safety precautions in the previous section, you'll do fine.

✔ **Follow these steps to open your computer:**

1. Turn off the computer and disconnect it from any power source, phone or network lines, and peripherals, such as a mouse or monitor.

2. On the right side of the back of your CPU, loosen the two screws (see Figure 16.5) with a flathead screwdriver. Note that the screws do not come out of their slots. They should just be loosened.

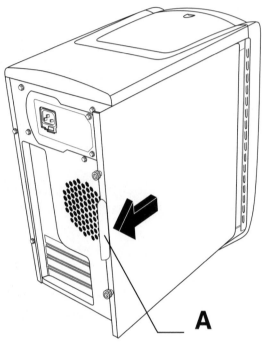

A

FIGURE 16.5 The right side panel gives you access to your computer workings (A).

3. Standing behind the back of the computer, put one hand on the top to hold it steady.

4. Grab the handle on the right side panel (see Figure 16.5) and pull it toward you.

5. Finally, lift the panel up and remove it from the CPU.

With some HP models, you also have to remove the fan duct to get at your memory slots. To do so, place the computer on its side and press the two tabs shown in Figure 16.6 down. Then, just push the fan (B) down and out.

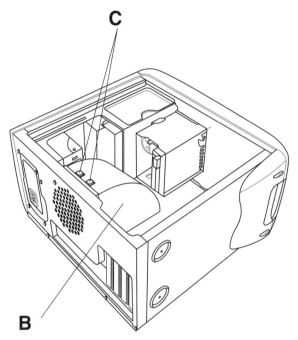

FIGURE 16.6   Push the tabs marked C in this illustration to remove the fan duct (B).

Adding Memory Modules

Now that you have your computer open, adding memory modules is a snap. The number of memory sockets will vary depending on which Pavilion model you have, but you can recognize memory sockets and modules by taking a look at Figure 16.7.

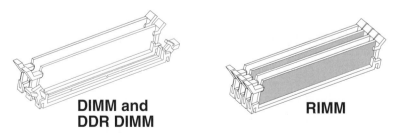

**DIMM and
DDR DIMM**

RIMM

FIGURE 16.7   DIMM and RIMM sockets look similar.

✔ **To add a memory module, follow these steps:**

1. Locate an empty memory socket and push down the retaining clips on either end.

2. Hold the module you want to insert by its edges (try not to touch the gold contact points) and line up the notches on the lower edge with raised areas in the socket (see Figure 16.8).

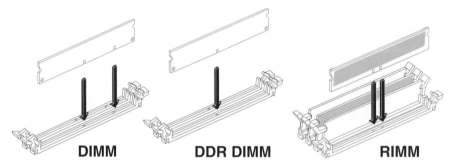

DIMM   DDR DIMM   RIMM

FIGURE 16.8 Each type of module has slightly different notches to line up with the memory socket.

3. Push the module into the socket until it is tightly in place. The clips at either end should click into place when it is inserted correctly.

That's it. Now you can replace the fan duct and side panel and reconnect your computer. When you reboot, Windows will recognize the additional memory.

Chapter Summary

In this chapter, you learned about how computer memory works. You checked your system to see how much memory you have available and learned about how you can free up hard disk space on your computer. Finally, you walked through the process of installing additional memory modules in your computer.

Upgrading Your Hardware

In this Chapter

✓ Replacing a disk drive

✓ Changing the optical drive

✓ Replacing the battery

W hen you have been using your Pavilion for a while, you may find that a piece of hardware in your CPU wears out, or you may want to replace an item with a newer technology. You can, for example, put in a new disk drive, change the CRW optical drive, or replace the battery that provides backup power to keep your computer's date and time calculations functioning.

Upgrading and Repairing

Upgrading or repairing your computer when there's a problem, rather than replacing your computer, makes as much sense as keeping your car in good repair rather than trading it in whenever you come across a mechanical problem. It can be even more cost-effective when you do it yourself, rather than taking it to the nearest computer shop. Knowing you can handle these functions yourself can also be satisfying, like the first time you figured out how to change the oil in your car.

Most common upgrades and repairs are really pretty simple to do, as long as you take a few simple safety precautions and avoid forcing delicate electronic parts to do things they don't want to do. Typically, all you need is a single screwdriver to remove the outer panel of your CPU and perhaps to remove some internal pieces. Most elements inside your Pavilion simply pop into and out of place in sockets, though occasionally you'll have to remove and then reattach cables.

Opening Up Your Computer

In Chapter 16, I outlined safety precautions you should use whenever opening up your computer. I'll repeat them here because they are very important:

- Remember that you're dealing with expensive equipment that has many small parts and that can hold an electrical charge even when it's turned off.
- Disconnect everything from the system, including phone lines, network connections, and power connections.
- It's a good idea to wear an antistatic wrist strap when working with electronic equipment and to use a foam pad of some sort to conduct any electricity away from you.
- Beware of sharp metal edges when removing the cover to your computer.

Now you're ready to begin. Whether replacing a disk drive, optical drive, or battery, the initial steps are the same. You have to open up the computer and remove the fan duct.

✔ **Follow these steps to open up the computer:**

1. Turn off the computer and disconnect it from any power source, phone or network lines, and peripherals.

2. On the right side of the back of your CPU, loosen the two screws (see Figure 17.1) with a flathead screwdriver. Note that the screws do not come out of their slots. They should just be loosened.

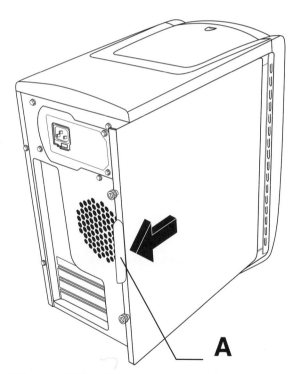

FIGURE 17.1 The right side panel gives you access to your computer workings (A).

3. Standing behind the back of the computer, put one hand on the top to hold it steady.

4. Grab the handle on the right side panel and pull it toward you.

5. Finally, lift the panel up and remove it from the CPU.

In some cases, you also have to remove the fan duct to get at your drives and battery. To do so, with the computer on its side, press the two tabs shown in Figure 17.2 down and push the fan down and out.

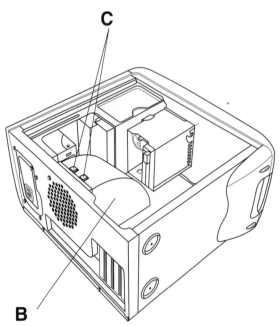

FIGURE 17.2   Push the tabs marked C in this illustration to remove the fan duct (B).

Replacing a Disk Drive

At some point, all drives wear out. If your disk drive isn't functioning properly anymore, or if you want to upgrade to a different model of drive, you can replace it. It's recommended that you purchase your replacement drive from HP. That way, you're ensured of equipment that will fit correctly into your CPU.

tip Click the Shops module of the HP Center to go to the online store where you can buy your equipment.

✔ **After you have purchased your replacement drive and have opened your computer, follow these steps to install the new drive:**

1. With the computer on its side, remove the power and Integrated Drive Electronics (IDE), or disk drive, cables that are on the back of the disk and hard drives (see Figure 17.3).

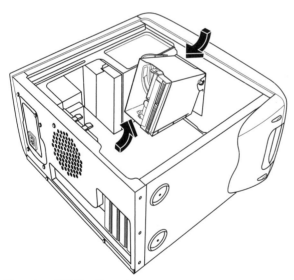

FIGURE 17.3 The drive cage houses the disk and optical drives.

2. Press the drive cage release tab as shown in Figure 17.3.

3. With the release tab still pressed down, move the cage upward and pull it gently out.

4. Take out the screw on each side of the disk drive and remove the drive.

5. Place the new drive into the drive cage so that the two screw holes match.

6. Replace the screws in each side of the drive cage.

When you're done, you can proceed to the "Closing Your Computer" section later in this chapter to close up your computer.

Changing an Optical Drive

Your Pavilion has two optical drives, in some combination of CD, DVD, or CD-Writer, depending on your specific model. You might decide that you'd like to upgrade to a drive with more capacity or that you'd like two CD-Writer drives, for example.

✔ **To replace an optical drive, follow these steps:**

1. With the computer panel and fan duct removed, and the computer on its side, unscrew the two screws on the bottom drive (marked C in Figure 17.4). If you want to remove the top drive, undo both screws B and C.

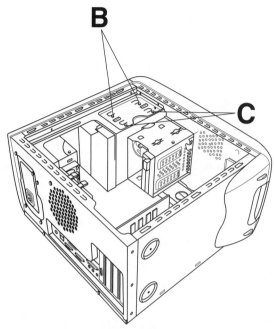

FIGURE 17.4 Either optical drive can be replaced.

2. Push one or both drives out through the front panel of the computer. There will be cables coming off the back of the drives.

3. Remove the cables that are attached to whichever drive you want to replace and pull the drive entirely free of the computer casing through the front panel.

4. Being sure that the jumper setting on the new drive you're going to install is set for Cable Select (CS), slide it through the front of the computer.

5. Reattach the cables to the drive and replace the drive in the casing.

6. Replace the two screws.

7. You're ready to close up the computer with the steps in the last section of this chapter.

tip Whenever you're detaching cables, make a little diagram for yourself or place colored tape on each cable and attachment point to identify where each reattaches.

Replacing the Battery

Your computer contains a battery that provides a backup specifically for your timekeeping feature (your date and clock). If you turn your computer off or your computer should crash, the battery ensures that these settings don't become inaccurate.

If this battery starts to go, you'll notice that your computer clock is no longer accurate. That's when it's time to replace it. Most Pavilions use a CR2032 lithium battery with a 3-volt, 220mAH rating, but just to be safe, verify this with the manual for your Pavilion model.

caution **If you don't use the right kind of battery, it could actually explode. Therefore, please, be sure you check your documentation and buy only the recommended battery type.**

✔ **Here's how you replace a battery:**

1. With the computer panel removed (note with some models the fan duct and drive cage might have to be removed as well), push gently on the metal latch that holds the battery in with a screwdriver until it pops out of its socket.

2. Place the new battery in the socket. Be sure the positive side faces up.

3. That's it. Now just reassemble your computer.

Closing Your Computer

To close your computer, depending on what you might have removed to do your upgrading task, you may have to replace the drive cage, replace the fan duct, and put the side panel back on.

Replacing the Drive Cage

The first thing to put back into place is the drive cage.

✔ **Follow these steps to put your computer back the way it was:**

1. With the drive cage held at a 45-degree angle, slide the two protrusions on the drive case into the slots in the chassis (see Figure 17.5).

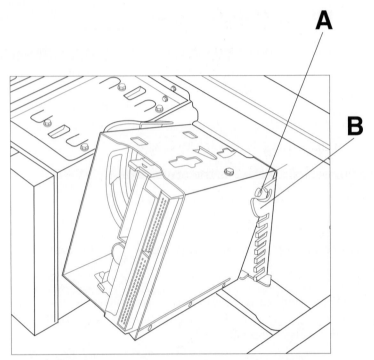

FIGURE 17.5 The protrusions, marked A, fit along the slots marked B.

2. Match the track on the side of the drive cage with the guide on the fixed drive cage (see Figure 17.6) and push them together as you move the drive into place.

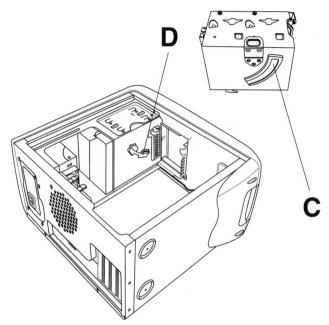

FIGURE 17.6 You need to align tracks C and D.

note **To test that you've got the drive cage in properly, try gently pulling it up. If it comes free without pushing on the release tab, it's not properly aligned, and you'll have to try again.**

Replacing the Fan Duct and Side Panel

Here are the last two steps in reassembling your computer. The fan duct has to slot over the fan that keeps your computer from overheating, and the side panel has to go back in place.

✔ **Follow these steps to reassemble your computer:**

1. Hold the fan duct at a 45-degree angle.

2. Line up the bottom of the duct with the hole on the fan base (see Figure 17.7).

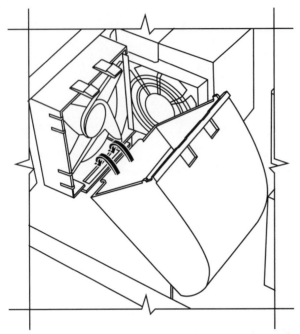

FIGURE 17.7 The fan duct cover should lock into place.

3. Turn the fan duct until it is in position and check that it's on there tightly.

4. Place the side panel on the CPU chassis, making sure the nodes on the panel match up with the holes in the chassis.

5. Slide the panel forward until it clicks into the proper closed position (see Figure 17.8).

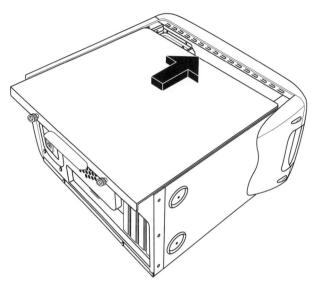

FIGURE 17.8 The panel should slide easily into place.

6. Tighten the screws on the panel.

   That's it!

Chapter Summary

In this chapter, you learned about some of the simple upgrading and repair techniques you can use to replace your disk or optical drives. You also learned how to replace your backup battery when it runs dry.

Supercharging Your Pavilion

In this Chapter

✔ Installing add-in cards

✔ Replacing your hard drive

✔ Networking your computers

Pavilions have plenty of power and features, but, if you've pushed your computer to the limit, you might find you'd like more hard drive space; more functionality, such as higher-end video graphics; or the ability to network two or more computers to orchestrate your computing power. This chapter looks at ways you can take your Pavilion to the next level.

Opening Your Computer

The steps involved in opening your computer and removing the fan duct and drive cage are covered in Chapter 17. Please refer to them to get ready to install an add-in card or hard drive. Also review the safety tips in that chapter. After the computer is open and the fan duct removed, you can proceed with the steps in this chapter.

Installing Add-In Cards

Add-in cards, also called expansion boards, are circuit boards that you connect to a computer to add functionality. Some commonly used add-in cards are video adapters to add video memory and graphics processing, sound cards to enable your computer to play and record sounds, and accelerator boards that enhance the computer processing speed.

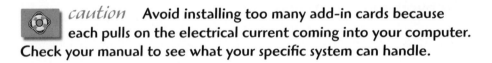 *caution*   **Avoid installing too many add-in cards because each pulls on the electrical current coming into your computer. Check your manual to see what your specific system can handle.**

✔   **If you want to replace a damaged expansion board or install a more sophisticated one, it's easy to do by following these steps:**

1.   With the computer panel off and the computer on its side, locate the card slots shown in Figure 18.1.

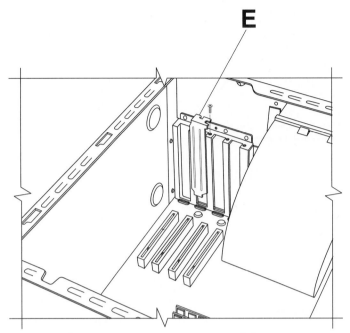

FIGURE 18.1   Empty slots have a cover (E) that you must remove.

2. Loosen the screw on the slot cover (E) and remove the cover.

3. Push the new card into the slot, with a downward motion (see Figure 18.2)

4. Reattach the screw to the card itself.

F

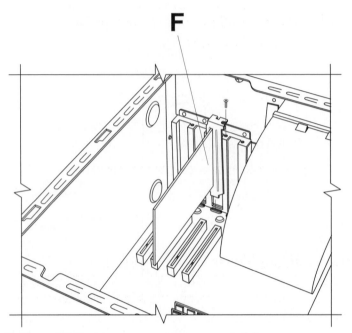

FIGURE 18.2 You can add several cards (F), but don't overextend your power.

5. Reassemble the computer.

note **If you're replacing a card that's already installed, after Step 1, you must remove the existing card by disconnecting any cables attached to it, unscrewing the bracket of the card, and removing it.**

Replacing the Hard Drive

The hard drive is the large storage medium on your computer. Hard drives shipped with Pavilions today have a very large capacity, but what's sufficient today might not be tomorrow. You might decide to replace your hard drive to put one with more capacity in its place or to replace a damaged hard drive.

✔ **The hard drive comes out of your computer quite easily with these few simple steps:**

1. With the computer open and the drive cage removed, unscrew the two screws on the top of the hard drive, as well as a single screw on the bottom.

2. Slide the old hard drive out.

3. Slide the new hard drive into place and reattach the screws.

4. Replace the drive cage and side panel.

Networking Your Computers

Do you want to create a home network of computers, including your HP Pavilion? Millions of households now have more than one computer and the benefits of networking them are many.

First, you can access the Internet from all your computers through a single connection. You can also send files to a printer or other hardware, no matter which computer it's connected to in your house. In addition, you can access files on your network from any computer, removing any need to email or hand-carry files from one computer to the other.

Typically, computers are attached in one of three ways: with network cables attached to the Network Interface Card (NIC) installed in each computer, through standard phone lines, or through a wireless connection device using infrared technology.

Choosing Your Network

There are several types of networks, such as Ethernet, Home PNA (using your home phone line), or Wireless HomRF. In choosing the type of network you want to install, you should consider how easy it is to connect the computers by cable, how fast you want your network to be, and cost.

Understanding Home Networks

In setting up a network, you have to be sure you have a network card and modem in each computer and make a choice of network method, either cables, infrared wireless, or through your phone lines. Visit *HPShopping.com* to view home networking products (see Figure 18.3). After you've purchased the option you prefer and followed manufacturer instructions to install network cards or cables, you're ready to set up your network using Windows XP's Network Setup Wizard.

 tip **You can follow the instructions earlier in this chapter for installing add-in cards to install your network card.**

FIGURE 18.3 HP offers solutions for networking that work perfectly with your Pavilion.

- Ethernet is the fastest type and is not all that expensive. However, if you choose Ethernet you must run cables from a central hub to each computer.
- If the computers are remote so that cabling is difficult, but each is near a phone line, you could use those lines to connect them. Note that you can then use your single phone line for voice calls and Internet access at the same time. However, this sharing can make for a slower connection.
- If your computers are not all near a phone line, wireless might be your only option. Here cost is a factor. Where an Ethernet connection might cost you $75 or so to connect two computers, a wireless connection might run almost $200. Also, wireless connections can be hampered by anything metal in your home, such as water pipes or door knobs.

caution **Wireless networks pose a standards challenge. Different vendors use different variations on the technology. If wireless is the way to go, find a wireless standard that several vendors support, such as Bluetooth, when purchasing your wireless network. Otherwise, if you want to expand your network someday, you may find yourself with a compatibility problem.**

Setting Up the Host and Guest Computers

✔ **The first step in setting up your network is to set up a host computer that gives access to the Internet and then to set up each computer in the network:**

1. Select Start, Control Panel.

2. Click Network and Internet Connections.

3. Click Set up or change your home or small office network. The Network Setup Wizard appears.

4. Click Next. The first window confirms that you have network cards, modems, and cables on all computers, and that all computers, printers, and external modems are on and connected to the Internet.

5. Click Next. The Select a Connection Method dialog box appears (see Figure 18.4).

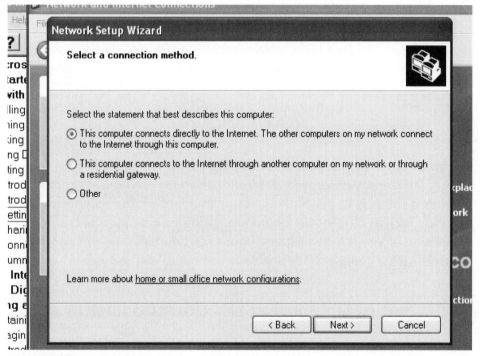

Network Setup Wizard

Select a connection method.

Select the statement that best describes this computer:

⦿ This computer connects directly to the Internet. The other computers on my network connect to the Internet through this computer.

○ This computer connects to the Internet through another computer on my network or through a residential gateway.

○ Other

Learn more about home or small office network configurations.

[< Back] [Next >] [Cancel]

FIGURE 18.4 The host will always be the computer on your network that has a direct Internet connection.

6. Click to select the first option, This computer connects directly to the Internet, and then click Next.

7. You are now asked to select your connection from a list of connections that Windows offers. Click your Internet provider, such as MSN Internet Access, and then click Next.

8. Type the word "host" in the computer description text box. If you want, you can also change the computer name.

9. Click Next. If you want, you can change the name of your network or accept the one that's listed.

10. Click Next. The next dialog box, shown in Figure 18.5, lists all the settings you've made.

FIGURE 18.5 Note that the Shared Documents folder has been set up to share with any printers.

11. Click Next, and all the settings will be configured. The final wizard page offers you the opportunity to configure your network to include computers that don't use Windows XP.

12. Assuming you have no non-Windows XP computers, click the Just finish the wizard option and then click Next.

13. Click Finish.

Now you have to set up each computer on the network to connect to the host using the Network Setup Wizard, which guides you through the process.

✔ **After all computers are set up, to view shared resources, follow these steps:**

1. Select Start, Control Panel.

2. Click Network and Internet Connections.

3. Click My Network Places.

4. Click View Workgroup Computers.

5. Double-click the Host computer. All shared resources are listed (see Figure 18.6).

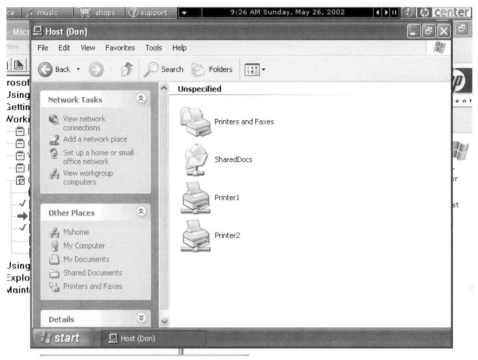

FIGURE 18.6 Now you can share files and hardware among all computers on the network.

Chapter Summary

In this chapter, you learned about installing add-in cards to add functionality to your computer. You also walked through the steps involved in replacing your hard drive, which you might do to increase your computer's storage capacity. Finally, you got a basic tutorial on home networking and the benefits it offers from shared Internet access and hardware.

19

Troubleshooting

In this Chapter

✔ Top tips from HP Technical Support

✔ Solving a problem with HP Help and Support

Your computer is the sum total of pieces of hardware, such as mouse, monitor, CPU, and keyboard; dozens of computer programs; and an operating system called Windows XP. All of that is connected to the Internet, where additional files are sent and received and downloaded all the time. The interaction of all of these components may occasionally cause you problems. For that reason, I've compiled some of the top tips of HP technical support folks to help you stay out of trouble or to solve problems when they arrive.

This chapter also walks you through solving a typical computing problem using the online HP Help and Support system so that you can see the many ways HP helps you to solve problems on your own.

Top Tips from HP Support

Here are some pieces of advice from the folks who help Pavilion users day in and day out. Following this advice might save you problems down the road, or get you out of trouble. Although HP Support people are some of the best in the business and love to help Pavilion owners have a positive experience, they like it even more when you can avoid problems altogether!

- *Tip 1*—HP consumer products work better together. Whenever possible, use HP hardware and drivers for peripherals you connect to your HP Pavilion. If you do use non-HP peripherals, always make sure you have the most current drivers for those products from their manufacturers. Most of these companies allow you to download the most recent drivers from their Web sites.
- *Tip 2*—You can get the most recent software for HP Pavilions from the HP Pavilion section of HP's Customer Care Web site (*www.hp.com/cposupport/eschome.html*) seen in Figure 19.1. Here you can get product-specific information and software. Enter your model information as specifically as possible, including product name and model number including any letters, such as Pavilion 520N, to get the most targeted results.

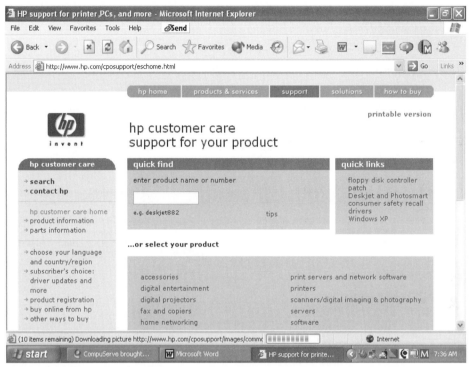

hp pavilion PCs

FIGURE 19.1 Search by product name to find recent software updates.

- *Tip 3*—You can use the HP Subscriber's Choice program to be notified automatically of new software versions for your Pavilion, get tech support alerts that relate to your product, or sign up for email newsletters that include product tips or project ideas. Go to http://www.hp.com/cposupport/eschome.html to sign up.

- *Tip 4*—If you have problems with non-HP software that was included with your Pavilion when you bought it, try visiting the software manufacturer's Web site. Most provide online support. A few addresses to help you out are the following: Microsoft for help with MS Works, Encarta Online Deluxe, Outlook Express, Internet Explorer, and Windows XP (*www.microsoft.com*); Corel for WordPerfect Office help (*www3.corel.com*); Music-Match for assistance with MusicMatch Jukebox (*www.music-*

match.com); and Adobe for support of Adobe Acrobat Reader (*www.adobe.com*).

- *Tip 5*—Turn on the Windows Update feature by selecting Start, Control Panel and clicking the Windows Update link (see Figure 19.2). With this feature, you can scan for any updates to Windows that should be downloaded to keep your system current, resolve glitches in the operating system software, or set yourself up for automatic updating.

FIGURE 19.2 Microsoft provides an update service to keep Windows XP current.

- *Tip 6*—When trying to resolve system problems, use the Three Strike Rule. First, use Microsoft System Restore to go back one day. If you still have a problem, use Microsoft System Recovery to go back one week. If that still doesn't work, try again, going back one month. If none of these works, then and only then should you use HP's nondestructive System Restore to restore your Pavilion's factory settings.

- *Tip 7*—If you're having trouble with video or sound devices, it's possible your hardware or its drivers aren't compatible with Windows XP. Microsoft maintains a list of products and drivers that have been updated for Windows XP and tested by Microsoft. If you are having a problem and can find a driver or product that has been determined to be XP compatible, it could solve your problem. Go to *www.microsoft.com/hcl/* to see listings such as the one shown in Figure 19.3.

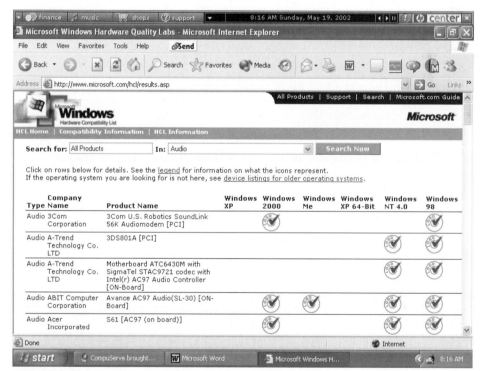

FIGURE 19.3 Look for an XP-tested driver from this list and download it.

Troubleshooting with HP Help and Support

It's one thing to show you how to navigate around a help system and another to show you how you can use the help system to run down a problem you're having. That's what this section is about. I've taken a typical problem—my modem isn't working—and written about the steps you can try to solve it. You'll find along the way that there is a wonderful combination of tools—from help text to automated diagnostic tests, Troubleshooter procedures, and instant live support to help you through. The exact steps you might use to solve this problem could differ, but here's one way to use the Help system to find a solution.

caution **If you were actually having trouble with your modem and couldn't connect to the Internet, some of the live support features wouldn't be accessible to you.**

✔ **To solve a problem with a modem, follow these steps:**

1. Select Start, Help and Support. The Help and Support Center appears.

2. Click the link for Fixing a Problem in the Pick a Help Topic section. The Fixing a Problem window shown in Figure 19.4 appears.

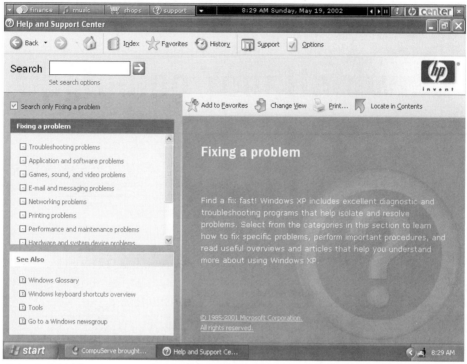

FIGURE 19.4 At this point, you could click the Troubleshooting problems link for general troubleshooting information.

3. Click the Hardware and System Device Problems link on the left side. (I chose Hardware and System Device Problems as being most specific to my problem.) The information in the right pane of this window changes to Hardware and System Device Problems.

4. Click the Modem Troubleshooter (see Figure 19.5). (Note that I could also have clicked the task, Test a Modem, at this point. Also, I could have reached this troubleshooter by choosing Troubleshooting problems, List of Troubleshooters, in Step 3 instead of clicking Hardware and System Device Problems. There are often several routes to the same solution.)

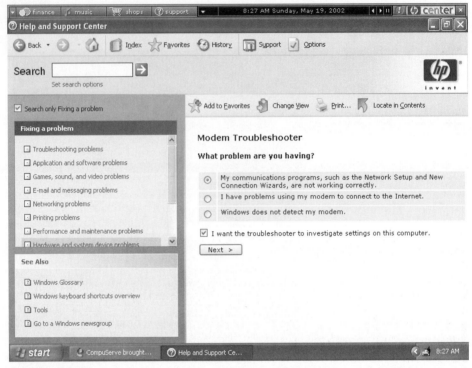

FIGURE 19.5 Troubleshooters are like wizards in that they walk you through a process step by step.

5. Because I was getting a message that no modem was detected when I tried to connect to the Internet, click the choice Windows does not detect my modem, and then click Next. The next step deals with the possibility that your connection to your modem or phone line is causing the problem.

6. Click No, my modem is connected correctly, but I still have a problem and then click Next. The window in Figure 19.6 appears.

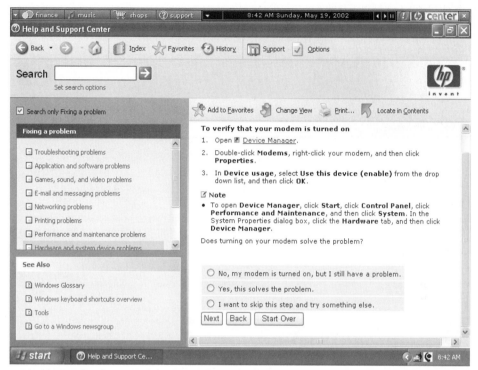

FIGURE 19.6 The Modem Troubleshooter is trying to isolate the problem based on your input.

At this point, you should note a few things. The Troubleshooter is suggesting there could be a setting you need to make in Windows XP, and it has provided a link to that setting (Device Manager) and directions on how to modify the setting. At any point during the Troubleshooter, you may solve the problem and indicate that by select the Yes, this solves the problem option.

On the other hand, if you continue to tell the Troubleshooter that you haven't solved the problem, you are presented with a final window, shown in Figure 19.7, that suggests you either check the Windows Hardware Compatibility List by following a link to it, or that you contact your modem manufacturer.

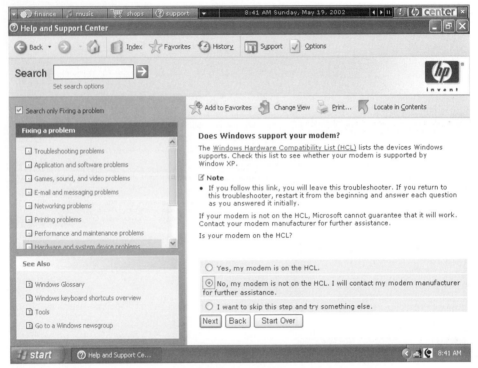

FIGURE 19.7 First the Troubleshooter identifies problems that can be fixed locally and then it directs you to online and manufacturer resources.

caution Sometimes when you go to a link in the Troubleshooter that is on the Internet, you can't get back to the Troubleshooter without starting to run it again from the beginning.

✔ **Take a look at a different way of solving this problem and a different tool:**

1. From the Help and Support Center main window, click Hardware.

2. On the window that appears, click Modems. The options in Figure 19.8 appear.

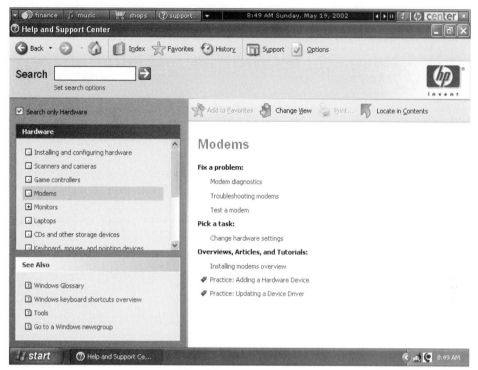

FIGURE 19.8 Modem-specific options are all together here.

3. Click Practice: Adding a Hardware Device. An interactive training module opens up (see Figure 19.9). You follow the steps in the printed and spoken instructions to see exactly how to complete a specific process.

FIGURE 19.9 You'll be asked to make specific choices to walk through a procedure in these tutorials.

A Variety of Tools

So far you've seen Troubleshooter routines that walk you through possible solutions and offer links to local and online resources, as well as an interactive tutorial. In addition to these, there are diagnostic tests, articles, and even a link to go to a Windows newsgroup to see what other users have said about your problem and its solution. There's also an HP Pavilion Frequently Asked Questions list that you can look at to see if your problem is included there.

 tip **Many of the windows in the Help and Support Center include a Related Topics link. If you didn't get exactly the answer you needed or it didn't give you all the information you**

need about a topic, clicking this link can be an easy way to find the exact information you want.

Troubleshooting Tips

The choices you make in the Help and Support Center will depend to some extent on the way you organize things in your own mind. For example, some windows will offer solutions organized by tasks or by the tools you'd use to fix a problem. If you think of problems in terms of tasks, such as the task of testing a modem, rather than in terms of a tool, such as Modem Troubleshooter, that's the option you're likely to pick. These may lead you to similar or identical solutions, but in a slightly different way.

There's no wrong choice to make in the Help and Support Center, but some paths are more direct or fruitful than others. Here are some tips to using the feature most efficiently:

- Try to make the most specific choice you can for your problem. For example, if you're having trouble installing an external modem, rather than clicking the Modems option on the Hardware list, you'd click the Installing and Configuring Hardware option.
- Use the Add to Favorites button to quickly return to information you encounter during a help search that you think you might like to come back to.
- If you are dealing with a topic that you have no knowledge about, look for Overview tutorials first to give you the context to understand more specific help information.
- If you encounter a term you don't understand, click the Index button to see a searchable list of terms to get more information about that item.

Ask a Friend

One feature that's definitely worth looking into is the Remote Assistance feature. This allows you to connect with somebody you trust who knows more about computers or the specific problem than you so that he or she can view what's on your screen. Your friend can even use his or her computer to take over yours (with your permission) and make changes for you.

To use this feature, you and the friend have to be using the Windows XP operating system. You must be using Windows Messenger, or an email program such as Outlook Express that is Messaging Application Programming Interface (MAPI) compliant. Finally, you both have to have an Internet connection.

✔ **Follow these steps to obtain help remotely using email:**

1. Select Remote Assistance from the Help and Support Resources area of the Help and Support Center.

2. Click Ask a Friend to Help. The form appears asking you to enter an email or Windows Messaging choice (see Figure 19.10).

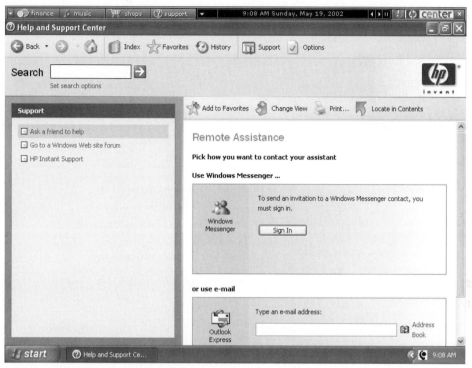

FIGURE 19.10 Your friend must be online to receive your invitation, which you can send using Windows Messaging or email.

3. Enter an email address and then press the arrow titled Invite this Person. The Invitation form in Figure 19.11 appears.

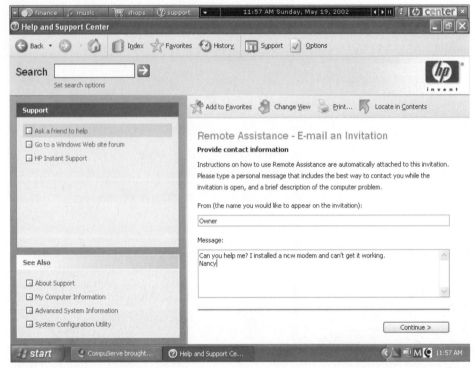

FIGURE 19.11 You and your friend both have to have Windows Messaging activated to use that feature. With email, you can invite anybody with an email address to help.

4. Change the name in the From box, if you like, and enter a message asking for help.

5. Click Continue. The window in Figure 19.12 appears, asking you to make settings for how long the invitation should be available and to enter a password the person must use to log onto your computer. Note that you'll have to contact the person to provide the password, but, because you're turning over access of your computer to someone else, using a password is a very good idea.

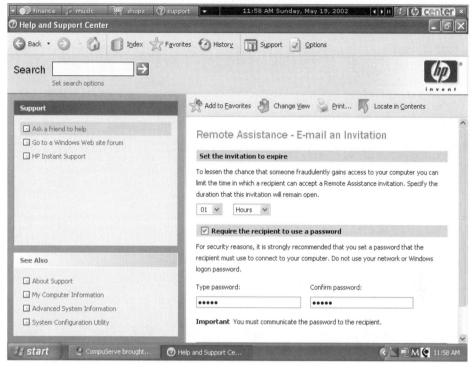

FIGURE 19.12 If your friend might not get online for another hour or two, set the availability of the invitation accordingly.

6. Click Send Invitation. An email is sent to the person, and a confirmation that your invitation was sent appears on your computer.

The other person will receive an email that looks like the one shown in Figure 19.13. This email contains your message and a link the recipient can follow to get instructions on how to proceed.

✔ **Here's what your friend must now do to help you out:**

1. Download the file that is attached to the invitation email and open it (rather than save it) when prompted.

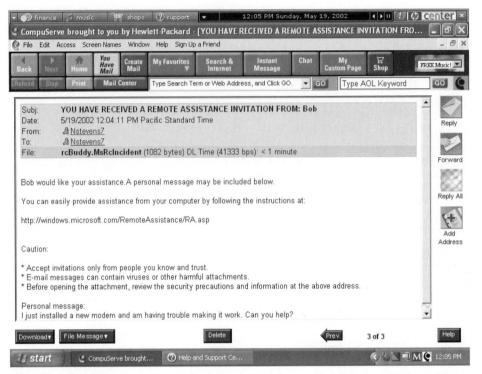

FIGURE 19.13 This email provides instructions for connecting to your computer.

2. Click Yes to accept the invitation. A prompt appears to connect to the sender's computer using a password, if that option was selected by you.

3. Enter the Password and click Yes. A dialog box appears confirming that you want to be connected to the person's computer. Click Yes.

   The dialog box shown in Figure 19.14 appears, with controls for talking, sending files, or controlling the settings on the requestor's computer.

  tip You can also use the Remote Assistance feature to allow an HP Technical Support person to take over your computer and make adjustments.

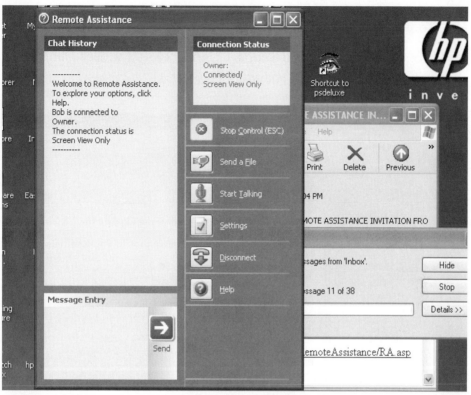

FIGURE 19.14 Use these controls to initiate chats or to look at computer settings.

HP Instant Support

HP Instant Support is a real-time exchange with an HP Technical Support person. You submit your question in writing and then wait a brief time for a response to appear. In essence, you can carry on a text-based conversation using this feature. The HP Support person will keep a log of your problem so that, if you must sign off to try a solution, you can come back. Whoever is available will have information about your problem.

✔ To use HP Instant Support, follow these steps:

1. From the HP Help and Support Center window, click HP Instant Support. The window shown in Figure 19.15 appears.

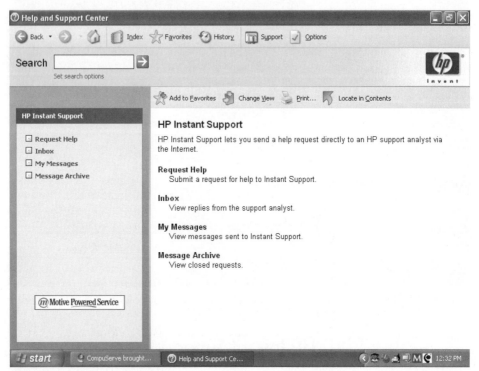

FIGURE 19.15 You can keep track of all your messages and responses from one of these four areas.

2. Click Request Help to initiate a session.

3. On the six-step Request Help procedure, Step 1, select a topic for your inquiry and click Next.

4. In Step 2, click Next (or, if you want to run a communications test first to ensure that you can connect with Support, click Run twice and then Next).

hp pavilion pcs

5. In Step 3, enter a description of the problem (Figure 19.16) and click Next.

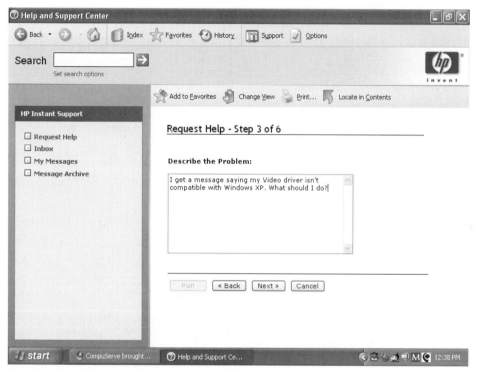

FIGURE 19.16 Try to make the description you enter here as concise, yet complete as possible.

Information is gathered about your system, and your message is sent to Support. In a few moments, you'll receive a response. Now you can follow directions provided, answer questions, ask more questions, and so on to solve your problem.

Chapter Summary

In this chapter, you got some insider tips from HP Technical Support about how to keep your Pavilion troublefree or to solve problems. Then, you walked through the process of using the wealth of help tools available for solving a typical computing problem.

More Goodies

Chapter 20: The Latest Pavilion Software

chapter
20
The Latest Pavilion Software

In this Chapter

✓ Getting smarter with Britannica Encyclopedia

✓ Instant virtual greeting cards using Greeting Card Creator

✓ Photo fun with Funhouse

If you purchased your Pavilion after the fall of 2002, you'll have a few new programs already loaded on your computer to help you be more productive and have fun. Britannica Encyclopedia replaced Encarta as your learning tool of choice in more recent models, offering online access to a world of learning. In addition, Funhouse now provides photo-imaging tools that allow you to put your own photos in built-in templates and easily email and share them with friends and family. Finally, Greeting Card Creator is an incredibly simple way to generate photo cards with audio greetings and instantly email them to anybody.

363

Learning Made Fun

A one year subscription to Britannica Online is included with all Pavilions shipped after September 2002. It's a wonderful resource to help kids do homework and to provide a wealth of material for everybody from the college-bound student and home businessperson to the soccer mom or dad.

When you log on to Britannica, you'll see the main window shown in Figure 20.1. Britannica doesn't just offer the renowned encyclopedia in an online format. There is also the Merriam-Webster dictionary on the site and headlines from *The New York Times*.

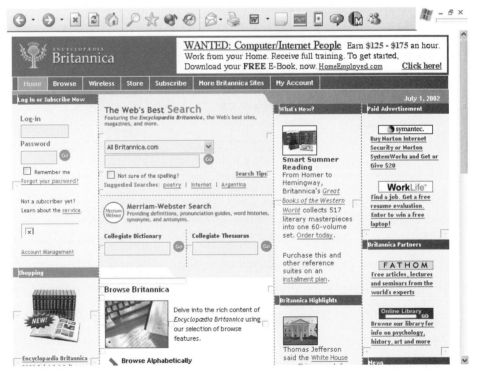

FIGURE 20.1 Browse the encyclopedia, read about current events, or shop in the Britannica store.

The World Atlas (Figure 20.2) includes data on culture, economy, history, major cities, and geography all in one easy-to-search format.

With the world changing so quickly these days, an online resource that is kept up to the minute is the best way to get information for your family or business.

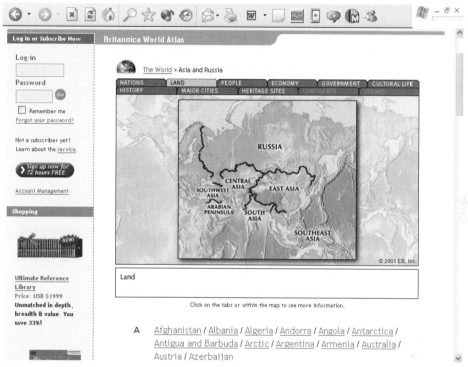

FIGURE 20.2 The world is at your fingertips with the Britannica Atlas.

To search the huge amount of information on Britannica, you can use the Search feature on the Britannica home page. Using the Search drop-down list, you can choose what to search: the entire Britannica site; the full encyclopedia; or just the concise or student editions, video and media collections, dictionary, or thesaurus. You can also search for other Web sites related to your search term.

Here are some tips for performing searches that find what you need:

- Select as specific a keyword as you can. If you're looking for information about sports cars, instead of entering the keyword "automobile", use "sports car".
- If you want a phrase (such as "sports car") searched exactly, rather than having the search engine look for results including either sports or car or both, enclose the words in quotes.
- Sometimes searches are case sensitive, meaning that, if you enter "Catholic", you may get very different results than if you entered "catholic".
- You can use wildcard characters to open up your search. For example, precede the word "boat" with an asterisk (*boat), and you can find information about various kinds of boats, such as sailboats, tugboats, rowboats, and so on.
- A search involving Boolean characters allows you to narrowly define a search. "Music and (piano or organ) not Bach" will get results about piano or organ music, but not results that include Bach.

✔ **To perform a search, follow these simple steps:**

1. Click the arrow on the Search box and choose a source for the search.

2. Type your keyword with any punctuation or Boolean operators you require.

3. Click Go. Your results will list all the applicable sources, as shown in Figure 20.3.

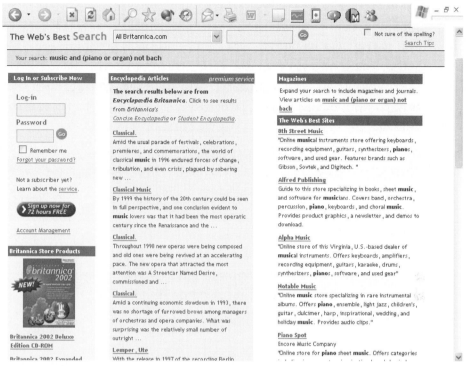

FIGURE 20.3 Articles, Web sites, and more may be included in your search results.

Greetings from Greeting Card Creator

There's nothing like a greeting card to make friends and family smile on a special occasion or when they need cheering up. Add a cheery audio greeting to your own pictures, and you have a personalized greeting that will have the recipient grinning from ear to ear.

Now there's no reason not to send this kind of customized greeting every day if you like. Greeting Card Creator from E-motional provides a simple-to-use format for combining photos, text, and audio greetings into a greeting card you can instantly email to anybody.

Project: **Create Your Own Greeting Card**

Next time you go on vacation, why not send back an audio greeting card? Gather the family around and brainstorm what you'd like to say, both in text and in an audio greeting, and then get going. Note that you'll need to connect a microphone to your computer to record the audio message.

1. Double-click the E-motional Greeting Card Creator icon on your desktop to begin the program.

2. At the opening window, click Next to begin creating your card. The window in Figure 20.4 appears.

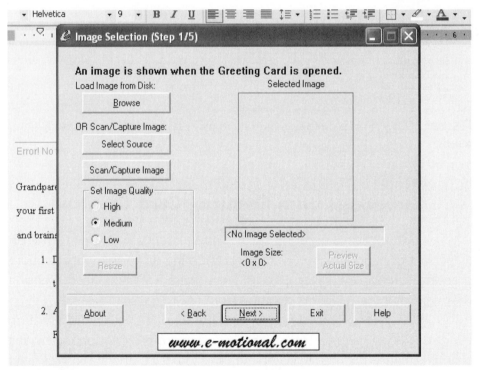

FIGURE 20.4   This is where you find a photo image to include in your card.

 tip If you have access to a scanner, you can scan an image in using the controls on this window.

3. Click the Browse button and use the Load Image dialog box to locate you're My Pictures folder (it's in the My Documents folder of Windows).

4. Double-click the Sample Pictures folder to open it, then click the Sunset image, and click Open. The image appears in the Greeting Card Creator preview.

5. Click Next.

6. Click Place Text Message on Image.

7. For the Placement of Text, click the Top of Image setting if it's not already selected.

8. Enter this text in the Enter Text Message box: "Having a wonderful time…wish you were here!"

9. Click the Select Font button and, in the dialog box that appears, select Comic Sans in the Font list and 26 point font in the Size list and click OK.

10. Click the Text Color button and then click the white sample on the palette that appears.

11. Click Next. The Audio Message window shown in Figure 20.5 appears.

FIGURE 20.5 Record your own audio message or load a sound file for music or even sound effects.

12. With Record from Microphone selected, click Record. Read this message (or one you've thought of yourself) into your microphone: "Hi, folks! We're having a great time swimming and sailing. See you next week."

13. If you want to listen to your message, click Play to preview it.

14. Click Next. You can record another greeting that plays when the card is closed. For now, skip that by clicking No Audio and then Next to continue.

15. Click the Browse button to locate your My Documents folder and click Save to save the card to your hard drive.

16. Click Create the Card. It takes a few seconds to create the card and then the Preview the Card button becomes available, as shown in Figure 20.6.

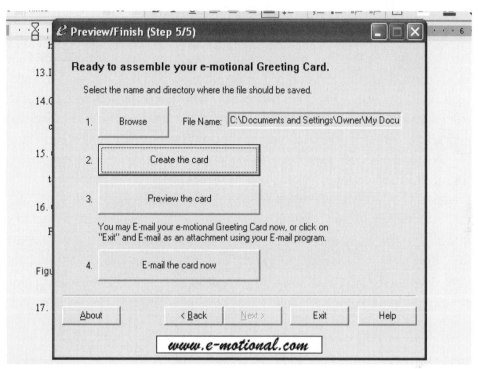

FIGURE 20.6 Take a look at your card before you email it to be sure it's what you wanted.

17. Click the Preview the Card button to hear your audio and see your text message. When it's done playing, click Close in the upper right-hand corner to close the preview.

18. Click E-mail the Card Now and a blank email message appears from your default email program (which is Outlook Express if you haven't set up another program).

19. Enter the address information and any message you like and then click Send.

Your card is on its way. Because it's been saved to your My Pictures folder, you can send it as an attachment to another email at any time.

Into the Funhouse

ArcSoft's Funhouse is a photo-imaging program that's strictly for fun. With this program, you can put your cat on a $10 bill, put your daughter's head on your dog, use more than 150 predesigned templates to insert your own photos, and then share the images using email. You can add text to images and can modify the font, size, color, and style.

With Funhouse, you can take a couple of photos and blur them together into a collage. You can easily resize, rearrange, and blend your image with the template to get a clean, seamless look.

One other great feature of Funhouse is that you can capture images from a video device connected to your computer, if it's compatible. Funhouse's easy and fun interface lets you use all these feature (see Figure 20.7).

hp pavilion pcs

FIGURE 20.7   Funhouse makes it easy to print or email your final photo to friends.

Chapter Summary

In this chapter, you learned the basics of searching for information on Britannica online. You created your own audio vacation postcard with Greeting Card Creator and emailed it to a friend. Finally, you got a glimpse of the easy-to-use photo imaging tools in Funhouse and learned the many ways you can use Funhouse to create personalized photo projects.

Index

hp pavilion pcs

hp pavilion pcs

Printing Projects Made Fun & Easy

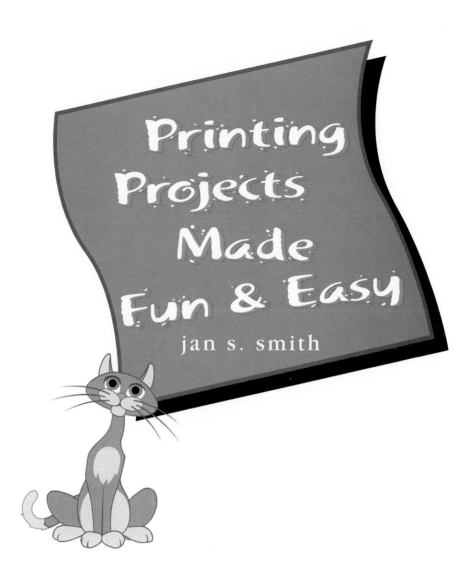

Printing Projects Made Fun & Easy

jan s. smith

the official hp guide

PRENTICE
HALL
PTR

Prentice Hall PTR   Upper Saddle River, NJ 07458   www.phptr.com

printing projects

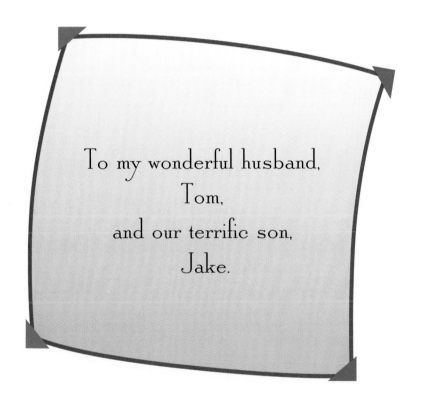

To my wonderful husband,
Tom,
and our terrific son,
Jake.

Table of Contents

printing projects

Foreword

Welcome to one of the most exciting books and CDs around!

At HP, we delight our customers with great imaging and printing products. Now it is our pleasure to share with you some of our customers' favorite printing projects. Author Jan Smith is a long-term HP employee who has personally completed each of these projects. I trust that you'll have great fun and be pleasantly surprised at just how easy these printing ideas are to create, thanks to HP products and Jan's terrific how-to advice.

So enjoy Jan's engaging book. You'll find it to be great fun.

Happy reading and printing!

Vyomesh Joshi
Executive Vice President
Imaging & Printing Group
Hewlett-Packard Company

Acknowledgments

A lot of wonderful—and wonderfully creative—people helped bring this book and CD into your home.

I'd like to thank a small but enormously talented group of artists, designers, illustrators, and animators, including Loren Weeks, Maiken Kling, Melissa Seifer, John Burton, Dan Mandish, Joel Mandish, Tim Larson, Kaci Kyler, Pamela Standley, Sean Fitzgerald, Danny Rubyono, and Tom Lakovic. Together, they helped bring much life and color and playfulness into this book and CD.

I would also like to express my sincere appreciation to Susan Rowe, Frank Rogers-Witte, and Vyomesh Joshi for encouraging me to follow my passion for printing. They've been just great!

For sheer inspiration, I looked to the fantastic Printsville team at HP. For years, they've been making the most awesome printing projects! And for all sorts of other great project ideas, I tapped into the skills of Jennifer Commons, Chad Summervill, Amy Kelm, Chris Morgan, Stacy Jones, Grace Harvester, Jill Kramer, Christi Putz, and Angela Wo.

Heartfelt thanks to my dear neighbors and friends, the Burkes, the Emerys, and the Wises, who make every day a day for joyous celebration! I've loved making all sorts of family calendars, banners, cards, and other arts and crafts projects with them.

And, as always, I want to thank Pat Pekary, who manages our HP Press, and Jill Harry, my Prentice Hall editor. They each provided terrific guidance and good cheer along the way.

About the Author

Jan S. Smith is a senior communications specialist for the Imaging & Printing Group at Hewlett-Packard Company. In that role, she has produced dozens of award-winning multimedia videos, films, CDs, and
television programs. Jan has worked for HP for 14 years. Before joining HP, she was a college professor for 11 years, teaching communications courses. Jan has a Bachelor of Arts degree in political science from the University of California, a Masters degree in journalism and advertising from the University of Oregon, and a Ph.D. in telecommunications from the University of Oregon. Jan is a mom and a wife, and loves to make all sorts of artsy-craftsy things using her home printer.

Introduction

I get the biggest kick out of making things with my printer—especially when the instructions are easy and the results look super snazzy!

Now you can experience all the same joys of printing. Just flip through the pages of *Printing Projects Made Fun & Easy*. Pick a great-looking project, pop in your CD, and follow the intuitive menu of options.

In a matter of moments, you'll be making all sorts of goodies that will bring smiles to the faces of your family members and friends. You'll be beaming with delight!

The CD is organized just like the book. On the home page, you will see five icons (each correlating to the five chapters in the book). If you click on one of these icons, a submenu of the different sections you can go to appears. From there you can go to a new page showing all the projects within that section. Once you find the project you want and choose the design, go ahead and print. And in case you get lost or aren't sure what to do next, there are hints along the bottom bar for extra help.

The project and instruction files are all printable Adobe pdf files. Adobe pdf file is a universal format—with all fonts, formatting, graphics, and color embedded into one nice, easy-to-use file. Some of the project pdf files on the CD are editable, so you can click, highlight, and type to customize them just for you. It's incredibly simple, lightning fast, and so much fun to use. If you are interested in learning more about Adobe® Acrobat® or have any other questions, there is free online support from Adobe; just visit: *http://www.adobe.com/support/readguide.html*.

Share some happiness! Share some color! Share some love!

With *Printing Projects Made Fun & Easy,* getting there is half the fun.

printing projects

Choosing the Right Paper and Ink for Printing

How to Select Paper

It's easy not to think about paper—just borrow what's in the copier machine, right? But if you've seen the difference that a quality paper makes—especially one designed specifically for your printer—you also know it's hard to go back to copier paper for anything but the most ordinary of documents. Paper designed for your printer looks and performs better every time.

Using special printer paper will not only give you better results, it will also be less costly: You'll have fewer paper jams, and your output will look great every time. But there's more to plain white paper than meets the eye. Here are the basics of using and selecting paper for general use and printing photos.

A Crash Course in Paper Basics

First take into account what you'll be printing. Black-and-white documents are quite different from full-color photos. Some papers are multipurpose and therefore good for both; but if you want crisp, vibrant photos that will last a long time, you should use paper that's designed just for photos.

If you're looking for good general-use paper, think about the following:

- *Weight.* Paper weight ranges from lightweight newsprint to very heavy cardboard. Most quality business paper is 20- to 24-pound (lb) bond, with greeting card papers at the heavier end of the scale, usually in the range of 60- to 65-lb cardstocks. Metric equivalents are expressed in grams per square meter, abbreviated as g/m2.

- *Thickness.* The thickness of a paper affects its handling and is most applicable to photo papers. Generally, thicker media will be stiffer and will resist creases and tears. Thickness is most often expressed as a unit of measure called a *mil.*

- *Brightness.* A higher brightness value means that more light is reflected from the surface of the paper, providing crisper text with better contrast and a brighter background for color and images. HP's brightest papers include Bright White for inkjet printing and Premium Choice for laser printing.

- *Finish.* Finishes for laser and inkjet papers are becoming increasingly sophisticated, with numerous choices for a variety of applications. They range from matte to glossy, with lessening degrees of glossiness, sometimes described as semigloss, soft-gloss, or satin-gloss. Many people prefer the mirror-like finish of high-gloss media for color photographs, and smooth matte finishes for black-and-white photographs and business documents. (Be careful with extremely smooth, shiny, or coated papers that aren't specifically designed for your printer. They can cause jams and even repel ink.)

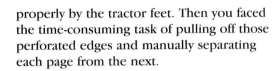
- *Opacity.* Opacity describes how well the paper blocks the passage of light through it. Highly opaque media prevent print from showing through to the other side and are considered good for printing on both sides —for example, for brochures, newsletters, calendars, and other similar applications.

Here's what to look for in paper for printing photos:

- *Whiteness.* For photo or picture printing, keep in mind that whiter papers produce sharper, more vibrant colors. Ink is translucent. Light passes through it and bounces off the paper, then passes back through the ink. The paper color therefore affects the color you see when you print.
- *Thickness.* Some photo projects—like calendars—require a heavier paper stock. But if it's too thick, it could jam up your printer.
- *Surface.* For printouts with crisp lines and intense, high-quality colors, the surface of the

paper is key. Glossy paper produces vibrant color but is susceptible to fingerprints, so matte paper might be a better choice for prints that will be handled often.

Your best bet is to buy a paper sampler with various weights and finishes. That way, you can see for yourself what kind of results you get.

Specialty Paper for Printing
Remember the old days when computer paper came in long, continuous sheets? You had to thread it carefully through the printer, making sure the holes along the edges were caught

properly by the tractor feet. Then you faced the time-consuming task of pulling off those perforated edges and manually separating each page from the next.

Paper has come a long way in the past two decades. Just about every mainstream printing device today uses some kind of plain bond paper in easy-loading paper trays, though there's nothing plain about the variety of specialty papers currently available for printers. A wide range is available to suit the needs of any and every computer user.

You can also save money by using the new specialty papers to print all sorts of things that you used to have to take to a professional printer. (Of course, before you start experimenting, be sure to check in your printer manual for paper compatibility.) Here's a rundown on papers that will fire your creativity.

Photo paper: Akin to paper used by film developers, photo paper is specifically designed to produce high-quality, color-rich images that are hard to distinguish from traditionally developed photographs. Most of HP's photo papers come in a choice of matte or glossy finishes and a variety of print sizes, including convenient 4 x 6 for affordable everyday prints and large portrait-size papers for studio-quality enlargements.

Greeting cards: Paper designed specifically for greeting cards is thicker, prescored (folded), and smaller than regular paper. You can personalize the cards with your own text and images. HP greeting card papers come in a variety of sizes, colors, and finishes—including linen in white and ivory—with matching envelopes. HP also has a card studio with free templates that let you create your own greeting cards in a snap.

Glossy paper: Glossy paper produces vibrant color but is susceptible to fingerprints. This paper has a shiny, coated surface on one or both sides and is ideal when you need a polished printout. For brochures, flyers, report covers, and special presentations, glossy papers produce colorful images and crisp text equal to professional printing. HP's line of brochure and flyer paper comes in a range of sizes to meet all of your printing needs.

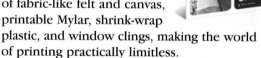

Transparencies: These clear sheets of plastic are used with overhead projectors for presentations.

Stickers and labels: Stickers and labels are available for mail, folders, diskettes, CDs, and whatever else you can think of. You can use fonts, images, and colors to customize them. Restickables allow for even more creative flexibility.

Craft papers: Specialty papers offer a wide range of possibilities to the craftsperson. HP's iron-on transfers make it easy to make your own T-shirts, photo pillows, and much more. Or get your message out loud and clear with HP banner paper. Also available are craft papers specially formulated for printers, such as vellum and parchment, printable sheets of fabric-like felt and canvas, printable Mylar, shrink-wrap plastic, and window clings, making the world of printing practically limitless.

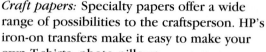

Again, remember to check for compatibility with your printer when you use specialty papers. Not doing so can lead to paper jams and other problems.

Ink and Toner Basics
You use them every day, but you probably don't think about them until they inconveniently run out in the middle of a large print job. Yes, we're talking about ink and toner. Whether you're printing straight black-and-white text or high-color photos, it's important to know that all inks are not created equal.

Inkjet Ink
To understand why some inks work better with your printer than others, it's necessary to understand a little bit about how ink is made. Traditional inks—like those used in your nice ballpoint pen—are oil-based and use dyes made of minuscule suspended particles for colorants. Using oil-based inks in a printer, however, can lead to trying maintenance problems, so instead most inkjet printers use

water-based inks. Unfortunately, in earlier inkjet printers, water-based inks would often bleed, smear, and run, particularly if the printed page was not allowed to dry properly or if it were to get wet.

In recent years, the chemistry of inks has improved considerably as manufacturers have developed ways to improve the vibrancy, clarity, and longevity of the printed product. Ink additives are used in varying amounts to control things like saturation, drying time, and resistance to fading.

But the improvements do not lie entirely in the ink. Preconditioned papers can help improve inkjet printing because they are primed with an agent that helps bind the

ink to the paper, reducing smearing and bleeding. When manufacturers recommend using only their ink and paper in your printer, it's not because they want to hold a monopoly on your purchases. It is because the three components—printer, ink, and paper—have been designed to work together to reach the most satisfactory results possible.

Laser Printer Toner
Unlike inkjet printers, laser printers use toner, a dry, powdery substance that is adhered to the paper using an electronic charge. It is specially designed to melt very quickly, and a component of wax makes the toner more

amenable to the process that fuses the toner to the paper. Monochrome printers use a single cartridge of black toner. Color models use four cartridges, one each of cyan, magenta, yellow, and black.

Like ink for inkjet printers, it is always best to use the toner recommended by the manufacturer, because the inner workings of the machine are designed to work with toner of a particular consistency and particle size. Using a different, lower-grade toner can result in smeared print outs (if the drum inside the printer isn't cleaned properly) or lead to jams and other internal problems.

Ink and Toner Refills
The temptation to purchase third-party cartridges or generic refills for your inkjet or laser printer can be strong, especially when the budget is tight. But in the end, the little bit you save in money will be lost in the quality of your end result. By following manufacturer recommendations, you can be sure you're getting the best out of your printer.

For fast, easy, online shopping for all of your inkjet and laser printing needs, come and visit *hpshopping.com*.

Chapter 1

HOME & FAMILY

Take a delightfully creative journey in and around your home. You'll find everything here but the kitchen sink!

Home & Family

Around the House

Home Sweet Home! Make it even sweeter with these delightful printing projects!

printing projects

Canning Kit

When you want your jar toppers, labels, and tags to look as delicious as the yummy foods you're craving, try printing these. You'll be berry glad you did!

Project 1: Jar Topper

A wonderful way to top off your hard work.

Materials Needed:

HP Bright White Inkjet paper

Scissors

Ribbon or raffia

Instructions:

1. Choose design and print pdf file.
2. Cut out paper topper along dotted line.
3. Place topper over jar.
4. Tie a piece of coordinating ribbon or raffia around jar lid to secure the piece of paper to lid.

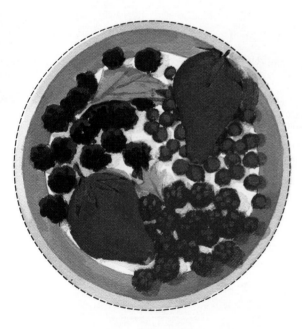

Project 2: Tags

A beautiful card for the chef to sign.

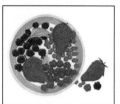
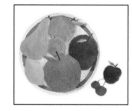

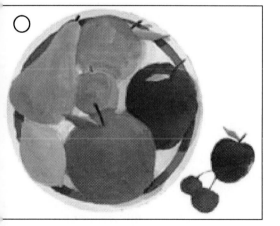

Materials Needed:

HP Card or Cover stock

Cutting mat, metal ruler, and X-ACTO knife

Hole punch

Instructions:

1. Choose design and print pdf file.

2. Trim where indicated.

3. Fold in half and punch where indicated.

4. Tie to raffia or ribbon on jar topper.

printing projects

Project 3: Jar Labels

Add a splash of color to your preserves.

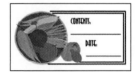 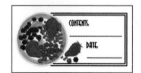

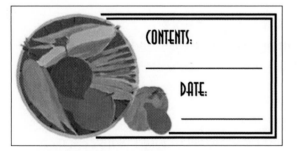

Materials Needed:

Full Sheet White Label stock

Cutting mat, metal ruler, and X-ACTO knife

Instructions:

1. Choose design and print pdf file.

2. Trim labels and fill in information.

3. Apply to jar and enjoy!

Note: Check your printer specifications on how to load special media such as label stock.

Project 4: Gift Labels

From your kitchen.

Materials Needed:

Full Sheet White Label stock

Cutting mat, metal ruler, and X-ACTO knife

Instructions:

1. Choose design and print pdf file.

2. Write your name, trim labels, and apply
   to jar.

3. Give to friends and family.

*Note: Check your printer specifications on how to
load special media such as label stock.*

Multimedia

When you want your videocassettes, audiocassettes, and CD-ROMs to look as colorful and professional as what you have on them, try one of these projects.

Project 1: CD Covers and Inserts

So easy to make.

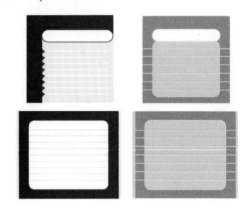

Materials Needed:

HP Inkjet Bright White paper

Cutting mat, metal ruler, and X-ACTO knife

Instructions:

1. Print pdf file.
2. Follow instructions on pdf file for trimming and folding.
3. Put into jewel case and enjoy.

Project 2: Audiocassette Case Covers

Mix and match to clearly identify your tapes.

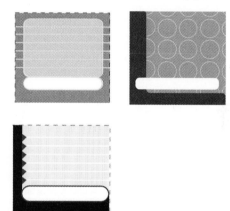

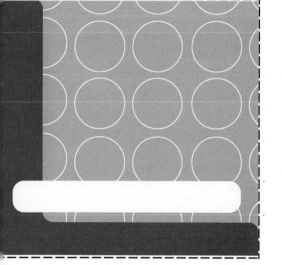

Materials Needed:

Full Sheet White Label stock

Cutting mat, metal ruler, and X-ACTO knife

Instructions:

1. Print pdf file.

2. Trim and fold where indicated.

3. Apply label to outside of cassette case.

Note: Check your printer specifications on how to load special media such as label stock.

printing projects

Project 3: Audiocassette Face Labels

The finishing touch.

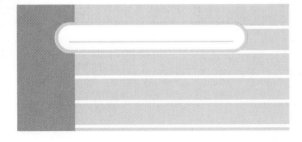

Materials Needed:

Full Sheet White Label stock

Cutting mat, metal ruler, and X-ACTO knife

Instructions:

1. Print pdf file.
2. Trim face labels.
3. Apply label to cassette face.

Note: Check your printer specifications on how to load special media such as label stock.

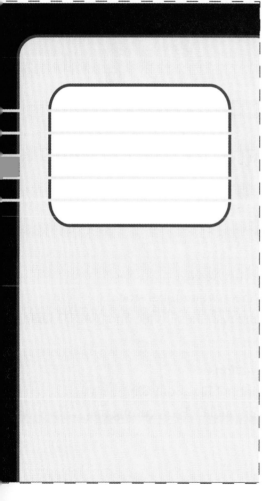

Project 4: Videocassette Case Covers

Organize your video library in no time.

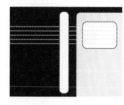

Materials Needed:

Full Sheet White Label stock

Cutting mat, metal ruler, and X-ACTO knife

Instructions:

1. Print pdf file.

2. Trim and fold where indicated.

3. Apply label to outside of cassette sleeve or in between clear cover and case.

Note: Check your printer specifications on how to load special media such as label stock.

printing projects

Project 5: Videocassette Face and Spine Labels

Cross your t's and dot your i's.

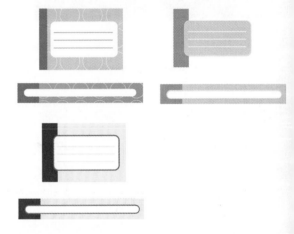

Materials Needed:

Full Sheet White Label stock

Cutting mat, metal ruler, and X-ACTO knife

Instructions:

1. Print pdf files from CD.
2. Trim out labels on cutting mat.

In the Garden

Everything's coming up roses, veggies, and cute little scarecrows when you let your imagination loose with these treats from the garden!

Project 1: Seed Packets

Now you can package your specialty seeds.

Materials Needed:

HP Bright White Inkjet paper

Cutting mat, metal ruler, and X-ACTO knife

Glue stick or double-sided tape

Instructions:

1. Print pdf file from CD.
2. Follow trim and folding instructions on pdf.
3. Tape or glue where indicated.
4. Share your crop with friends and family.

printing projects

Project 2: Iron-Ons

Make a special gift for a gardener you know.

Materials Needed:

HP Inkjet Iron-On Transfer material

Scissors and iron

Light colored cotton T-shirt

Instructions:

1. Print pdf onto transfer material (it will be backwards).
2. Cut out design, leaving 1/4" white space.
3. Iron transfer to T-shirt per box instructions.

Warning: Do not use iron-on transfer material with any laser printer or printer that uses heat to fuse the ink. It may melt the material and damage the printer.

Project 3: Garden Tags

No more confusion between plants.

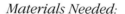

Materials Needed:

HP Card stock or Bright White Inkjet paper

Cutting mat, metal ruler, and X-ACTO knife

Wooden dowels or sticks

Self-laminating sheets (to protect ink)

Instructions:

1. If the pdf contains *Click Here to Edit* or similar instructions, edit the file on screen before printing, otherwise, go to step 2.

2. Print pdf file. Apply self-laminating sheets.

3. Trim tags and attach to sticks.

4. Put in your garden and enjoy!

printing projects

The Practical Home

Now let's see. First on my list for today: recipes for Mom, shopping for party, and maintenance on the house. So much to do!

Project 1: Herb Theme Recipe Cards

Mmm, yummy...

Materials Needed:

1 or more sheets of HP Card or Cover stock

Cutting mat, metal ruler, and X-ACTO knife

Instructions:

1. If editable: Type your recipe into the space provided on pdf file before you print. Or, delete the sample text and handwrite after.
2. Print the recipe cards onto card stock, and set them aside to dry completely.
3. Place the cutting mat underneath the printed card stock. Using the X-ACTO knife and the ruler as your guide, trim away the white areas from each card.
4. Share your delicious recipes with friends and family.

Note: Put your finished recipe cards in plastic sleeves or laminate them to protect from spills.

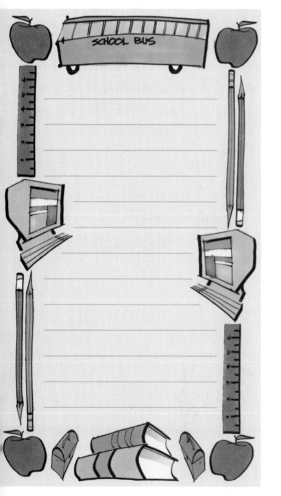

Project 2: Handy Lists

Something for almost everything.

Materials Needed:

HP Bright White Inkjet paper

Cutting mat, metal ruler, and X-ACTO knife

Instructions:

1. Print pdf file. Let dry.

2. Trim out and use.

Note: Not all designs shown. See CD for additional pdf files.

printing projects

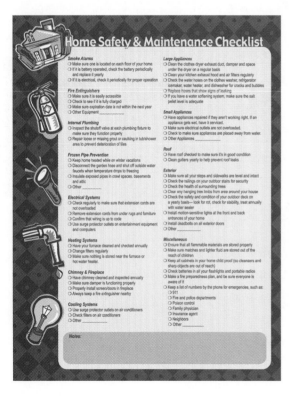

Project 3: Home Maintenance Checklist

A change of seasons is a great time to roll up your sleeves and clean house. It's also a good time to complete those home maintenance activities that must be performed if you want to avoid problems later—replacing smoke alarm batteries or cleaning the gutters. Most of the tasks are simple, requiring little effort.

The best way to remember your seasonal chores is to use a checklist. We've created one that should help you spend more time enjoying the seasons instead of dealing with unexpected issues.

Materials Needed:

HP Bright White Inkjet paper

Instructions:

1. Print pdf file.
2. Whistle while you work.

Project 4: Garage Sale Kit

Dazzle all the bargain hunters!

Materials Needed:

HP Bright White Inkjet paper, Card stock

Full Sheet Label stock (removable if available)

Cutting mat, metal ruler, and X-ACTO knife

Self-laminating sheets

Instructions:

1. If the pdf contains *Click Here to Edit* or similar instructions, edit the file on screen before printing, otherwise, go to step 2.
2. Print big sign and arrows on card stock. Let dry and laminate to protect ink.
3. Print price tags on label stock. Let dry.
4. Print item detail card on inkjet paper and dry.
5. Trim and fold where indicated.
6. Sell! Sell! Sell!

printing projects

Family Ties

Choose from among these memory makers for your journeys down Memory Lane.

Yesterday and Today

Something old, something new, something borrowed, something blue...

Project 1: 1940s Scrapbook Journal

Nostalgic pages for clippings and photos.

Materials Needed:

9 or more sheets of HP Card or Cover stock

Butter knife or bone folder

Glue stick

Cutting mat, metal ruler, and X-ACTO knife

Ribbon or raffia (24" long)

Clear nail polish

2 to 4 clothespins and hole punch

Clippings, letters, and photos for inside

Instructions:

1. Print artwork from pdf file. Let dry.
2. Follow instructions on CD for scoring and binding journal.

Project 2: 1940s Magnets

Your refrigerator never looked so good.

Materials Needed:

Printable Magnetic Inkjet paper

Cutting mat, metal ruler, and X-ACTO knife

Instructions:

1. Print pdf file onto magnetic paper.

2. Trim magnets and enjoy!

Note: Not all magnets shown. See pdf file on CD for complete designs. Check your printer specifications on how to use and load special media such as magnetic paper.

Project 3: Then and Now Activity Book

Fun for any generation.

Materials Needed:

6 to 10 sheets of HP Card or Cover stock

Glue stick and felt tip pens

3-hole punch

Instructions:

1. Print all pages of pdf file.
2. Hole punch and put into 3-ring binder, or use other binding suggestions on CD.
3. Fill out, glue photos, and enjoy.

Note: Not all pages shown. See CD for all pdf files.

Project 4: Photo Family Tree

Your photo family tree will be a wonderful centerpiece for your reunion.

Here's a great idea for your next family reunion

- Scan photos of family members into your computer. Use a photo-editing program to clean up old pictures. Remove scratches, repair torn edges, and adjust the colors if needed. Resize and crop photos so they focus on the people.
- Add captions to your photos, identifying the person or people in the image, and include details such as the date of the photo and where the photo was taken.
- Print the photos on photo-quality paper. HP has many to choose from. Trim away excess.
- On a piece of posterboard, draw a diagram of an ancestry chart, showing the various branches of your family. You can even draw or paint the outline of a tree around the chart. Write the family name in large letters at the bottom.
- Using mounting tape, attach the trimmed photos to the tree, starting with the oldest ones at the "trunk" and spreading out through the branches.

- Decorate the borders of the family tree with stickers, stamps, dried leaves and flowers, or family mementos.

More ideas for creative family memories

- Create a digital photo family tree using the collage function of your image editor. You can display this on a Web site, email it to family members, or print it out and frame it.
- Collect family stories from relatives. Using a word processor or desktop publishing software, assemble the stories with your photos and print them out in book form. Add a cover, and give it as a special gift.
- Create a calendar with your photos so that you can remember your family's history throughout the year. Copy houses can spiral bind them, or you can use metal rings to hold the pages together.

printing projects

Kids and Pets

Purr-fect printing projects for the little ones in your life!

printing projects

Kid's Table

When you want your kids to enjoy the dining experience as much as you want to enjoy the dinner, try one of these projects to keep their interest!

Project 1: Double-Sided Kid's Placemat

With so many fun games, your kids won't even have time to play with their food.

Materials Needed:

2 sheets HP Card or Cover stock

Glue stick

Self-laminating sheet

Instructions:

1. Print pdf files.
2. Glue pages back to back.
3. Put between self-laminating sheets to protect ink from spills.

Project 2: Lunch Bags

Package your kids' lunch in style.

printing projects

Materials Needed:

Standard white or brown lunch bag

Instructions:

1. Place a standard lunch bag face down on a piece of 8-1/2" x 11" paper.
2. Tape the top (open) edge of the bag to the top edge of the paper.
3. Insert the bag and paper into the printer with the bag side facing down.
4. Choose design, and print pdf file.
5. Pack a good lunch.

Nutrition Facts

Calories 10,986	
Total Fat 500g	99%
Sodium 3400mg	99%
Total Carb 800g	100%
Protein 0g	

INGREDIENTS: PIZZA, POTATO CHIPS, SOFT DRINK, CANDY BAR, POPCORN, DONUT.

CONTAINS NO SIGNIFICANT NUTRITIONAL VALUE AND CONSISTS ENTIRELY OF ARTIFICIAL INGREDIENTS.

Coloring

Hop to it! We have bunnies to print and bunnies to color!

Project 1: Bunny Coloring Pages

This is a honey-bunny of a project!

Materials Needed:

HP Bright White Inkjet paper

Colored pens, pencils, or crayons

Instructions:

1. Print pdf file. Let dry.

2. Give to someone to color.

Learning Fun

Let your imagination go wild—these alphabet magnets offer a whole zoo of learning and decorating fun!

Project 1: Animal Alphabet Magnets

You'll be magnetically drawn to these!

Materials Needed:

5 Printable Magnetic Inkjet sheets

Cutting mat, metal ruler, and X-ACTO knife

Instructions:

1. Print artwork pages from the pdf file. Let dry.
2. Trim and adorn your metal surfaces.

Note: See CD for complete alphabet. Check your printer specifications on how to use and load special media such as magnetic paper.

printing projects

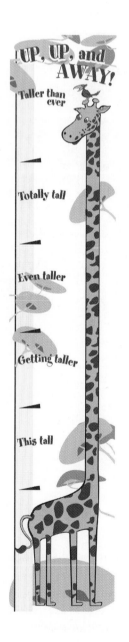

Growing Up

Use this fun wall chart to record your children's growth spurts. Note each child's initials next to the height marks.

Project 1: Giant Giraffe Growth Chart

They grow so fast!

Materials Needed:

HP Bright White Inkjet paper

Self-laminating sheets

Instructions:

1. Print each page of the pdf file. Let dry.
2. Tape ends together to make one tall giraffe.
3. Protect pages with self-laminating sheets, or take the taped-up giraffe to a copy house to have it laminated in one piece.
4. Hang on a wall or back of a door.

Pamper Your Pet

No bones about it—pets deserve the best! Read on for purr-fect ways to say "I love you" with some unique print projects.

Project 1: Pet Set ID Tags

Keep tabs on your furry friends no matter where they roam.

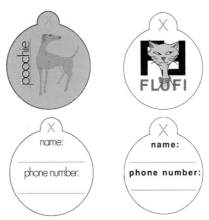

Materials Needed:

HP Card or Cover stock

Small sheets of laminate

Small split ring

Pen, scissors, and small hole punch

Glue stick

Instructions:

1. Print artwork from pdf file. Let dry.
2. Fill in pet information and trim both sides.
3. Glue front and back together.
4. Laminate the tag per instructions and trim, leaving 1/4" around design.
5. Punch hole where indicated and attach ring.
6. Put on your pet's collar.

printing projects

Project 2: Pet Set Food Dish Placemats

Spills are easy to clean with these mats.

Materials Needed:

HP Card or Cover stock

Self-laminating sheets

Instructions:

1. Print artwork from pdf file. Let dry.
2. Put between self-laminating sheets to protect ink from spills, or take it to your local copying store to have it laminated.
3. Ring the dinner bell.

Project 3: Pet Set Notecards

These notecards will be happily received by any friend or loved one.

Materials Needed:

HP Card or Cover stock

Scissors

Pen and envelope

Instructions:

1. Print artwork from pdf file. Let dry.
2. Fold and cut out the card where indicated (there will be a 1/2" tab left over to secure the open side).
3. Fill in your good wishes, use a Pet Set Sticker to seal, place in envelope, and send to a friend.

Note: Above thumbnails show card fronts only.

printing projects

Project 4: Pet Set Stickers

Accessorize anything with these darlings.

Materials Needed:

Full Sheet White Sticker paper

Scissors

Instructions:

1. Print artwork from pdf file. Let dry.
2. Cut out the stickers where indicated.

Project 5: New Pet Announcements

Notify everyone about a new arrival.

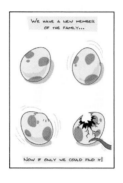

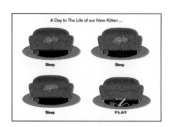

Materials Needed:

HP Card or Cover stock

Scissors

Pen and envelope

Instructions:

1. Print artwork from pdf file. Let dry.

2. Fold on center line and trim out cards where indicated.

3. Fill in your new pet's information and send.

Chapter 2

PHOTO FUN
& CRAFTS

Taking pictures is always fun. Turning
those pictures into keepsakes is magical!

Photo Projects

Print it, frame it, and glow with joy!

Memorabilia

You've taken beautiful pictures. Now what do you put them in? Use these projects and create real masterpieces.

Project 1: Photo Frames

Want to print your own frame? No problem!

Materials Needed:

HP Card stock or Printable Magnetic sheets

Cutting mat, metal ruler, and X-ACTO knife

Photo

Instructions:

1. Print pdf file onto desired paper. Let dry.
2. Trim white areas away from the frame, including the picture window.
3. If on card stock, tape photo to the back. If on magnetic paper, put your photo behind the frame and attach it to any metal surface.

Project 2: Mailable Photo Frames

A great surprise to find in the mailbox!

fold and tape ends together to create a stand

Materials Needed:

3 sheets of HP Card or Cover stock

Cutting mat, metal ruler, and X-ACTO knife

1 Full Sheet White Label stock

Double-sided tape

Butter knife or scoring tool

Spoon

Scissors and photos

Instructions:

1. Customize the photo frame by typing addresses where indicated, or delete to have a blank field.
2. Print pages 1 to 3 of the pdf onto card stock. Let dry.
3. Trim white areas away from each page.
4. See CD for complete assembly instructions, including scoring, folding, and taping tabs.
5. Print page 4 of the pdf file onto clear sticker paper. Let dry. Refer to CD for application.

Project 3: Photo Brag Book

Whether it's a trip to Tahiti, Junior's big recital, or your honeymoon, you've got plenty to boast about!

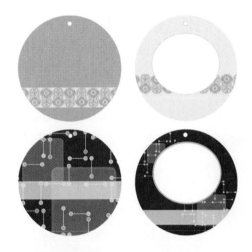

Materials Needed:

3 or more sheets HP Card or Cover stock

Cutting mat, metal ruler, and X-ACTO knife

Double-sided tape

Butter knife or scoring tool and spoon

Hole punch and scissors

Screw post or ribbon for binding

Photos

Self-laminating sheets (optional)

Instructions:

1. Customize the book cover (pg. 1) by typing your message in space provided. Or, select and delete for a blank field.
2. Print cover on card stock. Let dry.
3. Customize photo page (pg. 2) as above.
4. Print photo page on card stock. Let dry.

Project 3: Photo Brag Book

Instructions (continued):

5. Repeat steps 3 and 4 for all of your photos.

6. Print out the brag book back cover (pg. 3) on card stock. Let dry.

7. For easier folding, score all pages. See CD for details on how to do this.

8. Fold along scored lines, and crease with the back of a spoon.

9. Trim pieces of lamination to cover the circle on each page of your brag book.
    (This is optional, but will protect and extend the life of your book.)

10. Peel the backing from each sheet, one at a time, and place on top of the circles. See CD
    for how to completely seal to paper.

11. Cut the photo window from each of the photo pages.

12. From the back, tape your photos in place.

13. Apply double-sided tape to the back of each brag book circle. Fold each page in half
    along the crease and press firmly.

14. One at a time, trim white areas away from the circle using the cutting mat and X-ACTO
    knife.

15. Once all of the circles have been cut, punch out the gray dot at the top of each page.

16. To assemble the book, insert the screw posts through all of the pages and screw them
    together. If desired, a ribbon can be tied to bind the pages together instead.

Crafts

Have some intergalactic and soulful fun!

printing projects

Get Inspired

Sometimes an inspiring phrase or the sight of a beautiful flower is all it takes to bring a smile to a friend.

Project 1: Jewelry

Fun, playful, simply dazzling. You go, friend!

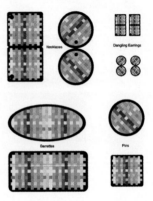

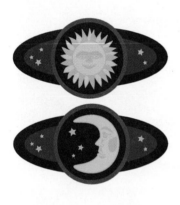

Materials Needed:

HP Bright White Inkjet paper or Card stock

Scissors and glue stick

Barrette backs, pins, earrings, and ribbon

Instructions:

1. Print pdf file. Let dry.
2. Trim away all white areas.
3. Glue pendants back to back and put on cord or ribbon.
4. Glue earrings back to back and put on metal earring hooks.
5. Attach pins and barrettes to back sides of other designs. Have fun!

Project 2: CD Clocks

Here's a colorful clock you can make yourself—and recycle an old CD at the same time!

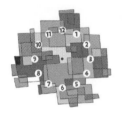 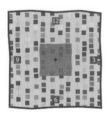

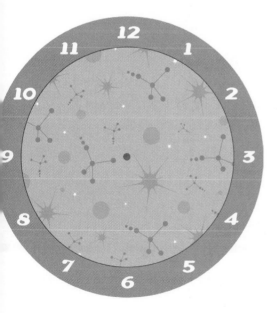

Materials Needed:

HP Card or Cover stock

Cutting mat, metal ruler, and X-ACTO knife

Double-sided tape (high tack)

Used CD

Fishing line and beads (optional for retro)

Clock movement and battery

Instructions:

1. Print pdf file on card stock. Let dry.
2. Trim away all white areas around face.
3. Cut out gray circle in center of clock face for clock movement to go through.
4. Unscrew the clock movement components from the shaft, then attach the CD to the front of the clock movement with double-sided tape. (CD will support clock face.)
5. Apply double-sided tape to the CD front and place clock face on top. Be sure clock face numbers are in position before pressing.
6. Assemble clock movement per instructions.
7. Put in batteries and hang up the clock.

Note: See special instructions on CD for retro clock.

printing projects

Project 3: Inspirational Art Mousepad

Words of inspiration at your fingertips.

Materials Needed:

HP Inkjet Iron-On Transfer material

Cutting mat, metal ruler, and X-ACTO knife

8" x 10" mousepad (or larger)

Instructions:

1. Print pdf file on iron-on transfer material. (Design will appear backwards.)
2. Trim art, leaving 1/4" white space around design.
3. Center design and follow iron-on transfer instructions from box.

Project 4: Inspirational Art Wallet Cards

Prose in your pocket.

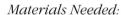

Materials Needed:

HP Bright White Inkjet paper

Cutting mat, metal ruler, and X-ACTO knife

Glue stick

Instructions:

1. Print pdf file. Let dry.
2. Trim where indicated and glue cards back to back. Or, trim outer edges and fold in half.

Project 5: Inspirational Art Notepaper

Beautiful words…beautiful paper.

"When you have decided what you believe, what you feel must be done, have the courage to stand alone and be counted."

— Eleanor Roosevelt

Materials Needed:

HP Bright White Inkjet paper

Cutting mat, metal ruler, and X-ACTO knife

Instructions:

1. Print pdf file. Let dry.

2. Cut sheet in half.

3. Enjoy!

Project 6: Inspirational Art Photo Frame

Framed to perfection!

 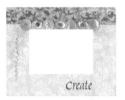

Materials Needed:

HP Bright White Inkjet paper

Cutting mat, metal ruler, and X-ACTO knife

Cardboard

Glue stick

Instructions:

1. Print pdf file. Let dry.

2. Paste entire printout onto cardboard

3. Cut out frame, including photo section.

4. Tape photo to back of frame.

5. To stand frame up, cut a triangle-shaped piece of cardboard and glue to back side.

6. To hang frame, loop a piece of string and tape to back.

printing projects

Iron-Ons and Textiles

Sew lovely! Sew nice! Sew playful!

Home Sweet Home

Be it ever so humble...

Project 1: Country Kitchen Aprons

The latest fashions for chefs everywhere.

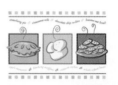 

Materials Needed:

HP Iron-On Transfer material

Scissors

White or light-colored apron

Instructions:

1. Print pdf file onto transfer material. Let dry. (Design will be backwards.)

2. Trim out design, leaving 1/4" white area.

3. Iron your design onto apron per transfer box instructions.

Project 2: Mother's Quilt

There's no one in the world like a mom. She nurtures, protects, and helps us out with homework. She teaches us right from wrong and how to learn from our mistakes. Here's a quilt that celebrates treasured family moments—a gift that will surely warm her heart!

Materials Needed:

HP Iron-On Transfer material

Scanner, digital camera, or digital photos

Sewing machine

12 fabric squares, 10-1/2" x 10-1/2"; use shades of white for photo transfers, solids and prints for a splash of color; 100% cotton or cotton/polyester blend works best on transfers

Fabric fixative and fabric adhesive

Buttons, fabric paints, beads, and ribbon

Instructions:

1. Print your images or art on iron-on transfer paper. (Remember to reverse the image.)
2. Run a bead of fabric fixative on edges of fabric squares. Let dry.
3. Fold under and press all four sides 1/4" (finished size will be 10").
4. Iron your transfer images onto the squares.
5. Organize your design by placing the finished squares on top of the throw (3" from the outer edges). Pin into place.
6. Sew the squares together either by hand or with a sewing machine (a topstitch or zigzag stitch works best.)
7. Add finishing touches to the squares using ribbon, beads, buttons, or fabric paint—get creative and experiment!

printing projects

Project 3: Dream Pillows

Just the thing to spin sleepy bedtime stories and sweet dreams.

dreamtime

dreamteam

dreammachine

make a wish...

night night

Materials Needed:

HP Iron-On Transfer material

Scissors and iron

Pillow cover or fabric square

Instructions:

1. Print artwork from pdf file onto iron-on transfer material. Let dry.

2. Trim out, leaving 1/4" white space around design. Iron to fabric square or pillow cover per transfer box instructions.

3. If on material square, turn edges under and press all sides. Sew finished transfer fabric square onto pillow.

Note: Not all pillow designs shown. See CD for more.

Special Considerations with Iron-Ons:

1. Warning! Do not use iron-on transfer material with any laser printer or with the HP DeskJet 1200C or HP DeskJet 1600C. The heating elements in these printers can melt the transfer paper and damage the printer. Refer to your printer manual if you are uncertain about yours.

2. For best results, use 100% cotton or cotton/polyester blend fabric.

3. If your fabric is dark colored, use dark iron-on transfer material.

4. Use standard ink when printing your transfer design. Photo and specialty inks are not recommended.

printing projects

Fuzzy Friends

Fun gift ideas and a moderately challenging sewing project.

Project 1: Beanbag Lizard

Fanciful lizard beanbag for fun!

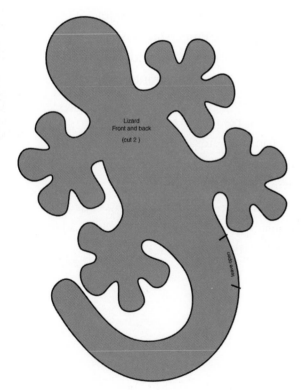

Lizard
Front and back
(cut 2)

leave open

Materials Needed:

HP Bright White Inkjet paper

Fabric (spandex recommended)

Sand or plastic pellets

Needle and thread

Straight pins

Scissors

2 small round black buttons, googly eyes, rhinestones, or fabric paint

Instructions:

1. Print out pattern from pdf file. Let dry.

2. Follow detailed instructions on CD.

Project 2: Beanbag Bunny

Who could resist this soft and loveable bunny!

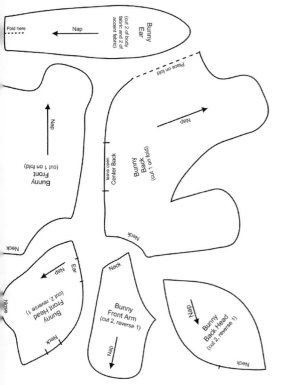

Materials Needed:

HP Bright White Inkjet paper

12" x 12" piece of white fabric (velour, terry cloth, twill, or nylon recommended)

2" x 12" piece of pink fabric (same as above)

Matching thread

1 1/2" white pom-pom

2 1/4" black pom-poms or small black round buttons

Brown and white embroidery floss

Plastic craft pellets

Fiberfill

Washable fabric glue

Scissors

Sewing machine

Instructions:

1. Print pdf file from CD. Let dry.

2. Follow detailed instructions on CD.

printing projects

Scrapbooks

Snap, Print, Pop!

printing projects

Photo Keepsakes

There are unlimited opportunities to share some of life's most treasured moments. Why not turn your memories into creative gifts? They'll be well loved because they come from the heart.

Project 1: Photo Collage

As rewarding to give as they are fun to create.

Materials Needed:

HP Bright White Inkjet paper

10 to 15 photos (depending on frame size)

Cutting mat, metal ruler, and X-ACTO knife

12" x 12" frame (or any size)

Poster board or foam core

Double-sided tape

Scissors (straight-edged or fancy)

Instructions:

1. Choose design and print pdf file.

2. Follow detailed instructions on CD.

Project 2: Graduation and Summer Camp Photo Book

Memory books to capture all the fun!

Materials Needed:

HP Bright White Inkjet paper

Cutting mat, metal ruler, and X-ACTO knife

Pencil and eraser

Acid-free parchment paper

Acid-free photo adhesive

Vellum or other decorative paper

One piece heavy black card stock

Self-adhesive photo corners

Hole punch

1/2 yard of 1" or thicker ribbon

Twenty-four 4" x 6" or smaller photographs

Preparation and Instructions:

1. The finished album will be 9-1/4" x 5". Trim the parchment paper and piece of card stock to those dimensions and set aside.

2. Print one of the pages of this pdf onto either vellum or another sheet of parchment paper. (Vellum will allow the first photograph to show through.) Trim to 9-1/4" x 5".

3. Draw a faint pencil line 1-1/4" from the left-hand sides of your trimmed sheets (the gutter).

4. Punch two holes into the gutter of each piece. They should be 1" from top and bottom, and centered in the gutter. Set the printed cover sheet and card stock aside until you get to step 6.

printing projects

Project 2: Graduation and Summer Camp Photo Book

Instructions (continued):

5. Place your photographs one by one in the remaining space (8" x 5") of your parchment paper. Make faint pencil marks around each photo to help center it. When the photo is centered, put a small piece of photo adhesive tape on the back of it and press into place. Peel off the backing of four self-adhesive photo corners and attach to the corners of your photo. Repeat this process with the remaining photos and pieces of parchment paper. Be sure to erase any pencil marks you made.

6. Arrange your finished stack of photos in the order you would like them to appear in your book. Place your printed cover sheet on top of the first photograph, using the card stock as the final page. Run a length of ribbon through the holes from front to back. Tie in a bow and trim ends on a diagonal. Apply no-fray fabric solvent or clear nail polish to ribbon edges so they don't fray.

Tip: If you're making multiple copies, you may want to scan your photos into your computer or use digital images rather than work with originals. You can use photo editing software for extra pizzazz.

Project 3: Beach and Camping Scrapbook Kits

Fun, fun, fun!

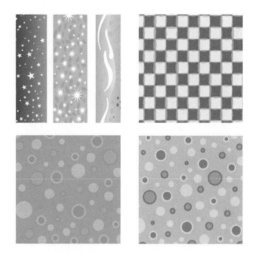

printing projects

Materials Needed:

HP Bright White Inkjet paper

Full Sheet White Label stock

Scissors (straight-edged or fancy)

Cutting mat, metal ruler, and X-ACTO knife

Photos, clippings, and memorabilia

Glue stick

Instructions:

1. If the pdf contains *Click Here to Edit* or similar instructions, edit the file on screen before printing, otherwise, go to step 2.
2. Print pdf file. Cut out stickers. Use backgrounds and borders to decorate pages.
3. Add your own photos and clippings.
4. Enjoy!

Chapter 3

SPORTS
& HOBBIES

Hobbyists and sports fans, rejoice!
Score the winning touchdown with
these printable goodies!

SPORTS & HOBBIES

Games

I see F*U*N in your future!

printing projects

Just for Fun

Whether on a road trip or at a family gathering, these games will add some extra fun to the event.

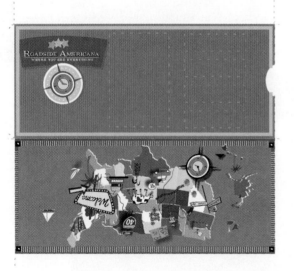

Project 1a: Roadside Americana Trivia Game Envelope

Materials Needed:

2 sheets of HP Card or Cover stock

Cutting mat, metal ruler, and X-ACTO knife

Double-sided tape and glue stick

Butter knife or scoring tool

Instructions:

1. Print pages 2 and 3 on card stock. Let dry.
2. Score the red dotted lines.
3. Cut along the black dotted lines.
4. Cut out the support rectangle and apply glue to one side. Glue the rectangle onto the back of the top part of the envelope.
5. Create windows in the envelope by cutting out the five boxes along the white dotted lines.
6. Fold the envelope flaps (A & B) along the scored lines, and crease. They should be folded away from the front of the envelope.
7. To hold the flaps in place, apply double-sided tape to flaps A & B. Then, fold the back of the envelope (with the map) on top and press firmly to hold in place.

Project 1b: Roadside Americana Trivia Cards

Test your knowledge of the offbeat destinations that make America like no other place on Earth.

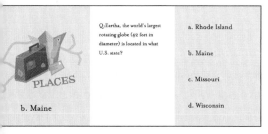

Materials Needed:

6 sheets HP Card or Cover stock

Cutting mat, metal ruler, and X-ACTO knife

Instructions:

1. Print pages 4 to 9 on card stock. Let dry.

2. Trim each card on dotted lines.

3. Slip the cards in the envelope (from Project 1a) and let the trivia challenge begin!

printing projects

Project 2: American Inventor Trivia Cards

Be inspired by the bright ideas of famous American inventors.

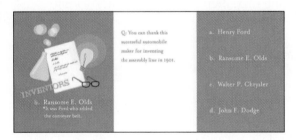

Materials Needed:

6 sheets of HP Card or Cover stock

Cutting mat, metal ruler, and X-ACTO knife

Roadside Americana Trivia Envelope

Instructions:

1. Use the same Roadside Americana Trivia Envelope as you created in Project 1a.
2. Print pages 4 to 9 on card stock. Let dry.
3. Trim each card on dotted lines.
4. Slip the cards in the envelope (from Project 1a) and let the trivia challenge begin!

Project 3: Magic Fortune Teller

Go ahead, ask your burning question…

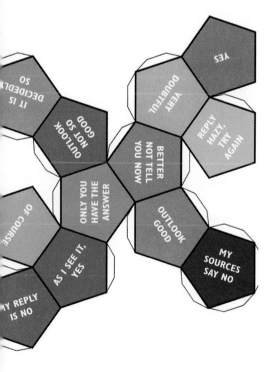

Materials Needed:

HP Card or Cover stock

Cutting mat, metal ruler, and X-ACTO knife

Thin double-sided tape

Instructions:

1. Print pdf file on card stock. Let dry.
2. Trim around outer black lines and fold on all black lines.
3. Apply double-sided tape to each tab to hold the ball together.
4. Ask a question and roll for the answer.

Hobbies

Decorate your garden and yourself!

CHAPTER 3 SPORTS & HOBBIES / Hobbies

printing projects

A Blissful Garden

Happiness is found in the garden. With these colorful projects, your creativity will surely bloom.

Project 1: Gardener's Gear Iron-On Designs

Create garden gear that inspires.

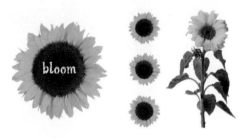

Get  your hands dirty.

Materials Needed:

HP Iron-On Transfer material

Cotton T-shirt, apron, baby onesie, or tote bag

Scissors and iron

Instructions:

1. Choose design and print pdf file. Let dry.
2. Trim around your design, leaving 1/4" white space.
3. Iron on design per transfer instructions.

Project 2: Garden Markers

Descriptive markers ready to grace your garden.

Materials Needed:

HP Card or Cover stock

Cutting mat, metal ruler, and X-ACTO knife

Self-laminating sheets

Wood or plastic plant labels

Instructions:

1. Print desired art from pdf file. Let dry.
2. Place a plant label on the back side of the marker card, pointed end down.
3. Following the laminate directions, sandwich the marker card and plant label together, covering all but the pointy end of the label. Leave enough space between each for trimming. Rub firmly on edges.
4. Cut out each marker, leaving 1/8".

Note: Not all designs shown. See CD for all pdf files.

Project 3: Garden Magnets

Bring a bit of nature into your home.

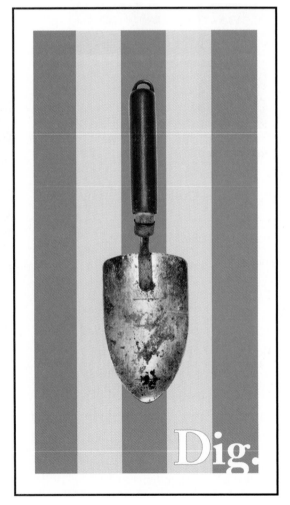

Materials Needed:

Printable Magnetic Inkjet paper

Cutting mat, metal ruler, and X-ACTO knife

Instructions:

1. Print page 2 of pdf file. Let dry.
2. Trim around each image where indicated.

Project 4: Garden Chart and Journal

Keeping track of your buds can be easy and fun!

Materials Needed:

HP Card or Cover stock

Cutting mat, metal ruler, and X-ACTO knife

Double-sided tape

Tape

3 screw posts or ribbon (1/2" wide, 18" long)

Hole punch

Garden photos

printing projects

Instructions:

1. Print cover from page 2 of pdf file. Let dry. Trim away white areas.

2. Print the garden chart (pg. 3) of pdf file. Print as many copies as you'd like of each. Let dry. Trim away white areas.

3. Print garden photo frame and frame back (pgs. 4–5) of pdf file. Let dry. Trim away white frame windows on all copies.

4. Choose photos and put behind windows in garden photo frame pages. Tape to back.

5. With the garden frame pages face down, apply double-sided tape to the backs.

6. Make sure the frame back art is oriented the same as the frame front. Carefully set the frame backs face up on top of the taped photo frame pages, and press firmly in place.

7. Punch holes in all the journal pages where indicated.

8. Stack the journal pages in order with the cover on top, photo pages on bottom.

9. See CD for detailed assembly and bindery directions.

Sports

Hit a grand slam with your printer!

printing projects

Baseball Party

Here's the pitch: We've got baseball projects to turn your next game or party into a major league celebration. Every fan in your neighborhood will be sliding into home (yours!).

Project 1: Invitation
It's party time!

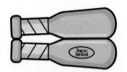

Materials Needed:

HP Card or Cover stock

Cutting mat, metal ruler, and X-ACTO knife

Instructions:

1. Print page 1 of pdf file. Let dry.
2. Turn 180° and place back in printer, printed side face up.
3. Print page 2.
4. Cut around outside of yellow circle.
5. Crease along each of the four sides of the green square to make flaps.
6. Start by folding in one of the flaps and continue around the square. To close, tuck the last flap under the first flap to seal.

Note: See CD for instructions for bat invitation.

Project 2: Magnetic Photo Frames

A great party favor to give away.

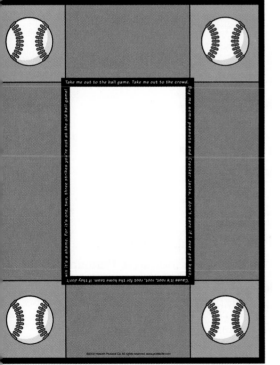

Materials Needed:

Printable Magnetic Inkjet paper

Cutting mat, metal ruler, and X-ACTO knife

Photo

Instructions:

1. Print pdf file on magnetic paper, or print onto HP Bright White Inkjet paper and paste to a magnetic sheet.

2. Cut out all white areas around frame, including interior photo area.

3. Place photo behind magnet and stick frame to a metal surface.

printing projects

Project 3: Stars Trading Cards

Make everyone at the party a star.

Materials Needed:

HP Card or Cover stock

Cutting mat, metal ruler, and X-ACTO knife

Team photos

Instructions:

1. Type in team name, player name, and number where indicated. Print and let dry.
2. Cut out all white areas around card, including photo window.
3. Tape photo to back of card.

Project 4: Baseball Trading Cards

Make them feel like a pro.

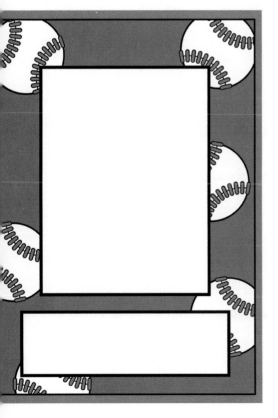

printing projects

Materials Needed:

HP Card or Cover stock

Cutting mat, metal ruler, and X-ACTO knife

Team photos

Instructions:

1. Type in team name and player's name and position on each card.
2. Cut out all white areas around card, including photo window.
3. Tape photo to back of card.

Project 5: Coasters

Catch those party spills with cool coasters.

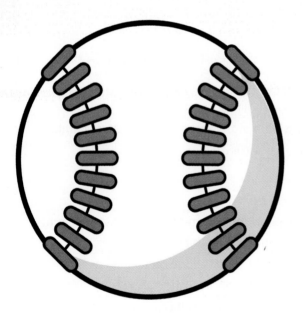

Materials Needed:

HP Bright White Inkjet paper

Scissors and glue stick

Cardboard

Self-laminating sheets

Instructions:

1. Print pdf file. Let dry.

2. Laminate printed sheets to protect ink.

3. Glue to cardboard.

Project 6: Window Cling

Funny when it's fake.

printing projects

Materials Needed:

Window decals for inkjet printers

Scissors

Instructions:

1. Print pdf file. Let dry.

2. Trim instructions off top and adhere to window.

Warning: Be sure to use materials designed specifically for your printer. To prevent damage, use window decals specifically designed for laser printers or printers that use heat to fuse the ink.

Project 7: Team Roster
Go, team, go!

Materials Needed:

HP Bright White Inkjet paper

Instructions:

1. Type in team name, players' names and stats, and coaches' names.
2. Print pdf file. Let dry.

Project 8: Catcher Game

Super fun and easy game for the party.

Materials Needed:

HP Bright White Inkjet paper

Self-laminating sheet

Instructions:

1. Print pdf file. Let dry.

2. Trim off instructions and laminate sheet.

3. Throw wet cotton balls at the target.

   Closest to the center wins.

printing projects

Project 9: Score Sheet
And reusable no less!

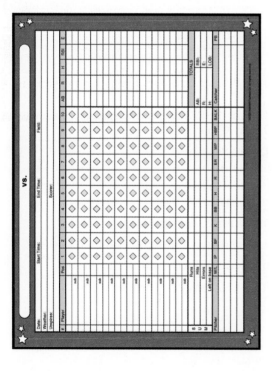

Materials Needed:

HP Bright White Inkjet paper

Self-laminating sheets (optional)

Instructions:

1. Print pdf file. Let dry.
2. If you want to reuse the score sheet, laminate and use removable overhead markers.
3. Keep score.

Project 10: Decorations and Shrinkables

Fun activities for the whole team.

Materials Needed:

White printable shrink sheets for inkjet printers

Scissors

Ribbon or raffia

Instructions:

1. Print pdf on the shrink material. Let dry.

2. Cut out and punch hole in each.

3. Follow instructions for baking that came in the shrink sheet box.

Warning: To prevent damage, be sure to use materials designed specifically for your printer.

printing projects

Project 11: Thank You Card
A perfect ending to a fun-filled party.

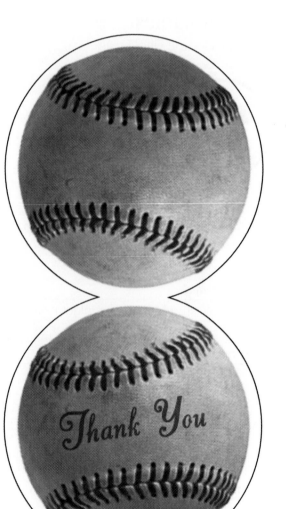

Materials Needed:

HP Card or Cover stock

Scissors

Instructions:

1. Print pdf file. Let dry.

2. Cut out where indicated and fold in half.

Soccer Kit

Stay on top of your game with cool soccer projects that coaches, parents, and kids will love. From practical to fun!

Project 1: T-Shirt Iron-On

Mix and match these icons for custom shirts.

Materials Needed:

HP Iron-On Transfer material

Scissors

Iron

Cotton T-shirt

Instructions:

1. Print pdf file onto transfer material. Let dry.
2. Follow iron-on instructions from transfer material box.

Warning: Do not use iron-on transfer material with any laser printer or printer that uses heat to fuse the ink. It may melt the material and damage the printer.

printing projects

Project 2: Yearbook

Use this scrapbook to capture all the season's highlights. There's room for memories, snapshots, clippings, autographs, and more!

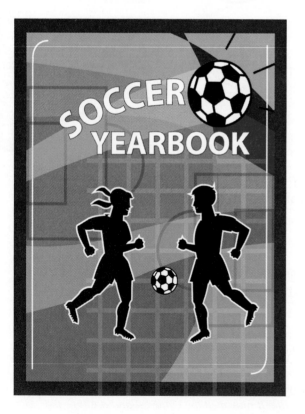

Materials Needed:

6 or more sheets of card stock

Full Sheet White Label stock

Cutting mat, metal ruler, and X-ACTO knife (or scissors)

Double-sided tape

Photos

Pens and markers

Hole punch (optional)

Screw posts, ribbon, three-ring binder, or other binding materials (optional)

Project 2: Yearbook
(continued)

Instructions:

1. Print the yearbook (pgs. 1–6) onto the card stock. Set them aside to dry completely.

2. Place the cutting mat underneath the first page. Using the X-ACTO knife and the ruler as a guide, trim the white areas away from each page.

3. To complete the friends page (pgs. 2–3), cut out the photo.

4. Using the double-sided tape, attach your photos to page 3 where indicated.

5. Apply double-sided tape around the photos on page 3, placing page 2 on top. Press the pages together firmly.

6. Fill in the information under each photo.

7. Print the stickers (pg. 7) onto the label stock. Set them aside to dry completely.

8. Using your pens, photos, and stickers, decorate the pages to create a scrapbook.

9. Decide how you would like to bind your pages and punch holes, if necessary.

printing projects

Project 3: Editable Soccer Trading Cards

Score big with your team with these cards.

Materials Needed:

HP Bright White Inkjet paper

1 or more sheets of Full Sheet Label stock

1 or more sheets of card stock

Cutting mat, metal ruler, and X-ACTO knife

Player photos (trimmed to 2" x 3-1/4")

Instructions:

1. If the pdf contains *Click Here to Edit* or similar instructions, edit the file on screen before printing, otherwise, go to step 2.
2. Print cards onto label stock. Let dry.
3. Trim out photo windows on each card and roughly cut out the trading card fronts.
4. Peel the paper backing from fronts of the cards and attach to photos.
5. Stick card fronts onto card stock.
6. Trim white areas away from each card.
7. Trim white areas away from card backs.
8. Peel paper backing from backs and apply to the corresponding fronts.
9. Trade cards with your friends and have fun!

Project 4: Editable Soccer Team Roster

Keep track of who's who with this handy tool.

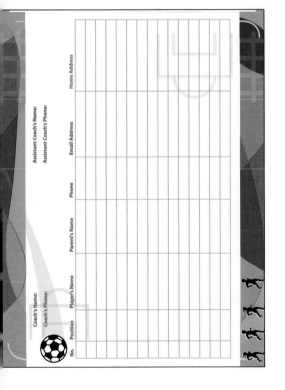

Materials Needed:

HP Bright White Inkjet paper

Instructions:

Edit the pdf file, then print it out. Or, if you'd like to print a blank roster and handwrite the information, highlight the editable text and delete.

Project 5: Editable Certificates

Make one for every player on the team!

Materials Needed:

HP Bright White Inkjet paper

Instructions:

1. If the pdf contains *Click Here to Edit* or similar instructions, edit the file on screen before printing, otherwise, go to step 2.
2. If you'd like to handwrite your certificates, just highlight the text in the pdf file and delete before printing.
3. Print pdf file. Let dry.

Note: Not all designs shown. There are boy and girl versions of each certificate pdf file on the CD.

The Sports Star

Is there a sports hero in your life? Give her or him some much-deserved credit with a sports-magazine picture frame. You can customize it to include your hero's stats!

Project 1: Sports Magazine Photo Frames

For the "professional" sports stars in your life.

Materials Needed:

Printable Magnetic Inkjet paper or card stock

Cutting mat, metal ruler, and X-ACTO knife

Photo

Instructions:

1. Customize and edit the frame before printing onto magnetic paper. Let dry.
2. Trim the white areas away from the frame, including the picture window.
3. If your frame is printed on card stock, tape your photo in place from the back.
4. If you printed the frame on magnetic paper, put your photo behind the frame and attach it to any suitable metal surface.

Note: See CD for additional frame designs.

printing projects

Chapter 4

CARDS & STATIONERY

Touch someone's heart with beautiful cards and stationery. Make these treasures right on your home printer!

CARDS & STATIONERY

Entertaining

Party on!

Invitations

Get creative and make your own invitations with your home printer. Here are a few of our ideas to get you started.

Project 1: Bridal Shower

I hear bells. Do you hear bells?

Materials Needed:

HP Matte Greeting Cards, 1/4-fold or 1/2-fold

Instructions:

1. If the pdf contains *Click Here to Edit* or similar instructions, edit the file on screen before printing, otherwise, go to step 2.
2. Set your print quality to *Best*.
3. Print a test invitation. If cropping occurs, select *Shrink to Fit*, and print again to ensure sizing.
4. Print your cards onto greeting card paper, and set them aside to dry completely.
5. Finish up by folding the cards in quarters or in half, depending on the layout.

Project 2: Baby Shower

First comes love, then comes marriage, then comes a baby in a baby carriage.

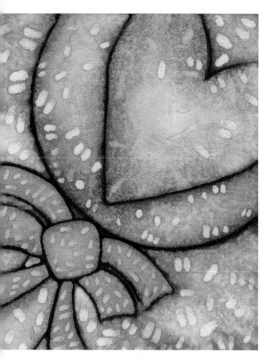

Materials Needed:

HP Matte Greeting Cards, 1/4-fold or 1/2-fold

Instructions:

1. If the pdf contains *Click Here to Edit* or similar instructions, edit the file on screen before printing, otherwise, go to step 2.
2. Set your print quality to *Best*.
3. Print a test invitation. If cropping occurs, select *Shrink to Fit*, and print again to ensure sizing.
4. Print your cards onto greeting card paper, and set them aside to dry completely.
5. Finish up by folding the cards in quarters or in half, depending on the layout.

Project 3: Kids' Party

The fun begins long before the party starts with these playful invites.

Note: See CD for pop-up invitation instructions.

Materials Needed:

HP Greeting Card paper, 1/4-fold or 1/2-fold

Instructions:

1. If the pdf contains *Click Here to Edit* or similar instructions, edit the file on screen before printing, otherwise, go to step 2.
2. Print a test of page 1. If cropping occurs, select *Shrink to Fit*, and print again to ensure sizing.
3. Print page 1 onto greeting-card paper, and leave it in the printer tray to dry.
4. Remove the printed page from the printer tray and, without turning the page over, return it to the loading tray.
5. Print page 2 and finish with a fold.

Baby Shower Party Kit

Fun games to play, guest lists and gift lists to keep you organized, and thank you notes to send afterwards. Oh baby!

Project 1: Memory Game

An easy and fun game for the group.

Materials Needed:

HP Bright White Inkjet paper

Pen

Instructions:

1. Print as many copies of the pdf file as needed. Let dry.
2. Instructions for game are at the top of the page. Enjoy!

Project 2: Unscramble the Word Game

Alphabet soup!

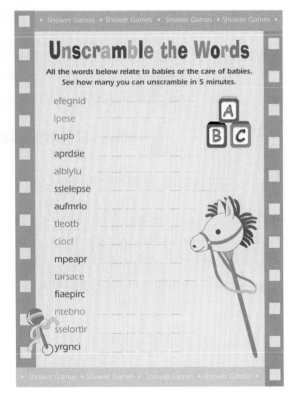

Materials Needed:

HP Bright White Inkjet paper

Pen

Instructions:

1. Print as many copies of the pdf file as needed. Let dry.
2. Instructions for game are at the top of the page. Enjoy!

Project 3: Guest List

Who's coming? Use this to keep track.

Materials Needed:

HP Bright White Inkjet paper

Pen

Instructions:

1. Print pdf file. Let dry.
2. Keep yourself organized and stress-free!

Project 4: Gift List

Organization help for the mom-to-be.

Materials Needed:

HP Bright White Inkjet paper

Pen

Instructions:

1. Print pdf file. Let dry.

2. Write in all the gifts received at the baby shower.

Project 5: Thank You Cards

A perfect ending…

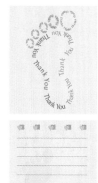 

Thank you!

printing projects

Materials Needed:

HP Greeting Cards, 1/4-fold

Instructions:

1. Print a test card. If cropping occurs, select *Shrink to Fit*, and print again to ensure sizing.

2. Print your cards onto greeting-card paper, and set aside to dry completely.

3. Finish up by folding the cards in quarters.

Fiesta Party Kit

Celebrate with a Mexican flair. This party kit includes everything you'll need for a great fiesta!

Project 1: Editable Invitations

Click, type, and print. As easy as flan.

Materials Needed:

HP Matte Greeting Card paper, 1/4-fold

Instructions:

1. If the pdf contains *Click Here to Edit* or similar instructions, edit the file on screen before printing, otherwise, go to step 2.
2. Set your print quality to *Best*.
3. Print a test invitation. If cropping occurs, select *Shrink to Fit*, and print again to ensure sizing.
4. Print your cards onto greeting-card paper, and set them aside to dry completely.
5. Finish up by folding the cards in quarters.

Project 2: 3D Centerpiece

Spice up the table with this decoration.

Materials Needed:

3 sheets HP Card or Cover stock

Scissors

Glue and double-sided tape

Instructions:

1. Print the centerpiece pdf onto three pieces of card stock. Set them aside to dry.
2. Cut out the pieces along the border.
3. Glue the front and back pieces of the cactus together.
4. Fold each triangular edge of the base piece up and together to form a pyramid.
5. Use the double-sided tape on the tabs of the base to hold the pyramid shape together.
6. Slide the cactus into the slit at the top of the pyramid.

Project 3: Editable Menu Cards

What's for dinner?

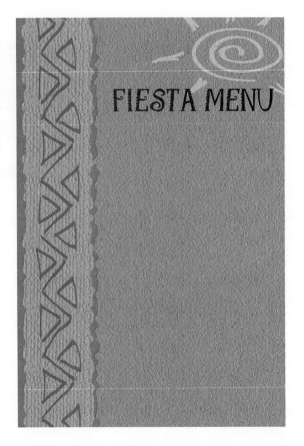

Materials Needed:

1 or more sheets HP Card or Cover stock

Cutting mat, metal ruler, and X-ACTO knife

Instructions:

1. Edit the menu cards on screen before printing. The type will repeat itself automatically in the second card.
2. Print the menu cards onto card stock, and set them aside to dry completely.
3. Trim away the white areas from each card.
4. Place a menu card at each table setting.

Project 4: Editable Place Cards

Fun and formal!

Materials Needed:

1 or more sheets HP Card or Cover stock

Cutting mat, metal ruler, and X-ACTO knife

Butter knife or scoring tool, spoon

Instructions:

1. Edit the cards on screen before printing.
2. Print the place cards onto card stock. Print one card for each guest, and set them aside to dry completely.
3. Score the cards with moderate pressure using the butter knife or scoring tool.
4. Trim away the white areas from each card.
5. With each place card face down, fold carefully along the scored edge. Crease the fold firmly with the back of a spoon.
6. Stand a place card at each person's plate.

printing projects

Project 5: Editable Table Tents

A fun and easy decoration for the table.

Materials Needed:

1 or more sheets HP Card or Cover stock

Cutting mat, metal ruler, and X-ACTO knife

Butter knife or scoring tool, spoon

Instructions:

1. Customize the table tents by typing your guests' names into the space provided. Or, to create a blank field, click on the text section to select it and then press delete.

2. Print the table tents on the card stock. Print as many as you need. There are four table tents per sheet. Let dry completely.

3. For easier folding, score the cards with moderate pressure using the butter knife or scoring tool.

4. Trim the white areas away from all the table tent pages.

5. With each place card face down, fold carefully along the scored edge. Crease the fold firmly with the back of a spoon.

Project 6: Fiesta Candle Lanterns

A glowing idea.

Materials Needed:

Vellum paper, 48 lb., clear

Cutting mat, metal ruler, and X-ACTO knife

Double-sided tape

Spoon

Glass candle holders and votive candles

Instructions:

1. Print out the lanterns on the vellum. Print as many as you like. For best results, manually feed one sheet of vellum at a time. Let dry.
2. For easier folding, score the lantern.
3. Trim the white areas away from all the lantern pages.
4. With the printed side facing down, fold carefully along the scored edges. Using the back of a spoon, press the fold firmly to crease.
5. Attach double-sided tape to the small fold on one side of the lantern. Press firmly to the other side of the lantern, creating a rectangular tube.
6. Light your votive candle and place the lantern around the candle.
7. Enjoy the glow!

Caution: Be sure to use votive candles in glass containers. Never leave the lanterns unattended. Keep out of the reach of children.

printing projects

Halloween Decorations

Calling all witches, goblins, ghosts and demons. These Halloween projects are guaranteed to raise your spirits. Throw a party and transform your home into a spooky haunted house!

Project 1: Spooky Music CD Labels

BOO! Spooky labels for your spooky sounds.

Materials Needed:

HP CD Label stock

Instructions:

Choose design. Print pdf file onto CD label stock. Let dry.

Project 2: Candy Bag Iron-Ons

Something for the sweet bag.

printing projects

Materials Needed:

HP Iron-On Transfer material

Scissors

Cotton pillowcase or tote bag

Instructions:

1. Print art pages onto iron-on material.

2. Trim around art, leaving 1/4" white space.

3. Follow instructions on transfer material box for ironing on your transfer.

Project 3: Costume Iron-Ons

A fun, fast costume for the little ones.

Materials Needed:

HP Iron-On Transfer material

Scissors

Cotton T-shirt

Instructions:

1. Print art from pdf files onto transfer material. Let dry.
2. Trim all the way around design, leaving 1/4" white space.
3. Follow iron-on transfer directions and iron design onto T-shirt or other material.

Project 4: Stickers

Stick some Halloween flavor anywhere.

Materials Needed:

Full Sheet Label stock

Scissors

Instructions:

1. Print pdf file onto label stock. Let dry.

2. Trim out and apply where desired.

printing projects

Project 5: Window Clings

Spooky from the outside...

Materials Needed:

Window decal material

Scissors

Instructions:

1. Print pdf file. Let dry.

2. Adhere to window.

Warning: Be sure to use materials designed specifically for your printer. To prevent damage, use window decals specifically designed for laser printers or printers that use heat to fuse the ink.

New Year's Decorations

Uncork the New Year right with lots of fun and easy printable projects!

Project 1: Editable Bottle Label

Cheers!

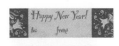

Materials Needed:

Full Sheet Label stock

Scissors or X-ACTO knife

Instructions:

1. If the pdf contains *Click Here to Edit* or similar instructions, edit the file on screen before printing, otherwise, go to step 2.

2. Print pdf file. Trim white areas away from art.

3. Apply to bottle and give to friends.

printing projects

Project 2: Balloon Danglers

Accessories even for balloons!

Materials Needed:

HP Bright White Inkjet paper

Scissors and glue

String and balloons

Instructions:

1. Print pdf file. Let dry.

2. Trim around outside edges.

3. Fold along center line.

4. Glue together and punch hole in top.

5. Tie balloon string to the top hole.

Project 3: Magnetic Resolutions

Fun, fun, fun!

Materials Needed:

Printable Magnetic Inkjet paper

Scissors

Instructions:

1. Print the artwork onto the magnetic sheets. Let dry.
2. Cut out each magnet as indicated.

Project 4: Masks

Masterfully mysterious!

Materials Needed:

HP Card or Cover stock

Scissors or X-ACTO knife

Ribbon, elastic cord, or wooden dowel

Hole punch

Instructions:

1. Choose design and print pdf file. Let dry.
2. Trim around outside of mask (including eyeholes).
3. Cut small holes on sides with hole punch.
4. Attach a string or elastic cord to side holes. Or, attach a wooden dowel to one side.

Project 5: Coasters
No party fouls in your house!

Materials Needed:
HP Bright White Inkjet paper

Scissors

Cardboard

Self-laminating sheets

Instructions:
1. Print on inkjet paper. Let dry.
2. Glue to cardboard and trim.
3. Laminate coasters to protect ink from spills and condensation.

printing projects

Correspondence

Everything's nicer when you use the write stuff!

printing projects

Stationery

With our colorful stationery and notes, you'll have lots to choose from to keep your pen pal interested.

Project 1: Fishing Stationery

Cast your every thought onto paper.

Materials Needed:

HP Bright White Inkjet paper

Instructions:

Print as many copies of the pdf file as desired. Let dry.

Project 2: Fishing Notes

Jot one on the fly.

Materials Needed:

HP Bright White Inkjet paper

Cutting mat, metal ruler, and X-ACTO knife

Instructions:

1. Print as many copies of the pdf file as you want. Let dry.
2. Art is set up 2 per sheet. Trim each page in half so the final size is 5-1/2" x 8-1/2".

printing projects

Project 3: Golf Stationery

A birdie told me to drop you a line.

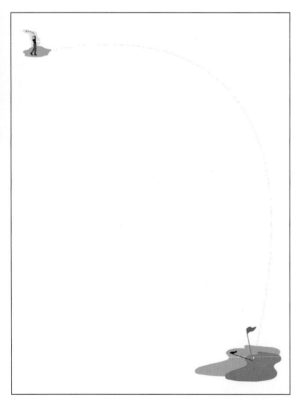

Materials Needed:

HP Bright White Inkjet paper

Instructions:

1. Print pdf file. Let dry.

2. Tell 'em about your last score.

Project 4: Golf Notes

Jot it down beFORE you forget it.

Materials Needed:

HP Bright White Inkjet paper

Cutting mat, metal ruler, and X-ACTO knife

Instructions:

1. Print as many copies of the pdf file as you want. Let dry.

2. Art is set up 2 per sheet. Trim each page in half so the final size is 5-1/2" x 8-1/2".

printing projects

Project 5: Nature Stationery
Bug someone with a letter on this.

Materials Needed:

HP Bright White Inkjet paper

Instructions:

1. Choose design and print pdf file. Let dry.
2. Write away.

Greeting Cards

Whether you want to say "thanks,"
"I miss you," "get well," or "happy birthday,"
these beautifully designed cards are the
perfect way to send your thoughts.

Project 1: Birthday Cards

Print one for a friend or family member.

Materials Needed:

HP Greeting Card paper, 1/4-fold or 1/2-fold
(ivory or white, matte or glossy)

See Greeting Card Instructions on page 139

*Note: Not all birthday cards shown. See CD for
additional designs.*

printing projects

Project 2: All-Occasion Cards

They're blank inside, awaiting your message.

Materials Needed:

HP Greeting Card paper, 1/4-fold or 1/2-fold
(ivory or white, matte or glossy)

See Greeting Card Instructions on page 139

Note: Not all cards shown. See CD for additional designs.

The following instructions are for HP color inkjet printers, which load from the front. If your printer loads from the back, please consult your printer's user guide. Try printing a test page before using the HP Greeting Card paper.

Greeting Card Instructions:

half-page card

1. Place a sheet of 1/2-fold HP Greeting Card paper (glossy or matte) in your printer tray, glossy/matte side down.
2. Set your printer to *Best* quality.
3. Print page, let dry, and fold in half. (If cropping occurs, select *Shrink to Fit* and reprint.)

quarter-page card

1. Place a sheet of 1/4-fold HP Greeting Card paper (glossy or matte) in your printer tray, glossy/matte side down.
2. Set your printer to *Best* quality.
3. Print page, let dry, and fold in quarters. (If cropping occurs, select *Shrink to Fit* and reprint.)

postcards or 1-panel cards

1. Place a sheet of HP Greeting Card paper (glossy or matte) in your printer tray.
2. Set your printer to *Best* quality.
3. Print the page. (If cropping occurs, select *Shrink to Fit* and reprint.)
4. Cut out card sections.

printing projects

Chapter 5

HOLIDAYS & EVENTS

Need a reason to celebrate?
Make one of these delightful projects
and you'll be jumping for joy!

Holidays & Events

Winter

Wrap up your winter wonderland!

printing projects

Christmas

Choose from a wide variety of holiday cards to send to friends and family.

Project 1: Christmas Cards

Spread some good cheer!

Materials Needed:

HP Greeting Card paper (1/2-fold or 1/4-fold)

See Greeting Card Instructions on page 139

Note: Not all Christmas cards shown. See CD for additional designs.

CHAPTER 5 HOLIDAYS & EVENTS / Winter

Hanukkah

Spice up your holiday mailings with customizable labels and cards made from the heart. They'll make every package and envelope sparkle with holiday cheer!

Project 1: Hanukkah Cards

Bring smiles to your friends and loved ones.

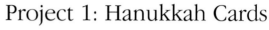

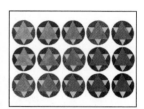

Materials Needed:

HP Greeting Card paper (1/2-fold or 1/4-fold)

See Greeting Card Instructions on page 139

printing projects

Project 2: Hanukkah Address Labels

To you.

Materials Needed:

Avery White Address Labels (#8162)

Instructions:

1. Customize your address labels before printing or delete to make blank.
2. Print pdf file. Let dry.
3. Use them for all your mailings.

Project 3: Hanukkah Return Labels

From me.

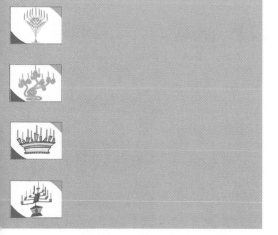

printing projects

Materials Needed:

Avery White Return Address Labels (#8167)

Instructions:

1. Customize your labels before printing. You only need to type it in once, and the rest of the fields will automatically duplicate.
2. Print pdf file. Let dry.
3. Use them for all your mailings.

Project 4: Hanukkah Shipping Labels

Special delivery with sparkle!

Materials Needed:

Avery White Shipping Labels (#8463)

Instructions:

1. Customize your shipping labels before printing, or delete to make blank.
2. Print pdf file on label paper. Let dry.
3. Use them for all your mailings.

Hint: Try using these as customized gift tags.

Kwanzaa

So festive! Bring vibrant colors to all of your gifts with these cute boxes.

Project 1: Gift Boxes

Make them cheer with joy.

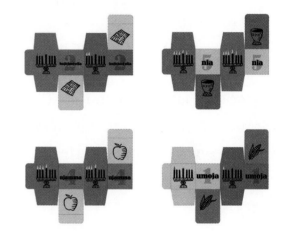

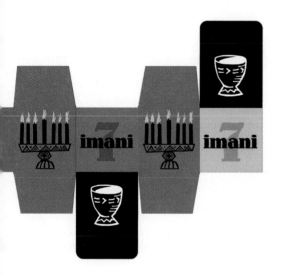

Materials Needed:

HP Card or Cover stock

Cutting mat, metal ruler, and X-ACTO knife

Glue or double-sided tape

Instructions:

1. Print pdf file on card stock. Let dry.
2. Cut out box around outside edges.
3. Fold along lines where indicated.
4. Apply glue or double-sided tape where indicated.

Tip: To make folding easier, score along lines with butter knife or scoring tool first. Not all boxes shown. See CD for additional designs.

printing projects

New Year's Supper Club Kit

If you're planning to host a dinner party, you can turn it into a truly festive affair. Here are some matching favors that will help you create a gathering to remember. Whether it's wine and cheese or a full buffet, your efforts will surely have them coming back for seconds.

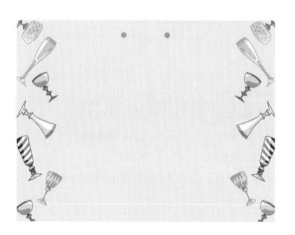

Project 1: Editable Invitation

This will get everyone in the mood.

Materials Needed:

1 or more sheets HP Card or Cover stock

1 or more sheets vellum paper, 48 lb., clear

Cutting mat, metal ruler, and X-ACTO knife

1/8" hole punch and scissors

Ribbon 1/4" wide (4" lengths)

A-7 envelopes (5-1/4" x 7-1/4")

Instructions:

1. Customize page 1 of the pdf (it will repeat automatically). Print on vellum and let dry. Print as many as you need (2 to a page).
2. Print page 2 onto card stock. Print the same number of sheets as page 1.
3. Trim white areas away from vellum.
4. Trim white areas away from card stock.
5. With the vellum and card stock face-up, center the vellum over the card stock piece.
6. Holding the two together, punch out the two gray dots at the top.
7. Cut the ribbon into 4" lengths (one for each invitation).
8. Thread ribbon through holes or tie a bow in front to hold the two pieces together.

Project 2: Editable Place Cards

Guests will feel special when they see their names on these cards.

Materials Needed:

1 or more sheets HP Card or Cover stock

Cutting mat, metal ruler, and X-ACTO knife

Scoring tool or butter knife

Spoon

Instructions:

1. Customize the cards before printing, or delete the fields to make them blank.
2. Print as many cards as you need. There are 4 cards per sheet. Let dry.
3. For easier folding, score the place cards. To do this, lay a ruler along each set of dotted lines and run a scoring tool along the ruler. Use medium pressure to make an indentation in the paper.
4. Trim away all white areas.
5. With each card face down, fold along the scored edge. Crease with the back of a spoon.
6. Stand the place cards at each person's plate.

printing projects

Project 3: Editable Menu Cards

Your carefully planned dinner will have a place of honor here.

Materials Needed:

1 or more sheets of HP Card or Cover stock

Cutting mat, metal ruler, and X-ACTO knife

Instructions:

1. Customize the menu card by typing your dinner menu in the first card. It will repeat itself automatically in the second card.
2. Print the menu cards on card stock. Print as many as you need (there are 2 cards per page). Let dry.
3. Trim away white areas from each page.
4. Place a menu card at each table setting.

Project 4: Glass Charms

Always know which drink is yours with these gorgeous, customizable glass charms.

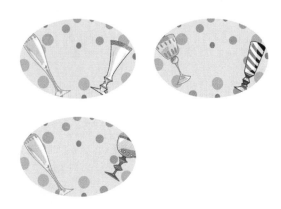

Materials Needed:

1 or more sheets vellum paper, 48 lb., clear

Scissors

Hole punch

Ribbon 1/4" wide (5" lengths)

Instructions:

1. Customize the charms before printing.

2. Print as many charms as you need on the vellum paper. There are 28 charms per sheet. For best results, manually feed one piece of vellum at a time. Let dry.

3. Using scissors, cut out each glass charm.

4. Punch a hole in the gray dot on each charm.

5. Cut 5" lengths of ribbon for each. Slip one end through the hole and attach each charm by tying a bow around the stem of the glass.

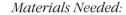

printing projects

Project 5: Lanterns

Light up the night like never before.

Materials Needed:

1 or more sheets of vellum paper, 48 lb., clear

Cutting mat, metal ruler, and X-ACTO knife

Double-sided tape

Spoon

Glass candle holders and votive candles

Instructions:

1. Print pdf file on the vellum. Print as many as you like. Print all three sizes or any combination. For best results, manually feed one sheet at a time. Let dry.

2. Score the lantern where indicated.

3. Trim away white areas from all pages.

4. With the printed side facing down, fold carefully along the scored edges. Crease with the back of a spoon.

5. Attach double-sided tape to the small fold on one side of the lantern. Press firmly to the other side, creating a rectangular tube.

6. Light your votive candles and place the lantern around the candle.

7. Enjoy the glow!

Caution: Be sure to use votive candles in glass containers. Never leave the lanterns unattended. Keep them out of the reach of children.

Project 6: Napkin Rings

Fold your elegant napkins in style.

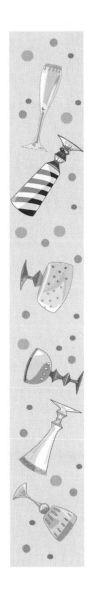

printing projects

Materials Needed:

1 or more sheets of vellum paper, 48 lb., clear

Cutting mat, metal ruler, and X-ACTO knife

Double-sided tape

Instructions:

1. Print as many napkin rings as you need on the vellum. Manually feed one sheet of vellum at a time. Let dry completely.
2. Trim away all white areas.
3. Wrap the napkin ring around a napkin.
4. Use the double-sided tape to attach both ends of the napkin ring together.
5. Set an elegant table for your guests.

Valentine Wrap Sets

Be still my heart!

Time to share the love.

Project 1: Wrapping Paper

Special paper for small, special packages.

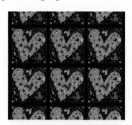

Materials Needed:

HP Bright White Inkjet paper

Instructions:

1. Print as many pages of wrapping paper as you like. Let dry completely.

2. Wrap up something special.

Tip: You can also use the wrapping paper for fun background paper in a scrapbook or journal.

Project 2: Gift Bags

Something for your sweetie.

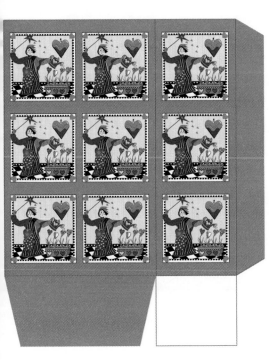

Materials Needed:

HP Card or Cover stock

Cutting mat, metal ruler, and X-ACTO knife

Double-sided tape

Scoring tool and spoon

Instructions:

1. Print two copies of pdf file. Let dry.

2. Trim around the outside edges.

3. Score and fold along all solid lines.

4. Glue the two sides together where indicated.

5. Fold in the white flap at bottom.

6. Fold in large flaps, gluing the back of the last one to seal the bottom of the bag.

printing projects

Project 3: Gift Tags

With hugs and kisses.

Materials Needed:

HP Card or Cover stock

Cutting mat, metal ruler, and X-ACTO knife

Scoring tool

Instructions:

1. Print pdf file on card stock. There are 2 cards to a page. Let dry.
2. Score where indicated.
3. Trim around outside of cards.
4. Fold in half and write your message.
5. Slip on top of a package or in a gift bag.

Project 4: Gift Boxes

Good things come in small packages.

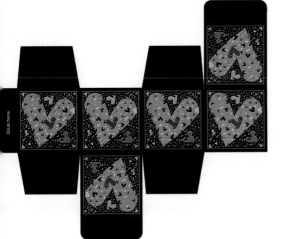

Materials Needed:

HP Card or Cover stock

Cutting mat, metal ruler, and X-ACTO knife

Scoring tool

Double-sided tape or glue

Instructions:

1. Print pdf file on card stock. Let dry.
2. Trim around outside edges.
3. Score and fold along lines where indicated.
4. Apply glue or double-sided tape where indicated.

printing projects

Spring

Colorful celebration goodies galore!

printing projects

St. Patrick's Day Tableware

It's our lucky day! Now you can share the magic with all of your visiting leprechauns.

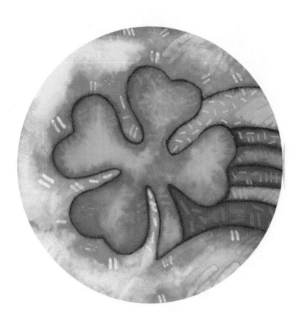

Project 1: Coasters

For your lucky lager.

Materials Needed:

HP Bright White Inkjet paper

Scissors

Self-laminating sheets

Instructions:

1. Print on inkjet paper. Let dry.
2. Cover with self-laminating sheets to protect ink from spills.
3. Glue paper to cardboard.
4. Cut out each coaster.

Note: Not all coasters shown. See CD for additional designs.

Project 2: Cup Wrappers

Make 'em festive.

Materials Needed:

HP Bright White Inkjet paper

Scissors

Tape

Instructions:

1. If the pdf contains *Click Here to Edit* or similar instructions, edit the file on screen before printing, otherwise, go to step 2.

2. Cut out artwork.

3. Tape ends together to form a circle.

Easter Decorations

The traditional egg hunt. The chance to wear your new bonnet. There is nothing like Easter. Here are some projects to boost up the fun level.

Project 1: Easter Stickers

A decorating shortcut to beautiful Easter eggs.

Materials Needed:

Full Sheet Label stock

Scissors

Instructions:

1. Print pdf file onto label stock. Let dry.
2. Cut out desired design and place on eggs or Easter baskets—anywhere you want a little color.

Note: Not all sticker designs shown. See CD for additional pdf files.

Project 2: Egg Dress-Up Kit

Your eggs can be works of art too.

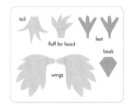

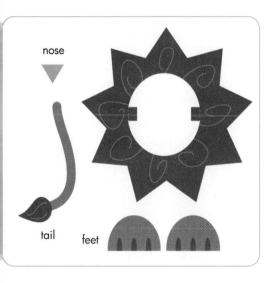

Materials Needed:

5 or more dyed eggs

2 or more sheets of card stock

Cutting mat, metal ruler, and X-ACTO knife

Butter knife or scoring tool

Pencil

Small hot-glue gun

Embellishments such as google-eyes, yarn

Tweezers (to hold small objects while gluing)

Instructions:

1. Print the egg decorations and stands onto card stock. Set aside to dry completely.
2. For easier folding, score all the tabs.
3. Trim the white areas away from all the decorations and stands.
4. Apply a small bead of glue to one end of an egg stand and connect the ends to form a ring.
5. Apply a dot of glue to your egg and then quickly add your decoration.

Note: Not all designs shown. See CD for additional pdf files.

printing projects

Project 3: Spring Pinwheels

Spring into breezy weather with these
colorful pinwheels.

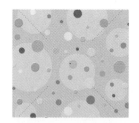

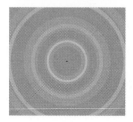

Materials Needed:

HP Premium Inkjet paper

Cutting mat, metal ruler, and X-ACTO knife

White craft glue

Wooden dowels

Push pins and straight pins

Spray adhesive and newspaper

Instructions:

1. Print pdf files. Let dry.

2. Cut out the squares.

3. Place squares face down on newspaper.
   Spray the backs with adhesive and let dry.

4. Place one square on top of the other. Line
   up edges and press firmly into place.

5. Cut along dotted lines to make spokes.

6. See CD for instructions to attach to dowel.

Earth Day

Every day is Earth Day!

In all things of nature there is something of the marvelous.

Aristotle

Project 1: Iron-Ons

Plant a tree and design a T-shirt!

Materials Needed:

HP Iron-On Transfer paper

Scissors

Iron and cotton T-shirt

Instructions:

1. Print pdf file onto transfer paper. Let dry.
2. Trim around design, leaving 1/4" white space.
3. Follow iron-on transfer box instructions for adhering to T-shirt.

Warning: Do not use iron-on transfer material with any laser printer or printer that uses heat to fuse the ink. It may melt the material and damage the printer.

printing projects

Cinco De Mayo

Celebrate this special day in style with our festive decorations.

Project 1: 3D Flowers

Accent walls, windows, and senoritas' hair!

Materials Needed:

HP Bright White Inkjet paper

Scissors

Glue or double-sided tape

Instructions:

1. Print one sheet for each flower you wish to make. Let dry.
2. Cut out all petals, leaves, and center.
3. Glue or tape petal to itself where indicated.
4. Arrange four petals on a table or other flat surface, and then tape the petals together at the points in the center.
5. Repeat step 4 for the other four petals.
6. Put the second group of four petals on top of the first group and attach.
7. Attach the center to the assembled flower petals.
8. Attach the leaves to the outside of the assembled flowers. Be artistic!

Project 2: Flags

For the fiesta.

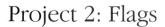

Materials Needed:

HP Premium Inkjet paper

Self-laminating sheets

Instructions:

1. Print as many copies of the pdf files as you like. Let dry.
2. Laminate flags to protect ink before using outside.
3. Decorate and use as is, or paste them back to back and attach wooden dowels to the side to make mini flagpoles.

printing projects

Mother's Day Gift Set

The colorful flowers adorning these items are sure to put a smile on Mom's face.

Project 1: Editable Card

So perfect.

Materials Needed:

HP Greeting Card paper, 1/2-fold

Instructions:

1. If the pdf contains *Click Here to Edit* or similar instructions, edit the file on screen before printing, otherwise, go to step 2.
2. Set your print quality to *Best*.
3. Print a test of page 1. If cropping occurs, select *Shrink to Fit*, and print again to ensure sizing.
4. Print page 1 onto greeting card paper, and leave it in the printer tray to dry completely.
5. Remove the printed page from the printer tray and, without turning the page over, return it to the loading tray.
6. Print page 2 and finish with a fold.

Project 2: Magnets

Attractive statements for Mom.

Materials Needed:

Printable Magnetic Inkjet paper

Cutting mat, metal ruler, and X-ACTO knife

Instructions:

1. Print the artwork onto the magnetic sheets. Let dry.
2. Cut out each magnet as indicated.

printing projects

Project 3: Photo Frame

Say cheese!

Materials Needed:

1 or more sheets of HP Card stock or Printable Magnetic paper

Cutting mat, metal ruler, and X-ACTO knife

Instructions:

1. Print the frame onto card stock or magnetic paper. Let dry.
2. Trim the white areas away from the frame, including the picture window.
3. If your frame is printed on card stock, tape your photo in place from the back.
4. If you printed the frame on magnetic paper, put your photo behind the frame and attach it to any suitable metal surface.

Project 4: Gift Tags

A snazzy topping to a gift.

printing projects

Materials Needed:

HP Card or Cover stock

Cutting mat, metal ruler, and X-ACTO knife

Instructions:

1. Choose design and print pdf file. Let dry.

2. Trim where indicated.

3. Write your message and attach to gift.

Hint: You can either fold these cards in half or leave them flat. Punch a hole in the card and tie to your package with ribbon or raffia.

Project 5: World's Best Mom T-Shirt Iron-On

Show the world she's the best.

Materials Needed:

HP Inkjet Iron-On Transfer material

Scissors

Iron and cotton T-shirt

Instructions:

1. Print pdf file onto transfer paper. Let dry.

2. Trim around design, leaving 1/4" white space.

3. Follow iron-on transfer box instructions for adhering to T-shirt.

Warning: Do not use iron-on transfer material with any laser printer or printer that uses heat to fuse the ink. It may melt the material and damage the printer.

Graduation

All the exciting parties and events at graduation can be remembered with this lovely keepsake.

Project 1: Gatherings Book

Gather friends…gather memories.

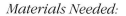

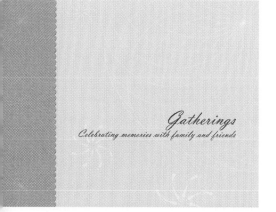

Materials Needed:

11 sheets of card stock

1 sheet of vellum paper, 48 lb., clear

Double-sided tape

Cutting mat, metal ruler, and X-ACTO knife

Butter knife or scoring tool

Spoon

Ribbon, 1" wide, 1-1/2 yards

Scissors

Photos

See Instructions on page 176

printing projects

Gatherings Book

(continued)

Cover and Spine PDF Instructions:

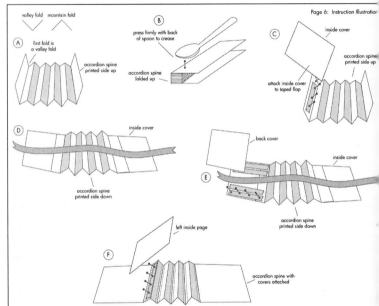

1. Print the book cover (pgs. 1–3 of pdf) onto card stock. Print page 3 twice. Let dry.
2. Trim the white areas away from covers.
3. Print the accordion spine (pg. 4 of pdf) onto the card stock. Let dry.
4. For easier folding, score the accordion spine. There are 9 lines to score.
5. With the accordion spine printed side up, fold up the first tab that is marked *tape inside cover*. Continue folding the scored lines back and forth. See illustration A.
6. Using the back of a spoon, press the folds firmly to crease. See illustration B.
7. Unfold the spine with printed side up. Place double-sided tape along the left tab marked *tape inside cover*. Attach one of the inside covers on the tape, carefully aligning the edge of the cover with the crease in the spine. Press firmly in place. See illustration C.
8. Repeat step 7 with the right tab and inside cover.
9. Flip the spine over, printed side down, and center the ribbon across the inside covers and spine. See illustration D.
10. Apply double-sided tape to the back of the inside cover on the left, leaving the area around the ribbon free from tape. See illustration E.
11. Place the back cover on top, aligning the purple band with the edge of the spine. Make sure the ribbon does not get stuck to the tape.

Gatherings Book

Instructions (continued):

12. Repeat steps 10 and 11 to attach the front cover.

Inside Pages PDF Instructions:

1. Print the inside pages (pgs. 1–6) onto card stock. Print pages 3 and 4 twice. Let dry.
2. Trim the white areas away from the inside pages. Keep the pages stacked in this order: 3, 1, 2, 5, 6, 4.
3. Place the spine, with covers attached, face up. Place double-sided tape on the left side of the first accordion peak where indicated. Attach the first left page from the stack, aligning the edge of the inside page with the white dotted line along the accordion peak. See illustration F.
4. Repeat step 3 for the next page by placing tape along the right side of the accordion peak. In addition, apply tape to the back of the left inside page to secure the pages together.

5. Attach the first right page from the stack, aligning the edge of the inside page with the white dotted line along the accordion peak. Press pages together firmly.
6. Continue attaching the rest of the inside pages by repeating steps 3 and 4.
7. Once complete, place your book out for family and friends to share their thoughts and memories.

Photo Corners Instructions:

1. Print the photo corners (pg. 5 of the cover pdf) onto the vellum paper. Let dry.
2. Trim the white areas away from art.
3. Make a slit along the dark line in each.
4. Slip one photo corner onto each corner of your picture.
5. Apply double-sided tape to the photo corners on the picture. Carefully place the picture and press the corners firmly.

Note: Instructions and full-size illustrated instruction diagram are on the CD.

printing projects

Father's Day Gift Set

Show your dad how much you love him with projects from this sophisticated-looking Father's Day kit.

Project 1: Greatest Dad Award

Show him he's special.

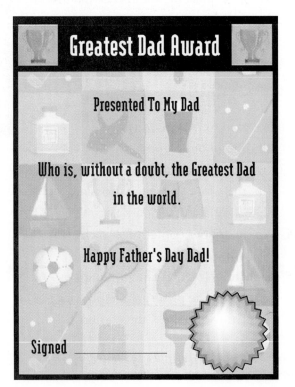

Materials Needed:

HP Premium Inkjet paper

Instructions:

1. After customizing your certificate, print your project. Let dry.
2. Present to your greatest dad.

Project 2: Greatest Dad Card

Let him know how important he is.

Materials Needed:

HP Greeting Card paper, ivory, 1/2-fold

Instructions:

1. Edit the pdf on the screen before printing. Or, delete the sample text to make blank.
2. Set your print quality to *Best*.
3. Print a test of page 1. If cropping occurs, select *Shrink to Fit*, and print again to ensure sizing.
4. Print page 1 onto greeting card paper, and leave it in the printer tray to dry.
5. Remove the printed page from the printer tray and, without turning the page over, return it to the loading tray.
6. Print page 2 and finish with a fold.

printing projects

Project 3: Greatest Dad Photo Frame

Just the two of you...

Materials Needed:

Printable Magnetic Inkjet paper or HP Card or Cover stock

Cutting mat, metal ruler, and X-ACTO knife

Photo

Instructions:

1. Print the frame onto magnetic paper or card stock. Let dry.
2. Trim the white areas away from the frame, including the picture window.
3. If your frame is printed on magnetic paper, put your photo behind the frame and attach it to any suitable metal surface.
4. If your frame is printed on card stock, tape your photo in place from the back.

Project 4: Magnets

Remind him everyday!

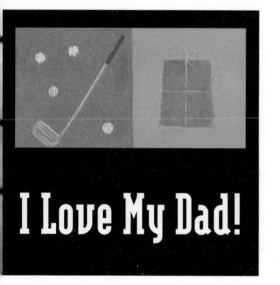

Materials Needed:

Printable Magnetic Inkjet paper

Cutting mat, metal ruler, and X-ACTO knife

Instructions:

1. Print the artwork onto the magnetic sheets. Let dry.
2. Cut out each magnet as indicated.

printing projects

Summer

Sunshine, lollipops, and rainbows everywhere!

printing projects

Lemonade Stand Kit

Hot off the press! Ice cold lemonade signs and banners!

Project 1: Signs

For the junior entrepreneur.

Materials Needed:

HP Bright White Inkjet paper

Instructions:

1. Print pdf files.
2. Hang them around the neighborhood and sell, sell, sell.

Project 2: Banner

This banner makes a statement.

Materials Needed:

HP Banner paper

HP Bright White Inkjet paper (optional)

Instructions:

1. Follow printer set-up instructions on the back of the HP Banner paper box.
2. Insert a four-sheet length of banner paper into the printer, with the top cut edge pointing toward the printer.
3. Open the banner pdf file on your screen. In the File menu, select *Print Setup*.
4. In Print Setup, select the *Properties* button.
5. In Properties, select the section on *Paper*.
6. In Paper, make sure *Banner* is selected under Paper Type. Click OK.
7. Click OK again to close the other window.
8. Print pages 2 to 5 of pdf file.

Option: If not using banner paper, print pages 2 to 5 of pdf on regular paper and tape pages together. You may need to trim edges and overlap the pages slightly to prevent gaps from showing.

printing projects

Fourth of July Decorations

Make some sparks at your next event. From T-shirts to string light covers, these projects are red hot and cool!

Project 1: Waving Flag T-Shirt Iron-On

Pledge allegiance to style with a design that explodes with color.

julyfourth

Materials Needed:

HP Inkjet Iron-On Transfer material

Scissors

Cotton T-shirt

Iron

Instructions:

1. Print pdf file onto transfer paper. Let dry.
2. Trim around design, leaving 1/4" white space.
3. Follow iron-on transfer box instructions for adhering to T-shirt.

Warning: Do not use iron-on transfer material with any laser printer or printer that uses heat to fuse the ink. It may melt the material and damage the printer.

Project 2: Pinwheels

Mix and match the patterns to make these festive favors.

printing projects

Materials Needed:

HP Premium Inkjet paper

Cutting mat, metal ruler, and X-ACTO knife

White craft glue

Wooden dowels

Push pins and straight pins

Spray adhesive and newspaper

Instructions:

1. Print pdf files. Let dry.

2. Cut out the squares.

3. Place squares face down on newspaper. Spray the backs with adhesive and let dry.

4. Place one square on top of the other. Line up edges and press firmly into place.

5. Cut along dotted lines to make spokes.

6. See CD for instructions to attach to dowel.

Project 3: Luminaria

Perfect for illuminating outdoor fun until the twilights last gleaming.

Materials Needed:

Lunch bags (brown or white)

Scissors

Glass candle holders and votive candles

Instructions:

1. Place a standard lunch bag (bottom flap down) on a piece of 8-1/2" x 11" paper.
2. Tape the top (open) edge of the brown bag to the top edge of the paper.
3. To print, manually feed the bag and paper into the printer with the bag side facing down. Set aside to dry completely.
4. Trim along top edge of artwork to create an interesting shape.
5. Put some sand inside the bag for weight.
6. Place a small candle in a glass holder inside the bag. Enjoy!

Caution: Be sure to use votive candles in glass containers. Never leave the luminaria bags unattended. Keep out of the reach of children.

Project 4: Table Tents

Great way to label Aunt Margo's potato salad at your next family reunion or potluck.

Materials Needed:

1 or more sheets of card stock

Cutting mat, metal ruler, and X-ACTO knife

Scoring tool or butter knife

Spoon

Instructions:

1. Customize the table tents before printing. Type your guests' names or menu items.
2. Print as many table tents on the card stock as you need. There are 4 to a sheet. Let dry.
3. For easier folding, score the table tents. To do this, lay a ruler along each set of dotted lines and, with medium pressure, run a butter knife or scoring tool along the ruler.
4. Trim the white areas away from all pages.
5. With each place card face down, fold carefully along the scored edge. Using the back of a spoon, press the fold firmly to crease.

printing projects

Project 5: String Lights

String them anywhere you want the soft glow of stars and stripes.

Materials Needed:

8 or more sheets of vellum paper, 48 lb., clear

Cutting mat, metal ruler, and X-ACTO knife

Tape

Butter knife or scoring tool

String of Christmas lights (white or green)

Instructions:

1. Print the art on vellum. Manually feed one piece at a time. There are 2 light covers per page. Let dry.
2. Score the covers where indicated.
3. Cut out the two light holes on each cover.
4. Cut along the slit where indicated.
5. Cut around outside edge of each light cover.
6. With art facing down, fold along scored lines.
7. Holding the light bulb facing the ground, take the short tab and slip over the bulb.
8. Fold the square in half, bringing the long tab over the wire towards you. Insert this tab into the slit. The entire length of the tab should be in the slit. Then fit the light hole from the long tab over the bulb on the interior of the light cover.
9. Bend and tape the top part of the long tab to the inside of the light cover. Secure in place with tape.
10. Plug in your lights.

Summer Grilling

The lazy days are upon us, which means it's time for that traditional rite of summer—barbecue. Kick off the grilling season in style!

Project 1: Apron Iron-On

Grill chefs will love this smokin' apron design.

Materials Needed:

HP Inkjet Iron-On Transfer material

Scissors

Cotton apron

Iron

Instructions:

1. Print pdf file onto transfer paper. Let dry.
2. Trim around design, leaving 1/4" white space.
3. Follow iron-on transfer box instructions for adhering to apron front.

Warning: Do not use iron-on transfer material with any laser printer or printer that uses heat to fuse the ink. It may melt the material and damage the printer.

printing projects

Project 2: Customizable Sauce Label

Whatever the ingredients, our red-hot label design will add zest to your special blend.

Materials Needed:

Full Sheet White Sticker paper

Cutting mat, metal ruler, and X-ACTO knife

Glass jar

Instructions:

1. Customize the labels by adding your name, sauce type, and date where indicated in the pdf file.
2. Print art onto sticker paper and let dry.
3. Cut out along the label edge.
4. Apply to the jar and give to friends and family.

Hint: To remove a label from a jar, simply soak in warm, soapy water.

Project 3: Recipe Cards

Customizable or with blank lines. Hot, hot, hot!

Materials Needed:

HP Card or Cover stock

Cutting mat, metal ruler, and X-ACTO knife

Self-laminating sheets (optional)

Instructions:

1. If the pdf contains *Click Here to Edit* or similar instructions, edit the file on screen before printing, otherwise, go to step 2.
2. Trim recipe cards where indicated.
3. Share your secrets with friends and family.

Hint: Store recipe cards in plastic sleeves or cover them with self-laminating sheets to protect from kitchen spills.

Fall

Back to school, and back to the kitchen!

printing projects

Tabletop Football

Play the classic tabletop football game using these printable football and goalpost projects.

Project 1: Football and Goalpost

Time for kick off!

Materials Needed:

HP Bright White Inkjet paper

Tape or glue

Cutting mat, metal ruler, and X-ACTO knife

Instructions:

1. Print one copy of football page. Let dry.
2. Cut out design along the outside black lines.
3. Fold in a triangular pattern five times (use the two black lines at the bottom as a starting point).
4. On the sixth fold, make a smaller triangular fold.
5. On the seventh fold, tuck the flap into the "pocket."
6. The "laces" should appear on either side.
7. Print two copies of goalpost page. Let dry.
8. Cut out both goalposts along outside edge.
9. Fold all of the white tabs back.
10. Fold along the black lines (on green rectangles) to form base.
11. Fold green base up and attach to pole.
12. Align the goalposts back to back and glue or tape matching tabs together.

Project 1: How to Play
(continued)

How to Play:

1. Find a flat, square-edge tabletop about two feet wide (like the school cafeteria kind), and have the players sit across the table from each other.

2. To kick off, use one finger to prop the paper football up on one point. Position the ball on the table near the edge you're kicking from. Use a strong finger-flick to "kick" the ball, trying to get it to land as far across the table as you can. If the ball goes over the opposite edge, it's a touchback and the other player gets the ball at his or her "20-yard line."

3. At the kickoff, if the ball lands hanging over the edge (in touchdown position) of the opposite side of the table, it's a safety. The kicker gets two points. The other player now has to kick off.

4. The player in control of the ball gets two flicks (also called downs) to try to score a touchdown. A touchdown is scored when you get the ball to hang over the other side of the table without falling off. Each time you flick the football, it's a "down."

5. If the ball falls off the edge of the table during a down, the opposing player gets the ball at his or her 20-yard line.

6. After a touchdown, have the opposing player try to flick the ball through the goalpost.

7. After a touchdown, a player can choose to "go for two" instead of kicking a field goal. In this case, the ball is placed on the 20-yard line near the other player's side of the table. If the player gets the ball to hang over the edge in a touchdown position in one flick, he or she gets two points.

Back to School

Help keep your student organized and in style with these binder covers that are both cool and functional.

Project 1: Binder Covers

Too cool for school!

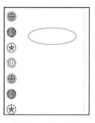 

Materials Needed:

HP Bright White Inkjet paper

3-ring binder with clear cover

Instructions:

1. If the pdf contains *Click Here to Edit* or similar instructions, edit the file on screen before printing, otherwise, go to step 2.
2. Print pdf file. Let dry.
3. Slide art under clear binder cover.

Halloween

Have you seen the costs of Halloween masks lately? Now, that's scary! Especially when you can make your own booootiful ones from home.

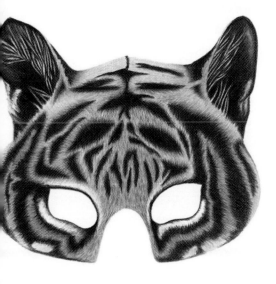

Project 1: Halloween Masks

Surprise someone with a new face.

Materials Needed:

HP Card or Cover stock

Scissors and hole punch

Elastic cord or string

Self-laminating sheets (optional)

Instructions:

1. Print pdf file. Let dry. Laminate page to protect ink from the elements.
2. Cut out masks and eyeholes.
3. Cut out small side holes with hole punch.
4. Attach string or elastic cord to side holes.

Note: Not all designs shown. See CD for all pdf files.

printing projects

Thanksgiving Kids' Table

Give the kids a special table of their own with all kinds of fun and entertaining decorations.

Project 1: Placemat Puzzles

Entertainment at the table.

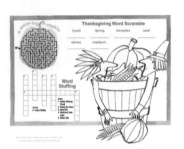

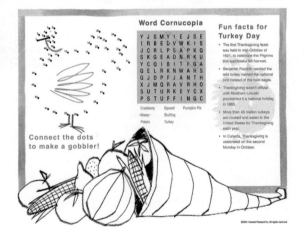

Materials Needed:

HP Bright White Inkjet paper

Pens or pencils

Instructions:

1. Print pdf files. Let dry.
2. Put on the table with pens and pencils for the kids to solve while they wait for dinner or dessert.

Project 2: Placemats

Have some fun with dinner.

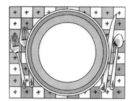 

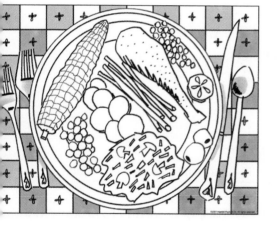

Materials Needed:

HP Bright White Inkjet paper

Scissors

Coloring crayons

Double-sided tape

Instructions:

1. Print the coloring placemat pdf. Let dry.

2. Print pages 1 to 2 of the the food cutout pdf file. Let dry.

3. Put on the table with crayons and double-sided tape. Let the kids be creative and have fun.

printing projects

Project 3: Table Decorations

Give thanks and have a little fun.

Materials Needed:

HP Brochure and Flyer paper

Scissors

Double-sided tape

Instructions:

1. Print headband pdf pages. Let dry.

2. Trim along dotted lines.

3. Attach back of headband to headpiece with tape at each end.

Note: Refer to specific instructions on the CD for turkey or pilgrim hat table decoration.

Project 4: Place Cards

Mix it up a bit!

Materials Needed:

HP Brochure and Flyer paper

Cutting mat, metal ruler, and X-ACTO knife

Instructions:

1. Edit the place cards before printing, or delete field to leave blank. Let dry.

2. Trim cards where indicated.

3. Fold in half

4. Put at each place setting.

printing projects

Project 5: Coasters

To catch those pesky drips.

Materials Needed:

HP Card or Cover stock

Scissors

Self-laminating sheets

Instructions:

1. Print pdf file. Let dry.

2. Cover with laminating sheets.

3. Cut out each coaster.

Project 6: Window Cling

Gobble. Gobble. Gobble.

Materials Needed:

Window decals for inkjet printers

Scissors

Instructions:

1. Print pdf file. Let dry.
2. Trim instructions off top and adhere to window.

Warning: Be sure to use materials designed specifically for your printer. To prevent damage, use window decals specifically designed for laser printers or printers that use heat to fuse the ink.

printing projects

About the CD

To install this software, place the CD into your CD-ROM drive. If you are using Windows, the Setup program should automatically start up (if it doesn't, just navigate to your CD drive under *My Computer* and double-click *Setup*). The Setup program will then guide you through the rest of the steps to install the software.

If you are using a Macintosh, just drag the *Printing Projects* folder onto your *Applications* folder on your hard drive.

In either case, you will need a minimum of 150 MB of free hard drive space to install all of these remarkable printing projects.

After you have installed the software, double-click the *Printing Projects* kitty icon (in Windows, a shortcut will be created on your desktop and a program group icon will appear under the Start/Programs menu) to run the program. *Please note: It may take a minute or two for the program to begin. Note, too, that the program runs off of your hard disk and you do not need the CD in your CD drive to run the program.*

The first time you run your *Printing Projects* program, it checks to see whether you already have Adobe Acrobat Reader installed. Acrobat Reader is needed to view and print all of the project files. If you don't already have it installed, your *Printing Projects* program will launch Adobe's (free) installer to allow you to install Acrobat Reader. If that is the case, you will need to re-launch *Printing Projects* after you finish installing Acrobat Reader, and the fun can then begin!

Using the program itself is very easy and intuitive. Just choose the project category you are interested in by clicking once on its icon. Submenus will appear to allow you to further refine your choice,

until you find just the project you are after. If you are confused at any step of the way, just look to the bottom of the screen where there will be a helpful hint to tell you what to do next. After you finally get a project open, you can print it by clicking on the Acrobat Reader printer icon (again, there is a hint in the program to show you how it looks). Some files have instructions included right in the project file. Some are more complex (such as iron-ons), and those will have separate (also printable) instructions. There are buttons for all such options along the top of the screen. One such button, the orange *Select a Project* button, opens a drop down menu that will allow you to select from different project variations or designs. Click on it to select a particular project.

Another button, the green *Helpful Products* button, suggests a few products that will help you create the project you are making. There's even a Web link there (in case you have Internet access) that takes you right to the Hewlett-Packard online store where you can shop for those products or other helpful printing products.

Also, there are *Back* and *Home* buttons that you can use to navigate back to a previous screen or to the home screen—just like a Web browser. Finally, use the *Exit* button to quit the program when you are finished.

It's all self explanatory, and LOTS of fun, so experiment, navigate, print, create, and have fun with *Printing Projects Made Fun & Easy.*

Technical Support: Prentice Hall does not offer technical support for this software. However, if there is a problem with the media, you may obtain a replacement copy by e-mailing us with your problem at: disc_exchange@prenhall.com.

printing projects

burn it!

creating your own great

dvds & cds

the official hp guide

mark l. chambers

PRENTICE
HALL
PTR

Prentice Hall PTR
Upper Saddle River, NJ 07458
www.phptr.com

This book is dedicated with all a father's love to my daughter,
Chelsea Chambers—"the Chelsea Girl."

dvds & cds

Contents

dvds & cds

dvds & cds

dvds & cds

dvds & cds

Preface

Who would have ever thought that DVD recording would be so affordable so soon? When I wrote my first book on the subject of optical recording in 1997, a CD recorder was out of budgetary reach for most of us—in fact, I had bought my own personal drive only about three months before! (I had gathered a year or two of previous recording experience, strictly from using a very expensive CD recorder that my company had bought to handle backups at the office.) From the first appearance of CD recorders in the late 1980s, it took a good chunk of a decade for CD recording technology to gain acceptance and hardware and software prices to drop.

Today, CD recording technology is "old hat"—if you're shopping for a computer these days, you'll find that virtually every model has a CD-RW drive as standard equipment. But, unlike the early days of CD recording, it took only a couple of years for affordable DVD recording hardware and software to arrive on the scene. DVD discs can store it all: gigabytes of high-quality digital video, thousands of MP3 audio files, and all of the digital images that a professional photographer can produce in an entire career! (Heck, rewriteable DVD discs are even well suited for mundane chores you've been performing all along, such as storing hard drive backup data.)

dvds & cds

In writing this book, I've made a serious—and I hope a successful—attempt at gathering together *all* of the information that a PC owner is likely to need to explore the exciting world of DVD recording. By the way, that includes several chapters that concern CD recording, as well—things such as disc label printing and standard Red Book audio CD recording—just in case you have to return to the "archaic" world of 700 MB from time to time.

Do I Need a Hewlett-Packard Recorder?

Definitely not! Don't get me wrong, I have an HP drive in my own PC—in my personal opinion, they make some of the best hardware on the planet—but like every title in the HP Books series, this book has been expressly written for all PC owners who want to record DVDs and CDs, using any recorder on the market from any manufacturer. In fact, I talk about specific hardware features in only one or two places in the book, and the recommendations and tips I mention will carry over to any recorder.

A Word About Organization

To be honest, this book makes a great linear reading adventure—but only if you're a novice when it comes to optical recording, and you're interested in what makes things tick. If you already have experience recording basic discs, your recorder is already installed, or you're just not interested in how your DVD recorder works, you may decide to skip the material at the beginning and return to it later. This section will help familiarize you with the design of the book.

The first group of three chapters explains how optical recording works—how your computer's CD-ROM or DVD-ROM drive reads files and music from a disc and how your recorder stores information on a blank CD or DVD. You'll also learn how to install an internal or external DVD recorder, using an EIDE, FireWire, or USB connection.

I'll show you how to prepare both your computer and your data before you record, assuring you of top performance, error-free operation, and the best organization for your finished discs.

The next three chapters provide you with complete, step-by-step procedures for burning basic audio and data discs with HP Record-Now, along with drag-and-drop recording within Windows, using HP DLA. I'll cover how you can create your own DVD Video discs for use in most DVD players, using MyDVD.

The final chapters cover the more exotic procedures and subjects in optical recording. You'll learn how to record digital video directly to disc, how to use PowerDVD to watch DVD movies on your PC, and how to print your own professional-looking custom disc labels and jewel box inserts. I'll discuss advanced formats, such as CD-Extra, Video CDs, and multisession discs, and show you how to create each one, step by step. I'll also show you how to create digital photograph slide show discs, how to edit your own digital video movies, and how to archive your existing vinyl albums and cassettes to audio CDs. You'll even learn how to design and produce a powerful menu system for your data discs with the same tools you use to create Web pages! Finally, I provide a software- and hardware-troubleshooting chapter as well.

At the end of the book, you'll find a helpful Glossary (which can aid you in keeping track of what strange term means what), as well as valuable recording and troubleshooting tips from Hewlett-Packard's technical support group. Just in case you haven't bought a recorder yet and you're shopping for one right now, I also provide a quick rundown of the features to look for in a recorder—as well as the "Do's and Don'ts" of buying any computer hardware online.

Watch For Helpful Icons!

Before I launch into Chapter 1, let me familiarize you with the special features you'll find in the text:

dvds & cds

- You'll find *Tips* that I've added to help you save time and money—as well as avoid potential pitfalls and recording errors.

- Pay close attention to any *Caution* icons in the text—whatever it is, you should definitely avoid it!

- Make sure that you have all of the *Requirements* that I've listed for a project before you begin the step-by-step procedure.

Where to Go Next

Here are my recommendations (don't forget to return later to read chapters that you've skipped):

- If you haven't bought your recorder yet, read through the chapter titled "Tips on Buying Your Recorder"—then begin with Chapter 1.
- If you've already bought your recorder but haven't installed it, begin with Chapter 2.
- If you're interested in mastering the basics of recording and your drive is already working, begin with Chapter 3.
- Finally, if you're already well experienced with burning audio and data CDs and you'd like to jump into recording digital video on a DVD, begin with Chapter 6.

It's my sincere hope that you'll find this book valuable: I hope it answers your questions, provides an occasional chuckle and—most of all—helps you have fun with your DVD recorder. If you have any questions or comments you'd like to send me, please visit my Web site, MLC Books Online, at http://home.mlcbooks.com.

And now…let's *Burn It!*

Acknowledgments

The arrival of this book is a very happy event—my first volume of computer lore for Prentice Hall—and an opportunity to thank several folks who have worked hard together as a team to produce a great book!

First, my appreciation to the great Production staff and editors at Prentice Hall; in particular, Faye Gemmellaro, my Production Editor (who took over the day-to-day schedule for this project at very short notice and did a fantastic job) and Roy Tomalino, my Technical Editor (who scanned every word for accuracy and provided me with cutting-edge information on DVD+R and the latest software)! I'd also like to thank Marti Jones, my Copyeditor, for her attention to detail and hard work in checking my grammar and spelling.

I also owe a great debt of gratitude to Jill Harry, Executive Editor at Prentice Hall PTR, for her tireless efforts during the design of the book and its contents! She coordinated this project from the beginning, and I have her to thank for the chance to work on this new HP title.

Speaking of Hewlett-Packard, I'd like to close these acknowledgements by expressing my heartfelt thanks to three of HP's best: Dean Sanderson, who provided me with technical information and artwork; Walt Bruce, my contact and advisor with HP Books; and finally, Pat Pekary, HP Books Publisher and Program Manager, for both her continued support and her friendship.

dvds & cds

About the Author

Mark L. Chambers has been an author, computer consultant, BBS sysop, programmer, and hardware technician for more than 20 years. (In other words, he's been pushing computers and their uses far beyond "normal" performance limits for decades now.) His first love affair with a computer peripheral blossomed in 1984, when he bought his lightning-fast 300BPS modem for his Atari 400—now he spends entirely too much time on the Internet and drinks far too much caffeine-laden soda. His favorite pastimes include collecting gargoyles, St. Louis Cardinals baseball, playing his three pinball machines and the latest computer games, supercharging computers, and rendering 3-D flights of fancy with TrueSpace—and during all that, he listens to just about every type of music imaginable. (For those of his readers who are keeping track, he's up to 1,200+ audio CDs in his collection.)

With a degree in journalism and creative writing from Louisiana State University, Mark took the logical career choice and started programming computers...however, after five years as a COBOL programmer for a hospital system, he decided there must be a better way to earn a living, and he became the documentation manager for Datastorm Technologies, a well-known communications software developer. Somewhere between organizing and writing software manuals, Mark began writing computer books; his first book, *Running a Perfect BBS*, was published in 1994.

Along with writing several books a year and editing whatever his publishers throw at him, Mark has recently branched out into Web-based education, designing, and teaching a number of online classes—called WebClinics—for Hewlett-Packard.

dvds & cds

Mark's rapidly expanding list of books includes the *Office v. X for Mac OS X Power User's Guide, Building a PC for Dummies, Scanners for Dummies, CD and DVD Recording for Dummies, The Hewlett-Packard Official Printer Handbook, The Hewlett-Packard Official Recordable CD Handbook, The Hewlett-Packard Official Digital Photography Handbook, Computer Gamer's Bible, Recordable CD Bible, Teach Yourself the iMac Visually, Running a Perfect BBS, Official Netscape Guide to Web Animation,* and the *Windows 98 Troubleshooting and Optimizing Little Black Book.*

His books have been translated into 12 different languages so far—his favorites are German, Polish, Dutch, and French. Although he can't read them, he enjoys the pictures a great deal.

Mark welcomes all comments and questions about his books—you can reach him at mark@mlcbooks.com.

How Does DVD Recording Work?

In This Chapter

✓ Understanding binary language

✓ Reading data from a DVD

✓ Explaining the recording process

✓ Selecting the correct media

✓ Handling and storing your discs properly

✓ Understanding copy-protected discs

✓ Explaining DVD recording formats

Before you jump into installing your DVD recorder and burning your first discs, you should be properly introduced to the world of the digital versatile disc: how information is stored on a DVD and retrieved, what types of media your DVD recorder can use, how to handle your discs properly, and so forth.

dvds & cds

In this chapter, I'll provide you with an overview of what's happening behind the scenes and the basics of DVD storage.

The Language of Computers

Whoa! You may be saying to yourself, "This sounds like we're ramping up to a discussion full of techno-speak." Don't worry, I'll keep things in honest-to-goodness English. In fact, the binary language used by computers is the simplest language ever devised. (Look at the size of this section: It can't be too complex!)

Computers read, write, and communicate to each other using binary, which has only two values: zero and 1, as illustrated in Figure 1.1, just like a light switch. Your computer stores files and programs as long strings of binary data—and the music on an audio compact disc is also recorded in binary (it's the job of an audio CD player to read the digital information on a disc and convert it back to an audio signal).

Using binary, your computer can store audio and video as data files—in fact, you can even store a "snapshot" of the entire contents of a CD or DVD as an image file on your hard drive (provided that you have enough space). You can use this binary image to make copies of a CD or DVD whenever you need them.

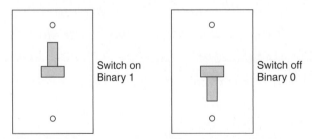

FIGURE 1.1   There are only two values in the binary language of computers and audio CD players.

Reading Data from a Disc

So how does a DVD (or an audio CD) store binary data? (By the way, DVD actually stands for *digital versatile disc,* although many folks now seem to think it stands for *digital video disc* instead. Just another example of how even the acronyms that techno-types use can change over time.)

Here's why a DVD recorder is technically called an *optical* storage device: the "on" and "off" states of binary information are represented by the presence of (or lack of) laser light. As you can see in Figure 1.2, a commercially made DVD disc is actually composed of several layers. One (or more) of those layers is highly reflective; this aluminum surface is covered by a groove with microscopic *pits,* and these pits are arranged so that they can be read by a laser beam.

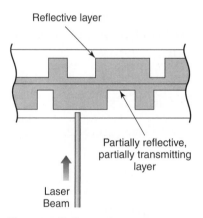

FIGURE 1.2   Although a DVD disc looks like a solid piece of plastic, it's actually more like a sandwich.

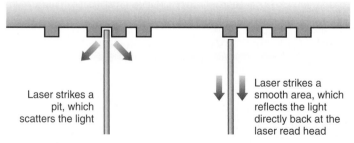

FIGURE 1.3   The basics of optical storage: A laser beam "reads" the pits and lands in a disc.

As you can see in Figure 1.3, when the drive's laser beam hits a pit, it scatters, and most of it isn't reflected back—this represents a zero in binary data. However, when that same laser beam hits one of the flat surfaces (called a *land*), it's reflected cleanly back (much like your reflection in a mirror), and the drive registers that the beam has been returned. This transition between a pit and a land (or, if you remember our light switch, the difference between darkness and light) represents a 1 in the stream of binary data.

Once the drive has read the data, it sends the binary data over a cable connection to your computer. If you're copying a file from a disc, all of those ones and zeroes are saved as a file on your hard drive; if you're running a program directly from the disc or loading a program directly from the disc, the data is piped directly to your computer's processor.

Sounds simple, doesn't it? This manipulation of laser light is used by both computer DVD drives and your home DVD player to read the binary data encoded on a disc as pits and lands.

Recording DVDs and Audio CDs

"Now I understand how a DVD disc is read, but how can I *record* one?" As you might have guessed, your DVD recorder must somehow create the equivalent of pits and lands on a blank disc. As you can see in Figure 1.4, a recordable blank disc is composed of layers, as well; one of those layers is *reactive* (meaning its physical properties can be altered).

The reactive layer is made from either a special dye or a special crystalline compound (depending on the type of disc you're recording). When the dye layer is struck by a laser beam, it permanently discolors. When the crystalline layer is hit by a laser beam, it changes, as well. (In the case of rewriteable CDs and DVDs, the crystalline layer can be "reset" later by the same beam and used again.)

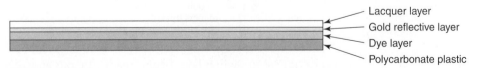

Lacquer layer
Gold reflective layer
Dye layer
Polycarbonate plastic

FIGURE 1.4   A recordable disc contains a layer of dye or a crystalline compound.

The laser beam in a DVD recorder can be set to both low and high power settings; the high power setting is used to create the nonreflective "pit" (Figure 1.5), whereas the low power setting makes no change to the disc, leaving it a land (Figure 1.6).

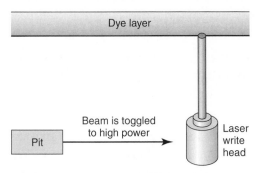

FIGURE 1.5 A high-powered laser beam creates a pit in the dye layer of a recordable disc.

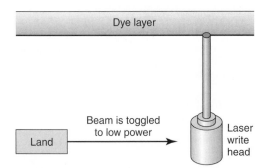

FIGURE 1.6 A low-power laser beam makes no change to the disc, leaving the surface as a land.

When you read a recorded DVD disc, the drive's laser beam strikes the reactive surface, and one of two things happens:

- If the reactive layer has not been changed, the beam is returned by the reflective layer behind it, acting just like a land in a commercially made disc.
- If the reactive layer has been altered, the beam is scattered as it would be by a pit in a commercially made disc.

As I mentioned before, the crystalline layer used by some discs can be altered back and forth between clear and opaque, over and over, so the disc can be completely rewritten; however, these discs must be formatted before they can be reused. This formatting process is very similar to the formatting you've probably performed on a hard drive: It clears the entire surface of the disc, essentially returning the disc to a "factory-fresh" state. (Note that this formatting will begin immediately upon the loading of a DVD+RW disc if you're using an HP DVD-Writer drive—in effect, it happens in the background, so there's no need to worry about formatting.)

Some programs refer to this formatting step as "erasing" the disc; for example, Figure 1.7 illustrates the options you can set in Roxio's Easy CD Creator while erasing a CD-RW disc. (I cover Easy CD Creator in detail later, in Chapter 10, in the section titled "Introducing Easy CD Creator 5.")

FIGURE 1.7   Formatting a CD-RW disc in Easy CD Creator.

Identifying Your Media

If you've been shopping for optical media lately, you know there's a confusing forest of acronyms and incompatible standards that you must brave before you can click the Buy button—or, if you're in an actual brick-and-mortar store, hand the box to a salesperson. Don't panic, however: In this section, I'll explain the advantages, drawbacks, and compatibilities of each of the major types of CD and DVD media.

CD-R and CD-R/W

CD-R (short for *compact disc recordable*) was the first recordable disc available, and at the time of this writing, it's still the most popular and the least expensive. Currently, a stack of 100 CD-R discs should cost you anywhere from $30 to $50. A typical CD-R disc can store up to 700 MB of computer data or 80 minutes of audio. Because CD-R discs use a dye layer, the data and audio you burn to a CD-R is permanently recorded and can't be erased or formatted.

CD-R discs are the most compatible of CD media because of their high reflectivity. Any CD-ROM drive—no matter how old—can read CD-R discs, and they're the only type of discs that will play in *every* home or car audio CD player.

CD-RW, which stands for *compact disc rewriteable*, is the standard for reusable CD recording; they can store 650 MB of data or 74 minutes of audio. At current prices, a box of 25 CD-RW discs should cost you around $60. As I mentioned earlier in this chapter, you can erase the contents of a CD-RW disc by formatting it, which returns the disc to a blank state, ready to be used again. Unfortunately, the crystalline layer used by a CD-RW disc makes it incompatible with virtually all audio CD players.

DVD+R, DVD-R, DVD+RW, and DVD-RW

DVD+R and DVD-R (predictably, that's short for *DVD recordable*) are often referred to as "write-once" discs. DVD-R is probably the most popular recordable DVD media available at the time of this writing; it was the first to arrive on the market, and it offers the best compatibility with both DVD set-top players and computer DVD-ROM drives.

dvds & cds

Both DVD+R and DVD-R have higher compatibility than do rewriteable DVD media because they have higher reflectivity. (However, neither DVD+R nor DVD-R media can be used with a standard CD-ROM drive or audio CD player.) DVD-R discs typically sell for about $20 for a pack of 10 discs, whereas the newer DVD+R discs sell for around $5 each at the time of this writing.

Like a CD-R disc, DVD+R and DVD-R discs can be recorded only once. However, a single-sided disc can hold 4.7 GB, whereas a double-sided disc can hold 9.4 GB of data. A double-sided DVD doesn't have a standard label; printing can appear only around the spindle hole, because a label would interfere with the laser. (You may have already noticed this if you have a DVD player, because many DVD movies have a widescreen version of the film on one side and a standard ratio version on the other side.)

DVD+RW and DVD-RW (which stands for *DVD rewriteable*) are relatively new arrivals on the DVD recording horizon. Many drives capable of writing DVD-R discs also write DVD-RW discs. DVD+RW hit the market slightly later than the DVD-RW products, but it's already making a name for itself among a number of DVD recorder manufacturers and has been chosen by several large PC manufacturers as a component in high-end PCs. Like a CD-RW disc, DVD+RW can be reformatted and reused up to 1,000 times. DVD+RW and DVD-RW discs can store 4.7 GB per side and are compatible with most DVD players and DVD-ROM drives. Naturally, the DVD+RW and DVD-RW discs you record can't be read on a standard CD-ROM drive or audio CD player.

The only drawback to DVD+RW and DVD-RW technology is the price of the media: currently, anywhere from $8 to a whopping $20 per 4.7-GB disc! Rewriteable DVD media (just like its cousin, CD-RW media) is more expensive to manufacture and, therefore, more expensive than DVD+R and DVD-R media. However, the convenience of erasing and rewriting the discs make them well worth the extra expense. As more of these discs are produced, they'll be easier to find, and I predict that their price will drop as rapidly as DVD-R discs have done.

DVD-RAM

DVD-RAM discs are reusable and, like DVD+RW and DVD-RW, they can store up to 9.4 GB of data, using both sides. Like DVD-R, DVD-RAM is a well-established standard, and DVD-RAM discs are popular for system backups and portable mass storage. When you consider the megabyte/dollar ratio, they're significantly cheaper than other types of rewriteable DVD storage, currently averaging about $10 for a double-sided 9.4-GB disc.

However, DVD-RAM is compatible with very few DVD players and no DVD-ROM drives (hence the advantage of the newer DVD+RW and DVD-RW discs), making them a poor choice for creating DVD video discs. A few late-model (also called "fourth-generation") DVD players can read a DVD-RAM disc, as well.

tip **Due to the wide disparity in manufacturers, I can't tell you whether your current DVD player will read a DVD-R, DVD+RW, or DVD-RAM disc—and you may not be able to test its compatibility easily unless you happen to have friends with all three types of drives! Therefore, it's a very good idea to check your DVD player's manual and its specifications for any word on recorded DVD media. Also, you can check the manufacturer's Web site to see whether there's any information on media compatibility.**

Caring for Your Optical Pets

You've probably been handling CDs for many years now—and because DVDs look so similar and work the same way, you might think you can handle and store them in the same way. As you've learned in this chapter, however, DVDs carry a lot more information than do those "antique" compact discs, and they do it by compressing more pits into a smaller area. Therefore, a simple fingerprint, a speck of dust (or, in the worst case, a scratch) can result in read problems that you wouldn't encounter with a CD.

In this section, you'll learn the correct way to handle, clean, and store your DVDs.

dvds & cds

DVD Handling 101

Let's begin with the Golden Rule of DVD: *Never allow anything to touch the reflective surface of your discs!* A disc that's smudged by fingerprints, grease, or oil may be unreadable, because the laser beam in your DVD player must be able to pass through the surface of the disc *twice* to read it. Even the cleanest set of fingertips can transfer all sorts of contaminants when you hold a DVD incorrectly.

There are two proper methods of holding a disc: by the outside edge and by inserting a finger into the spindle hole, as shown in Figures 1.8 and 1.9.

Things to Avoid

DVDs have four arch enemies that you should avoid at all costs:

- **Heat.** If you have a car audio CD player, you already know how important it is to protect discs from high temperatures; a slight warping caused by overheating can render a disc unreadable. Therefore, direct sunlight should also be avoided.

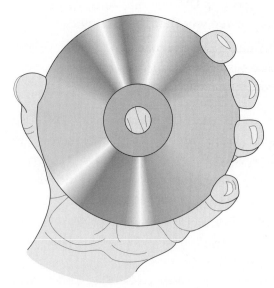

Fingers grip on outside edge

FIGURE 1.8   Holding a DVD by the outside edge.

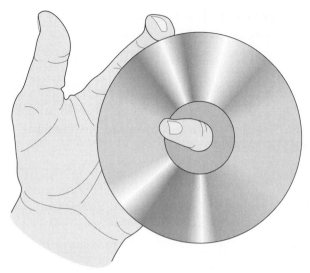

FIGURE 1.9   Hold a disc using the spindle hole (for those with smaller fingers).

- **Sharp objects.** Scratching the surface of a disc can result in read errors (or, in the worst case, ruin the disc if the scratch is deep and wide enough).

tip **You can write on the label side of a single-sided DVD disc— as long as the manufacturer says you can print on the surface— but don't use a ballpoint pen! The sharp point of a ballpoint pen can easily damage the disc. Instead, use a quick-drying, soft-tip permanent marker to label your discs. Slow-drying markers may contain solvents that can eat through or etch the outer layer of the disc.**

- **Liquids.** Although some disc cleaning systems use liquids (usually based on an alcohol solution), they're not necessary. Other liquids should be wiped off as quickly as possible, using the technique I will demonstrate later in this section.
- **Dust.** Because DVDs store information based on reflected light, dirty discs tend to skip in an audio CD player (or end up unreadable in a DVD player). Keep your discs in their jewel cases or store them properly to keep them free of dust.

dvds & cds

tip **Never set a DVD on a table! If you need to set a disc aside—even just for a few seconds—always put it back in its jewel case.**

caution   **Do not use a "laser lens cleaner" in your DVD recorder or your DVD player—you could damage your drive! The laser and lens system inside these units doesn't require any cleaning and can be easily damaged by fibers or abrasives.**

Storing Your Discs

Most folks use the jewel box or plastic case that a disc comes with to store it. This is fine, but there are other methods of storing your discs that take up less room. For the best protection for the most discs in the least space, I recommend a DVD disc binder, which stores each disc in an individual plastic sleeve, so you can toss the jewel case. DVD disc binders are available in sizes that range from 10 to more than 250 discs.

You'll also find a bewildering variety of plastic and cloth cases—accordions, clamshells, zippered books, and many more. These "hi-tech" storage units are fine, as long as they're specifically designed for use with DVDs: Never store a DVD in a jewel box or case that's meant for a standard CD. Although the hole in the center of a CD and DVD are the same, a jewel case for a DVD will have a slightly smaller hub diameter (making it easier to remove to avoid flexing). If the disc is flexed, it should be allowed to stabilize and become flat again before trying to read or write to it.

Whatever storage method you choose for your discs, make sure that it meets these three criteria:

- It must be closed to dust and dirt.
- It must protect your discs from scratches.
- It must be expandable (or at least store enough discs to provide for some future additions)!

Cleaning Discs the Right Way

Although there are expensive DVD disc cleaning machines, I don't recommend them, and they're really not necessary—if you follow the Golden Rule, hold your discs correctly, and store them in their cases, they simply don't need cleaning!

However, accidents do happen. If a disc picks up fingerprints or dust, use a lint-free photographer's lens cloth—if necessary, you can also apply a spray or two of disc cleaning fluid if the disc has picked up a stain.

It's very important to wipe the surface of your discs properly: *Never wipe a compact disc in a circular motion!* (Figure 1.10) Wiping in a circle is more likely to scratch a larger portion of the disc's surface and result in read errors; always move from the center spindle hole straight toward the outside of the disc (Figure 1.11), applying only fingertip pressure to avoid scratches.

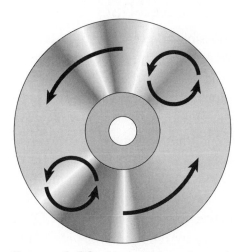

FIGURE 1.10 Never wipe a disc with a circular motion!

FIGURE 1.11 To avoid scratches, wipe discs from the center toward the outside of the disc.

A Word about Copy-Protected Discs

DVD-Video movies are practically impossible to copy: Some discs are protected by the addition of unreadable areas on the disc during manufacture (because your DVD recorder can't read these areas, it also can't duplicate them). Other protection schemes involve encrypted key codes that your DVD player must recognize in order to play the disc. Sure, it's possible to copy the digital video stream from a DVD disc, but it takes hours of time, specialized software, and quite a bit of technical knowledge; the quality of the video is likely to be significantly degraded, too. (I don't think I need to underline the fact that it's also illegal.) There are programs that advertise that they can "copy" DVD movies, but the result is far lower in quality than the original video (and you don't get any of the extras, such as interviews, subtitling, and alternate soundtracks).

But I'll be honest—there's a much more mundane, low-tech reason why copying DVD movies is a waste of time. Currently, a blank DVD-R disc typically costs around $2, but the hassle involved in producing a low-quality dub of a DVD movie can tie up your computer for a day or two (yes, it actually takes that long). If you can buy a legal copy of a movie for $15, is it really worth it?

To sum it up: A DVD recorder is perfect for recording your own home video, but don't expect to use it to copy commercial movies.

DVD Formats on Parade

As I close this chapter, I'd like to introduce you to the three DVD *formats* you'll be using with your new recorder. A format is a standardized "road map" used by hardware manufacturers around the world that details what data goes where on a recorded disc—without the proper format, your disc would be unreadable in any other device, so you couldn't use it in your DVD player or your computer's DVD-ROM drive. I'll try to keep the technobabble to a bare minimum while we cover these three important formats!

DVD-V

A commercially manufactured DVD movie disc is often called a DVD-ROM (that's short for *DVD read-only memory*)—technically, however, a DVD-ROM can also be called a DVD-V disc, which is short for *DVD video*. The DVD-V format describes a DVD-ROM that holds broadcast-quality digital video in a special compressed format called MPEG-2. As I mentioned earlier, DVD-V discs can also include high-tech features such as Dolby audio, surround sound, subtitles, and different aspect ratios—and you can even run programs from a DVD-V disc if it's being played in a computer DVD-ROM drive.

If you're using a DVD recorder, it is possible to record a DVD-V disc that delivers the quality of a commercially made DVD-ROM—in fact, I'll be showing you how to do just that later in the book, using the HP DVD-Writer and a selection of home movies I've taken with my DV (*digital video*) camcorder.

DVD-A

Here's a riddle for you: What looks like an audio CD but features up to 4 hours of stereo music, interactive animated menus (much like the current crop of DVD-V discs), and even the ability to store video clips? The answer is DVD-A, which stands for *DVD audio*! You also get the mind-boggling addition of surround sound, which provides unparalleled

dvds & cds

realism and depth to your music. DVD-A discs will not be compatible with your current audio CD player, but your collection of traditional audio CDs should work fine in a DVD-A player.

The future of DVD-A is somewhat cloudy, because it may take a number of years to match the popularity of the familiar audio compact disc, and it's now receiving stiff competition from the new Super Audio CD (or SACD) format that's currently in development.

UDF

Our last—but by no means least—recording format is called UDF (short for *Universal Disc Format*). You're also likely to hear UDF called by another common name, *packet-writing*, which dates back to the days when it first appeared in CD recording software. UDF recording allows you to write files to a DVD-R/DVD-RW, DVD+R/DVD+RW, or DVD-RAM just as you would write files to your hard drive, using Windows Explorer, the Mac OS Finder, or any of your favorite applications. If you can write the file to your hard drive or a floppy, you can write it directly to DVD. Files can be added (or deleted) one at a time or in groups, without having to record the entire disc at one sitting. In effect, UDF turns your DVD recorder into a gigantic, superfast, removable disc that can store at least 4.7 GB of data. Figure 1.12 illustrates the formatting utility you'll use with the popular UDF recording program DirectCD, which ships with Easy CD Creator; HP DVD-Writer owners can use the HP DLA program, which I'll be covering later, in Chapter 5 ("Drag-and-Drop Recording with HP DLA").

Later in the book, we'll encounter a number of other different formats that apply to computer CD-ROMs and audio CDs; your drive can record these formats, as well, and we'll use them for several projects.

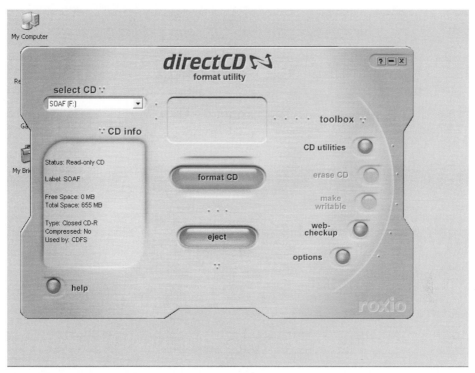

FIGURE 1.12   Preparing a disc for UDF recording using the DirectCD formatting utility.

Summary

This chapter introduced you to the basics of DVD recording, beginning with the binary language of optical storage. I discussed how data is burned and retrieved from a recordable DVD disc. You learned about the different types of DVD media, including their strong and weak points. I covered the proper methods of handling and storing your discs, and touched on the topic of copy-protected DVD discs. Finally, I discussed the three recording formats you'll use when creating DVD discs.

dvds & cds

2

Installing Your DVD Recorder

In This Chapter

✔ Checking installation requirements

✔ Preparing for the installation

✔ Determining the right jumper settings

✔ Installing your new EIDE drive

✔ Connecting a FireWire or USB recorder

✔ Troubleshooting EIDE hardware

✔ Troubleshooting FireWire and USB hardware

Most internal CD and DVD recorders available for today's computers use an EIDE connection—for technical types, that stands for Enhanced Integrated Drive Electronics, a type of connection that's supported by all of today's PCs. Luckily, however, normal human beings need only remember the acronym (and only when shopping, just to make sure that you've bought a drive with the right kind of connection).

dvds & cds

19

Although EIDE hardware is very easy to install, there are still jumpers to configure, cables to connect, and a drive that needs to find its way into your computer's case—and that's what this chapter is all about. I'll show you how to install both your drive and the bundled software that came with it…and don't worry, you don't have to be a computer technician to install a DVD recorder. As a matter of fact, if you can handle a screwdriver, you already have all the tools you need!

By reading the instructions that came with your recorder and by following the step-by-step procedures in this chapter, *anyone* can install their own drive (and brag about it afterward).

If you've decided to add an external drive to your system using FireWire or USB, things are much easier: You won't have to remove your computer's case, move jumpers, or worry about "which end of the cable is up." However, there are still one or two possible pitfalls you may encounter, so I'll also cover the connection of an external recorder.

Before We Begin

In this chapter, I'm going to demonstrate how to install both the Hewlett-Packard DVD-Writer DVD200i—an internal EIDE device—and an external FireWire or USB drive such as the HP DVD200e. Although it's harder to install an internal drive than an external recorder, the step-by-step procedure in this chapter should be all you need. If you have another brand of EIDE DVD recorder, *you don't have to skip this material!* EIDE devices are very standardized (they have to be to be so compatible); therefore, the steps you'll read here will also work with virtually every combination of EIDE DVD recorder and a PC.

There is the possibility that your drive may require special software or use a different jumper configuration than the DVD200i recorder. Because of the chance that you'll encounter something different, I strongly recommend that you read the installation instructions for your recorder! Once you're familiar with the installation instructions for your particular drive model, you can follow the steps I provide in this chapter—and if the installation instructions for your drive differ significantly from mine, you can follow them instead.

What Do I Need?

Let's consider the basic requirements for installing your new DVD recorder; if your PC doesn't meet these minimum standards, you'll have to upgrade your system before you can use your drive. An EIDE recorder requires:

- **An EIDE cable with an open connector.** Most PCs built in the last five years or so have four available EIDE device connectors: a *primary* master and slave on one cable, and a *secondary* master and slave on another cable. (If that sounds like Greek to you, don't worry—you'll learn more about master and slave settings later in this chapter). Your new drive requires one connector. If your PC has only one hard drive and one CD-ROM drive on the primary cable, you may have to buy another EIDE cable for your secondary connector; many PC manufacturers don't provide a cable if the secondary connector isn't being used.
- **An empty drive bay.** Your case must have one 5.25-inch drive bay available that's open to the front of your case; it's the same type of drive bay your CD-ROM drive uses. Most PC cases have at least two of these bays.
- **An unused power connector.** Your new recorder needs an available connector to your computer's power supply, such as the one illustrated in Figure 2.1. If your computer no longer has a spare power connector, you can buy a power splitter (also called a *Y connector*) at your local computer store; these special plugs convert one power cable into two.

dvds & cds

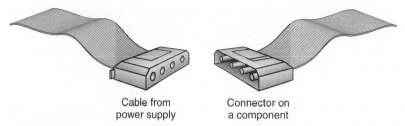

Cable from   Connector on
power supply   a component

FIGURE 2.1   Your PC's power supply must have an available power cable to install your drive.

If you're installing an external FireWire or USB drive, you'll need the following:

- **An open connector.** At the time of this writing, there's only one standard for a FireWire (also called IEEE-1394) connection, so you can be reasonably sure that you've got the right hardware. FireWire is used for everything from high-speed external hard drives and recorders to DV cameras and scanners. Things aren't quite as simple on the USB side of the fence, however, because there are now two versions of the Universal Serial Bus: the original standard, which has been around since the late 1990s, and the much faster version 2.0 standard. Luckily, version 2.0 cables and devices are backward-compatible with original USB hardware, so everything will still work—your connection won't be anywhere near as fast, though, and you probably won't be able to record at the full speed possible with your drive. Therefore, if you have a recorder that supports USB 2.0 (such as the HP DVD200e), make sure that the USB ports on your computer conform to the new 2.0 standard so that you can take advantage of the faster data transfer rate. (Many manufacturers are already selling USB 2.0 adapters for PCs, so you can add these ports to your computer for about $150.)
- **An open AC wall socket.** Unlike an internal drive (which draws its power directly from your PC's power supply), an external recorder has its own power cord.

tip Like any other piece of expensive external hardware—your printer, for example, or your scanner—you should connect your external recorder to a surge protector. If you have the cash to spare, a UPS (or Universal Power Supply) is even better: Not only will you protect your system from brownouts and surges but, in case of a power outage, you can continue to run your computer for a number of minutes. If you're recording a disc when the lights go out, those extra minutes can mean the difference between a successful recording and a disc that's headed for the trash can!

- **An appropriate location.** Find the right spot for your external recorder! Keep it several inches away from your computer's case and monitor, which ensures proper ventilation, and make sure the drive tray has the room to extend fully. Also, make sure that it's safe from vibration; for example, don't place that sensitive drive on top of your PC's subwoofer!

Next, let's turn our attention to the requirements you'll need for a typical suite of DVD recording software. Your PC should have a minimum of the following hardware:

- **128 MB of RAM.** Today's recording software needs elbow room to work. If your computer has less than 128 MB of RAM, take advantage of today's low memory prices and upgrade your PC; more memory will allow all versions of Windows and your application programs to run faster, too.
- **Pentium III or faster CPU.** For error-free video recording to a DVD drive, I recommend a minimum of an 800-MHz Pentium III computer; anything slower, and your computer will likely not be able to record successfully. (For simple data recording, you can get by with a minimum of a 450-MHz Pentium II computer.)
- **Windows 98, Me, XP, or Windows 2000.** HP supports Windows 98 Second Edition, Me, 2000, and XP (Windows NT and the advanced server versions of 2000 and XP are not supported). If you're using Windows 95, it's definitely time to upgrade!

dvds & cds

- **5 GB of free hard drive space.** Wow! Those DVD+RW discs can really hold a huge amount, but you typically have to store all that data on your hard drive first. If you want to record your own DVD video and your hard drive doesn't have 10 GB available, you'll have to either delete existing software to make room or buy a new drive (either to add to your system or to upgrade your current hard drive). For regular data recording to a CD-R or CD-RW, it's good to have at least 1 GB free.

- **Video capture hardware.** To create DVD-V discs using your own video clips, you'll need either a FireWire port on your PC or a video capture card.

Be Prepared

It works for Boy Scouts, and you'll find that good preparation can also help keep your installation short and smooth. I recommend the following preparations before you pick up your screwdriver:

- **Set up a stable surface, such as a tabletop or workbench.** If you need to protect the top of your work surface, such as the kitchen table, spread newspaper on top. Do not use cloth, which can result in static electricity!

- **Keep a good light source handy.** You can't work on something that you can barely see; I use an old-fashioned gooseneck desk lamp on my workbench.

- **Use a parts bowl.** What's a parts bowl? Nothing exotic—just a plastic bowl or wide-mouth container that can hold all of the screws and parts that you remove (either temporarily or permanently). Once the installation has been finished, anything left over in the bowl can be saved for future installations and repairs; you'll be surprised at just how good it feels to have the right spare part!

- **Reserve plenty of time.** No one wants to be rushed while installing computer hardware: You're more likely to overlook a step or leave a cable unattached. If you've never installed a drive before, allow yourself at least three or four hours of uninterrupted time.

tip **Do you have a friend who's knowledgeable about computer hardware? If you'd like a "safety net" while you install your first EIDE drive, it's a good idea to enlist that person to help.**

Time to Determine Your Settings

As I mentioned earlier, most PCs can handle up to four EIDE drives, with two drives on each of two cables. How does your PC keep track of which devices are connected? By the use of jumper settings. A *jumper* is a tiny wire-and-plastic electrical crossover that connects pins on your recorder's circuit board. You can move a jumper to different positions to connect different sets of pins, which in turn changes the drive's EIDE configuration. (Tweezers come in handy if the jumper is particularly small.)

Determining Jumper Settings for an HP DVD-Writer

Hewlett-Packard includes a software utility with the DVD-Writer DVD200i drive that can recommend which jumper settings you should use. To use this program, you should install the software that came with the DVD-Writer now, before you even open your computer's case!

✔ **Follow these steps:**

1. Load Software Disc 1 into your PC's CD-ROM drive, and you'll see the screen shown in Figure 2.2.

2. Click Start Installation to begin, and follow the on-screen instructions to install the various programs that you received with your DVD-Writer.

dvds & cds

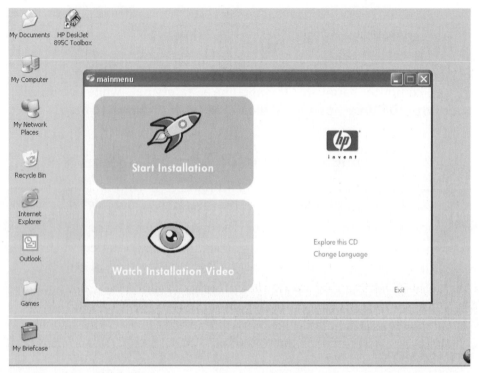

FIGURE 2.2   The Welcome screen from the HP DVD-Writer software installation
program.

tip **During the software installation, it's a good idea to accept
all of the defaults (especially which programs you'll install and
where they'll be stored)—this ensures that you'll have all the software
you'll need for many of the projects I'll be showing you later. Also, you
should install DirectX8.1 when prompted, because you'll need it for
advanced video work.**

3. Once the software has been installed, you'll see the screen shown
    in Figure 2.3—the software has recognized that you haven't yet
    installed the drive itself. Click Next to continue.

4. The installation program displays the screen illustrated in Figure
    2.4, where you'll decide whether to keep your PC's existing CD-
    ROM or replace it with the DVD-Writer. (Personally, I recommend
    that you keep your existing CD-ROM drive if you have an open bay

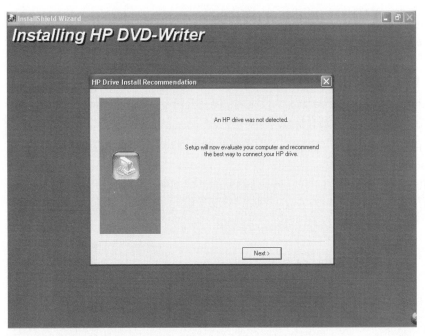

FIGURE 2.3 Beginning the Install Recommendation portion of the installation.

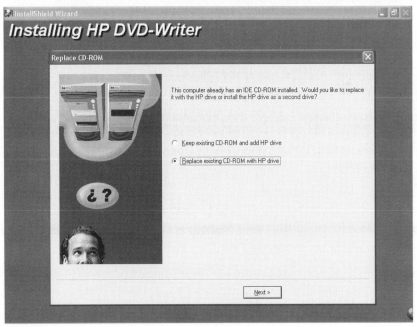

FIGURE 2.4 To add or switch—that is the question!

dvds & cds

available. Of course, if you don't have a spare open bay, you'll have to replace your CD-ROM drive.) Click the desired option and click Next to continue.

5. The program displays a customized screen like the one in Figure 2.5 that shows you the correct jumper settings, cable, and EIDE connector you should use. Write down this information, or click Print to send it to your system printer. Click Next.

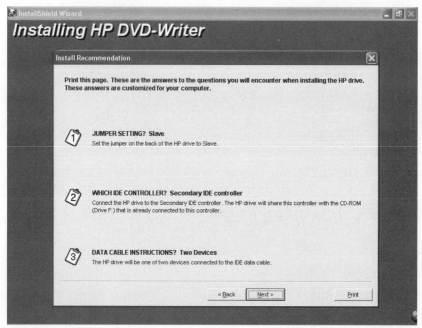

FIGURE 2.5   The installation program displays the settings you'll need for your hardware.

6. The final installation screen you see in Figure 2.6 offers several options. Click Review the drive Install recommendation to return to the Recommendation screen shown in Step 4. Click Watch the tutorial install Video to see a 10-minute animated video overview of the hardware installation process—I highly recommend watching this video, it's very well done, and it's a good preparation for the steps to come. To begin the hardware installation process immedi-

ately, click Shutdown Now; to install the hardware later, click Shutdown later (remember, however, that you *must* install the drive before you can restart your PC again, because programs that check for the drive have already been installed).

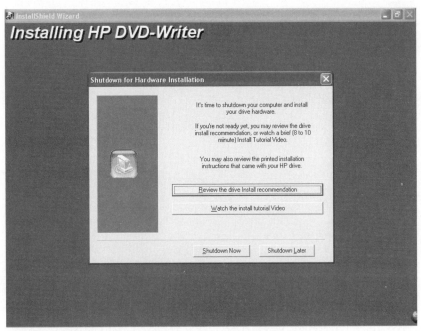

FIGURE 2.6   Finishing the software installation.

If you decide to shut down later, you'll see two new icons on your Windows desktop, as shown in Figure 2.7: PowerDVD and HP DVD-Writer!

FIGURE 2.7   Your desktop sports new icons.

Determining Jumper Settings for Other DVD Recorders

If you're using another brand of drive, you'll probably have to determine the jumper positions you should use for your existing EIDE hard
drive, your existing CD-ROM or DVD-ROM drive (if you have one),
and your new recorder. Table 2.1 should help you decide which settings are correct; the different "master" and "slave" positions are
printed on most EIDE drives, and they can also be found in your
hardware documentation.

> *tip* If all else fails and you can't locate the jumper settings for
> an older hard drive or CD-ROM drive, visit the manufacturer's
> Web site and check its technical support area, or call its voice technical
> support number for help.

TABLE 2.1   EIDE Master/Slave Jumper Settings

One Hard Drive	One Hard Drive and One CD-ROM on the Same Cable	One Hard Drive and One CD-ROM on Different Cables
Set the hard drive as "multiple drive, master unit" and set your recorder as "multiple drive, slave unit."	Set your recorder as "single drive, master unit" and connect it to the secondary EIDE cable. No changes are required to the existing drives on the primary EIDE cable.	Set your recorder as "multiple drive, slave unit" and connect it to the EIDE cable that the hard drive is using. The hard drive must be set to "multiple drive, master unit." No changes are required to the CD-ROM drive on the secondary EIDE cable.

Installing an Internal Drive

Ready to install your new DVD recorder? Is your work surface prepared, well lit, and equipped with a parts bowl? In this section, I'll take you step by step through the entire process.

caution Static electricity can damage any exposed electronic components you touch, including your PC's motherboard and adapter cards! Therefore, always take a moment to discharge any static electricity before touching the interior of your PC or any hardware—touch a nonpainted metal surface (such as the back of your computer or your computer's case) often before and during the installation.

✔ **Follow these steps to install an internal drive:**

1. Shut down your computer and unplug it from the AC wall outlet.

2. Unplug all of the various cables from the back of your PC (if necessary, take a moment to label them or draw a diagram of the cable connections before you unplug them).

3. Remove the screws that secure the cover to your computer and put them in your parts bowl. Take off the cover and set it aside.

4. Set the jumpers on the back of your recorder according to the recommendations made by the HP software or your drive's documentation. Figure 2.8 shows the three possible settings for the HP DVD-Writer drive. (Remember, you may have to change the settings for other EIDE devices that are already installed in your PC—if so, make those changes now, as well.)

5. Select an open drive bay for the recorder that offers access to the front of the case. If the bay is covered by a plastic insert, remove it by pushing on it from inside the case, as shown in Figure 2.9. Some of these inserts are snapped into place, so you may have to bend the insert to remove it; if so, be careful not to gouge or scratch your case in the process.

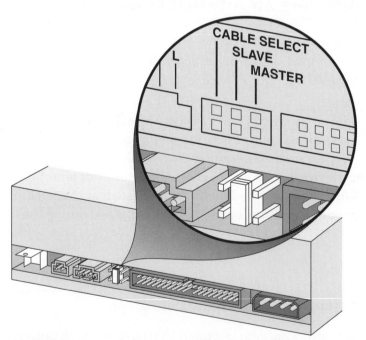

FIGURE 2.8   Setting the master/slave jumper on an HP DVD-Writer drive. *Image courtesy of Hewlett-Packard.*

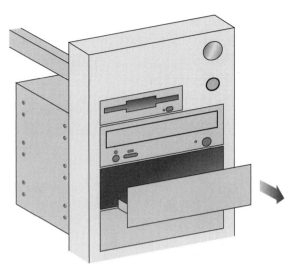

FIGURE 2.9 Removing the plastic insert covering a drive bay. *Image courtesy of Hewlett-Packard.*

6. Once the bay is open, slide the drive into it from the front of the case, as shown in Figure 2.10. The end with the connectors should go in first, and the drive should be facing upright (check the printing or lettering on the front of the recorder to make sure that the orientation is correct).

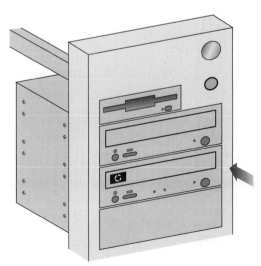

FIGURE 2.10 Introducing the drive to its new home. *Image courtesy of Hewlett-Packard.*

dvds & cds

7. Slide the recorder back and forth in the drive bay until the screw holes in the side of the bay line up with the screw holes on the drive. Attach the recorder to the bay with the screws supplied with the drive, as shown in Figure 2.11. Although you should try to add all four screws, it may be harder to reach some of them (with at least two screws, the recorder will be fine).

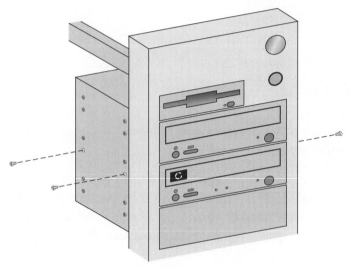

FIGURE 2.11   Securing the drive. *Image courtesy of Hewlett-Packard.*

8. Connect a power cable from your PC's power supply to the recorder's power connector, as shown in Figure 2.12. Don't be worried about plugging the power cable in the wrong way—the connector fits only one way, so there's no chance of making a mistake! (I'd like to thank the engineer who designed these.)

9. Now it's time to attach the EIDE data cable coming from the computer's EIDE connector to the data connector on the back of the recorder, as shown in Figure 2.13. If your new drive will use a cable by itself, you may have to connect the cable to your computer's motherboard, as well—check your motherboard manual to determine where the secondary IDE connector is located. If your recorder will share a cable with an existing EIDE device, simply fol-

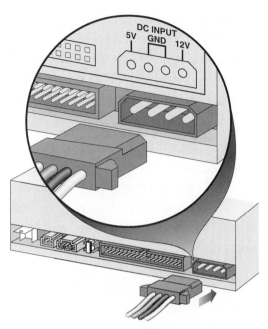

FIGURE 2.12 Providing power to your new recorder. *Image courtesy of Hewlett–Packard.*

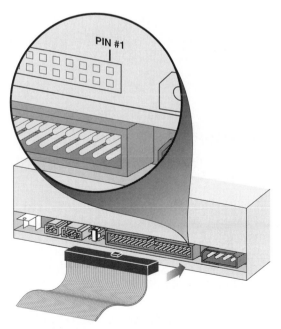

FIGURE 2.13 Connecting the data cable. *Image courtesy of Hewlett–Packard.*

dvds & cds

low the cable from the back of that device until you find the second connector. Again, this cable should fit only one way; a small notch on the cable connector must line up correctly with a matching cut-out on the drive's connector, and Pin 1 normally lines up with the side with the power connector. Once you're sure that the alignment is correct, press the connectors firmly together.

10. If you plan to play audio CDs using your DVD-Writer, you must connect the cable from your sound card to the port on the back of your drive, as shown in Figure 2.14. If you're going to keep your existing CD-ROM drive, this cable is probably already attached, and you can either move it to your DVD recorder or leave it connected to the CD-ROM. (If you choose the latter, you should continue to listen to audio CDs with your CD-ROM drive.) PCs manufactured by HP usually ship with sound cards that have two audio cables; in this case, use both.

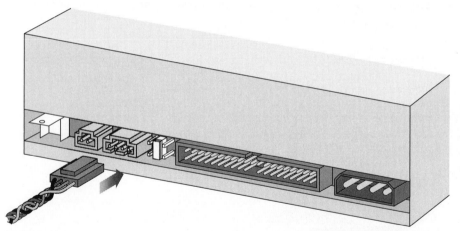

FIGURE 2.14 Connecting the audio cable. *Image courtesy of Hewlett–Packard.*

11. Check all connections to each device (even the cables you didn't touch)—it's very easy to inadvertently unplug a cable while working inside your PC.

12. Replace your PC's cover and fasten it with the original screws from your parts bowl.

13. Plug all of the cables from your other devices back into your PC.

14. Plug in the power cable and turn on your computer.

Remember, if you're installing a DVD recorder other than an HP DVD-Writer, you may have additional software that you have to install.

Installing an External Drive

If you've bought a USB or FireWire external drive, there's no need to disassemble anything...in fact, you don't even have to turn off your PC!

✔ **Follow these steps to connect the drive to your computer:**

1. Connect the drive's power cord to the AC wall socket.

2. Connect the USB or FireWire cable to the drive and turn it on.

3. Plug the cable from your drive into the corresponding USB or FireWire port on your computer.

4. If you're connecting the drive for the first time, load the driver disc when prompted (or install the software that came with your drive).

Once you've successfully connected the drive for the first time and loaded any required software, you can put the manufacturer's disc away—it's necessary only when loading software the first time.

Troubleshooting EIDE Installation Problems

Although EIDE drives are the industry standard, there's still the possibility that your new recorder will sit motionless like a silicon brick when you try to use it—if so, it's time to exercise your troubleshooting skills to determine the problem and fix it. Never fear, I won't abandon you in your time of need! I'll cover the most common installation glitches you may encounter and their solutions.

My new recorder doesn't eject or show a power light.

- **Power cable loose or unplugged.** If the drive's tray doesn't eject when you press the Eject button, check the power connector—even if the jumper settings aren't correct, your drive should still be able to eject the tray, as long as it's receiving power.

Windows no longer boots—my hard drive is no longer recognized.

- **Cables improperly connected.** This can happen if you've accidentally moved your PC's hard drive from the primary to the secondary controller cable—the hard drive must be the master device on the primary EIDE controller cable.

I get power, but Windows doesn't recognize my new drive.

- **Master/slave jumpers are incorrectly set.** This is a classic symptom of an improper jumper setting. If your new DVD recorder is sharing a cable with another EIDE device, make sure that you've correctly set the master/slave jumpers for *both* drives.
- **Data cable loose or unplugged.** Check the ribbon cable connection to both the drive and the motherboard, and make sure that the cable is firmly seated on both ends. (If the drive is sharing a cable with another EIDE device and that device is working fine, the culprit will be the connection to the DVD recorder.)
- **Required software drivers haven't been loaded.** Check to make sure that you've run the complete software installation process for your new drive.

I get a weird message about something called a BIOS error.

- **Incorrect BIOS configuration.** PCs made within the last three or four years will automatically detect changes in your

EIDE setup and add (or remove) devices from your BIOS configuration—if your PC doesn't do this by itself, however, you can make the required changes manually. Check your PC's documentation for the key that you need to press during the boot sequence to edit your system BIOS—when you've displayed the BIOS, use the update function to add the recorder to your active EIDE device list.

Troubleshooting USB and FireWire Installation Problems

You've already seen that USB and FireWire connections are about as trouble-free as you can get—but, like every other piece of hardware on the planet, it's possible that things may not work as advertised. In this last section, I'll discuss common problems with external drives and the proper way to handle them.

My new recorder doesn't eject or show a power light.

- **Power cable loose or unplugged.** Just like an internal recorder, your new external drive needs power! Check the AC cable and make sure that it's snugly connected to the drive.

tip Some USB 2.0 drives may not use a separate power supply—instead, they may draw power directly from the port itself. Unfortunately, not all USB ports can provide that much juice (some are provided only for connecting a keyboard and a mouse); this is the likely problem if you find that your drive works fine when connected to one computer but doesn't seem to be getting any power at all when connected to another system.

I get a message about a missing driver.

- **USB/FireWire software drivers corrupted, incompatible, or not installed.** The culprit is the manufacturer's driver program: It may have been damaged, or you may not have installed it on this computer. Alternately, your recorder's driver may not work with your operating system (a classic problem that often occurs when you've just completed an upgrade to your operat-

dvds & cds

ing system). Try reinstalling the manufacturer's software—if the driver doesn't work with your operating system, it's time to visit the drive manufacturer's Web site to hunt for an updated driver.

I get power, but Windows doesn't recognize my new drive.

- **Cabling problems.** This problem is usually traced to a faulty cable or a faulty hub (a separate piece of hardware that allows you to connect multiple USB or FireWire devices to a single port). Try connecting the drive with a different cable.
- **No power when daisy-chaining.** If you've connected your recorder to a USB or FireWire device that has a "passthru" or "daisy-chain" port, make sure that *both* external devices are switched on! Most USB and FireWire hardware won't pass a signal to further devices if they're turned off.

Summary

In this chapter, you installed your new DVD recorder and its software. I discussed the requirements for adding both an internal and an external DVD recorder to your PC, as well as the preparations you should take before beginning the installation. I then provided step-by-step instructions, using the HP DVD-Writer as an example. Finally, I discussed the most common problems you might encounter during the installation of an EIDE, USB, or FireWire device, and I provided possible solutions for each problem.

3

Preparing Your Computer and Material

In This Chapter

✓ Reducing hard drive clutter

✓ Defragmenting your hard drive

✓ Preventing interruptions from scheduled programs

✓ Adding memory to improve performance

✓ Converting files to archival formats

✓ Organizing your files for easy retrieval

Many folks ask me, "Can't I just record whatever's on my hard drive?" The answer, of course, is yes—once your DVD recorder and its software have been successfully installed, you're "technically" ready to burn discs. However, I don't recommend that you rush right into recording without taking a few simple steps first—without this preparation, you may:

· Run out of space to hold the files you want to record (or your recording software may run out of temporary file space in the middle of a burn, which is even worse).

dvds & cds

- *Degrade the performance of both your recorder and your entire system.*
- *Record documents and files that you may not be able to read five years in the future.*
- *Record files haphazardly, making it harder to find the files you're looking for when you need them the most.*

In this chapter, I'll show you the preparations you should take before you record your first disc—these steps will reduce the possibility of recording errors and speed up the burning process. You'll also find tips and tricks you can use to organize and standardize your files…it's a good bet that you'll benefit from these preparations the next time you load one of your discs!

Freeing Up Space on Your Hard Drive

Today's hard drives provide dozens of gigabytes of storage, but they aren't limitless. Today's 3D games often require 700 MB of space, and a lengthy digital video clip can easily gobble a gigabyte, so it's actually more important than ever to make sure you've got enough open territory on your hard drive! Besides the space required to hold your material, you also need free space because:

- Your recording software will need additional space for temporary files; these files are deleted once the recording has finished.
- Your computer may need space to convert files from one format to another (such as WAV audio files to MP3 audio) or compress digital video before it can be recorded.
- Windows will need additional space for *virtual memory* (hard drive space Windows uses as "temporary RAM" when your PC runs out of memory). Figure 3.1 illustrates how virtual memory works.

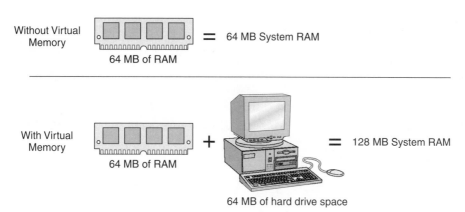

FIGURE 3.1   With virtual memory, a PC can run programs that use more memory.

Naturally, you won't want to simply drag a gigabyte's worth of files straight to the Recycle Bin! In most cases, you can safely delete these types of files:

- **Files stored in your Recycle Bin.** Those files stored in your Recycle Bin are actually still taking up space on your hard drive, and because you've already deleted them, it's safe to release that space. Right-click the Recycle Bin icon; Figure 3.2 illustrates the pop-up menu that appears. Select Empty Recycle Bin to delete the files.

- **Windows temporary files.** Windows 98, ME, and XP create all sorts of temporary files that can clutter up your hard drive. To clean up these derelicts, use the Windows Disk Cleanup Wizard. Under Windows XP, for instance, you would click Start | All Programs | Accessories | System Tools | Disk Cleanup, which runs the Wizard you see in Figure 3.3.

tip If you're familiar with the XP Disk Cleanup Wizard, you may have noticed that it offers you the opportunity to compress older, seldom-used files to regain space. This is a good idea—on a larger drive of 40 GB or more, compression is likely to save you at least 1 GB—and it won't affect your recording performance.

dvds & cds

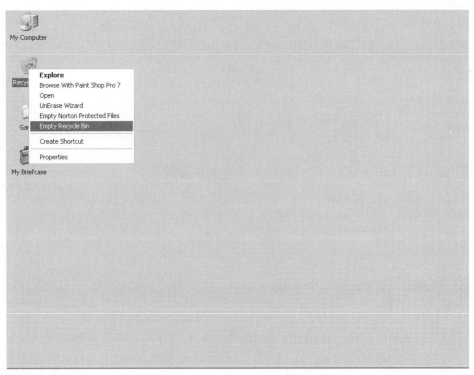

FIGURE 3.2   Need more space? Empty your Recycle Bin.

- **Unnecessary programs, game demos, shareware, and sample files.** Whether the programs are applications that you no longer use, forgotten game demos, or shareware you decided not to buy, they're prime targets for removal. Also, if an application has example files or sample documents that you know you won't need, you may be able to trim them—check the program's documentation or README file for details.

caution   Never simply drag a program's folder to the Recycle Bin—instead, click Start | Control Panel | Add and Remove Programs (Figure 3.4)! If you remove a program without allowing Windows to uninstall it, you may cause your PC to lock up or cause other programs to stop running. Older Windows programs may have their own uninstall programs in the Start menu, as well.

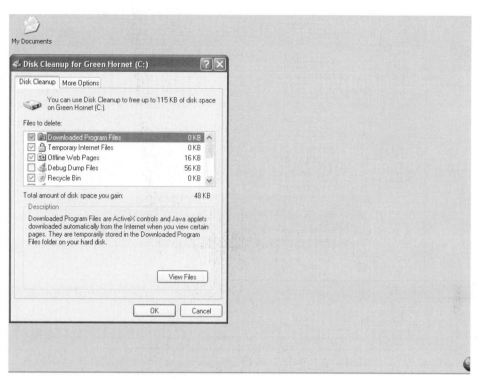

FIGURE 3.3   The Disk Cleanup Wizard may be buried in menus, but it's worth the trip.

- **Browser cache files.** If you spend hours browsing the Web, Internet Explorer may be eating up dozens of megabytes with its temporary files! To get rid of these files, run Internet Explorer, click Tools, and choose the Internet Options menu item. Click the General tab on the Internet Options dialog to display the settings you see in Figure 3.5. Click Delete Files, and click OK on the confirmation dialog.

If you can't find enough space on your system to use your new DVD recorder, it's time either to swap your existing drive with a larger one or to add a second drive to your system. Luckily, an EIDE hard drive is installed just like your DVD recorder, so you can follow the procedure in Chapter 2 in the section titled "Installing an Internal Drive" (and you won't need a device bay that's open to the front of the computer, because a hard drive has no tray to eject).

dvds & cds

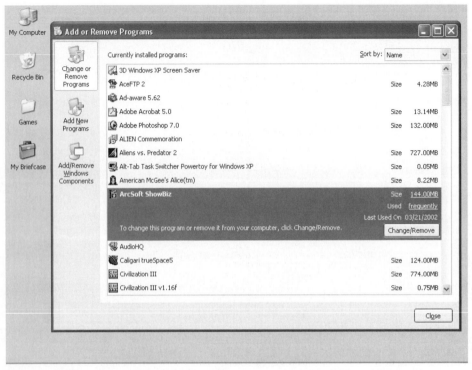

FIGURE 3.4   Deleting Windows applications using the Add and Remove Programs dialog.

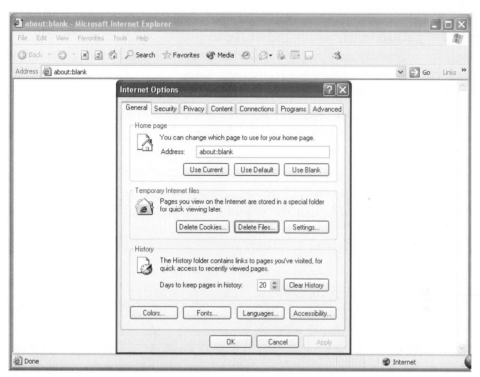

FIGURE 3.5   Deleting those pesky Web browser temporary files.

Defragmenting Your Hard Drive

Defragmenting is an easy step that you can take that will boost performance on any PC—and it can help eliminate DVD recording errors on older computers!

What is fragmentation, and why is it a problem? To answer those questions, you'll have to return to the days when you first began using your computer's hard drive. At that time, files were written contiguously (all in the same area and unbroken from beginning to end). As your drive stored more data, however, Windows started to save new files in the space freed when you deleted other files: Larger files can no longer be saved contiguously. Instead, a larger file is broken up into smaller pieces that fit into those "holes" left by deleted files, and it is saved in pieces (or segments) on your drive. The segment locations are saved, so your drive knows where all the parts of a particular file are

dvds & cds

stored. When a program wants to read that file, Windows and your drive's controller work together automatically to combine all the smaller segments of the file back into their original order; then Windows sends the restored file to the program.

It's a pretty neat process and invisible to both you and the programs you run—but the process isn't perfect. As you can see in Figure 3.6, it takes more time for Windows to "reassemble" the file, and the delay grows if there is a large number of segments that are spread out all over your drive. This is the ongoing process of fragmentation, and it gets worse over time—more files become more and more fragmented, and they take longer and longer to reassemble, which translates into slower disk performance. Disk performance is critical when you're recording a CD or DVD on a slower computer (especially when you're using Direct-to-Disc recording, as I will demonstrate in Chapter 7, "Direct-to-DVD Recording").

To optimize your drive, you need a defragmenter: a utility program that reads in the files on your drive and rewrites them in contiguous form, one after another. Figure 3.7 shows that same file after a defragmenter has done its work—our file is now contiguous, so it takes far less time for Windows to read it and send it to your recorder. It also means there's less chance that the next file you save to disk will become fragmented.

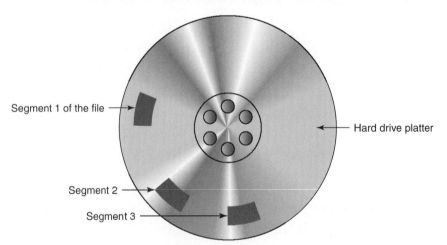

FIGURE 3.6   A fragmented file actually resides in segments on your hard drive.

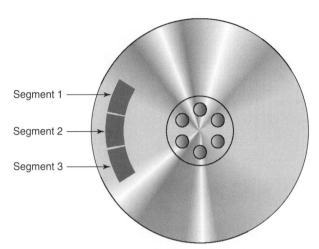

Segment 1

Segment 2

Segment 3

FIGURE 3.7   After running a defragmenter, the file is contiguous and loads much faster.

A defragmenter has been included with Windows 98, ME, and XP, as well as with Windows 2000—unfortunately, many folks don't know it's there and have never run it! I recommend running this program at least once a month.

✔ **To run Defragmenter under Windows XP, follow these steps:**

1. Click Start | All Programs | Accessories | System Tools | Disk Defragmenter. The Disk Defragmenter screen shown in Figure 3.8 appears.

2. Click the hard drive you want to scan. (If you have more than one drive, choose the drive that holds the files you'll be recording; however, it's always a good idea to defragment all of your hard drives.)

3. Click Defragment to begin defragmenting your drive. If you like, watch as Defragmenter does its thing—once the program has completed, you'll see by the graph that virtually all of the files on your drive are now contiguous.

dvds & cds

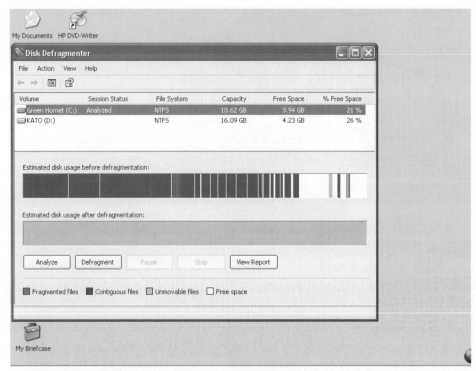

FIGURE 3.8   Windows XP includes a defragmenter—thanks, Microsoft!

Disabling Scheduled Programs

Not every Windows program is "well behaved." (Programmers would love you to think so, but it's not true.) Some of your favorite applications may be downright obnoxious; for example, a misbehaving program may prompt you for input without allowing other programs running simultaneously to continue in the background (effectively halting your entire system). Other programs may simply lock up from time to time. These types of interruptions during a recording session likely spell doom for that disc—if you're recording a CD-R, another ruined coaster hits the bottom of your trash can. (CD-RW and DVD+RW discs can simply be reformatted.)

To make sure your recordings aren't interrupted, you should disable any program that may kick in during a recording session, as well as other programs that may be running minimized or in the background. If a program isn't necessary to Windows or your recording software, disable or exit that program before you launch your recording software—and that includes programs running under Windows 2000 or XP Professional.

These programs can include:

- **MP3 or DVD players.** It's never a good idea to access any type of multimedia while you're recording. For example, playing a movie in Windows Media Player (shown in Figure 3.9) usually entails a great deal of hard drive and DVD-ROM access, and some MP3 players can cause your PC to freeze for a second or two at the beginning or ending of a song.

FIGURE 3.9   Avoid the popcorn—never watch a DVD while recording.

dvds & cds

- **Disk and system monitoring software.** It's important to scan your hard drives for errors, but do it before you start recording, not *during*! Also, system monitoring programs, such as Norton System Doctor (Figure 3.10), are great for checking the overall performance of your PC, but they're also infamous for slowing down older computers and automatically running programs (neither of which is recommended during a burn).

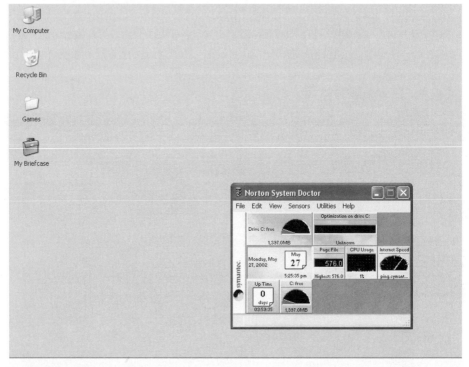

FIGURE 3.10 Disable monitoring programs, such as Norton System Doctor, while recording.

- **Screensavers.** Pretty to look at, but they can turn a fast Pentium III or Pentium 4 processor into a paperweight—especially multimedia screensavers that feature digital video or animation. Under Windows XP, right-click the desktop and choose Properties, then click the Screensaver tab (Figure 3.11) and set your screensaver to None.

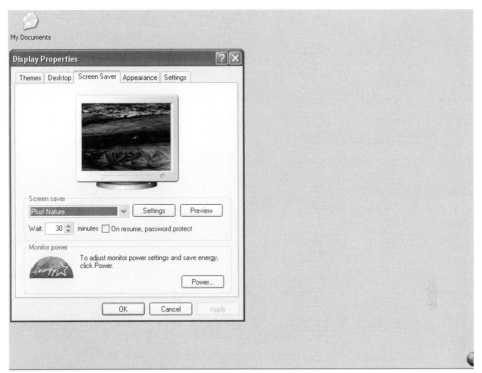

FIGURE 3.11 Turning off the screensaver in Windows XP.

• **Fax programs.** Fax programs can be performance-intensive, so be sure to disable your fax program's receive and scheduled send functions before you record.

You can usually disable or exit an unnecessary background task by right-clicking its taskbar icon and selecting Quit or Disable from the pop-up menu, as shown in Figure 3.12.

I also recommend pausing the Windows Task Scheduler (Figure 3.13) while you're recording—this prevents it from automatically launching programs without warning right in the middle of a burn. Right-click the Scheduler icon in the taskbar, and select Pause from the pop-up menu. (Don't forget to select Continue Task Scheduler after you've finished recording!)

dvds & cds

FIGURE 3.12 Turning off an unnecessary background task.

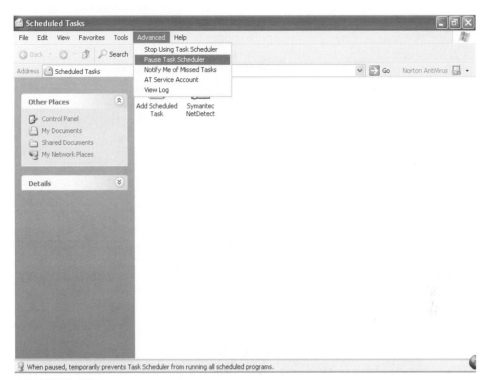

FIGURE 3.13 Pausing the Task Scheduler in Windows XP.

Adding System Memory

I'll be blunt here: At the time of this writing, memory is *dirt cheap*. If you're running Windows 98, I recommend at least 128 MB of RAM; if you're running Windows NT, ME, 2000, or XP, I wouldn't settle for less than a minimum of 256 MB of system RAM. If your computing budget allows more than these minimums, then by all means add more!

If you're unsure how much memory is available to Windows, right-click on the My Computer icon and select Properties from the pop-up menu. Figure 3.14 illustrates the System Properties dialog that appears in Windows XP; as you can see, this particular machine has 384 MB of RAM.

Why am I so enthralled with PC memory modules? Simple: No matter which version of Windows you're running, it will *always* per-

dvds & cds

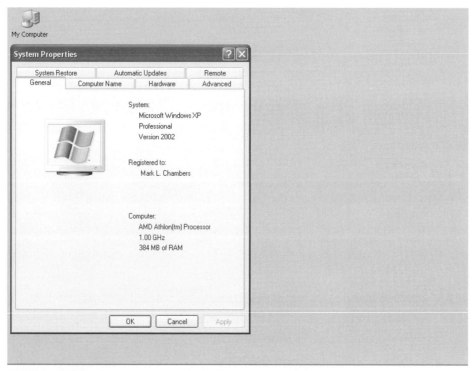

FIGURE 3.14 My machine has 384 MB of system memory.

form better overall with each extra megabyte of RAM you add. In fact, short of a processor upgrade, additional memory is the most effective upgrade you can perform when it comes to speeding up your system.

Also, adding more memory is very easy to do. If you like, you can bring your PC into your local computer store and have them perform the upgrade for you, but installing additional memory is much easier than installing your recorder; the entire process should take less than 10 minutes. Most of today's PCs use DIMM memory modules (there are a number of varieties, some of which are faster and more expensive than others).

✔ **To add a DIMM module to your PC, follow these steps:**

1. Shut down your computer.

2. Touch the metal chassis of your computer to dissipate any static electricity from your body, then unplug it from the AC wall outlet.

3. Unplug all of the cables from the back of your PC.

4. Remove the screws holding the cover and put them in your parts bowl. Take off the cover and set it aside.

5. Locate the DIMM memory slots; typically, they're located at one corner of the motherboard, or close to the CPU itself. Your motherboard manual should include a drawing that will help you find the memory slots.

6. Align the connector on the bottom of the memory module with the socket and push down lightly to seat the chip; make sure that the notches cut into the module connector match the guides in the memory sockets. (These guides ensure that you won't install your memory modules the wrong way!)

7. Make sure the two levers at each side of the socket move toward the center—these levers at the ends of the chip lock it into place.

When the DIMM is correctly installed, it should set vertically on the motherboard, with the two levers flush against the sides of the module.

tip When buying memory for your PC, make sure that you're buying the right type (older computers may even require that you upgrade memory modules in pairs). Bring your PC's manual to the store, or check the manufacturer's specifications for the right type of memory to use. (If you're totally stumped as to what to buy, you can even remove the existing modules and bring them with you—make sure they're wrapped in a static-free plastic bag.) The manufacturer's Web site often carries memory upgrade information for discontinued PC models.

dvds & cds

Converting Files to Other Formats

First, a quick definition: If you've never heard of file *conversion*, it's the procedure you follow when you change a file from one format to another. Many computer applications understand only one or two file formats, whereas others can understand many—and that's the reason behind this section.

When you choose documents and files that will be saved on DVD and used for many years, it becomes important to save those files in the right format; this can help ensure that you'll still be able to watch your digital video, listen to your music, or open your Letter to the Editor in 10 years as easily as the day after tomorrow. Formats do "die out" over the years—this makes perfect sense, because everyone tends to standardize on one or two very successful and popular formats. After that decade has passed, you definitely want your music saved in MP3 format and not SND format. (Never heard of SND format? Gotcha! It's an older, once-popular Macintosh sound recording format that has all but disappeared, and it's the perfect proof of my point.)

There's another reason why you might convert files before record-ing them on a disc: If you're creating a cross-platform disc that will be read by Macintosh owners (or Linux technowizards), you'll save those people quite a bit of trouble if you choose a format that's just as popular in their computing world as in the Windows world. Don't leave an image bound for a Macintosh in Windows Bitmap format, for exam-ple—instead, do the job yourself and convert that file to JPEG or TIFF (both of which are popular in the Mac world and well recognized by Macintosh applications).

Here are the best choices for formats for each of the major types of files you're likely to record, along with the best programs for converting file formats under Windows:

- **Images and photographs.** Use either JPEG or TIFF—JPEG is the most widely recognized image format out there (and it's the format of choice for Web pages), and TIFF is almost as well known. TIFF images provide better quality than JPEG, but they're much, much larger. Use Paint Shop Pro from Jasc (Figure 3.15) for conversions; it's inexpensive shareware, it's fast, and it

FIGURE 3.15 Converting images using Paint Shop Pro.

recognizes a huge number of formats! Jasc's Web site is located at www.jasc.com. Adobe Photoshop (Figure 3.16) is another perennial favorite, capable of converting all sorts of exotic and complex formats.

- **Music and audio.** MP3 is the clear winner here, and just about all audio programs recognize it on all computers. Microsoft's WAV format is also a good pick for files that will stay in the Windows world, but a WAV file is huge, compared with the same music saved as an MP3 file. To convert other formats and copy tracks from an audio CD to MP3, I use Musicmatch Jukebox Plus (www.musicmatch.com), shown in Figure 3.17; the basic version is available for free!

- **Video.** Your best choices for storing digital video on the PC are Microsoft AVI format or MPEG format—personally, I prefer

dvds & cds

FIGURE 3.16 If you use Adobe Photoshop, put it to work when converting formats.

MPEG format, which is widely used on the Web and is almost always recognized by video editors running on all different types of computers. (If you're recording digital video for use on a Macintosh, consider QuickTime MOV format.) Adobe Premiere makes a great conversion utility, because it's available on both the PC and Macintosh. Figure 3.18 illustrates the familiar face of Premiere.

tip   One type of video conversion that you may need to make from time to time is a switch from the PAL video standard used in Europe to the NTSC video standard used in the United States. ArcSoft ShowBiz comes in handy as a conversion tool for this job. For more information on this conversion, see Chapter 12, "Making Movies with ArcSoft ShowBiz," where I give you all the details on ShowBiz.

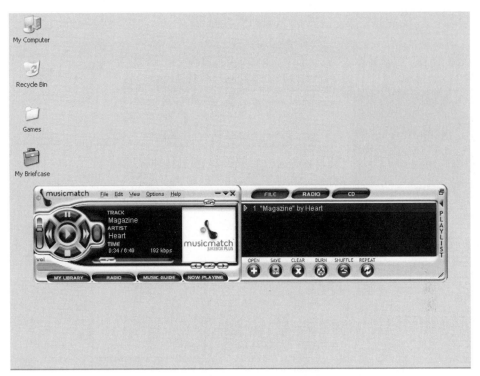

FIGURE 3.17 Musicmatch Jukebox Plus is a great MP3 conversion tool.

- **Documents.** Microsoft Office (Figure 3.19) is the obvious choice here—it's available on both the PC and Mac, and it includes a dizzying array of options for importing, converting, and exporting all sorts of document formats. Microsoft has a passion for preserving older Office document formats, which bodes well for your Word documents in a decade or two.

dvds & cds

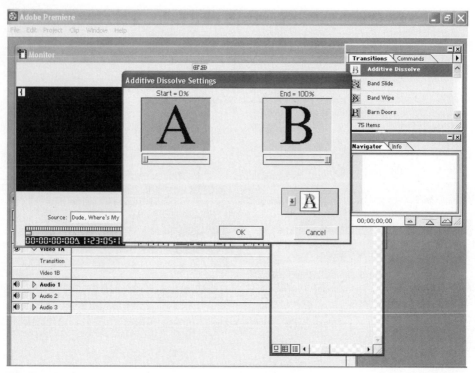

FIGURE 3.18   Adobe Premiere is available for both the PC and the Macintosh.

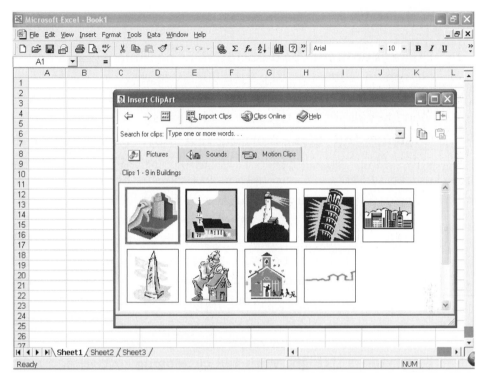

FIGURE 3.19 If you're an Office owner, you already have a great document conversion tool.

Organizing Files

Along with conversion, I strongly recommend that you take a few minutes to plan the arrangement of a data CD before you record it. Sure, you can lump 50 files in the root directory of a DVD and read them without a problem...but will it be easy to find what you're *looking for* in six months?

With convenience and ease of use in mind, here are a few guidelines you can follow:

- **Use folders to store your files.** Grouping your files in folders makes them easier to locate, and some types of discs have a limit to the number of files you can place in the root directory of the disc.

- **Make your names as descriptive as possible.** For example, a file named "State Tax Reports 2001" is easier to locate and easier to comprehend than a file named "STXR2001." (Luckily, Windows allows you to use long filenames.)

- **Organize your files according to a "key."** If you've ever created a database, you know what a key is—it's the data that you use to search your information (whether it be a person's last name or an order number). Arranging files in folders on your disc using a key makes it much easier to locate a specific file in years to come. For example, your key could be the type of file, and all JPEG images would be grouped together. By adding another key—for example, the subject of the image—you can create a folder just for images of your family in JPEG format. (You'll know precisely where all your pictures of Uncle Milton are stored: They're in the folder called "JPEG Family Shots.")

- **Keep things straight with file cataloging software.** At the simplest level, you can use the Windows Search feature to look for a specific filename on your discs—however, there are also shareware and commercial disk cataloging programs that can search for a file through multiple discs and hard drives (even the ones that aren't loaded). Also, you can use a program such as Media Center Plus (again, from Jasc Software at www.jasc.com)—this great utility creates albums of all your multimedia files and allows you to search visually through thumbnails. Figure 3.20 illustrates a thumbnail album from one of my discs. Media Center Plus can also catalog video clips, sounds, and MP3 files, and you can play them back within the program to check out their contents.

FIGURE 3.20 With Media Center Plus, you can catalog all of your images, sounds, songs, and video.

Summary

In this chapter, I covered the preparations you should make before you launch your DVD recording software. You learned how to optimize the performance of your hard drive by defragmenting and how to add extra memory to speed up your entire system. I discussed how you can delete programs safely to open up additional free space on your hard drive and how to disable the Windows Task Scheduler to prevent interruptions while you're recording. Finally, you learned how to organize files on your discs and how to convert those files to other formats, if necessary.

4

Burning Discs with HP RecordNow

In This Chapter

My second car was a 1979 Ford Pinto hatchback—it was the definition of a basic automobile, with no luxury items besides a cup holder and an AM radio, but I loved that vehicle. (And no, it never showed signs of exploding.) Why do I have such fond memories of my Pinto? To wit, it never broke down, it delivered great gas mileage, and it was easy to drive. Also, I got it for practically nothing.

Those same qualities will endear you to Hewlett-Packard's RecordNow program—well, all except the great

dvds & cds

gas mileage, anyway. RecordNow is included with the DVD-Writer drive, so you can use your new recorder the minute you install it. RecordNow is very easy to operate, as well. Although RecordNow doesn't deliver the exotic formats of programs such as Easy CD Creator, it does produce most of the basic discs you're likely to need: data DVDs and CDs, audio CDs, and copies of existing discs. I've found RecordNow to be as reliable as my Pinto, and I use this great program every day.

In this chapter, I'll use RecordNow to demonstrate how you can burn each of these standard disc types, and I'll also provide two step-by-step projects: one to record an audio CD from MP3 files and one to burn a disc to carry data while I'm traveling on the road.

Introducing HP RecordNow

You can run RecordNow directly from the Windows Start menu—click Start | All Programs | HP RecordNow | RecordNow—but the easiest way to run the program is simply to load a blank CD, DVD+R, or DVD+RW disc into the DVD-Writer, which automatically displays the Create dialog you see in Figure 4.1. Click HP RecordNow, and click OK when the program recommends a CD-R disc; the RecordNow window appears, as shown in Figure 4.2.

tip **Are you running Windows XP? If so, you may find that Windows displays that irritating "What Should I Do?" dialog (shown in Figure 4.3), along with the Create dialog. If so, you can easily "teach" Windows not to repeat this annoying performance: Click the Take no action entry from the list and click the Always do the selected action checkbox to enable it, then click OK.**

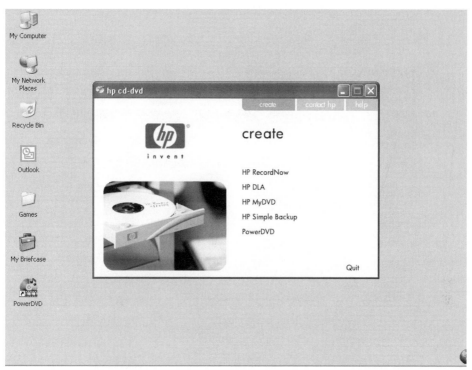

FIGURE 4.1   Loading a blank disc displays the Create window.

As you can see, RecordNow—like my trusty Pinto—includes just what you need, and the program couldn't be easier to use. Because the program doesn't have a traditional menu bar, however, there are two features that may not be immediately apparent:

- The RecordNow Help system appears when you press F1 or when you click the Help button at the top of the window. You can find details on everything the program can do (as well as a direct link to the HP RecordNow support site on the Web) from this menu.
- Click Options to set up general program preferences, advanced recording options, and links to the Internet audio CD database. I'll be discussing many of these options later in this chapter, but make note of the Options menu now, in case you need to change your RecordNow configuration.

dvds & cds

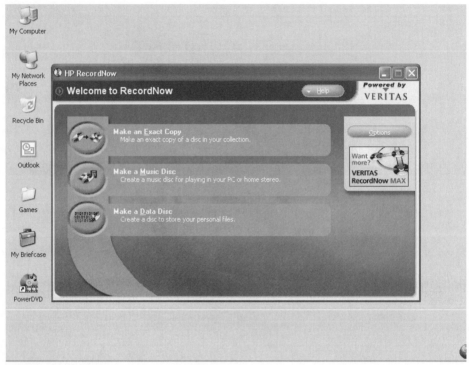

FIGURE 4.2   The main RecordNow window.

tip One option that you'll either love or hate is the "Eject drive trays automatically" checkbox; by default, RecordNow will eject the drive tray when a disc needs to be loaded. This is a boon for the inexperienced users who have multiple drives, but you may want to disable this option if your PC has a door or cover that hides the recorder from view! (There's nothing quite like the sound of your DVD recorder's drive tray making contact with another surface.)

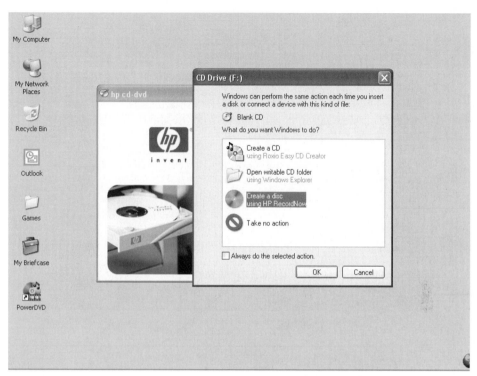

FIGURE 4.3 Windows XP tries to make things easier...no thanks.

Putting Computer Files on a Disc

If your hard drive is running out of room or you want to archive files from your computer for safekeeping, look no further than RecordNow: The program can create data discs using CD-R, CD-RW, and DVD+RW media. (If you've bought an HP DVD-Writer DVD200-series drive, you can also use DVD+R media.)

✔ **Follow these steps to create a data disc:**

1. Click Make a Data Disc; RecordNow displays a wizard window prompting you to insert a blank disc (as shown in Figure 4.4). If you ran the program by loading a blank disc in the first place, continue by clicking Next; if you ran RecordNow from the Start menu, load a blank disc in your drive and click Next.

dvds & cds

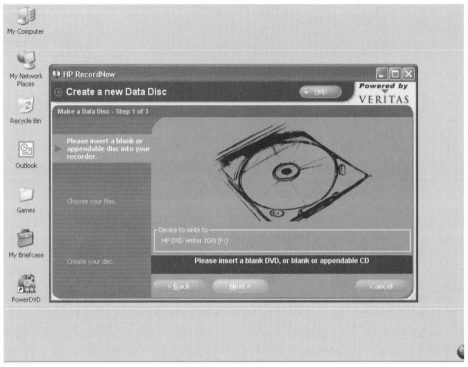

FIGURE 4.4   Time to load a blank CD or DVD, if necessary.

2. Time to select the files you want to add to your data disc: Record-Now supports "drag-and-drop" file selection from the Windows Explorer, so you can select files and folders and drag them to the wizard window shown in Figure 4.5. Alternately, you can click Add Files and Folders—RecordNow displays the familiar Windows file selection dialog, where you can navigate to the files and folders you want to add, select them, and click Add. Whichever method you use, RecordNow displays the files you've added in the window and updates the amount of space remaining on the disc. To rename a file or folder, click the name once, press F2, and type the new name. When you've added all of the files you want to add to your data disc, click Next to continue.

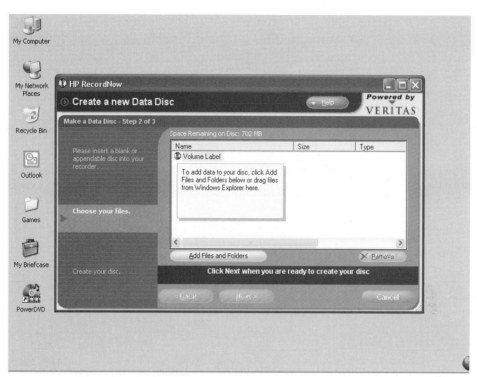

FIGURE 4.5 Drag and drop files on this window, or use the Windows file selection dialog.

tip **To change the volume label displayed for the disc under Windows—commonly called the "name" of a data CD—click on the words *Volume Label* next to the disc icon, press F2, and type a new label, then press Enter to save it.**

3. RecordNow displays a warning dialog, explaining that recording errors can occur if you start new applications while the disc is burned. Generally, this is a good idea if your recorder doesn't offer burn-proof recording—however, because all DVD-Writers support burn-proof recording, you can effectively ignore this warning if you need to take care of other tasks. (To disable this warning, click the Don't show me this dialog again checkbox.) Click OK to continue, and sit back and relax while the recording process begins.

dvds & cds

tip By default, RecordNow verifies the data it's written to the disc by comparing the files on the disc with the files on your hard drive—a good way to guard against media defects. Because this can take half as long as the actual recording, you may want to disable verification: Click Options on the RecordNow main window and click the Verify the data written to the disc after write checkbox to disable it, then click OK to save your change.

4. Once the data has been successfully written and verified, Record-Now ejects the disc and displays the dialog you see in Figure 4.6; you can click Make Another to create another copy of the same disc or click Done to return to the RecordNow main window.

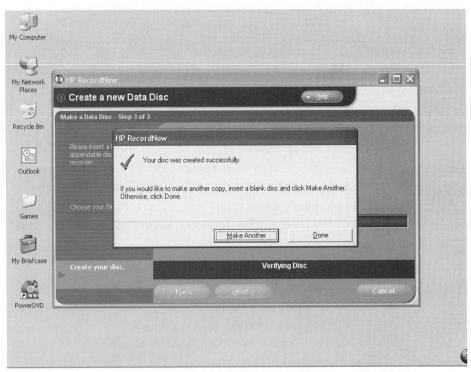

FIGURE 4.6   Another successful burn—I love that Big Green Check!

Recording Your Music

RecordNow makes a great tool for burning audio CDs for use in your home and car audio CD players. The program can create three different types of audio CDs:

- A standard audio CD using MP3 and WAV format digital audio tracks from your hard drive
- A standard audio CD using individual tracks you've copied from existing CDs (a process popularly called *ripping*)
- A special MP3 disc for use in MP3 audio players; these discs can't be used in a standard audio CD player, but they can contain much more music than a standard audio CD. This type of disc is actually not an audio CD at all; instead, it's a data CD that can be read by the improved electronics inside today's MP3 audio players. In effect, the player reads the music files just as your computer does when it plays MP3 audio directly from your hard drive!

tip **If you choose one of the first two types (those that create a standard audio CD), RecordNow will first convert the audio files into WAV format before they're recorded, so avoid burning audio CDs when your drive is very low on free space.**

To burn an audio CD, run RecordNow and click Make a Music Disc. RecordNow prompts you for the type of disc you want to create, as illustrated in Figure 4.7. Click the desired type, and follow the corresponding steps in the next section.

caution **Unless your audio CD player specifically supports CD-RW discs, you should always use CD-R discs to record standard audio CDs! Most audio CD players can't read an audio CD recorded using a CD-RW disc. (Note that MP3 music discs are the exception to the rule, because virtually all MP3 audio players can read CD-RW discs.)**

dvds & cds

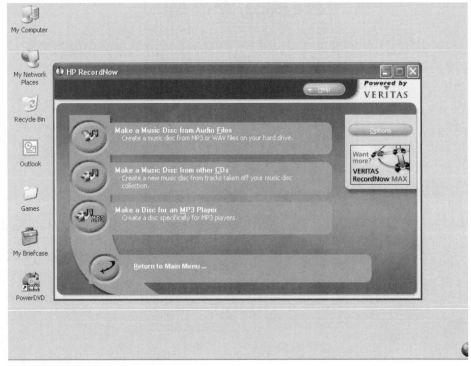

FIGURE 4.7   Selecting a music disc.

Recording with Digital Audio Files

✔ **Follow these steps if you clicked Make a Music Disc from Audio Files or Make a Disc for an MP3 Player:**

1. RecordNow displays the same wizard screen you saw in Figure 4.4, prompting you to insert a blank disc; if necessary, load a blank disc in your drive and click Next.

2. To search for MP3 and WAV digital audio files on your system, click Yes at the prompt; RecordNow will find all digital audio files in these two formats on your hard drive. If you have an Internet connection

active, the program will also attempt to identify the tracks, using the CDDB Internet database.

tip Are you a game player? If you choose to search for files, be prepared for a long wait—and several dozen MP3 and WAV files that you probably don't want to record to an audio CD. (Most of the PC games written today use MP3 audio for background music and WAV files for sound effects.) In fact, Windows itself ships with a number of WAV files that will also show up. The moral of the story? If you know what audio files you want to record and where they are, click No at the search prompt and skip to step 3.

3. RecordNow displays the layout wizard screen you see in Figure 4.8. If you searched for audio files, the files that were found are listed in the Music on System list at the left; you can click a filename to select it in this list and click Add to add the song to your music CD layout. To add specific files from your hard drive, you can drag and drop files from the Windows Explorer; alternately, you can click Browse to display the Windows file selection dialog, where you can navigate to the audio files, select them, and click Add. The files you add appear in the list on the right, and RecordNow updates the amount of time remaining. When you've finished adding tracks, click Next to begin recording.

tip You can rearrange the order of the tracks in the layout by dragging a filename to the desired location. To preview an audio file, click the desired filename to select it and click the speaker icon under the Music on System list.

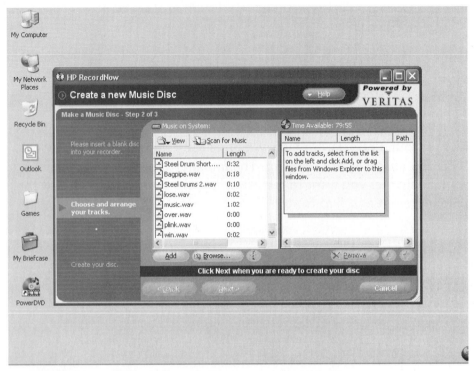

FIGURE 4.8   Adding MP3 and WAV digital audio to a CD.

Recording Tracks from Existing Audio CDs

✔ **Follow these steps if you clicked Make a Music Disc from other CDs:**

1. RecordNow automatically ejects the disc tray and displays the wizard screen shown in Figure 4.9, prompting you to insert a music CD. Load the first disc containing the music you want to record and click Next.

2. RecordNow displays the layout wizard screen—the tracks on the CD you loaded are listed in the Music CD Tracks list at the left; click a track name to select it in this list and click Add to add the song to

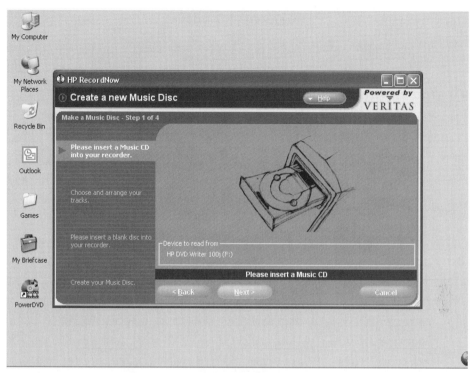

FIGURE 4.9   Load your music and prepare to rip.

your music CD layout. Remember, to preview a track, click the desired track name to select it and click the speaker icon under the Music CD Tracks list (click the button again to exit preview mode). The files you add appear in the list on the right, and RecordNow updates the amount of time remaining.

3. When you've finished adding tracks from the current audio CD, click Next CD to load the next source disc. RecordNow temporarily copies the tracks you selected to your hard drive.

4. When you've finished adding tracks, click Finish. RecordNow prompts you to load a blank CD to begin recording.

Copying a Disc

✔ **You can also use RecordNow to make an exact duplicate of an existing data or audio CD. Follow these steps:**

1. Run RecordNow and click Make an Exact Copy; RecordNow automatically ejects the disc tray and prompts you to load the disc you want to duplicate.

2. Load the source disc and click Next.

3. RecordNow displays a progress bar as it copies the contents of the source disc to a temporary image file on your hard drive. Once the original disc has been copied to the computer's hard drive, the program ejects the tray and prompts you to load a blank CD to begin recording. If you use a second CD-ROM drive to read the source disc while your DVD-Writer concentrates on recording, no disc swapping is necessary: Simply congratulate yourself for your foresight and consider yourself a "Power Ripper."

tip **Don't attempt to copy a "copy-protected" CD or DVD disc with this program (such as a DVD movie or a game CD-ROM). Naturally, RecordNow is not meant for duplicating these discs, and the result will be a shiny coaster.**

Project: **Recording a "Road Trip" Audio CD**

What could be better on a long drive than a collection of your disco favorites? (Don't answer that...there's always the Partridge Family.) Anyway, in this project, we'll burn a "Road Trip" audio CD, using tracks taken from several different existing audio CDs: The resulting disc can be played in any car or home audio CD player.

Requirements

- A collection of audio CDs
- Blank CD-R disc

✔ **Follow these steps to create your compilation audio CD:**

1. Run RecordNow and click Make a Music Disc, then click Make a Music Disc from other CDs.

2. RecordNow automatically ejects the disc tray and prompts you to load the first of the existing audio CDs. Load the first disc containing the music you want to record and click Next.

3. Figure 4.10 illustrates the tracks from my first source CD; let's add *A Fifth of Beethoven* and *Play That Funky Music*. Click *A Fifth of Beethoven*, hold down the Ctrl key, and click *Play That Funky Music* to select both tracks, then click Add. Note that RecordNow indicates we have 66 minutes and 5 seconds of time remaining on this disc.

4. Click Next CD to load the next source disc; RecordNow takes a few seconds to copy those first two tracks temporarily to your hard drive, then ejects the drive tray. Load the next disc and click OK.

5. Repeat steps 3 and 4 until you've added all of the desired tracks; for example, Figure 4.11 illustrates my completed disco audio CD layout, using selected tracks from three different audio CDs. However, I've decided that I'd rather start the disc with *YMCA*—I'll click on the name *YMCA* in the track list and drag it to the first position in the list.

6. Time to burn this disco inferno! Click Finish. RecordNow prompts you to load a blank CD, and the recording begins.

dvds & cds

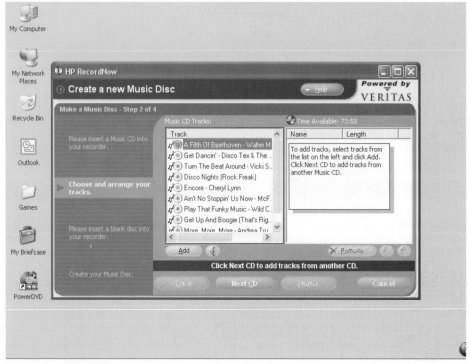

FIGURE 4.10 Selecting the perfect disco tracks.

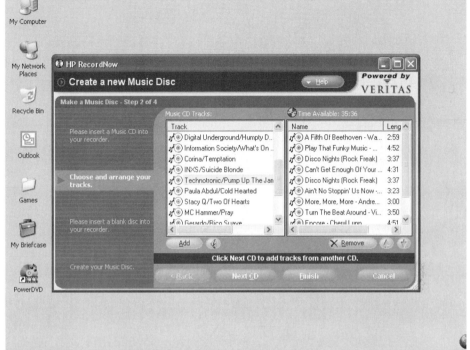

FIGURE 4.11 A completed disco disc layout.

Project: Creating a "Briefcase Backup" DVD

Next, I'll record what I like to call a *Briefcase Backup* (if you've read other books I've written, you'll probably recognize the term). A Briefcase Backup is a disc that you record to augment your laptop's hard drive; for example, when I travel, I store all of the data I'll need (including things such as PowerPoint presentations, Excel worksheets, books in PDF format, and digital video samples) on a CD-RW disc. (I could do the same thing with a DVD+RW disc, but I don't need to haul around that much data yet!) A Briefcase Backup has a number of advantages for the road warrior:

dvds & cds

- Most laptops (especially older models) have smaller hard drives—rather than use up that valuable space, you can store 700 MB of your traveling data on a disc instead.
- In case of a damaged or lost notebook, you still have a backup if you carry the disc in your luggage.
- If you need to transfer that data to a client's PC, there are no silly cables or network cards needed; you can load the disc in any PC with the proper drive.

In this case, I'll record all of the files necessary to recreate this entire book to a Briefcase Backup—that includes Word documents, templates, and every single figure, all of which fit comfortably on a single DVD+RW disc!

Requirements

- Blank CD-R, CD-RW, DVD+R (if you're using a DVD-Writer DVD200 drive), or DVD+RW disc

✔ Follow these steps to record data:

1. Run RecordNow and click Make a Data Disc, then load the blank disc (if necessary) and click Next to continue.

2. I'll use drag-and-drop file selection from Windows Explorer; Figure 4.12 shows Windows Explorer open, displaying the folder with the files I need to record. Select the desired files—remember, you can hold down Ctrl while you click to select multiple files, then click and drag the files to the wizard window. To rename a file or folder, click the name once, press F2, and type the new name.

3. Before I record a Briefcase Backup disc, I usually name it with a description of the contents; in this case, we'll change the volume label to DVDREC. Click on the words Volume Label next to the disc icon, press F2, type DVDREC, and press Enter. That completes the data layout, so click Next to continue.

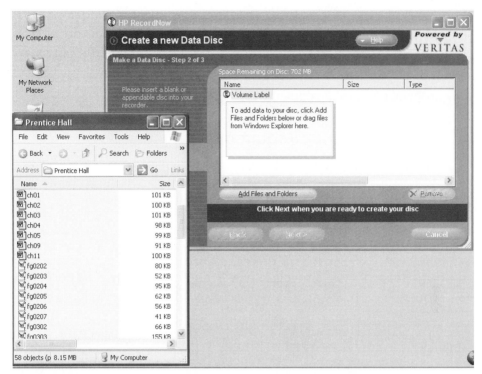

FIGURE 4.12 Ready to drag and drop files on the RecordNow wizard window.

4. If you haven't disabled the warning dialog, click OK to continue. RecordNow begins burning our disc.

5. When the verification completes successfully, our new Briefcase Backup disc is ejected from the drive. RecordNow prompts you for additional copies of the same disc. Because we need only one copy, click Done to return to the RecordNow main window.

Project: **Copying a Backup Data CD for Archiving**

To close this chapter, let's prepare your company's data (or the data from your home office computer) against the worst by creating a second copy of your hard drive backup disc for storage off site. There are numerous companies that can perform this operation for you and store

dvds & cds

your archival copy—for a hefty fee, of course—but by using your DVD or CD media and RecordNow, you can make a copy and store it in your safety deposit box at your bank. Total cost? Probably less than $5—and, if you use rewriteable media, you can continue to update your archival copy on a regular basis!

Requirements

- The original disc
- A blank DVD+RW or CD-RW disc

✔ **Follow these steps to record data:**

1. Run RecordNow and click Make an Exact Copy; RecordNow prompts you to load the original data disc, as shown in Figure 4.13.

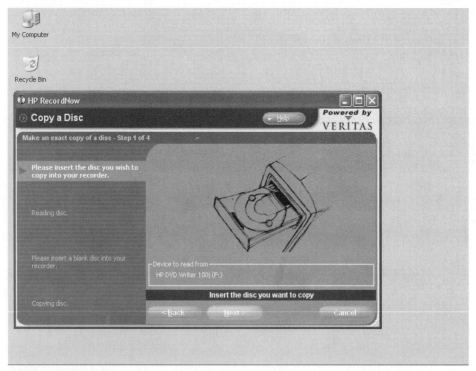

FIGURE 4.13 RecordNow prompts you to load the source disc for duplication.

2. Load the source disc—in this case, the backup data disc—and click Next to close the drive door and begin the duplication.

3. If you're using two drives (your DVD recorder and a CD-ROM or DVD-ROM read-only drive for the source) to copy, just load the blank disc in the recorder and grab yourself a cup of coffee or refill your soda—there's no need to swap discs, so your job is finished.

4. If you're using only your DVD recorder, sit back and relax while RecordNow copies the contents of the backup data disc to your hard drive (Figure 4.14)—this image will be used as the source when you load the blank disc into your recorder.

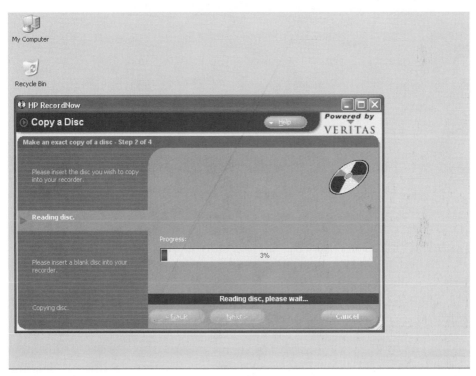

FIGURE 4.14 When copying with only one drive, the data is first copied to your hard drive.

5. If you're using one drive, the program ejects the tray, once the original backup data disc has been copied to the computer's hard drive, and prompts you to load a blank disc to begin recording (as shown in Figure 4.15).

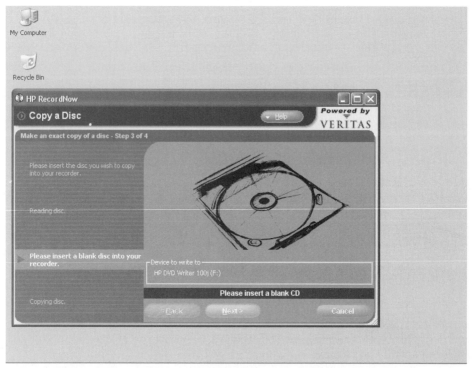

FIGURE 4.15   Load a blank disc, and RecordNow does the rest!

Summary

In this chapter, you learned how to create the "bread-and-butter basics" of CD and DVD recording: data discs (created from files and folders on your hard drive), audio CDs (burned from digital audio files on your hard drive or tracks ripped from existing music discs), and MP3 discs (data discs that contain digital audio files for use in MP3 audio players).

chapter

5

Drag-and-Drop Recording with HP DLA

In This Chapter

✓ Formatting and writing DLA discs

✓ Ejecting a DLA disc

✓ Adding files to an existing DLA disc

✓ Project: Creating a Genealogy Archive Disc

✓ Project: Recording and Finalizing a PowerPoint Presentation Disc

UDF (short for Universal Disc Format) recording, also called packet writing, is practically the perfect method of burning data files over an extended period of time. You can copy files to or delete them from a CD-R (or, if you're using the HP-Writer DVD200-series drive, a DVD+R) UDF disc as you would a floppy drive, a ZIP drive, or a hard drive. In fact, if you can save a file using drag-and-drop, Windows Explorer, or any other Windows application, everything is transparent—you don't have to worry about running a separate program, creating a layout, or recording a session.

dvds & cds

Naturally, UDF can team up with rewriteable CD-RW and DVD+RW discs, too—most computers with a DVD-ROM drive running Windows or Mac OS can read a DVD+RW UDF disc, and any computer with a MultiRead CD-ROM drive can read a CD-RW UDF disc. Because both of these media types can be reformatted and used again, your DVD+RW drive becomes what many computer owners consider the "perfect" removable media drive!

The Hewlett-Packard DVD-Writer drive comes complete with HP DLA (short for Drive Letter Access), a complete UDF formatting and burning application; I'll use this program while covering how to format a UDF disc, how to copy files to it, and how to eject it properly when you're done. Our three projects for this chapter illustrate how you can create a removable disc for carrying files between your work and your home computers, how to record a DVD genealogy archive disc that you can update whenever you like, and how to burn a PowerPoint presentation disc that's finalized for use in any PC CD-ROM drive.

Formatting a DLA Disc

Like any floppy disk, ZIP disk, or hard drive, a UDF disc must first be formatted before you can write to it. You can do this from the Toolkit, which is available from the Windows Start menu—click Start | All Programs | HP DLA | DLA Toolkit.

Of course, the easier this task is, the better—therefore, you can also simply load a blank CD or DVD disc into the DVD-Writer, which automatically displays the familiar Create dialog. Click HP DLA, and click OK when the program recommends a CD-R or DVD+RW disc— I actually use UDF more often with rewriteable media, such as CD-RW or DVD+RW discs.

Figure 5.1 illustrates the Toolkit window that appears regardless of which method you choose to display the program.

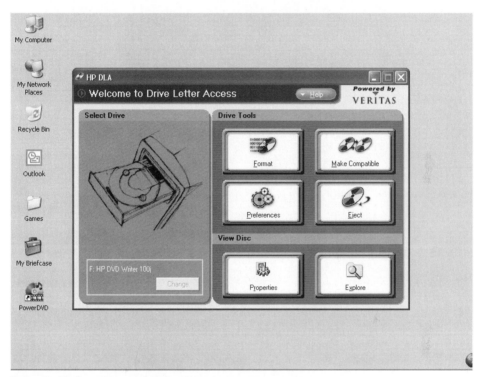

FIGURE 5.1   The main DLA Toolkit window.

✔ Follow these steps to format a disc for use with HP DLA:

1. Click Format; the Toolkit displays a wizard window prompting you to insert a blank disc (as shown in Figure 5.2). If you ran the program by loading a blank disc in the first place, continue by clicking Next; if you ran DLA from the Start menu, load a blank disc in your drive and click Next.

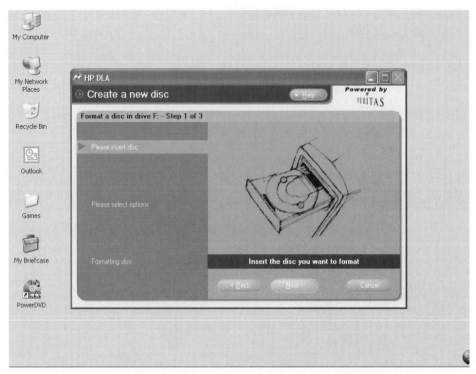

FIGURE 5.2   DLA prompts you to load a blank disc.

2. Next, it's time to configure the disc. First, click in the Volume Label field and type a name for the disc; this is the name that will appear with the DLA drive in Windows Explorer.

3. DLA can use either of two formatting modes: You can choose between a *quick format* and a *full format*. As the name implies, the Quick format is much faster (taking less than a minute), but it can be used only in certain cases: if you're formatting a CD-R disc for the first time or if you're reformatting any type of rewriteable media. On the other hand, the Full format must be used if you're formatting a CD-RW or DVD+RW disc for the first time.

tip Generally, I use Full format only when initially formatting CD-RW or DVD+RW discs; however, if you have a rewriteable disc that returns errors when you try to read it (or can't be read at all),

you should always use Full format before using it again. Such errors can occur because of a power failure or lockup while your PC is writing to the disc.

4. Finally, click the Enable compression checkbox if you'd like to increase the capacity of the disc (generally by a ratio of 2:1, depending on the type of data you're storing)—however, enabling compression means that other computers will need HP DLA installed before they can read your disc. Without compression, any computer with a compatible drive that supports UDF discs will be able to read the disc—this includes all current versions of Windows, as well as Mac OS 9.x, Mac OS X, and most "flavors" of UNIX and Linux. Figure 5.3 illustrates the settings I'm using for a DVD+RW disc. Click Next to continue.

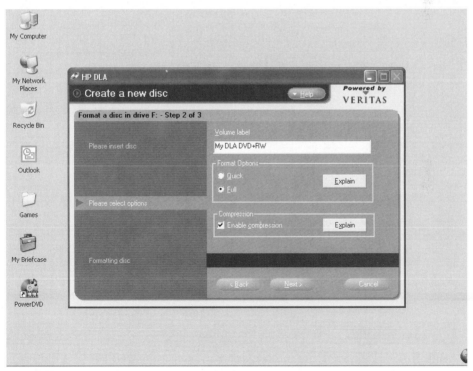

FIGURE 5.3   Configuring the formatting settings for a DVD+RW disc.

dvds & cds

5. The Toolkit program displays a progress bar and an approximate time remaining to complete the format; once the disc has been successfully formatted, you're returned to the Toolkit main window. To display the capacity, compression settings, and volume name, click Properties to display the Properties dialog (Figure 5.4). Click Close to return to the Toolkit window.

tip **If you've enabled compression on your DLA disc, you may be wondering where all that extra space comes in—because the compression is applied when the files are written, DLA can display only the used space and an *approximation* of the free space remaining. It pays to keep an eye on the free space for a UDF disc after writing to it, because Windows can only estimate the amount of space left.**

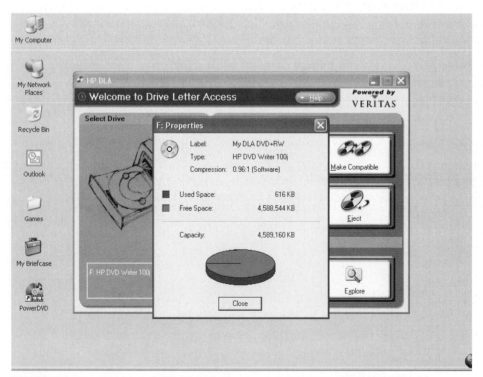

FIGURE 5.4   Displaying the properties for a newly formatted HP DLA disc.

Writing Files to a DLA Disc

Don't expect to find complex procedures in this section! DLA operates *entirely* in the background—nearly invisibly—while you use your new CD or DVD disc. You can read, copy, and move files to your HP DLA disc using the same standard Windows menu commands, keyboard shortcuts, and drag-and-drop mouse operations that you're already using—you can also delete files from the DLA disc (although you can't reclaim the space occupied by the deleted files if you're using CD-R or DVD+R media).

tip **DLA discs are data-only: you can't create an audio CD using HP DLA, and they're not suitable for use in audio CD players. However, you can use a DLA disc to store MP3 files for later. (When you have the chance, you can copy the digital audio files to your hard drive and burn them to a music disc, using HP RecordNow.)**

Your applications can open and save data to documents on a DLA disc, just as they would with a hard drive—you can also use the Send To option that appears when you right-click on a file or folder to copy a file to your DLA disc. Even if you use Windows Explorer or another file management program, there are no settings to change or adjustments to make to use a DLA disc; it's all taken care of by the HP DLA program, and that's all there is to it! Figure 5.5 illustrates how the DLA disc that I formatted in the last section looks in Windows XP's My Computer window.

✔ **For example, if you have a file saved on your Windows desktop, follow these steps to copy it to your DLA disc:**

1. Double-click My Computer to open it and display your drive icons.

2. To copy the file into a folder on your DLA disc, double-click the icon for your DLA disc and double-click the desired folder to open it.

dvds & cds

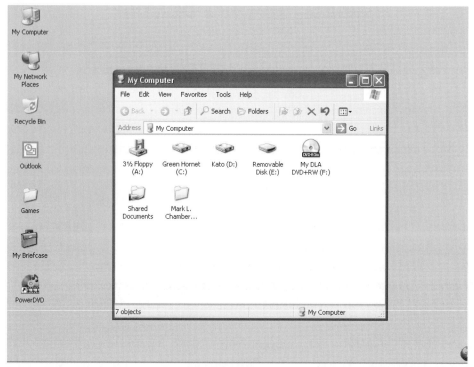

FIGURE 5.5   To Windows XP, my DLA disc is just another removable disc.

3. Click the file you want to copy and continue to hold down the mouse button. Drag the file to the DLA folder window to copy it.

Ejecting a DLA Disc

In most cases, ejecting a DLA disc is no different from ejecting a regular read-only CD or DVD. You can:

- Press the Eject button on your drive.
- Right-click on the disc icon in the My Computer window.
- Run the HP DLA Toolkit application and click the Eject button.

Note that DLA may require a few seconds to prepare the disc before it's ejected (depending on whether the drive is still writing data).

tip **If you're planning on reading the disc on a computer that's not running a UDF-compatible operating system (for most of us, this means Windows 95 and earlier versions or Mac OS 8.5 and earlier versions), you should make your UDF disc *compatible* first—I'll discuss this feature a little later in this chapter.**

Recording Additional Files to a DLA Disc

"Can I add more files to a DLA disc after I've ejected it?" You bet! In fact, this is yet another reason why I call creating discs with UDF programs such as HP DLA "the perfect method of burning data files." As long as you don't make your DLA disc compatible (as I show you in the next section) and your disc has free space remaining to fill, simply load your disc back in the drive, and DLA will automatically recognize it.

In fact, with HP DLA, this process of "mounting" a UDF disc operates totally "behind the scenes"—unlike some other UDF programs, HP DLA doesn't display a dialog or any indicator that it's working, so you just load the disc and go.

Making a DLA Disc Compatible

If there's any drawback at all to a DLA disc, it's the fact that you can't read the contents of that disc in two situations:

1. If you've used compression on the disc and the computer you're using doesn't have HP DLA installed

2. If the computer doesn't support UDF discs (remember, this means Windows 95 and earlier versions or Mac OS 8.5 and earlier versions)

To be honest, there's not much you can do in the first situation—if you've chosen compression, HP DLA *must* be installed on the PC, or you won't be able to read your DLA disc, period. However, there is hope in the second situation: If you want to make a DLA disc readable

dvds & cds

on older versions of Windows and Mac OS, you can make the disc *compatible*, effectively turning your UDF disc into an *ISO 9660* disc. (ISO 9660 is a universal disc format that's recognized by just about every computer with a CD-ROM drive on the planet.)

To make a disc compatible, you must be using a CD-R disc, and the disc must be formatted *without* compression—also, making a disc compatible will close (or finalize) the disc, which prevents you from writing additional data to it. Therefore, never make a disc compatible until you've finished writing all of the files you want to the disc.

✔ **Follow these steps to make a DLA CD-R disc compatible:**

1. Double-click on My Computer and right-click on the DLA disc icon; select Make Compatible from the pop-up menu.

2. HP DLA displays the confirmation dialog you see in Figure 5.6. Click Start to begin the compatibility processing.

3. Once the compatibility procedure has completed, HP DLA displays a status dialog, and you can eject the disc.

Note that making a disc compatible will shorten long file names, and directories nested more than 30 folders deep will not be readable. Compatible discs cannot be read by Windows when you're using DOS mode. If you're using CD-RW or DVD+RW discs, you can quick-format them and reuse the discs after they've been made compatible.

FIGURE 5.6   Are you absolutely, positively sure you want this disc compatible?

Project: **Recording a DVD Genealogy Archive Disc**

I can't think of a better use for a DLA disc than a genealogy archive—your valuable data is stored safely, but you can update the disc with additional information that you turn up with continuing research. (Come to think of it, the same is true for your Quicken data files and TurboTax returns for the last five years…but we'll stick with the genealogy project, because I thought of it first.) With compression, you may be able to store 5 or 6 GB of data on one disc; that's enough space for reunion videos, a library of voices in WAV format, and a high-resolution Windows bitmap image of every member of your clan!

dvds & cds

Because you won't be distributing this disc to others, you can safely use compression and a DVD+RW disc. We'll assume that your blank DVD+RW disc is unformatted.

Requirements

- A collection of genealogical data files
- A blank DVD+RW disc

✔ **Follow these steps to create your genealogical archive:**

1. Run the DLA Toolkit and click Format. Load a blank disc in your drive and click Next.

2. Click in the Volume Label field and type the name Family Data for the disc. Because this is the first time you've used this DVD+RW disc, click Full format. Click the Enable compression checkbox to turn on software compression. Click Next to continue.

3. Once the formatting process has finished, you're ready to copy your data files! Click Explore from the Toolkit window to display the contents of the Family Data disc—naturally, it's currently empty. Double-click the My Computer icon on your desktop and navigate to the location of the files you want to store, then select them and drag them to the Family Data window (Figure 5.7).

4. Once you've finished copying files to the archive disc, you can eject it and store it for later use; when you're ready to copy additional files to the DLA disc, just load it in the DVD-Writer drive again, and HP DLA will recognize it. For example, if you want to save a copy of a Word document that you've just written, click File and choose Save As, then navigate to your DLA disc and click Save.

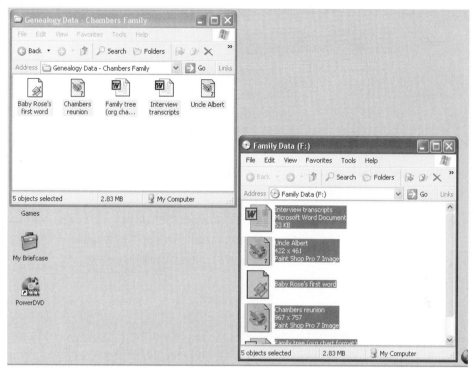

FIGURE 5.7   Storing family data optically for generations to come.

Project: **Recording a "Working Copy" UDF Disc**

Now let's consider what I call a "working copy" disc: It's a disc with your current project and data files that you carry with you between your computer at home and your computer at work. (A working copy disc also does double duty as a simple backup in case one of these two computers goes haywire.) We'll assume that one of your computers uses HP DLA, but the other does not have the program installed; naturally, this means you can record additional files on only one computer.

In this situation, we want to leave the disc compatible with a computer that's not running HP DLA, and we also don't want to finalize it. This way, you can continue to add (and overwrite) files until you've reached the maximum capacity of a CD-R disc.

Requirements

- Programs and data from your home or office
- A blank CD-R disc

✔ **Follow these steps to record data:**

1. Run the DLA Toolkit and click Format. Load a blank disc in your drive and click Next.

2. Click in the Volume Label field and type the name *Working Copy* for the disc. Click Quick format, and make sure the Enable compression checkbox is turned off. Click Next to continue.

3. Use drag-and-drop or the Send to menu item from the right-click menu to copy files.

4. When you're ready to take the disc to your other computer, eject it. Additional files can be recorded to the disc by simply reloading it in the computer that's running HP DLA.

Project: **Recording and Finalizing a PowerPoint Presentation Disc**

Our third project in this chapter is a little trickier: You need to create a CD-R containing your PowerPoint presentation files that you can send to your company's overseas branch. Unfortunately, not all the files have been assembled yet—you're still waiting for logos and artwork from the marketing department—and you're not sure what type of computer will be reading the disc at the overseas office.

Fear not! HP DLA comes to the rescue again: You can create the presentation disc in segments, saving the files you have on hand until they're all assembled. In addition, you can make the resulting disc compatible, and virtually any computer (including Macs and Linux machines) should be able to read it.

Again, we'll use a blank CD-R disc straight from the spindle.

Requirements

- PowerPoint data files
- A blank CD-R disc

✔ **Follow these steps to record data:**

1. Run the DLA Toolkit and click Format. Load a blank disc in your drive and click Next.

2. Click in the Volume Label field and type the name PowerPoint Project for the disc. Click Quick format (when you're formatting a CD-R DLA disc, you can use this time-saver), and make sure the Enable compression checkbox is turned off—remember, you can't make a disc compatible if it's formatted with software compression! Click Next to continue.

3. Use drag-and-drop or the Send to menu item from the right-click menu to copy the first batch of data files to the new DLA disc, then eject it until the remaining files arrive.

4. Finally got those graphic files from Marketing? Load the Power-Point Project DLA disc in the DVD-Writer drive and copy the updated presentation to your disc; feel free to "delete" older versions of the presentation. (As I mentioned earlier, this won't reclaim the space, but with 700 MB of elbowroom, you can probably fit several iterations of a typical PowerPoint project on a single CD-R DLA disc.)

5. When the disc is complete and ready to send, double-click on the My Computer icon on your desktop and right-click on the Power-Point Project disc icon; select Make Compatible from the pop-up menu.

dvds & cds

6. Click Start on the confirmation dialog to begin the compatibility processing.

7. Once the compatibility procedure has completed, eject the disc, and you're ready to send it! (If you like, you might also make a backup copy that you can store; run the HP RecordNow program and use the Make an Exact Copy feature to create an exact duplicate of the disc, as I demonstrated earlier in the book in Chapter 4, "Copying a Disc.")

Summary

We explored the convenience and ease of UDF recording in this chapter—you learned how to use HP DLA to create "removable media" discs for your own use, and I showed you how to make your DLA discs compatible in case you need to swap them with other computers and "foreign" operating systems.

6

Recording a DVD with Existing Files

In This Chapter

MyDVD is a great example of the new generation of DVD recording software—like Apple's iDVD on the Macintosh side, MyDVD makes it easy for anyone to create a DVD Video disc, complete with basic interactive menus! No longer do you need years of film editing experience, $20,000 of hardware and software, and the eye of a "starving video artist." MyDVD takes video clips directly from your hard drive and allows you to choose things such as backgrounds and buttons from an easy-to-use menu system; there's even a helpful wizard to guide you through the entire process, if you like.

dvds & cds

n this chapter, I'll show you all of the features of MyDVD, and we'll create a DVD with video clips of your family's summer vacation taken from your hard drive.

Introducing MyDVD

As you can see from Figure 6.1, there are actually two components to MyDVD: the menu bar and toolbar, which stretch across the top portion of the screen; and the menu editor, which occupies the center of the screen in its own movable dialog. You can resize the menu editor by dragging the lower right corner of the editor window. MyDVD also includes a wizard that we'll use to create a DVD later in the chapter. To run MyDVD from the Windows XP Start menu, click Start | All Programs | MyDVD | MyDVD.

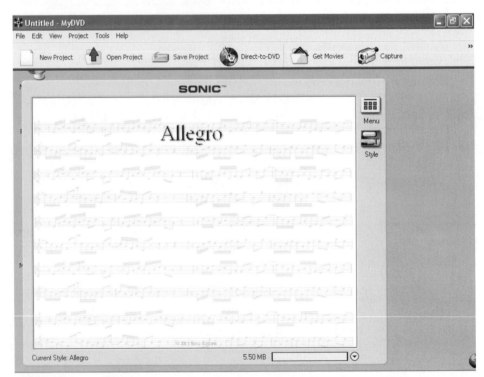

FIGURE 6.1   The MyDVD toolbar and menu editor.

MyDVD can operate in two modes: You can either edit and record existing clips (or clips that you've captured beforehand) or you can record directly from a video source to a DVD. In this chapter, we'll cover the first mode of operation; I'll cover direct-to-DVD recording in Chapter 7, "Direct-to-DVD Recording."

You can even use MyDVD to edit and "remaster" DVDs that you've already created—this is a great way to create an "open-ended" family video, where new scenes can be added and the disc recorded again with the new material (naturally, the rewriteable nature of DVD+RW comes in handy for this kind of project).

As a reminder, both DVD+RW and DVD+R discs are compatible with most DVD players and computer DVD-ROM drives, but there are exceptions; generally, the older the DVD player, the less likely it will be able to read DVD+RW and DVD+R media. Therefore, it's a good idea to verify that you can use DVD+RW or DVD+R discs with the equipment that you'll use to view your DVD movies. The easiest way to do this is to burn a quick test disc and try it out on your DVD player or DVD-ROM drive—you can also check the Web site of the manufacturer of your DVD hardware for a compatibility listing. (If you're interested in using CD-R discs instead, MyDVD can also produce a cDVD disc, which will be compatible with most computer CD-ROM and DVD-ROM drives.)

Using the Wizard

By default, the MyDVD Wizard greets you each time you open the program; Figure 6.2 illustrates the opening Wizard screen. From this screen, you can choose to:

- Record direct-to-DVD (which I will explain in the next chapter)
- Create a new project with existing photos and video clips
- Open an existing project and continue working on it
- Edit an existing DVD

dvds & cds

You can also run the program's tutorial from this screen—like many online help systems these days, the tutorial is in HTML format (the same language used to create Web pages), so MyDVD opens your Web browser of choice when you click the Tutorial button. Figure 6.3 illustrates the opening page of the MyDVD tutorial, which you can navigate simply by clicking on the links.

tip **Once you're familiar with using the manual features in MyDVD, you can click the Always show this wizard when MyDVD starts checkbox to disable it, which will take you directly to the MyDVD screen layout I showed you earlier. (This setting can also be toggled on and off from the Preferences dialog, which you can display by clicking File and choosing the Preferences menu item.) Alternately, click Cancel on this opening Wizard screen, and the program will return you to the MyDVD menu bar and menu editor.**

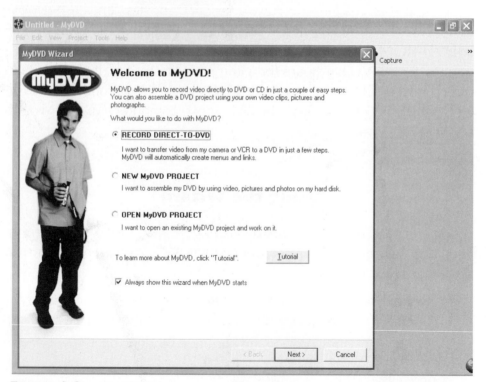

FIGURE 6.2   The Wizard screen is ready to help as soon as you run MyDVD.

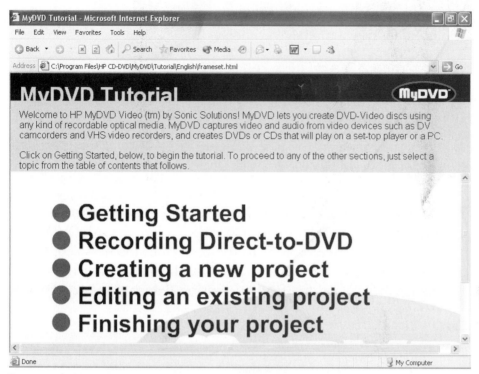

FIGURE 6.3   The MyDVD tutorial uses your Web browser.

I'll describe the Wizard in the project at the end of this chapter—for now, just remember that the process of starting a project can be automated through the Wizard.

Adding a Menu Manually

Like commercial DVD movies, you can create menus with MyDVD that allow branching movement (where you move from menu screen to menu screen by pressing a button on your DVD player's remote control)—each one of these submenu screens can also display buttons that can display photos or run video clips. In this way, you can build a simple menu tree; for example, you might have a Title screen with two submenu buttons. One button takes the viewer to a submenu screen ded-

dvds & cds

icated to videos of the family pet, and the other submenu screen would include videos of your family vacation.

✔ **MyDVD makes it easy to create menus. Follow these steps to add a menu:**

1. Click the Menu button at the upper right corner of the menu editor window. MyDVD adds the Untitled Menu button you see in Figure 6.4.

2. Double-click on the Untitled Menu button to display the new submenu screen, as illustrated in Figure 6.5. Note that MyDVD automatically adds two buttons to the bottom of the new screen: the Home button (which takes you back to the main Title screen of the menu system) and the Previous button (which takes you back to the previous screen).

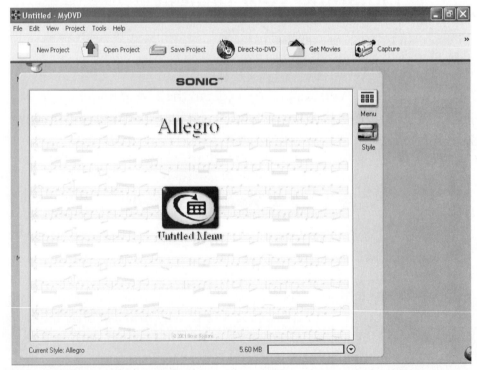

FIGURE 6.4   Adding a menu to a screen adds an Untitled Menu button.

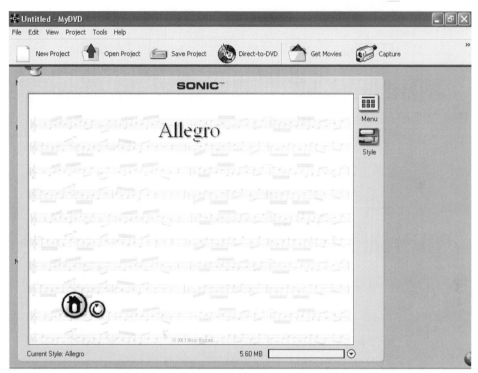

FIGURE 6.5   MyDVD automatically creates a submenu when necessary.

tip As you add menus, photos, and video clips, you'll note that the bar graph at the lower right corner of the menu editor will indicate how much space the project will occupy on a disc. If you're designing a disc with several large clips, it's a good idea to keep an eye on this gauge to make sure that your project doesn't exceed the capacity of a blank disc. (You can click on the drop-down button next to the gauge to switch between the 4.7-GB capacity of a DVD and the 650-MB capacity of a CD.)

3. Next, change the text on the menu button you've just created. Double-click on the Previous button—because we've added only one submenu, this button will take you back to the Title screen, as well. Click on the text "Untitled Menu" under the button you added, and MyDVD opens a text editing box (shown in Figure 6.6). Type the new label for the button and press Enter to save it.

dvds & cds

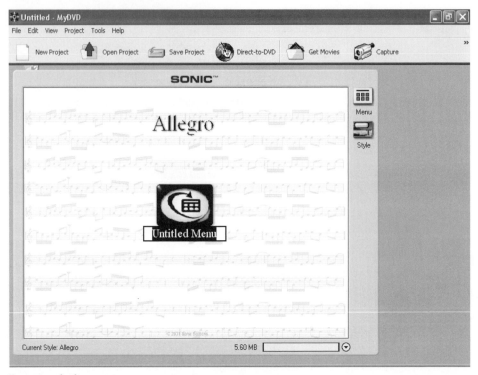

FIGURE 6.6   Editing the text for a menu button.

You can delete the currently displayed menu by right-clicking on the menu background—choose Delete Menu. If the current menu contains one or more buttons (either submenu or movie buttons), MyDVD prompts for confirmation; click OK, and all of the menu and movie buttons (and anything they are linked to) are deleted from your project.

To delete a menu button, right-click on it and choose Delete Button—again, MyDVD prompts you for confirmation, because you'll lose the submenu and anything linked to the button.

Adding Video Clips Manually

✔ **Buttons on a MyDVD menu can also display video clips from your hard drive. Follow these steps to add movies to your DVD project:**

1. Click the Get Movies button on the MyDVD toolbar—the program displays the contents of the My Documents\My Videos folder in the Add movies to menu dialog (Figure 6.7). Navigate to the location where you've saved your movies, select one or more files, and click Open.

 tip **You can also add movies by dragging the files directly from the Windows Explorer onto the menu editor.**

FIGURE 6.7 Selecting video files from the My Videos folder.

dvds & cds

2. Neat! MyDVD automatically adds a button that displays the movie, complete with a thumbnail image from the beginning of the video file (as shown in Figure 6.8). The movie's filename is used as the default button; as with a menu button, you can click on the label and type your own text, then press Enter to save it.

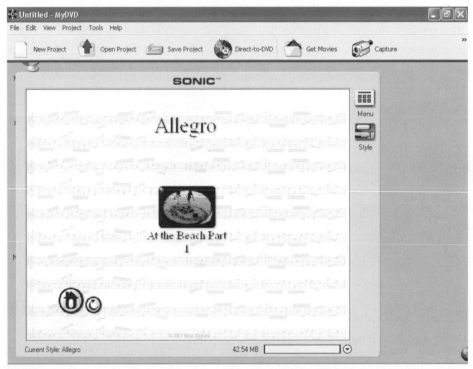

FIGURE 6.8   Our new video clip button looks very professional, don't you think?

3. It's often necessary to *trim* a video clip so that extraneous material at the beginning or ending of the movie doesn't appear in your project; consider this somewhat similar to cropping a digital photo using Paint Shop Pro or Photoshop. (Note that this process *does not* actually remove any frames from your digital video! It only "marks" the beginning and ending of the clip for your MyDVD project.) To trim the clip, double-click on it; MyDVD displays the Trim dialog you see in Figure 6.9, with thumbnail images of the start and ending

frame, along with the duration, starting time, and ending time (If you're not familiar with the time notation used in video editing, everything is in hours:minutes:seconds:frames.) A Hollywood film has 24 *frames per second* (or FPS); PAL video has 25 FPS; and NTSC video has 30 FPS (it's actually 29.97, but everyone rounds it upward.)

4. To select the beginning point for your clip, click and drag the green slider (for the start frame) to the desired location—MyDVD updates the starting thumbnail preview image so that you can tell where you are within the video clip.

5. Select the ending point for your clip by clicking and dragging the red slider (for the end frame) to the desired location—again, the ending thumbnail preview image is updated as a reference.

FIGURE 6.9   Trimming excess from the beginning and ending of our clip.

dvds & cds

tip For more precise control, click on the slider you want to move and press the left and right arrow keys to move backward and forward.

6. Satisfied with the trimmed video clip? If so, click OK to return to the menu. To cancel your changes without saving them, click Cancel—or, to start over with the trimming process, click Reset.

7. If you like, you can specify the thumbnail you want to display from anywhere within the video clip.

To delete a movie button, right-click on it and choose Delete Movie—note that this simply removes the button and the linked video clip, it does not delete your original video clip from your hard drive.

tip **MyDVD has a limit of six buttons (of either type) on a single menu; if you attempt to add more than six buttons, the program automatically displays a dialog explaining that a new *continue* menu has been created, and adds your button on the new menu. (In this case, *continue* means that the new menu is not a submenu but a continuation of the previous menu.) You can always tell when you're on a continue menu, because MyDVD adds the previous and next buttons to the lower right corner of the menu. You can double-click on these navigational buttons to move to the previous and next menus in the continuous series.**

Changing Menu Styles

In MyDVD, a *menu style* is a combination of these separate choices:

*   The background image
*   The border around menu and movie buttons
*   The fonts
*   The color scheme

Although Allegro, the default menu style, is a great choice for a DVD with video clips from a piano recital, it's certainly not appropriate for a birthday party! Luckily, MyDVD doesn't restrict you to just one menu style; there are 27 preset menu styles to choose from, with designs for holidays, family events, and themes such as TV shows, nature trails, and rainy days. You can also create your own custom menu styles by combining elements from the preset menu styles.

✔ **To change the menu style for your MyDVD project at any time, using one of the preset styles, follow these steps:**

1. Click the Style button at the top right corner of the menu editor window. (You can also press Ctrl+L.) MyDVD displays the Select a Style dialog, as shown in Figure 6.10.

FIGURE 6.10 Choosing a preset menu style.

dvds & cds

2. Scroll through the style thumbnails until you find the one you want to use with this project. Click on it to highlight it.

3. You can specify whether you want to add a 3-D drop shadow effect to the buttons and text on your menus; by default, the option is turned on. (Personally, I prefer it with the drop shadows, but it makes the text hard to read on some televisions.) To turn this option off, click the Add drop shadows to buttons and text checkbox to disable it.

4. Click OK to use the new menu style; Figure 6.11 illustrates the "Halloween 01" menu style.

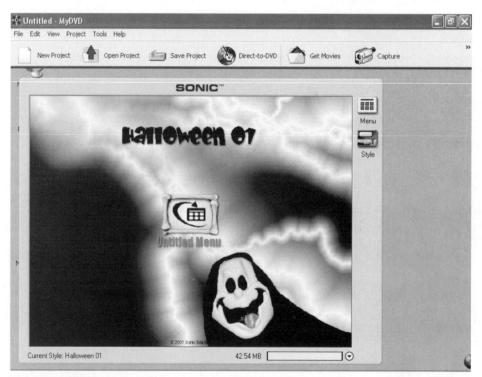

FIGURE 6.11 With a click of the mouse, our project is ready for Halloween!

✔ Follow these steps to create a custom menu style:

1. Click the Style button at the top right corner of the menu editor window to display the Select a Style dialog.

2. Click the New Custom Style button to display the New dialog, illustrated in Figure 6.12, and type a new name for your custom style. Click OK to continue.

3. MyDVD displays the dialog you see in Figure 6.13—note that the Category has changed to Custom. Click the Browse button to select a background, and navigate to the desired Windows bitmap or JPEG image. Click it to select it and click Open. MyDVD updates the thumbnail preview image to reflect your change.

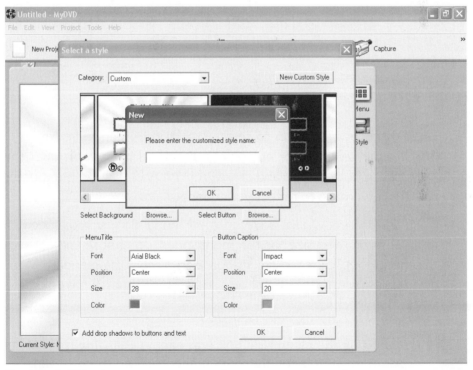

FIGURE 6.12 Entering a new name for a custom menu style.

dvds & cds

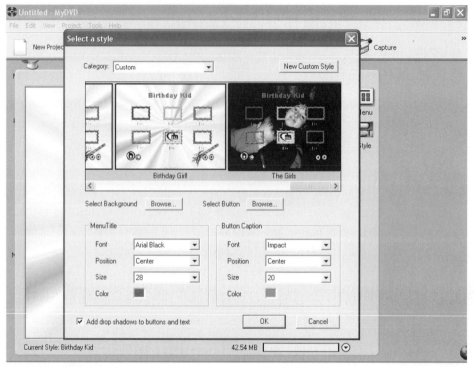

FIGURE 6.13   Preparing a custom menu style.

4. Click the Browse button to select a button border style. MyDVD displays the selection of buttons you see in Figure 6.14; click the appropriate button style and click OK. MyDVD updates the thumbnail preview image to reflect your change.

5. Click the drop-down list boxes in the MenuTitle group to specify a font, position, and size for the menu titles. To choose the color of the menu font, click the color square to display the standard Windows color palette selector shown in Figure 6.15; click the color you want, then click OK.

tip **Editing the menu title text is as easy as changing the captions on your menu buttons: Simply click on the title and type the new text.**

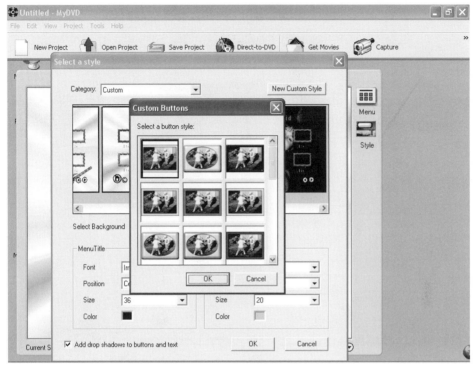

FIGURE 6.14 Choosing a button border style.

6. Click the drop-down list boxes in the Button Caption group to specify a font, position, and size for the captions that appear under your
   menu buttons. To choose the color of the caption font, click the
   color square to display the (now familiar) standard Windows color
   palette selector; click the color you want, then click OK.

7. By default, MyDVD adds a 3-D drop shadow effect to the buttons
   and text on your menus—to turn this option off, click the Add drop
   shadows to buttons and text checkbox to disable it.

8. Click OK to save the custom menu style; Figure 6.16 illustrates a
   custom style I created for a video tour of WWII military airplanes,
   using my own photo as a menu background. You can now choose
   the custom style any time you display the Select a Style dialog.

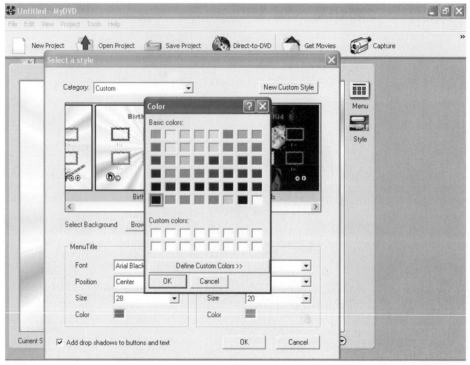

FIGURE 6.15   What color goes best? Use the Windows color selector to choose your color.

FIGURE 6.16 My custom menu background.

Checking the Safe Zone

So what's a *safe zone*, anyway? That's a term that video editors use when referring to the dimensions of your television screen. You may not know it, but the image designated by the signal that's beamed to your television is actually larger than the television screen; the additional area around the outside of the image that you can't see takes care of distortion (call it the "ragged edge" of the TV image).

When you're creating a MyDVD disc, the safe zone refers to that part of the video clip that will actually appear on screen, and it's important to verify that your movies are correctly displayed in the safe zone before you record them. MyDVD can display a rectangle that signifies the safe zone: To display it, click View and choose the Show TV Safe Zone menu item. Figure 6.17 illustrates the dashed line that appears to indicate the safe zone.

dvds & cds

FIGURE 6.17 Displaying the safe zone around a menu.

To hide the safe zone border, click View and choose the Show TV Safe Zone menu item again.

tip As a general rule, while you're filming, try to keep the subjects of your movies in the center of the frame—this will keep them from being "chopped" outside the edge of the safe zone.

Previewing Your Work

Okay, you've created all of your menus, added and trimmed all of your movies, edited the text of your menu titles and buttons, and checked the border of your project, using the safe zone display. Are you ready to burn? Technically, you are indeed finished and ready to record your disc; however, MyDVD offers a Preview player that can display your project as it will appear on the finished disc, complete with a "virtual" remote control that simulates the remote for your DVD player!

To enter Preview mode at any time, click Preview on the MyDVD toolbar (or press Ctrl+P). The project appears in the menu editor, with the remote control pad shown in Figure 6.18. Click on the remote control buttons just as you would press the buttons on your DVD remote control.

To jump directly to the Title menu, click the Title button—clicking the Menu button displays the last menu you used.

When you're done previewing your project (and you want either to record the disc or to edit the project further), click the Close button on the remote control.

FIGURE 6.18 Doing a little testing in Preview mode before I record.

Recording the Disc

When you're ready to record your project, MyDVD gives you three choices:

1. **Make a CD.** If you record your project to a CD-R or CD-RW disc, MyDVD creates what's called a *cDVD* (a trademark of Sonic, the makers of MyDVD)—these discs will play on virtually all computer CD-ROM and DVD-ROM drives, using a free viewer program that MyDVD automatically adds to the disc.

2. **Make a DVD.** If you record using a DVD+RW or DVD+R disc, your disc will play in most DVD players and computer DVD-ROM drives.

3. **Make a DVD to hard disk.** Select this option to create a *DVD volume* in the folder you specify, which is something like a disc image— although a DVD volume can be recorded to a disc later, it's often used to create a DVD volume for use with software DVD players, such as PowerDVD and WinDVD.

✔ **Follow these steps to record your project:**

1. Load a blank disc of the proper type into your recorder—no disc is necessary if you're going to create a DVD volume.

2. Click the Make Disc button on the MyDVD toolbar, and MyDVD prompts you to save the project. Choose a filename and a location, and click Save.

3. The Make Disc Setup dialog shown in Figure 6.19 appears. Click the desired media type; if you have more than one recorder on your system, you can also choose which drive will be used. Leave the Write Speed setting at Auto.

4. Click OK to begin recording!

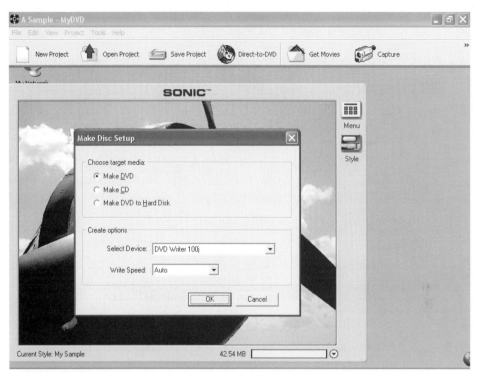

FIGURE 6.19 Preparing to record my project.

Project: **Recording a DVD Video Disc with MyDVD**

In this project, we'll take video clips that you've stored on your hard drive and create a family DVD Video disc that you can watch on your DVD player.

Requirements

- MPEG, AVI, or MOV digital video clips
- Installed copy of MyDVD
- A blank DVD+RW or DVD+R disc

✔ Follow these steps:

1. Click Start | All Programs | MyDVD | MyDVD to run the program.

2. From the initial Wizard menu, click the New DVD Project option and click Next to continue.

3. The Wizard prompts you to choose a menu style for your project (Figure 6.20). For this project, I'll click the Summer Fun thumbnail to select it. Click Finish, and the MyDVD toolbar and menu editor appear with the style you've selected.

FIGURE 6.20   Selecting a menu style using the Wizard.

4. For this project, I'll add two buttons: One will feature a clip with the family dog, and the other will have two clips from summer vacation. Click twice on the Menu button to add two buttons to the layout.

5. Let's change the menu title and the captions for both buttons. Click on the menu title, type "Our Family's Summer 2002," and press Enter to save the change. Click on the caption for the left button and type "Let's Wash the Dog"—press Enter to save the change. Finally, click on the right button caption and type "Summer at the Beach" and press Enter. Figure 6.21 illustrates our completed Title menu.

6. Next, double-click the left button you added—note that MyDVD automatically updates the title of this menu to match the button that links to it. Click the Get Movies button on the MyDVD toolbar. Navigate to the location of your video clip, click it once to highlight it, and click Open to add the video button.

FIGURE 6.21   The Title menu looks great.

7. The clip you've just added has a 4-second title and transition that we no longer need, so double-click on the movie button to display the Trimming dialog you see in Figure 6.22. Note that I've moved the green slider 4 seconds to the right to eliminate the beginning title. Click OK to continue.

8. To return to the Title menu, double-click on the Home button.

9. Double-click the right button you added. We'll add two movies to this menu. Click the Get Movies button on the MyDVD toolbar. Navigate to the location of the clips and hold down Ctrl while you click both filenames, then click Open to add two video buttons. Double-click on the Home button to return to the Title menu.

10. Next, let's check the safe zone for our project: Click View and click Show TV Safe Zone to toggle this feature on. As you can see in Figure 6.23, our title and buttons fit well within the safe zone border.

FIGURE 6.22 Trimming the first 4 seconds from one of our video clips.

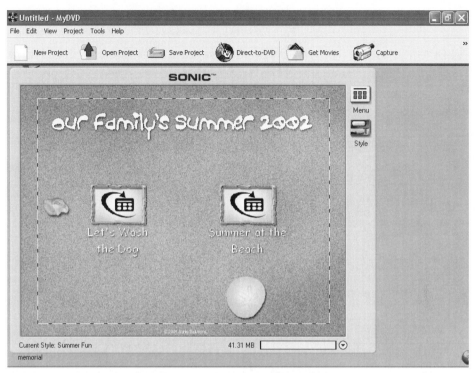

FIGURE 6.23 Checking the safe zone around our menu.

11. Finally, let's preview our disc before we record it—click Preview on the MyDVD toolbar, then use the controls to change menus and run each of the movies. (Note that the remote control also displays the elapsed time for the clip you're viewing.) If everything checks out okay, click the Close button on the MyDVD remote control to return to the menu editor.

12. We're ready to record! For this project, I'll load a blank DVD+RW disc into my drive.

13. Click the Make Disc button on the MyDVD toolbar, and MyDVD prompts you to save the project. Choose a filename and a location, and click Save.

14. MyDVD displays the Make Disc Setup dialog. Click the DVD option.

15. Click OK and sit back while your DVD masterpiece is created.

dvds & cds

Project: **Recording a cDVD with a Custom Menu**

As I mentioned earlier, MyDVD can create a cDVD using a CD-R or CD-RW disc; I'll design and build a cDVD in this project, using a custom menu design.

Requirements

- MPEG, AVI, or MOV digital video clips
- Installed copy of MyDVD
- A blank CD-R or CD-RW disc

✔ **Follow these steps:**

1. Click Start | All Programs | MyDVD | MyDVD to run the program.

2. From the initial Wizard menu, click the New DVD Project option and click Next to continue.

3. The Wizard prompts you to choose a menu style for your project—because we're going to change the design, you can select any style (I used the first one, Allegro), then click Finish.

4. Click the Style button at the top right corner of the menu editor window to display the Select a Style dialog.

5. Click the New Custom Style button to display the New dialog, and type a new name for your custom style. Click OK to continue, and click the new style thumbnail to select it.

6. On the Select a Style dialog, click the Browse button to select a background, and navigate to the desired Windows bitmap or JPEG image (Figure 6.24). Click it to select it and click Open; in this case, I'll choose one of the default background bitmap images that comes with Windows XP.

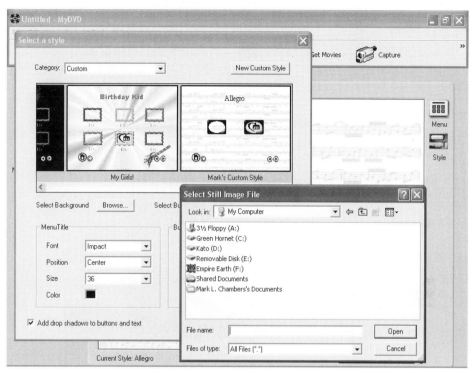

FIGURE 6.24 Locating a background image for our custom style.

7. Next, click Browse and select a button border style. I'll click the light blue oval button border. MyDVD automatically updates the thumbnail preview image.

8. For this project, I'll choose the Rockwell font for my menu text, and I'll set the font size at 28.

9. Because I like matching fonts on a menu, let's also click the Font drop-down list box for the button captions and specify Rockwell; however, I want white button captions, so click the color square to display the standard Windows color palette selector. Click white and click OK to save the change.

10. We're done! Click OK to save the custom menu style; the new design is shown in Figure 6.25 (perfect for a camping trip video).

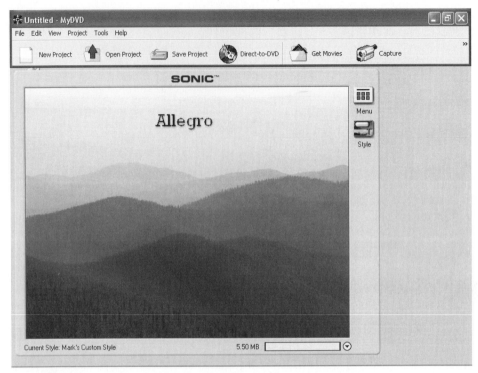

FIGURE 6.25 Our new custom style.

11. I have only one clip to add to this disc (because it's a cDVD disc, we have less space to work with)—it will feature digital video that I took on our last family camping trip. Click on the Menu button to add a single button to the layout.

12. Next, it's time to change the menu title and the captions. Click on the menu title, type "Roughing It" and press Enter to save the change. Click on the caption for the button and type "Camping in the Ozarks"—press Enter to save the change. Figure 6.26 illustrates our completed Title menu.

13. Double-click the button you added and click the Get Movies button on the MyDVD toolbar. Navigate to the location of your video clip, click it once to highlight it, and click Open to add the video button.

14. That completes our menu design! To return to the Title menu, double-click on the Home button.

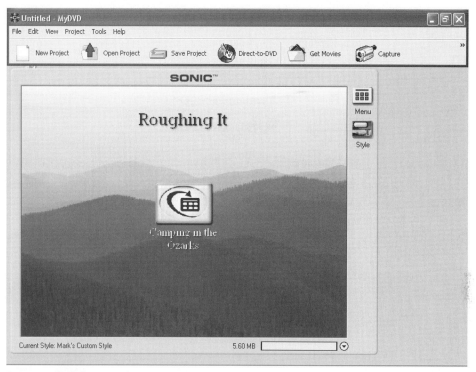

FIGURE 6.26 The camping video Title menu.

15. Click View and click Show TV Safe Zone to make sure that both the title and the button fit within the safe zone border—no problem with this project, because we needed to add only a single button.

16. We're ready to burn—but first, click Preview on the MyDVD toolbar and use the remote control to check the menu and watch the video. If you like what you see, click the Close button on the MyDVD remote control to return to the menu editor.

17. Because we're recording a cDVD, load a blank CD-R disc into the drive.

18. Click the Make Disc button on the MyDVD toolbar, and MyDVD prompts you to save the project. Choose a filename and a location, and click Save.

dvds & cds

19. MyDVD displays the Make Disc Setup dialog. Click the cDVD option.

20. Click OK, and recording begins!

Summary

In this chapter, you learned how to design, edit, and produce your own DVD and cDVD discs using MyDVD and digital video clips stored on your hard drive.

7

Direct-to-DVD Recording

In This Chapter

✔ **Connecting your equipment**

✔ **Selecting capture settings**

✔ **Setting chapter points**

✔ **Project: Recording a DVD from a DV Camcorder**

In the previous chapter, you learned how to record a DVD (or cDVD) disc using MyDVD and digital video files from your hard drive—this is likely to be the route that most of us will take with our digital video footage.

However, MyDVD also offers a direct-to-DVD mode, where the video input from sources such as a digital camcorder or VHS VCR can be burned directly to a DVD. No editing required!

dvds & cds

In this chapter, I'll discuss the process of direct-to-DVD recording using MyDVD, and we'll burn a DVD disc using this technique (with the help of the MyDVD Wizard). By the way, you can also record a CD-R or CD-RW directly from your DV source, but I wouldn't recommend it unless you're going to be recording less than 30 minutes of uncompressed footage.

Connecting to the Source

In videospeak, a *source* (or, as MyDVD calls it, a *video device*) is any piece of hardware that can send one of two types of signals to your computer:

1. A digital video signal, using a FireWire (or IEEE-1394) connection to your computer. This is the method you'll use to connect a DV camera to your PC. This type of connection is pure joy: It's *plug-and-play* (meaning that your PC automatically detects that you've connected your DV camcorder), and you don't have to reboot after you plug in the FireWire cable.

2. An analog video signal, using a DirectShow-compatible video capture device. You'll need this hardware if you want to connect a VCR, VHS camcorder, or TV (with Video Out) to your PC.

tip Do you have an older PC that doesn't have a built-in FireWire connector? Don't panic—no need to buy another computer just to connect your DV camcorder! Instead, you can add a FireWire card to your existing PC; these cards usually cost under $100. You'll also need an open PCI slot in your computer where you can install the card. (Most video capture cards will also need the same type of PCI slot.) If your recorder uses a USB 2.0 connection, you can also install a FireWire/USB 2.0 combo card and take care of both requirements with one piece of hardware.

Unfortunately, there's no one "standard" way to connect an analog device—you'll have to refer to the manual that accompanied your video capture card to determine how to connect your analog video source to your computer. Note also that you may require a separate connection for the analog audio signal, as well.

Configuring Windows for Direct-to-DVD Recording

Unlike the recording from files that I covered in the last chapter, direct-to-DVD recording is much more demanding on your entire system—therefore, it's important to make sure that your computer and its operating system have been correctly optimized for best performance. In this section, I'll discuss the three important steps you should take before attempting a direct-to-DVD session.

Using DMA Mode

DMA stands for *Direct Memory Access*, and it's the fastest method of transferring data directly from your computer's memory to your recorder (without processing it or routing it through the CPU beforehand). To record directly from a video source to your recorder successfully, you should enable DMA on your primary hard drive.

✔ **Follow these steps:**

1. Log onto Windows as Administrator (or as a user with Administrator privileges).

2. Right-click on My Computer and choose Properties from the pop-up menu to display the System Properties dialog (Figure 7.1).

3. Click the Hardware tab to display the hardware controls (Figure 7.2).

dvds & cds

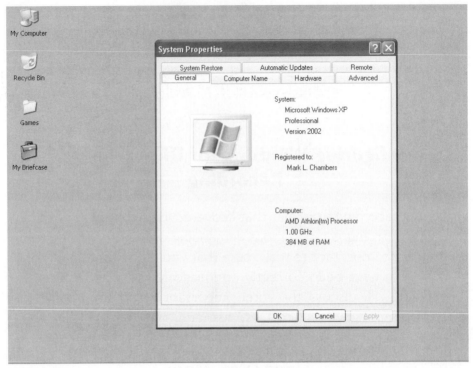

FIGURE 7.1   The System Properties dialog within Windows XP Professional.

4. Click Device Manager to display the window you see in Figure 7.3.

5. Click the plus sign next to the IDE ATA/ATAPI controllers entry to expand it, as shown in Figure 7.4. (Note that the hardware listed under the entry may not exactly match what you have on your system.)

6. Right-click on the Primary IDE Channel entry and choose Properties.

7. Click the Advanced Settings tab to display the options you see in Figure 7.5.

8. Click on the Transfer Mode drop-down list for Device 0 and choose DMA if available.

9. Click OK to return to the Device Manager, then click the Close button on the Device Manager window to return to Windows.

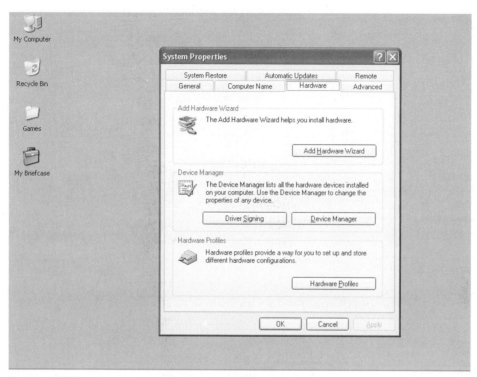

FIGURE 7.2　The System Properties Hardware panel.

Defragmenting Your Drive

I discussed how and why you should defragment your hard drive in Chapter 3, so I won't go into it here; suffice it to say that you'll need to fine-tune and optimize your hard drive to get the top performance you need for error-free direct recording.

If you missed my sage advice on defragmenting—as well as the step-by-step procedure to follow—turn back to the section titled "Defragmenting Your Hard Drive" in Chapter 3. We'll wait for you here!

Avoiding Multitasking

Finally, it's very important to avoid running any other programs at the same time you're using MyDVD to record direct-to-DVD. Multitasking

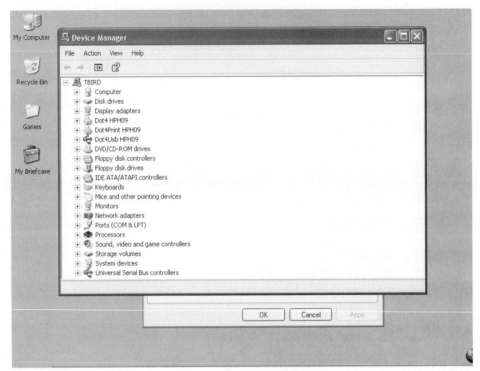

FIGURE 7.3   The Windows XP Device Manager revealed.

with a "performance sloth" such as Word or Photoshop, for example, will be a serious drain on your PC's memory and hard drive resources; the older the computer, the more likely that this performance hit will adversely affect the recording session and MyDVD will abort the recording.

Therefore, before you begin direct-to-DVD recording, make sure that MyDVD is the only application running under Windows, and shut down as many of the background programs running in the Windows taskbar as possible.

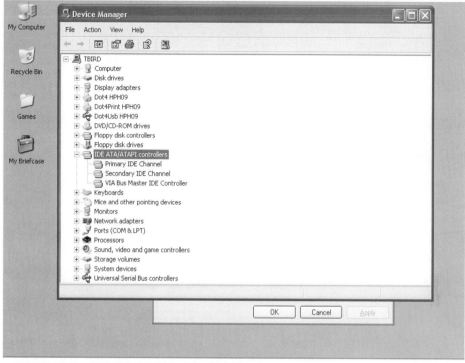

FIGURE 7.4   Displaying the controllers on your system.

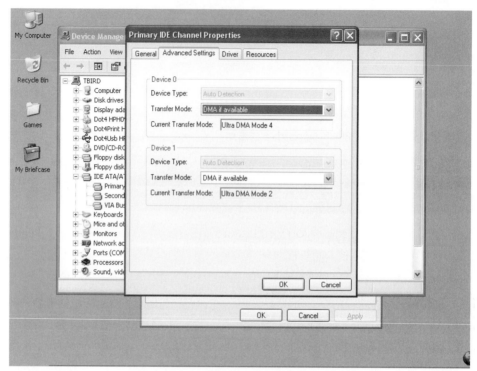

FIGURE 7.5   Enabling DMA transfer mode for my hard drive.

Selecting Capture Settings

If you've connected a single FireWire device, MyDVD will automatically recognize it as a source, and you can skip this section—it's possible, however, that you have either connected an analog device or you have multiple sources connected to your PC. If so, you must select the video and audio devices that Windows will use as the source for your recording. Note that you must have already successfully installed the capture device within Windows, or the connection won't show up during this procedure.

tip It's very important to keep your capture hardware updated with the latest Windows drivers—check the capture hardware manufacturer's Web site at least once a month. Current drivers will go a long way toward assuring trouble-free operation—that applies to all of your PC's components!

✔ **Follow these steps:**

1. Click Tools and choose the Capture menu.

2. Click Change to display the current video device—to select a new device, click on the entry that corresponds to the hardware you've connected.

3. If the video device you've chosen has multiple input connectors—for example, a capture card that can handle multiple sources—choose the entry for the input you'll use from the source list.

4. If the Configure button is enabled, click it and set the video configuration to NTSC, 720 ∞ 480, and use either I420 or IYUV for the color model/image format setting. Click OK to save your changes. (Note that these settings apply within North America, whereas many other countries around the world use PAL or SECAM, a derivative of PAL. The software defaults to NTSC; however, if you change the selection, it will default to the last setting used. MyDVD will inform you if you are trying to import a PAL clip into an NTSC project; you can convert clips between NTSC and PAL using ShowBiz.)

5. If the Select button is enabled, click it and set the configuration to the input you're using and NTSC. Click OK.

6. Click on the entry that corresponds to the audio device you'll be using.

7. If the audio device you've chosen has multiple input connectors, choose the entry for the input you'll use from the source list.

8. Click OK to save your changes and return to MyDVD.

dvds & cds

Whew! You can see why the DV-FireWire route is so popular in the world of video recording; because it's automatic, you can avoid a lot of these settings altogether.

Setting Chapter Points

MyDVD allows you to set chapter points for your disc that operate just like those in a commercial DVD movie: You can jump directly to a chapter point at any time. MyDVD can create chapter points automatically at timed intervals in your recording—just enable the Create Chapter Points checkbox within the direct-to-DVD Wizard, and choose the interval time (either in seconds or minutes). When capturing from DV, the program can be set to create chapter points automatically where the tape was started and stopped.

 tip **To set a chapter point manually while you're recording, press the spacebar.**

Project: **Recording Directly from a DV Camcorder**

Let's record a DVD directly from a DV camcorder, using MyDVD and a FireWire connection.

Requirements

- DV camcorder and FireWire cable
- Installed copy of MyDVD
- A blank DVD+RW (or DVD+R disc, if you're using the DVD-Writer DVD200)

✔ **Follow these steps:**

1. Click Start | All Programs | MyDVD | MyDVD to run the program.

2. From the initial Wizard menu, click the Record Direct-to-DVD option and click Next to continue.

3. The Wizard prompts you to enter a name for the project—type a name and click Next to continue.

4. Next, the Wizard displays the screen you see in Figure 7.6. Because we're recording to a DVD disc, click Make DVD. Click on the Select Device drop-down list and choose your drive; leave the Write Speed option set to Auto. Click Next to continue.

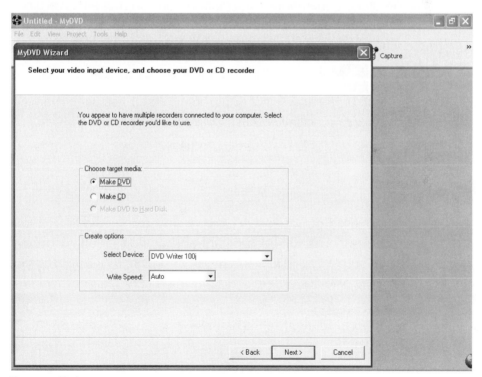

FIGURE 7.6 Choosing the target drive and media.

5. Choose a menu style by clicking on the thumbnail—or, if you prefer to burn a disc without menus, click No menus. You can add drop shadows to buttons and text if you like. Click Next to continue.

6. The next screen allows you to record just the video signal from the source—a good option when audio isn't important, because it will save a significant amount of space on the disc—as will the video quality option you choose. (At Best quality, you can fit only about 60 minutes of video on a 4.7-GB DVD; at Good quality, you can fit a whopping 180 minutes.) You can also set MyDVD to create chapter points automatically.

7. Because we're using a FireWire connection as our source, you can actually control your DV camcorder through the Wizard by using the VCR-style controls; note that you can move backward one frame by clicking the minus button, and you can move forward one frame by clicking the plus button. Using these controls, move to the frame where you want to begin the recording.

8. Click Record—MyDVD will automatically start the camcorder.

9. MyDVD will buffer the signal until the disc limit has been reached, then the actual recording process will begin.

Summary

This chapter covered direct-to-DVD recording using MyDVD; I discussed the requirements for both digital and analog video recording, along with the steps you should take to optimize Windows before recording. Finally, we recorded a disc using a DV camcorder as a source.

8

Watching DVD Video with PowerDVD

In This Chapter

✔ Loading and playing a DVD movie

✔ Using the standard DVD player controls

✔ Using bookmarks

✔ Viewing subtitles

✔ Watching DV files from your hard drive

✔ Project: Capturing and E-mailing Images from Digital Video

When you bought your DVD recorder, you may not have considered the primary "fringe benefit" of that purchase: the ability to watch DVD-Video discs on your computer. In fact, many videophiles prefer the sharper picture you'll get with a computer monitor over a standard TV set; if you've spent the money on a sophisticated surround sound speaker system and subwoofer for your PC, you may also enjoy better audio during the movie by watching it on your computer. These days, some DVD movie discs even come

dvds & cds

with programs such as trivia games and 3-D models that you can run only if you've loaded the disc in a DVD drive.

In this chapter, I'll use the PowerDVD software viewing program that accompanies the HP DVD-Writer drive: You'll learn how to operate the same "virtual" controls on your screen (using your mouse and your keyboard) that you would find on an actual DVD player remote control. In addition, I'll also demonstrate how you can display digital video files straight from your computer's hard drive—something that your mundane DVD player can't do—and how you can capture images directly from the display and e-mail them to friends and family. Gather the family around that 19-inch monitor and fix a bowl of popcorn—PowerDVD is about to turn your computer into a movie theater!

Loading and Playing a DVD Movie

Your set-top DVD player is simple to operate, and PowerDVD is just as easy to run. There are three methods of starting PowerDVD:

1. **From the Start menu.** Click Start | All Programs | Cyberlink PowerDVD | PowerDVD.

2. **From the desktop shortcut.** The PowerDVD installation program places a shortcut icon on your Windows desktop—double-click it to start the application.

3. **Automatically upon loading a DVD.** You can configure Windows XP to run PowerDVD automatically each time you load a DVD movie. The first time you load a movie, you'll see the infamous "What Should I Do?" dialog (shown in Figure 8.1). Click the Play DVD Movie using PowerDVD entry from the list and click the Always do the selected action checkbox to enable it, then click OK.

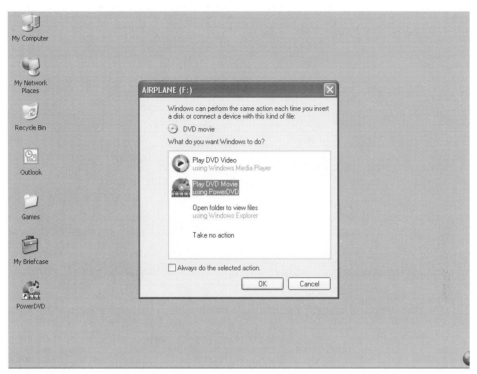

FIGURE 8.1 Configuring Windows XP to run PowerDVD automatically when you load a DVD movie.

Once PowerDVD is running, you'll either see the program's display window and control panel (shown in Figure 8.2) or the movie will begin playing automatically—the result depends on the setting you've selected in the General configuration dialog, which I'll explain later in the chapter). If the movie doesn't begin playing automatically, check the Mode button and make sure PowerDVD is in Disc mode (click the Disc/File Mode button to cycle to Disc mode, if necessary), then click the Play button; Figure 8.2 also shows both of these controls. When the DVD movie's menu appears, click on the desired menu option to select it.

If all you want to do is simply watch a movie, that's all there is to it! However, if I stop here, we're left with a two-page chapter, and you won't learn about all of the other great features included in Power-DVD. Therefore, watch a movie or two, or three (if you have to get the

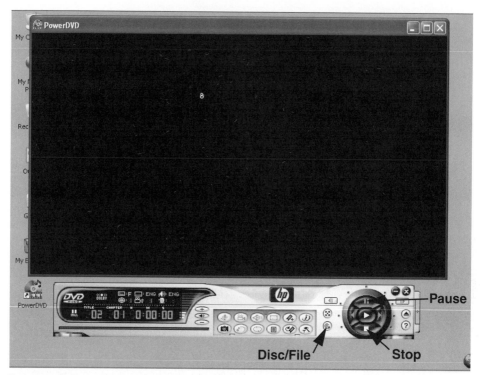

FIGURE 8.2   PowerDVD is ready to go.

novelty out of your system first), then come back, and I'll describe the rest of the program.

Basic Video Controls Explained

Most of the controls you'd expect to find on a good DVD player are available within PowerDVD, along with several features that are unique to the PC that may be unfamiliar to you. In this section, I'll cover these common controls and demonstrate how they're used.

tip PowerDVD provides a control menu that's always active— even in full-screen mode, when you normally can't see the control panel. To display the control menu, right-click the mouse and choose the desired option.

Note that PowerDVD usually provides both *on-screen* controls (on either the control panel or the right-click menu) and *keyboard* controls (which you can use at any time) for each feature.

Showing and Minimizing the Panel

Although the control panel is handy to have around, it can get in the way of the action when you're watching a movie full-screen. To minimize the panel, click the button with the minus sign at the top right corner of the control panel, as shown in Figure 8.3 (or press the Ctrl+N keyboard shortcut).

 tip **If you're viewing a movie full-screen and the Ctrl+N shortcut doesn't work, use Alt+Tab to switch to the panel.**

Switching Between Window and Full Screen

Personally, I prefer watching my movies full-screen, which takes advantage of my 19-inch monitor; however, if you like to leave a movie running in a window, it's possible to work on a document or use another application while you're screening an old favorite from your DVD collection. (That is, of course, if you can actually concentrate on your work while Sigourney Weaver is toasting aliens with a flamethrower.)

Like any well-mannered Windows program, you can resize the PowerDVD display window by dragging the right corner of the window border; PowerDVD will automatically adjust the resolution and aspect ratio of the display window to make the best use of the new window dimensions.

To switch PowerDVD between full-screen and windowed display, use the Zoom button (Figure 8.3), or display the right-click menu and choose Zoom.

dvds & cds

FIGURE 8.3   The PowerDVD window controls.

Pausing and Stopping the Movie

It never fails: The phone rings, there's a meeting to attend, or you have to sign for a FedEx package just as the action really gets good. You don't have to miss a second of your movie if you pause PowerDVD: If the control panel is visible, click on the Pause button (Figure 8.2), or display the right-click menu and choose Pause. You can also press the spacebar to pause the movie, or click on the Shuttle dial at the top position (more on the Shuttle dial in the next section).

If you need to stop the movie completely, you can either:

• **Exit PowerDVD.** Press Ctrl+X or click the Exit button on the control panel, as shown in Figure 8.3. (You can eject the disc by pressing Ctrl+E.)

- **Stop the movie.** You can also stop the movie without exiting PowerDVD. Click the Stop button (Figure 8.2), press S or right-click and choose Stop.

While the movie is paused, you can step forward or backward one frame at a time—this is a great way to view a particularly complex or extremely fast action sequence in "slow motion." (For example, I'll step forward quite a bit while watching one of my Bruce Lee movies!) To step, click either the Step Backward or Step Forward buttons (shown in Figure 8.4), or display the right-click menu and choose Forward or Backward. The key sequences are Ctrl+B for a backward step and T for a forward step.

Step Backward   Step Forward

FIGURE 8.4   Use these PowerDVD controls to navigate through a movie.

dvds & cds

Fast-Forward and Rewind

Most of today's DVD players offer a circular control called a *Shuttle dial* that you use to fast-forward and rewind through the movie while it's playing, and PowerDVD uses a Shuttle dial, as well (as shown in Figure 8.4). The Shuttle dial is active only when the movie is playing.

To use the dial, just click on one of the dots that appear around the outside edge: Each dot corresponds to a specific speed in either the forward or reverse directions. For example, clicking the outside edge of the dial at the top position—the one directly above the Pause button— actually has the same effect as the Pause button. Clicking any position to the left of this top position rewinds the movie, and the farther down along the edge of the dial you click, the faster the rewind speed. Clicking the right side of the dial moves forward—again, the farther down the edge of the dial, the faster the forward speed.

To help you visualize the operation of the Shuttle dial, Figure 8.4 illustrates four positions: 8X rewind at the bottom left of the dial, 1X rewind at the top left, 1X forward at the top right, and 8X forward at the lower right. The other dots along the edge of the dial correspond to 2X and 4X rewind and forward speeds.

When you click on the Shuttle dial, PowerDVD places a green dot at the position to indicate the shuttle direction and speed.

Selecting a Chapter

Today's DVD movies are divided into *titles* and *chapters*, making it easy to start at specific points in the movie or jump from one part of the film to another to view your favorite scenes. A title is a named section of the film—for example, in *Gone With the Wind*, one title might read "A Party at Tara"—and each title usually includes a number of chapters, each of which you can jump to directly. Most of the DVD movies available today use an interactive menu that appears before the movie actually begins, and one menu item allows you to watch the movie beginning at any chapter point you choose.

Because the DVD interactive menu appears when I load a movie, I usually use it to make my initial chapter choice; PowerDVD displays the menu, and you simply click on the desired chapter thumbnail image. However, there's a faster alternative you can use to select a specific chapter: Use the PowerDVD shortcut menu. Right-click on the Play button at the center of the Shuttle dial, and PowerDVD displays the chapters in the film (organized as submenu items under the title names, as shown in Figure 8.5).

Unfortunately, the shortcut menu doesn't display the thumbnail images you'll get from the DVD menu's built-in chapter selector…but if you know a film by heart, you may even learn the chapter numbers, as well!

You'll note that the shortcut menu also displays a Browser option—select it, and PowerDVD opens the dialog you see in Figure 8.6. The Browser is essentially a graphical representation of the same title and chapter hierarchy that's available from the shortcut menu, but I find it easier to use; to choose a specific chapter, just double-click on it. (You can also use your cursor keys to navigate the Browser tree.)

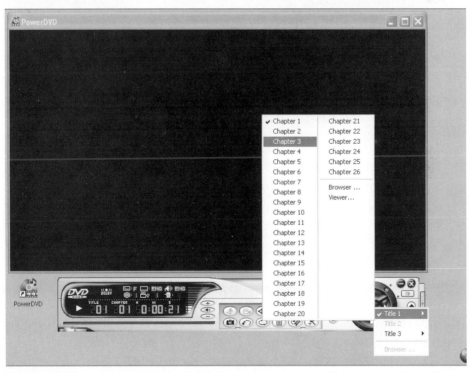

FIGURE 8.5   The titles and chapters available for the DVD edition of the film *Airplane!*

dvds & cds

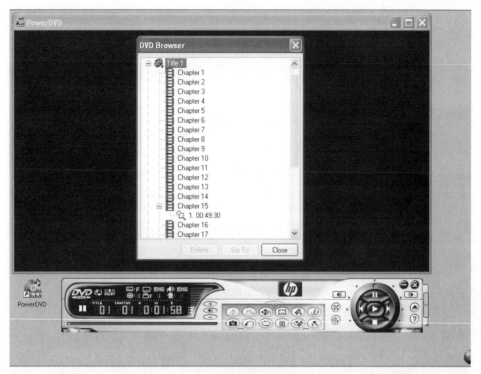

FIGURE 8.6   Selecting a chapter from the Browser dialog.

Using Next and Previous

Are you tired of a particular scene but don't want to jump elsewhere in the film or lose the flow of the plot? You can skip from one chapter to the previous or next chapter using the Next and Previous buttons (shown in Figure 8.4) or display the right-click menu and choose Next or Previous from there. The keyboard shortcut buttons for Next and Previous are N and P, respectively.

Using Repeat

You can repeat the display of an individual chapter or a title: Click the Repeat button (Figure 8.7) once to repeat (or loop) the current chapter. Click the button twice to repeat the current title; clicking the Repeat button again turns the function off. You can press Ctrl+R from the keyboard, as well.

PowerDVD doesn't stop there, however; you can set your own specific scenes to repeat, using the program's AB Repeat feature.

✔ **Follow these steps to set a custom repeat while you're watching a movie:**

1. Click the AB Repeat button (Figure 8.7) or press X to mark the start of the segment (point A).

2. When the movie reaches the point where you want the segment to end, click the AB Repeat button or press X again to set the end of the segment (point B). PowerDVD will immediately begin looping the segment you've marked.

3. To cancel the AB repeat, click the AB Repeat button again.

dvds & cds

FIGURE 8.7   The PowerDVD repeat and audio controls.

Setting the Volume Level

Although you can set the volume level in Windows using the taskbar Volume Control—display the taskbar at the bottom of the screen and click on the speaker icon—PowerDVD offers a more elegant and convenient solution with its own volume controls. Figure 8.7 illustrates the three audio level controls:

1. Click the Increase Volume button or press the plus (+) key on your keyboard to turn up the audio.

2. Click the Decrease Volume button or press the minus (-) key on your keyboard to turn down the volume.

3. Click the Mute button or press the Q key on your keyboard to temporarily turn off the audio altogether.

Selecting an Audio Stream

Many DVD movies feature a number of different *audio streams*—for example, a movie can include the dialog spoken in French or Spanish, commentary from the actors and director, or even a complete alternate soundtrack. Some discs may also include specialized audio streams with playback modes such as Dolby surround sound or Dolby Pro-Logic (whereas older discs offer only plain-and-simple stereo).

The selection of audio streams that you can choose from in Power-DVD while watching a DVD movie depends on three criteria:

1. The sound card you've installed in your computer

2. The speaker layout you're using

3. The DVD movie itself (what audio streams the studio decided to add for this specific movie)

You can choose an audio stream from the DVD's own interactive menu, or you can put PowerDVD to work. Click the Audio Streams button shown in Figure 8.7 to toggle between the different streams, or press H.

Switching Angles

If you're watching a DVD disc that features multiple camera angles, click the Angle button shown in Figure 8.8 to switch between the different angles, or press A.

Bookmarking Scenes

Earlier, I mentioned AB Repeat; in that same vein, *bookmarking* a scene is another PowerDVD feature designed to make it easy to locate a specific scene in your favorite movie. To add a bookmark, you click the Set Bookmark button on the control panel (Figure 8.8) or press Ctrl+F2 at the desired moment in the film; you can do this as often as you like, and PowerDVD keeps track of each bookmark.

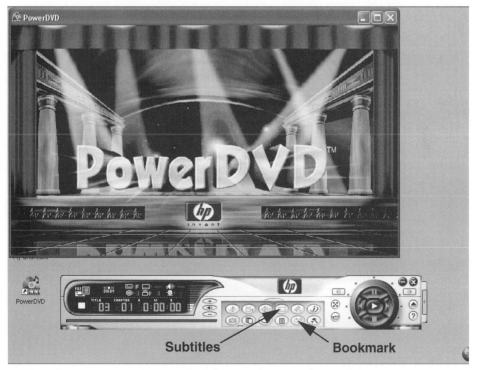

FIGURE 8.8   PowerDVD's bookmark, angle, and subtitling controls.

There are four methods of selecting a bookmark that you've set:

1. Press the F2 button or click the Go To Bookmark button to toggle through your bookmarked scenes.

2. Right-click the Go To Bookmark button and choose a bookmark from the pop-up menu.

3. Right-click the Go To Bookmark button and choose Browse to display the Browse dialog, which looks very much like the Chapter Browse dialog—double-click on the desired bookmark (they look like pushpins, and they appear underneath the chapters).

4. Right-click the Go To Bookmark button and choose Viewer (for the thumbnail viewer you see in Figure 8.9)—double-click on the desired bookmark thumbnail.

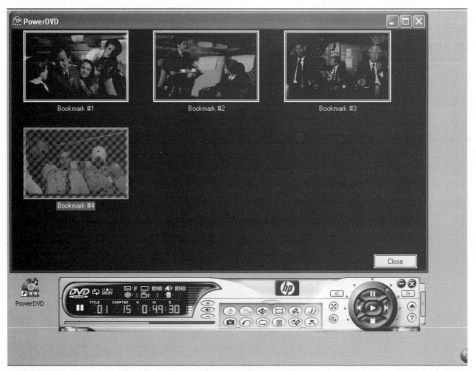

FIGURE 8.9   Selecting a bookmarked scene using the Viewer.

Displaying Subtitling

Like audio streams, most of today's DVD movies feature subtitles—usually, you'll get subtitles in English and one or two other languages, but I've seen as many as five different subtitle selections for one film. Figure 8.8 illustrates the Subtitles button, which you can click while the movie is playing to toggle between the different subtitles available on the disc—from the keyboard, press the U key to toggle the subtitles.

You can also right-click on the Subtitles button to display a pop-up menu—click on the specific subtitling you want from the menu to select it.

tip **If your DVD movie also provides closed captioning, you can toggle this feature on, using the Subtitles button; right-click on it and choose Closed Captioning from the Secondary Subtitles section.**

Using File Mode

As I mentioned at the beginning of the chapter, PowerDVD isn't limited to displaying only DVD movies; you can also listen to audio CDs and display video CDs (also called *VCDs*) using the same controls as DVD movies—a neat feature and one you'll likely use often.

But why limit yourself to discs? You can view MPEG, QuickTime MOV, and Windows AVI-format video directly from your hard drive! (In fact, most DVD movies are "assembled" and burned from hard drives.) To view digital video files from the hard drive, you must switch PowerDVD to File mode.

Follow these steps to switch to File mode and to load files from your hard drive (or other source, such as a ZIP disk or a CD-ROM):

1. Click the Disc/File Mode button (Figure 8.2) or press O to toggle the button to File mode (the button graphic changes to a file folder).

dvds & cds

2. Click the Menu/Playlist button to display the Edit Playlist window you see in Figure 8.10.

3. Use the tree display at the left side of the window to locate the digital video files you want to play—click on the plus sign next to a drive or folder to expand it. When you've located a digital video file that the program can play, it will appear in the Path list at the top right of the window.

4. Click the desired video file in the Path list and click Add to add it to the Playlist at the bottom right of the window. To add more video files to the playlist, repeat steps 3 and 4—PowerDVD will play them in the order they appear in the playlist.

5. Once you're done with the playlist, click OK, and click the Play button on the control panel to start the show.

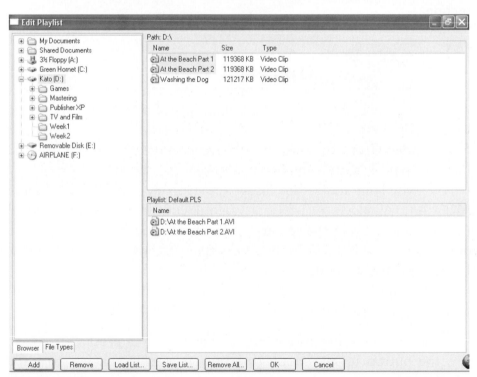

FIGURE 8.10 Choosing a digital video file from my hard drive.

Using the Menu Pad

As I've mentioned earlier, most DVD movies display an interactive menu that you can use to select different features—you can simply click your mouse pointer on a menu option to select it, but PowerDVD also provides a slick menu pad that simulates the keyboard pad on a standard DVD player remote control. Because some DVD movie menus may use "hotspot" buttons that aren't easily found on the screen, you can save yourself the trouble of hunting for those hotspots and use the menu pad to navigate the menu, instead.

To display or hide the menu pad, click the vertical button at the far right end of the control panel—you can also press the slash (/) key. Figure 8.11 illustrates the extended menu pad. Click on the desired directional button to navigate around the DVD movie's menu system (the button at the center of the pad is the Enter button, which usually activates the active menu command).

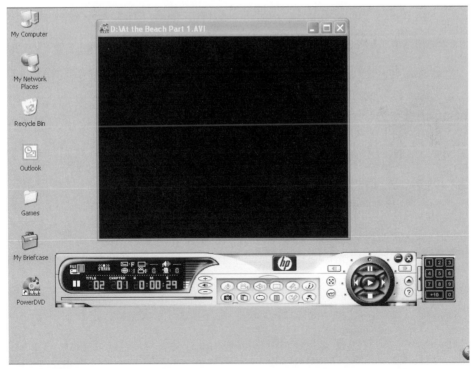

FIGURE 8.11 Using the menu pad to select a DVD movie menu option.

dvds & cds

Project: **Capturing and E-mailing Images from Digital Video**

So you've used your new digital camcorder to film your daughter's first birthday, and some of the footage is priceless—I know the feeling! Let's assume that you want to e-mail selected images from the video to other family members, *without* sending them the entire 400-MB MPEG file. PowerDVD comes to the rescue, allowing you to capture images directly from your digital video and save those images as still photos—which you can then send through e-mail as attachments.

Because you may not be familiar with e-mail attachments, this project will take you all the way from capturing the image to sending the message; I'll be using Outlook Express to send the images.

Requirements

- A digital video file on your hard drive (or a DVD movie disc)
- Outlook Express or other e-mail program

✔ Follow these steps:

1. Run PowerDVD—if the program is in Disc mode, click the Disc/File Mode button (Figure 8.2) or press O to switch to File mode.

2. Click the Menu/Playlist button to display the Edit Playlist window.

3. I'll navigate to the digital video file "Family Birthday"—because PowerDVD recognizes the format, it appears in the Path list. Click the entry for Family Birthday in the Path list and click Add to add it to the Playlist.

4. Click OK to return to the PowerDVD control panel, then click Play to begin watching the video.

5. When you reach the scene that you want to capture as a still image, click Pause, then right-click the Capture button on the control panel

(Figure 8.12). Choose Capture to File—by default, this saves the image in the My Pictures folder in your my Documents folder under Windows XP. You can take as many images as the free space on your hard drive allows; PowerDVD names the first image PDVD_000.BMP and increments the number as you save successive photos.

FIGURE 8.12 The Capture and Configuration buttons on the PowerDVD control panel.

tip To save the image to another directory, click the Configuration button on the control panel (Figure 8.12), and click the Capture tab to display the settings you see in Figure 8.13. Click Browse and navigate to the directory where you want your images saved, then click OK to save your changes, and click OK to exit the Configuration dialog.

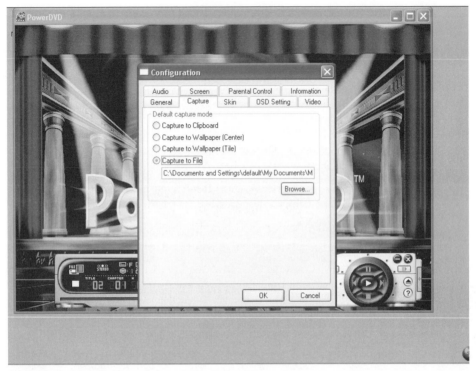

FIGURE 8.13 Changing the default Capture settings.

tip PowerDVD saves your still images in Windows bitmap format, which (depending on the size of the video frame) may be too large to send as an e-mail attachment—in general, I never send a message with more than a total of about 500 KB attached to it, because many Internet Service Providers will not allow large attachments. (You'll know that this is the case if you receive an error message from your e-mail server saying that the message couldn't be delivered or was too large.) However, there are two solutions to this problem of attachment "elbowroom": you can use a ZIP archiving utility, such as WinZIP (www.winzip.com), to reduce the file size, or you can load the image into an image editing program, such as Paint Shop Pro (www.jasc.com) or Photoshop, and convert it to a JPEG image.

6. Now that you have your images saved to your hard drive, it's time to send that e-mail. Run your e-mail program and compose a new

message; in Outlook Express, for example, you would click the Create Mail button on the toolbar.

7. Fill out the To and Subject fields as you normally would, and enter the text of your message. In Outlook Express, click the Attachment button on the New Message dialog toolbar to attach one of your images to the message.

8. Navigate to the location of the image files and click on one or more of the desired filenames, then click Attach. As you can see in Figure 8.14, the files appear in the Attach field. (Note that the file sizes are listed, too—remember, try to keep the total size of all attachments for a single message under 500 KB. If you need to, you can always send multiple messages with one image attached to each message. If the recipient is using a dial-up modem connection, it's a good idea to send the smallest attachments possible!)

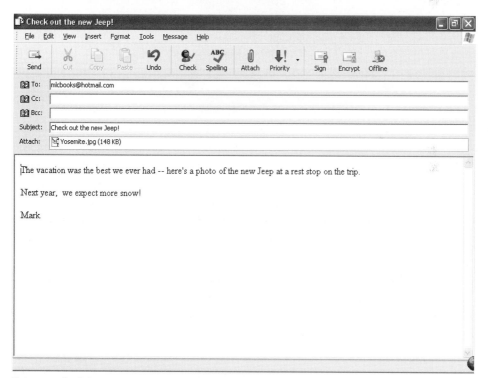

FIGURE 8.14 I've attached an image to this e-mail message.

9. Click the Send button in the toolbar to send the message.

10. If you've sent your images in Windows bitmap or JPEG formats and the recipients are running Windows ME or XP, they should be able to simply double-click on the icon for each attachment when they open the message. Figure 8.15 illustrates our attached image after I've opened it in Microsoft Outlook.

FIGURE 8.15 Voilà! The image from your digital video has crossed the Internet via e-mail.

Summary

In this chapter, we covered the features of PowerDVD, and you learned how to view DVD movies and digital video clips using this powerful application. I also demonstrated how to capture high-quality still images from DVD movies and digital video clips.

9

Printing Disc Labels and Inserts

In This Chapter

✔ Determining whether a disc needs a label or inserts

✔ Applying labels the right way

✔ Designing inserts

✔ Project: Creating a CD Label

✔ Project: Creating a CD Case Cover and Insert Set

Nothing adds a professional appearance to a CD you've recorded better than a custom label—except, perhaps, a custom label and case inserts! As long as you label your recorded discs in some fashion and protect them somehow, you've taken care of the basics; however, a felt-tipped permanent marker and an empty compact disc "jewel box" case won't make a great impression on anyone.

dvds & cds

n this chapter, I'll demonstrate how you can use Roxio Easy CD Creator and your computer's printer to turn out CD labels and case inserts that are both attractive and informative—in addition, I'll show you how to apply a custom CD label properly.

Do I Need Labels and Inserts?

If you're recording only DVD+RW discs, you should think twice before applying a paper label. For example, Hewlett-Packard includes this warning with each HP DVD+RW disc:

caution   **Never use a ball point pen or adhesive labels on DVD+RW media—there's too high a risk of damaging the disc! Any change you make to the balance of the disc (no matter how slight) will likely render a disc unreadable. Remember, DVD technology packs more data on the same disc because the track containing the pits and lands is far smaller, so there's less room for error.**

Therefore, this chapter applies only to those folks who are using their DVD recorder to burn data and audio CDs using CD-R and CD-RW discs, as well as those who want to create custom case inserts for their DVD cases.

With that said, when should you take the time to create custom labels and inserts? I recommend them when:

- You're recording discs for distribution—for example, if you're a shareware author or a musician recording demo discs. A label is also a good idea if you're sending beta copies of software to testers or distributing a disc among your customers.
- You're presenting a disc as a gift.
- You'd like to document the contents of a data or audio CD fully. Because you can add a surprising amount of text to both the label and case inserts, you can even include luxuries such as track times and liner notes.

tip Labels are a great idea when creating hard drive backup sets using CD-RW discs—with a label, you'll have more space to add dates and hard drive information.

- You simply want the best appearance for your collection of recorded discs.

Naturally, I don't create disc labels for every project—but when you take the time to create labels, they can really make an impression! (And add convenience, as well; for example, all of my home movie DVD discs have custom case inserts with thumbnail images from the video clips. I can find the right disc in seconds.)

Applying Labels 101

Two different types of CD labels are available: those that are designed to be applied by hand and those that are designed for application using a device such as the two-piece NEATO CD labeling machine in Figure 9.1 (www.neato.com).

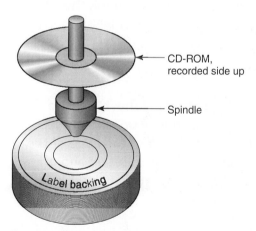

CD-ROM, recorded side up

Spindle

Label backing

FIGURE 9.1   Applying a CD label using the NEATO CD machine.

dvds & cds

If you choose labels that are applied by hand, leave the disc inside its jewel case; this helps steady the disc and allows better alignment. In fact, most of these labels include a border that acts as a visual guide— you match it to the edge of the case. With hand-applied labels, it's important to smooth the label slowly across the face of the disc, eliminating bubbles as you go.

caution   **Never attempt to remove a paper label from a disc unless the manufacturer specifically calls the labels "removable"! Most CD labels use permanent adhesive, and you're likely to damage the disc beyond repair; in addition, a badly-aligned label can throw your disc out of balance and ruin it. (Yet another reason to be careful when aligning and smoothing a disc.)**

The NEATO device (which dates back to the mid-1990s) is a little more hi-tech, and it guarantees correct alignment with very few bubbles: The disc is placed upside-down on the spindle with the reflective side facing up, and the printed label is placed on the base with the adhesive side facing up. The label is applied by pushing the spindle into the base and pressing down.

Which type of labels is best for you? Personally, I think the labeling device is worth the extra investment if you need to label your discs quickly or if you produce a large number of discs at one time. A label applicator is a must for the best quality of work.

tip   **When peeling the label off the backing sheet, here's a trick that will prevent the label from "rolling up" into a tube: Turn the sheet upside down and lift up a small area of the edge of the label, then hold that down against a table. Pull the sheet up and off the label, and you'll be left with the label on the table sticky side up and flat as a pancake!**

Project: **Creating a Label**

Enough talk: Let's print a custom label for an audio CD! In this project, you've created a "Greatest Hits" birthday collection from a friend's favorite CDs, and you want to present it as a gift so it can be played during the party. I'll be using CD Label Creator, which is included in the popular Easy CD Creator recording software from Roxio (www.roxio.com).

Requirements

- Computer with a laser or inkjet printer
- Installed copy of Easy CD Creator 5
- Recorded audio CD

✔ Follow these steps to design and print your label:

1. Click Start | Programs | Easy CD Creator 5 | Applications | CD Label Creator to run CD Label Creator. Click the CD Label icon to select it at the left side of the screen, which displays the blank layout shown in Figure 9.2.

2. If you recorded your audio disc with CD-Text, you can import the title and artist name automatically—click the Contents toolbar button. (If you didn't use CD-Text or the program can't find the disc in the Internet CD database, you'll have to do things the old-fashioned way: Double-click in each of the fields and type the information manually. Press Enter to update the field once you've entered the text.)

3. Click the Theme toolbar button to select one of Roxio's preset themes. The Change Theme dialog appears, as illustrated in Figure 9.3.

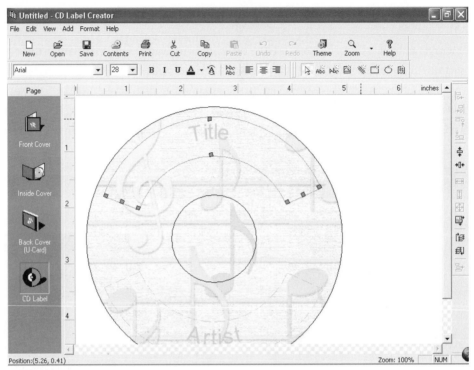

FIGURE 9.2   Roxio's CD Label Creator, ready for action.

4. Note that each of the themes listed in the Available Themes list is followed by either "Audio" or "Data"—this indicates which type of disc is preferred for use with that theme. (Any theme can be used for either type of disc, but these tags indicate which type of information will be automatically updated. If you use an audio CD theme with a data CD-ROM, you'll have to do more work and create all of the fields manually.) For our festive party, let's choose the Whirl theme—click Whirl in the list, which updates the Preview pane, and click OK. Our CD label layout now looks like the one you see in Figure 9.4.

tip To view just the themes for an audio CD or a data CD-ROM, use the Show Audio Themes and Show Data Themes checkboxes at the top of the dialog box.

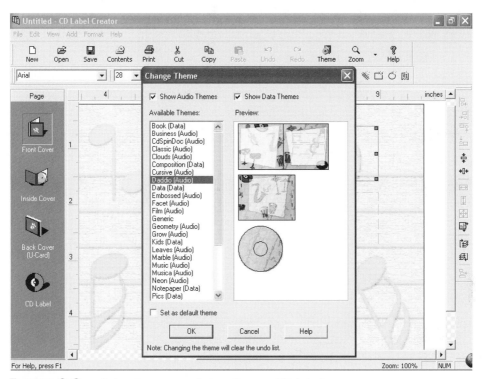

FIGURE 9.3 Selecting a new theme for our CD label.

5. CD Label Creator uses the rusty, tried-and-true default font of Times New Roman—boring! Because you can make changes to the text box that's currently selected, let's choose a new font and make things a bit more interesting visually. First, click on the Title box to select it, then click on the Font drop-down list box and click on a font name. To change the font size, click on the Points drop-down list box (the program automatically wraps words that are too big for the text box).

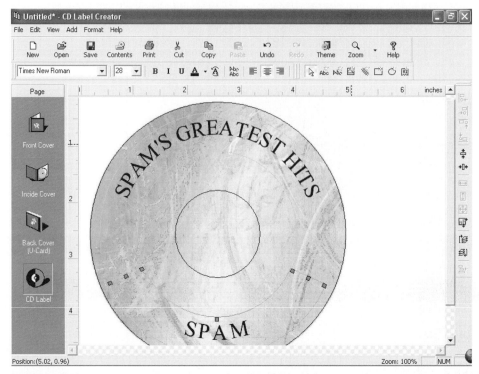

FIGURE 9.4   The Whirl theme has been applied to our CD label layout.

6. Click on the Artist text box and choose the same font and point size. Figure 9.5 shows our disc sporting text using the Mickey font, which is much more fitting for a party.

7. Our gift needs a little personalization. To add a text box, click Add and choose Text. Click and drag to move the text box below the spindle hole, as shown in Figure 9.6. You can also click and drag the *handles*—those small squares on the border of the text box— to resize the box.

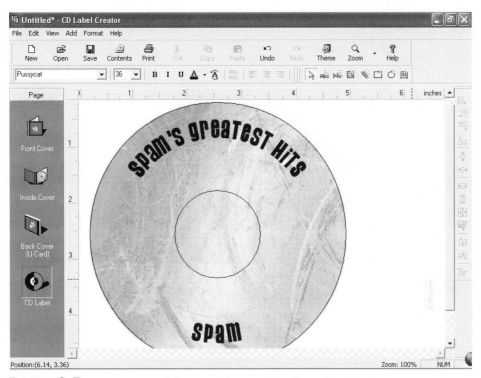

FIGURE 9.5   A change of font can do wonders for a disc label.

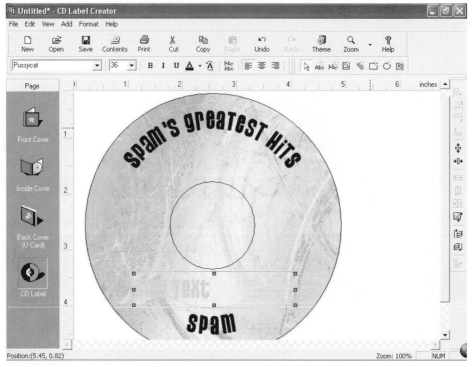

FIGURE 9.6   Adding a new text box to the layout.

8. Double-click in the box and type the text, then press Enter to save your changes. Figure 9.7 illustrates our completed label design, ready to print or save to your hard drive.

9. Load your CD label blanks into your printer as instructed by the manufacturer—make sure the labels are facing in the right direction, and the correct edge is facing away from the printer.

10. Click File and choose Print Preview (Figure 9.8) to check the appearance of the label. To make changes, click Close and return to the layout.

11. Click Print on the toolbar to print your labels.

FIGURE 9.7   A completed label design can be saved or printed.

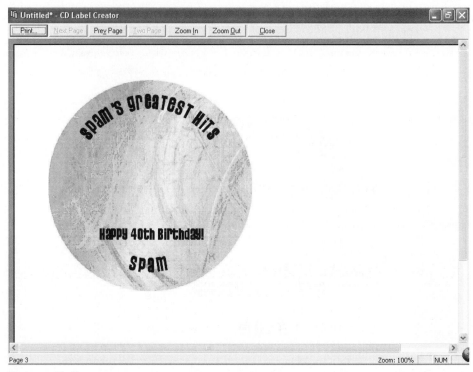

FIGURE 9.8   Why waste expensive labels? Use Print Preview to check your design.

Project: **Creating an Insert Set**

Now let's turn to another fun project that's easy to print with CD Label Creator: this time, a set of inserts for a DVD home video disc that I've just recorded. I want to use thumbnails from the video as artwork, and each clip will be noted on the back.

Requirements

- Computer with a laser or inkjet printer
- Installed copy of Easy CD Creator 5

✔ **Follow these steps:**

1. Click Start | Programs | Easy CD Creator 5 | Applications | CD Label Creator. Click the Front Cover icon to display the layout you see in Figure 9.9.

2. Let's select a new theme—the default, Music, doesn't work well for our DVD inserts. Click Format and choose the Change Theme menu item.

3. Click on the Pics entry to select the Pics theme, as shown in Figure 9.10—CD Label Creator automatically updates the Preview pane so you can see the theme—and click OK to accept it.

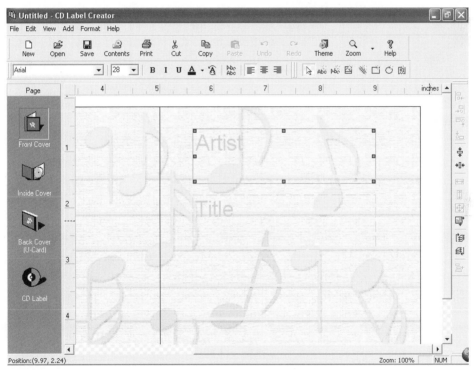

FIGURE 9.9   A new blank front cover layout.

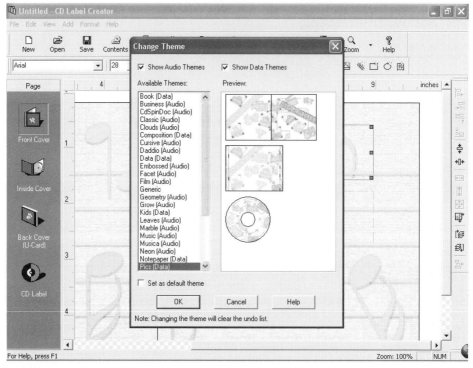

FIGURE 9.10 The Pics theme is perfect for a home video DVD.

4. Double-click directly on the Title field. An edit box appears, and you can type the title directly in the field. Press Enter to save your changes.

tip **Made a mistake while editing your layout? Use the Undo button on the toolbar to backtrack from your last action.**

5. Double-click in the Contents field and enter the name of each video clip on the disc—I usually add the date each clip was taken, as well as the subjects. Press Enter to save your changes. Your layout should now look something like mine in Figure 9.11.

6. Let's add a piece of clip art—in this case, a thumbnail image from the video. Click Add and choose the Picture menu item to display a standard File Open dialog. Navigate to the location of the image,

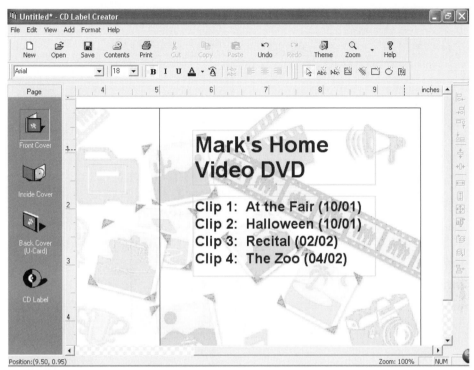

FIGURE 9.11 The completed text fields for my DVD home video disc.

click on the filename to highlight it, and click Open. CD Label Creator can use both Windows bitmap and JPEG image formats.

7. As you can see in Figure 9.12, the image is already selected. You can resize it and move it just like a text box. To resize the image, click on one of the square "handles" on the edge of the window and drag to resize that edge. To move the entire image to another spot on your layout, click in the middle of the selected image and drag it to the desired spot.

8. Don't forget the inside cover and back cover! Click on the desired icon in the Page view on the left side of the screen, and you'll find that you have quite a bit of additional space that you can fill with text and graphics. For this project, I'd like to add a quick description of each of my video clips on the back cover, so I'll click the Back Cover (U-Card) icon. CD Label Creator switches to the Back Cover layout

dvds & cds

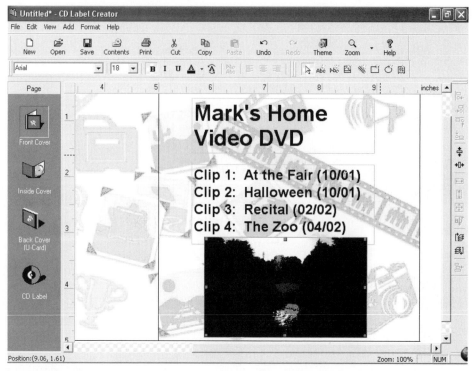

FIGURE 9.12 Adding a thumbnail image to my DVD insert layout.

you see in Figure 9.13—note that some of the information from the front cover has already been automatically imported.

9. To add a new block of text on the back cover, click Add and choose Text or Curved Text. A text block appears, and you can resize and relocate it as usual. To enter text, double-click in the desired text box and type; press Enter to save your changes. Figure 9.14 illustrates my completed back cover.

10. Ready to print? You can use either plain paper or precut insert paper—if you have insert paper, load it into the printer as instructed by the manufacturer.

11. To check your work before you print, click File and choose Print Preview. If everything looks good, click Print on the toolbar; to make changes or add more information to the inserts, click Close and return to the layout.

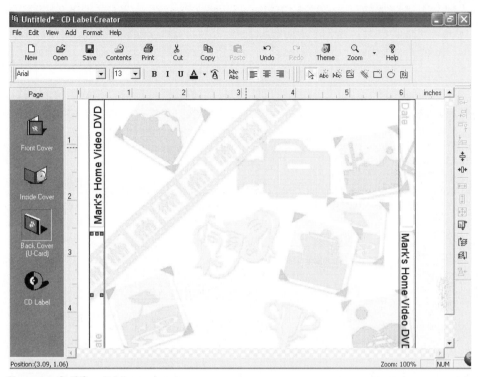

FIGURE 9.13 Adding a back cover to my insert set.

FIGURE 9.14 The back cover insert, ready to print.

Summary

We covered the world of CD labels and inserts in this chapter: when you should use them, how to apply them, and how to design and print them, using Roxio's CD Label Creator.

10

Recording Advanced Formats and Video CD Discs

In This Chapter

✓ Comparing Video CDs and DVD Video discs

✓ Understanding mixed-mode recording

✓ Understanding multisession recording

✓ Recording with a disc image

✓ Project: Creating a Video CD with Digital Video

✓ Project: Recording a Promotional CD-Extra Disc

✓ Project: Burning a Bootable CD

Throughout most of the earlier chapters, I've focused on recording standard DVD data and video formats, as well as basic data and audio CDs. However, there's an entire chapter's worth of advanced CD recording formats that have been popular for many years that I need to discuss— you might not need one of these specialized disc formats every day, but it's important to know how to create video CD, mixed-mode, bootable, and multisession discs when the situation calls for them.

dvds & cds

My application of choice for this chapter is Roxio's Easy CD Creator Platinum, which ships with many CD and DVD recorders; you'll also learn how to create copies of a CD or DVD using a disc image. Our three projects will demonstrate how to record a standard Video CD disc, a CD-Extra disc that can be used with DVD players and audio CD players, and a bootable data CD.

Note that MyDVD version 3.5 will also create a proprietary type of Video CD disc called a cDVD disc; for more information on burning cDVDs with MyDVD, see the section titled "Recording the Disc" in Chapter 6.

Introducing Easy CD Creator 5

Figure 10.1 illustrates the main window from an old friend of mine: version 5 of Roxio's Easy CD Creator Platinum, which I've been using for about six years now. (Coincidentally, I also wrote my first book on the topic of CD recording in 1997. I'll bet you can guess which program I covered in that book.)

Easy CD Creator is a complete recording application—the Platinum version includes a number of standalone utilities that can produce:

- CD labels and jewel box inserts (as you saw in Chapter 9, "Printing Disc Labels and Inserts")
- UDF (packet-writing) discs using DirectCD, which operates very much like HP DLA
- Digital photograph albums and video postcards (more on this in Chapter 11, "Recording Digital Photographs on CD")
- Audio CDs from cassettes and albums, using your home stereo
- Hard drive backups using CD and DVD discs (such as HP Simple Backup)

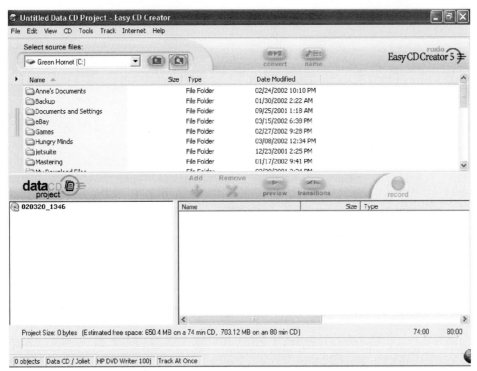

FIGURE 10.1 The Easy CD Creator main application window.

Although you can configure a disc format manually if you like, Easy CD Creator comes with a great "front-end" wizard program that can help automate the setup for many types of discs: We'll use the Roxio Project Selector (shown in Figure 10.2) often during this chapter. The Project Selector automatically starts Easy CD Creator with the proper settings for the standard formats you've learned about throughout earlier chapters.

If you've installed Easy CD Creator Platinum already, you can run the Project Selector in Windows XP by clicking Start | All Programs | Roxio Easy CD Creator 5 | Project Selector.

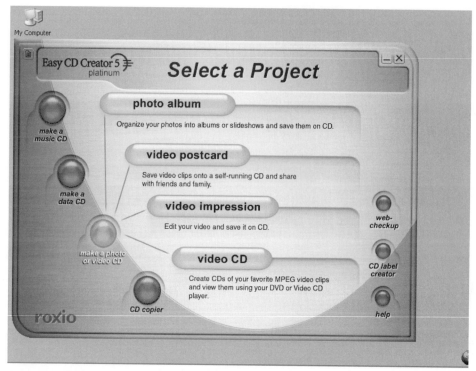

FIGURE 10.2 The Project Selector shows off the different video and photo discs it can create.

Video CDs vs. DVD Video Discs

"Mark, why do I need to record a video CD, anyway? Aren't DVD Video discs far superior to anything that's come before?" Good question, and the answer is a definite "yes"—DVD video discs are the best medium for carrying high-quality, high-resolution digital video.

However, not everyone has a DVD player or a DVD-ROM drive, and that's where the video CD still comes in handy! A video CD can't carry anywhere near the same amount of digital video, and the quality is significantly lower than a DVD Video disc—however, most computers with a standard CD-ROM drive can read a video CD, and many DVD players are also compatible with video CDs. Before the advent of DVD, many manufacturers turned out video CD players and CD-I players that will accept this format, as well. As you learned in the section titled "Loading and Playing a DVD Movie" in Chapter 8, Power-DVD can display video CDs on your computer.

Therefore, here's one of Mark's Patented Recording Rules: *Burn DVD Video discs when you're sure a DVD player or DVD-ROM drive (that you know is compatible) will be handy, and burn video CDs for friends and family who aren't prepared for DVD yet!*

Depending on the compression scheme you're using, you can usually fit anywhere from 45 to 75 minutes of MPEG video on the standard video CDs produced by Easy CD Creator. Note that I said MPEG video—in order to record video clips in Windows AVI or QuickTime MOV formats, you'll have to convert them to MPEG format first. (In some cases, Easy CD Creator can do this for you automatically.) A video CD can even include a rudimentary menu system that will allow you to select the clip you want to watch (when used on compatible DVD, video CD, and CD-I players).

Introducing Mixed-Mode Recording

In earlier chapters, you learned the differences between recording audio and data CDs—oil and vinegar, right? Never will the two mix. (I love this part.) Unless, of course, you move to *mixed-mode* recording! A mixed-mode CD-ROM actually has both digital audio tracks and a data track on the same disc; a good example is a multimedia CD-ROM game title that includes digital video, a computer application, and several tracks of digital audio. Just like English in elementary school: There's an exception to every rule!

To illustrate how this magic is performed, check out Figure 10.3: You'll note that the first track on the disc is computer data, and the following tracks are recorded separately as digital audio.

Naturally, an idea this good doesn't come without caveats. Before we get too excited about mixed-mode recording, here's the downside:

dvds & cds

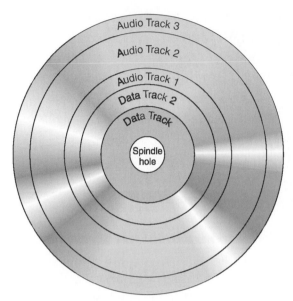

FIGURE 10.3 Merging computer data and digital audio on the same mixed-mode disc.

- **Older hardware may not recognize a mixed-mode disc.** If an older PC is using a CD-ROM drive that's 4X or slower (or if you scavenged such a drive from a garage sale or an eBay auction), it probably won't be able to read either the data or the digital audio from a mixed-mode disc.

- **Older operating systems may not recognize mixed-mode discs.** Older versions of UNIX, Mac OS, and DOS won't be able to read a mixed-mode disc—luckily, these relics don't really have the horsepower to play digital video or high-quality audio anyway, so good riddance!

- **You can't play a standard mixed-mode disc in your audio CD player.** Remember that the first track of a standard mixed-mode disc is still computer data, so your audio CD player will spit it out (or play some incredibly bad audio). You can get around this problem by recording a very useful variant of the mixed-mode standard disc: The *CD-Extra* (also called *Plus* or *Enhanced*) disc shown in Figure 10.4 is recorded with the audio

Data Track

Audio Track 2

Data Track 2

Spindle hole

FIGURE 10.4 Your audio CD player accepts a CD-Extra mixed-mode CD-ROM without any trouble.

tracks appearing first on the disc, so it can played on a standard audio CD player. (Your audio CD player simply ignores the data track that appears at the end of the disc.) Bands such as the Rolling Stones and Smash Mouth have released CD-Extra discs that include the music, a music video, and all of the song lyrics on the same disc! We'll record a CD-Extra disc in one of the projects at the end of this chapter.

Introducing Multisession Recording

A traditional single-session data CD-ROM has only a single recording session—the disc is then fixed and closed so that it can't be recorded again. With a multisession disc, however, you can record it once, use it, then record on it again; for instance, you could record your tax returns on the same disc, "appending" them each year until you fill the entire disc.

dvds & cds

In multisession recording, you can record separate sessions (think of them as separate volumes on the same disc), or you can "update" the same session with new information. Each session you record is separated from the previous section by an area of empty space (which can range anywhere from 14 to 30 MB, depending on its position on the disc surface). Because of this lost space, you never get the storage capacity from a multisession disc that you get from a single-session disc. It's a good idea to avoid recording a session that contains only a small amount of data, because you're guaranteed to lose at least 14 MB when you add another session!

You can record two different types of multisession CD-ROMs, using Easy CD Creator:

1. **Incremental.** An incremental multisession disc makes it easy to "update" previous data that you've recorded, because all the information that you've recorded within the previous session is available; as the name suggests, you can add files to that existing information. Easy CD Creator includes an Import Session function that enables you to read the contents of the previous session into your data CD layout. Incremental discs are fast to create, too, because the information in the previous session is not actually rerecorded. Instead, the session's directory information is retained and updated with the new data; however, your drive can read only the latest session you've recorded.

tip **You can even "delete" files from an incremental multisession disc! (Actually, files deleted from this type of disc are not erased and you don't regain any of the space they used; instead, the location of the file isn't updated in the disc's Table of Contents, so it effectively disappears and can't be recovered.) This trick was used often in the days before UDF (or packet-writing) became common.**

2. **Multivolume.** Data on a multivolume multisession disc is arranged in separate sessions, and you can switch between volumes whenever you like—however, you can read data from only one volume at a time, and you can't modify the data stored on a

session. Note that older, first-generation CD-ROM drives may not be able to read all of the sessions on a multivolume disc—instead, they may be able to access only the first or the last session on the disc. (Consider an incremental multisession disc if your CD-ROM will be read on older computers.) Figure 10.5 illustrates multivolume recording at work.

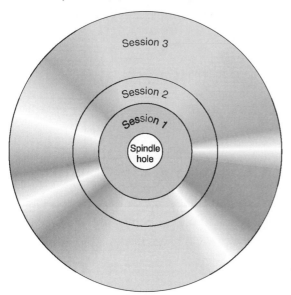

FIGURE 10.5 *Separate sessions store discrete data in a multivolume multisession recording.*

Recording an Incremental Multisession Disc

To burn an incremental multisession disc with Easy CD Creator, you need a disc with an existing session that you've recorded earlier. This disc must have been recorded with the Record Method set to *Track-at-Once* and *Finalize Session, Don't Finalize CD*. (These settings appear when you click the Options button on the Record CD Setup screen, as shown in Figure 10.6.) If you've created the first session on the disc with another recording program, make sure you don't *finalize* (or close) the disc, or you won't be able to write to it again!

dvds & cds

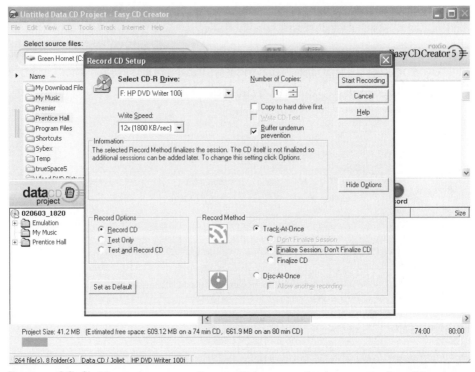

FIGURE 10.6 The proper recording options to use for incremental multisession recording.

✔ **To record an incremental multisession disc:**

1. Load the disc with the existing session into your drive. Easy CD Creator automatically displays the Roxio Project Selector.

2. Place your mouse pointer over Make a Data CD to display the different types of data disc you can record.

3. Click Data CD Project to load the Data CD Layout screen.

4. Before you add any files or folders to the empty layout, click the File menu and select CD Project Properties to display the dialog you see in Figure 10.7. Verify that the *Automatically import previous session check box is enabled*—if not, click the check box to turn the feature on—and click OK.

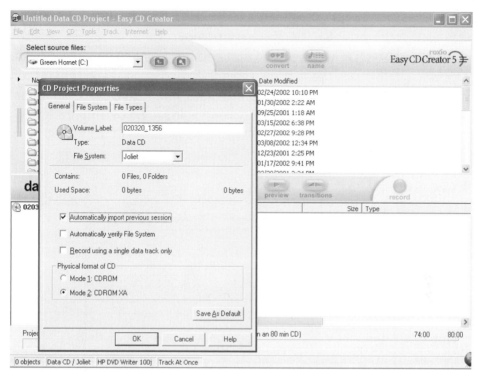

FIGURE 10.7   Setting Easy CD Creator to automatically import our existing session.

5. Build the layout for the new session: Navigate to the files and folders you want to add in the top portion of the window, highlight them, and click the Add button in the middle of the window to move them to the layout below. When you add the first new file or folder, Easy CD Creator automatically imports the files and folders recorded during the previous session.

    tip   **Things are very similar to Windows Explorer in the world of Easy CD Creator: For example, you can double-click on a file or folder name in the layout portion of the window to rename it, and you can drag and drop files in the layout to rearrange them as necessary.**

6. Click the big red Record button at the center of the screen to display the Record CD Setup dialog. If you'll be adding more data to

dvds & cds

the disc later—in other words, if this isn't the last incremental session you'll add to the disc—remember to once again set the Record Method to *Track-at-Once* and *Finalize Session, Don't Finalize CD*. (If this is the last session you'll record on this disc, you can set the options to *Track-at-Once* and *Finalize CD*.) Click Start Recording to burn, and the progress dialog appears (Figure 10.8)!

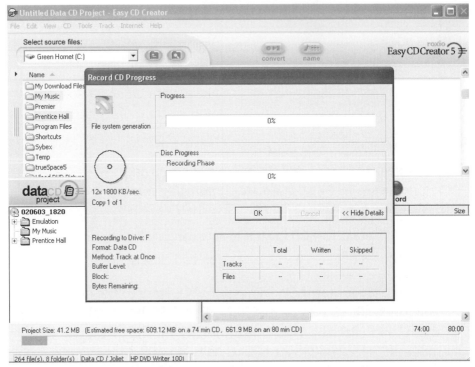

FIGURE 10.8   The progress dialog appears while recording an incremental multisession disc.

Recording a Multivolume Multisession Disc

To record a multivolume multisession disc, you'll once again need a disc with an existing session recorded with the Record Method set to *Track-at-Once* and *Finalize Session, Don't Finalize CD.*

✔ **Follow these steps:**

1. Load the disc with the existing session into your drive. Easy CD Creator automatically displays the Roxio Project Selector.

2. Place your mouse pointer over Make a Data CD to display the different types of data disc you can record.

3. Click Data CD Project to load the Data CD Layout screen.

4. Before you add any files, click the File menu and select CD Project Properties—verify that the *Automatically import previous session* check box is enabled. (If not, click the check box to turn the feature on.) Click OK.

5. Build the layout for the new session as I described in the previous section.

6. Click the big red Record button at the center of the screen to display the Record CD Setup dialog. (If you'll be adding more data later, remember to once again set the Record Method to *Track-at-Once* and *Finalize Session, Don't Finalize CD.*) Click Start Recording.

7. Easy CD Creator prompts you to confirm that you want to add a new volume to the disc. Click Yes to begin the recording.

Selecting a Session from a Multivolume Multisession Disc

The Platinum version of Easy CD Creator also includes Session Selector, a useful little utility application for selecting and reading a different volume.

dvds & cds

✔ **To choose a new session from a multivolume disc, follow these steps:**

1. Run Session Selector from the Start menu by clicking Start | All Programs | Roxio Easy CD Creator 5 | Applications | Session Selector. The program displays the main window shown in Figure 10.9.

2. Click the correct CD-ROM drive in the left pane of the window. Session Selector displays the sessions on the selected disc in the right portion of the window.

3. The current session being read is reported with a drive letter. To select another session, click the desired session in the list to highlight it, click Tools, and choose Activate Session.

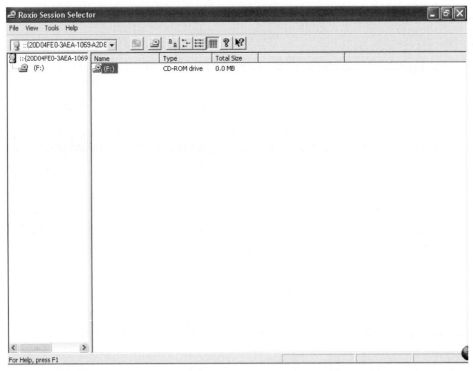

FIGURE 10.9 Using Session Selector to choose a session from a multivolume disc.

4. Click File and select the Close menu item to return to Windows.

tip **You can also select another session from the disc and automatically open it within Windows XP using Windows Explorer. To do this, click the session to highlight it, click the Tools menu, and choose Explore.**

Recording with a Disc Image

Consider a *disc image* as a single file on your hard drive that contains all of the information necessary to create a disc. There are several reasons why you may decide to create a disc image instead of actually recording a disc itself:

*   **Security.** If you record a CD or DVD disc from a disc image, you can be sure of the stability of the disc (none of the files were altered or updated by mistake in the interim)—an important point for software developers, for example.

*   **Speed.** If you have an older computer with a faster recorder that doesn't have burn-proof protection, you may experience recording errors (especially if you're recording a large number of small files) because of the slower data transfer rate. Recording your data as an image first will significantly reduce the chance of recording errors, because the image is a single continuous file; your hard drive doesn't have to read all those smaller files and send them to your recorder.

*   **Convenience.** If you must record the same disc from time to time but don't want to create a batch of several copies at once, use a disc image; if the disc changes, you won't waste additional discs you recorded before the change.

*   **Mobility.** Let me guess: no recorder on your laptop? (Or perhaps you're sharing an external CD recorder with others?) Record a disc image to your hard drive, and when the external drive is available, just record the disc from the image.

tip **Make sure that you have at least 800 MB of free space on your hard drive for a full CD-R or CD-RW disc image—that's about 700 MB for the image itself, along with a little left over for Windows and Easy CD Creator to use.**

As you can see, a disc image is useful in all sorts of situations!

Saving a Disc Image

✔ **To save a disc image to your hard drive, follow these steps:**

1. Run Easy CD Creator by clicking Start | All Programs | Roxio Easy CD Creator 5 | Applications | Easy CD Creator.

2. Click File and select New CD Project, then select Data CD from the pop-up menu. (This is another method of starting a new project.)

3. Build your CD layout.

4. From the File menu, choose the Create CD Hard Disk Image menu item. Easy CD Creator displays the familiar Image File dialog box shown in Figure 10.10.

5. Navigate to the location on your drive where you want to store the disc image, and type a filename. (The CIF extension is automatically added by Easy CD Creator.)

6. Click Save.

7. Take a soda or coffee break while Easy CD Creator "records" the image to the hard drive.

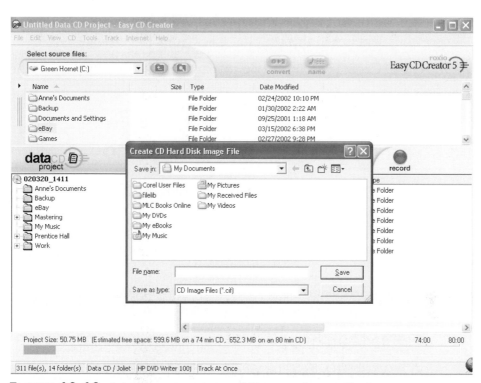

FIGURE 10.10 Selecting a location and filename for our disc image.

Recording a CD from a Disc Image

✔ **To record a disc from an existing disc image on your hard drive:**

1. Run Easy CD Creator.

2. Click File and select the Record CD from CD Image menu item.

3. Easy CD Creator displays the Image File dialog box.

4. Locate the disc image you want to record on your hard drive. Highlight it and click Open.

dvds & cds

5. Easy CD Creator displays the Record CD Setup dialog you used in previous sections in this chapter. Click Start Recording.

6. Easy CD Creator prompts you to load a blank disc and records the disc.

Project: **Creating a Video CD**

In this project, we'll create a video CD using MPEG format digital video files you've recorded with your digital camcorder.

Requirements

- MPEG digital video clips
- Installed copy of Easy CD Creator 5
- A blank CD-R disc

✔ Follow these steps:

1. Load a blank CD-R disc into your drive—avoid using CD-RW discs, because they're not compatible with most video CD hardware. Easy CD Creator will detect this and automatically display the Project Selector screen.

2. Move your mouse pointer over the Make a Photo or Video CD button, and click the Video CD button that appears.

> *tip* **If you need to fix a mistake you made on an earlier screen, you can click Back at any time to return to previous screens.**

3. Easy CD Creator loads the first wizard screen from the stand-alone program VCD Creator, as shown in Figure 10.11. Click Next to continue.

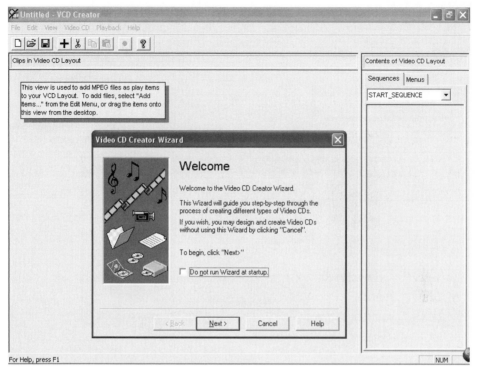

FIGURE 10.11 The Easy CD Creator VCD Creator wizard.

4. For this project, we'll use the Simple Video Sequence type—it provides the highest level of compatibility with DVD players and older CD-ROM drives. Choose Simple Video Sequence and click Next.

5. Click Add to select the MPEG video clips from your hard drive; VCD Creator displays the Add Play Items dialog shown in Figure 10.12. Navigate to the location of the MPEG files and double-click the first file to open it.

6. The clip is loaded and displayed in the Add New Play Item dialog, where you can watch the clip frame by frame, by dragging the slider bar under the preview window. Click OK to accept the clip. VCD Creator displays a thumbnail of the clip in the Video CD layout screen (Figure 10.13).

dvds & cds

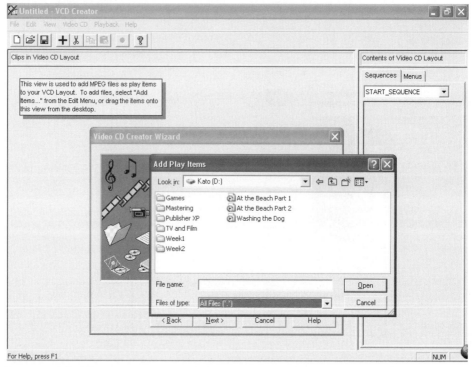

FIGURE 10.12 Selecting an MPEG video clip.

7. Repeat steps 5 and 6 as necessary to load each of the desired video clips into the VCD Creator layout screen.

8. Once you've added all of the clips, click Next to continue. Click Next again on the Creating Play Sequence screen.

9. It's time to set up the order (or play sequence) for the clips you've selected. Click the thumbnail image in the left column for the clip that should appear first and click Add (Figure 10.14). Continue this process until you've added all the clips in the order they should appear. If you need to remove a clip from the sequence you're building—or you want to remove the clip from the sequence and place it elsewhere—click the thumbnail in the START_SEQUENCE column to select it, and click Remove. Once you've added and arranged all of the clips in the order that

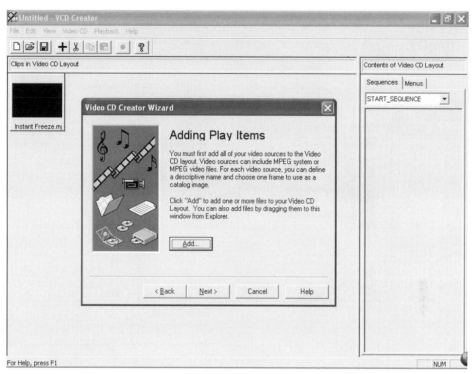

FIGURE 10.13 Our first video clip has been added to the Video CD layout.

you want them in the START_SEQUENCE column, click Next to continue.

10. Here's a nice feature: VCD Creator allows you to preview the video sequence you've created before you burn the disc! Click Playback, and VCD Creator displays the control panel shown in Figure 10.15—if you've used a VCR before, these controls should be quite familiar. You can use these to play, pause, or skip to the next or previous clip. Once you've finished the playback, click Close on the MPEG Playback panel, and click Next to continue.

11. Time to burn your disc—click Create the CD now on the final wizard screen (Figure 10.16), and click Finish to start the process.

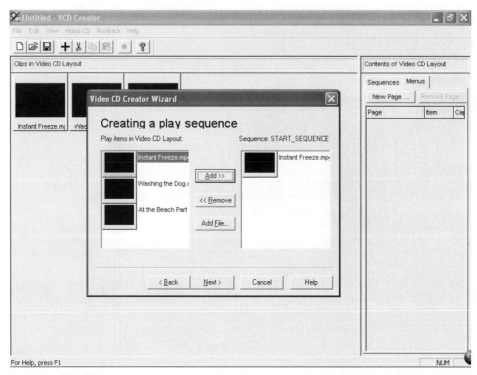

FIGURE 10.14 *Specifying the sequence for my video CD clips.*

Note that VCD Creator must create the video clip sequence file first, before the actual recording begins—depending on the speed of your PC, this can take a few minutes (especially if you've selected a large number of clips). When the video sequence is ready, you'll see the same familiar Record CD Setup dialog, and the rest of the process is the same as I've already described earlier in the chapter.

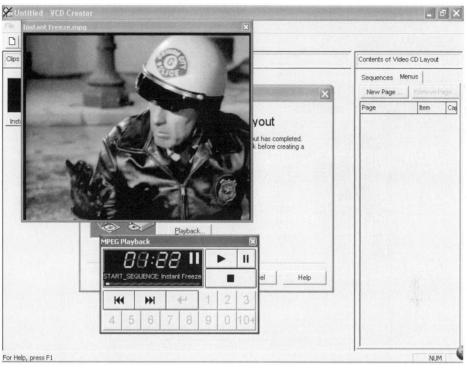

FIGURE 10.15 Previewing the video sequence, complete with VCR controls.

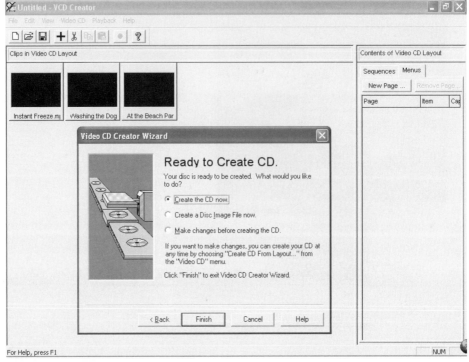

FIGURE 10.16 You're set to record!

Project: **Recording a Promotional CD-Extra Disc**

Here's a project for readers who've joined an up-and-coming garage band—I'll show you how to create a professional-quality CD-Extra demo disc for your up-and-coming rock band, with a number of audio tracks taken from MP3 files, followed by a data track containing the band's latest video and promotional information!

Requirements

- An MPEG, AVI, or MOV digital video clip
- A number of digital audio files
- Audio tracks taken from existing audio CDs

- Installed copy of Easy CD Creator 5
- A blank CD-R disc

✔ **To record music and video on a CD Extra disc, follow these steps:**

1. Run Easy CD Creator—from the Windows XP Start button, click Start | All Programs | Roxio Easy CD Creator 5 | Applications | Easy CD Creator.

2. Click the File menu, select New CD Project, and choose Enhanced CD (the other common name for a CD-Extra disc) to display the layout shown in Figure 10.17.

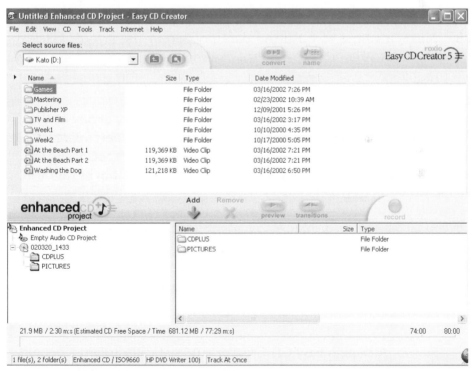

FIGURE 10.17 The beginning of a CD–Extra layout.

3. Click the Empty Audio CD Layout entry in the CD Layout window to add your audio tracks.

4. Navigate through your system and locate the audio files you want to record, using the Explorer display at the top of the window. You can also copy tracks from an existing audio CD by loading it and selecting that drive to display the tracks. We'll use five tracks in MP3 format, which Easy CD Creator will automatically convert during the recording process.

5. Click the audio files to highlight them. To select multiple files, hold down the Ctrl key while you click.

6. Click the Add button in the center of the window to copy the files.

7. Repeat steps 4, 5, and 6 until you've added all the tracks you want to the audio layout.

8. Next, it's time to build the data portion of the layout. Click the disc icon in the CD Layout window to add files and folders to the disc.

caution   **Don't delete the CDPLUS directory or any of the files it contains, and don't place any files or folders inside it! This folder is automatically added by Easy CD Creator specifically to hold any CD-Text information you enter for the audio tracks (as I will demonstrate in step 12).**

9. Navigate through your hard drive, using the Explorer display at the top of the Layout window, and locate the files and folders to record. Click the icon for the file or folder you want to add to your data CD to highlight it; hold down the Ctrl key while you click each icon to highlight multiple files and folders.

tip   **Although Easy CD Creator automatically assigns a default volume label for the data session, you can change it if you like by clicking the label and typing a new one.**

10. Click the Add button to add the files and folders to the data portion of the layout. In this case, I'm adding both a digital video clip and a promotional brochure about the band in Adobe PDF format.

11. Repeat steps 9 and 10 until you've added all the files you want to the layout—Figure 10.18 illustrates a completed CD-Extra layout.

12. If you like, you can enter additional information that can be displayed by audio CD players that support the full CD-Extra format: Click File, choose CD Layout Properties, and click the CD-Extra tab to display the dialog box shown in Figure 10.19. All fields in this dialog box are optional. Click the Created: and Published: drop-down list boxes to choose the desired date from a calendar pop-up display, and type text directly into the other fields. Once you're done, click OK to save the information to your layout.

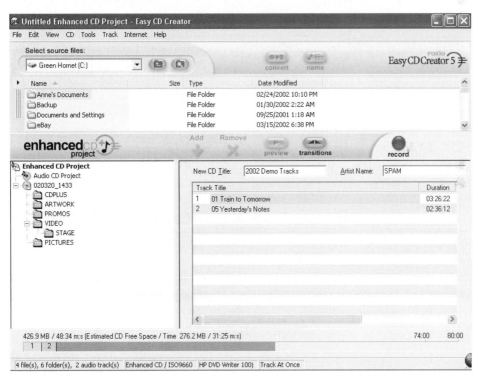

FIGURE 10.18 Our CD-Extra layout is complete.

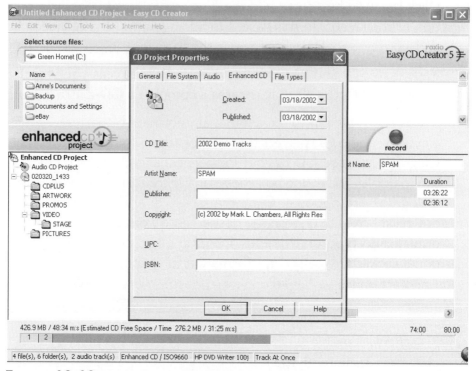

FIGURE 10.19 Adding audio CD text to our layout.

13. Click the big red Record button and complete the recording process, as demonstrated earlier in this chapter.

Project: **Recording a Bootable CD-ROM**

Most normal human beings will likely never need to actually record a *bootable* CD-ROM—a disc that contains the operating system files required to boot your computer—but if your hard drive fails or you're a computer technician, you'll find this specialized format invaluable! (Here's a piece of absolutely meaningless-but-fun trivia: Bootable CDs use the *El Torito* format standard. I don't know where that name came from, but it really adds sparkle to this discussion, don't you think?)

Anyway, most operating systems are shipped on bootable discs—for example, the Windows XP install disc is a bootable CD-ROM—and many Windows utilities are also designed to work from a bootable CD (such as Norton Utilities and Norton AntiVirus). If you bought your PC within the last three years or so, it probably supports a bootable disc—check your computer's manual or display the BIOS options the next time you turn on your PC, and look for "CD-ROM" as a startup boot drive option.

Because bootable CD-ROMs can hold over 600 MB, you can usually store all of the operating system files you need on one disc, as well as any hardware drivers you'll use, utility software, and troubleshooting programs.

caution   **As you might expect, it requires more expert technical knowledge to create an El Torito bootable CD than any other type of CD format I discuss; therefore, I recommend that you try this project only if you're an experienced PC technician or power user.**

To record a bootable CD, you'll need a bootable floppy "master" disk ready that contains all the files necessary during the boot process; check your operating system help files to determine how to format a bootable system disk. (You can also use an Easy CD Creator disc image that you built earlier.)

tip   **If you use a floppy to create a bootable CD and you're running Windows 98/Me, XP, NT, or Windows 2000, you'll be limited to DOS as the operating system for a bootable CD-ROM (because the complete operating system won't fit on a single floppy). Therefore, you should create and include AUTOEXEC.BAT and CONFIG.SYS files on your floppy disk if you want to configure your system automatically during the boot process.**

Requirements

- A bootable floppy
- Additional programs and data files

- Installed copy of Easy CD Creator 5
- A blank CD-R disc

✔ Follow these steps to record a bootable CD-ROM:

1. Run Easy CD Creator—from the Windows XP Start button, click Start | All Programs | Roxio Easy CD Creator 5 | Applications | Easy CD Creator.

2. Click the File menu, select New CD Project, and choose Bootable CD to display the dialog shown in Figure 10.20.

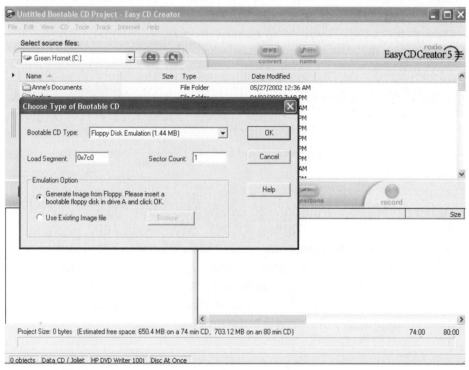

FIGURE 10.20 Selecting the options for a bootable CD.

3. Because we're creating a bootable CD from a DOS system disk, leave all of the settings as they are and load the bootable floppy disk into your floppy drive. Click OK.

4. The files are read from the floppy disk and stored in two special files within your CD layout: BOOTCAT.BIN and BOOTIMG.BIN.

5. Load a blank CD into your recorder.

6. From this point on, you can add any remaining files to your layout normally, just as you would for a standard data CD-ROM. You can create folders if necessary.

7. Once the layout is complete, click Create CD to record the disc.

Summary

You learned all about a number of advanced recording tricks and specialized CD formats in this chapter, including video CDs, disc images, bootable CD-ROMs, CD-Extra discs, and multisession recordings.

dvds & cds

chapter

11

Recording Digital Photographs on CD

In This Chapter

Although a recorded CD doesn't have anywhere near the capacity of a recorded DVD, there are still some applications that are better suited for CD-R or CD-RW—for example, most audio is still recorded on CD-R. CD-RW discs are also great for recording digital photographs, because today's typical digital camera produces a JPEG image of under 200 KB. With the file sizes for photographs so small, you can fit thousands of images on a standard CD-ROM—and you can be assured that any computer with a CD-ROM drive can display your photographs, too.

dvds & cds

221

his chapter includes two step-by-step projects for
storing both digital photographs and digital video on
CD—the former as a slide show, and the latter as a neat
"video postcard" that you can view on your computer. I'll
be using a great program called PhotoRelay, from ArcSoft
(www.arcsoft.com)—it's included as part of Easy CD
Creator Platinum.

Introducing PhotoRelay

To run PhotoRelay, click Start | All Programs | Roxio Easy CD Cre-
ator 5 | Applications | PhotoRelay. The main program window
appears, as shown in Figure 11.1. The PhotoRelay toolbar includes most
of the common functions you're likely to need; to display the function
of a toolbar icon, move your mouse pointer over the icon and check
the status line at the bottom for its description.

PhotoRelay applies the familiar concept of a traditional paper photo
album to your digital photographs: You create an *album* that contains
pictures from your hard drive (either from a single folder or from different locations). When you display the contents of an album, each photograph is represented by a thumbnail image; this makes it easy to scan
your pictures quickly for a particular shot. Once you've created the
catalog, you can also:

- Attach audio clips to pictures in your album
- Print selected pictures or the entire album
- Sort the images in your album
- Build an automated slide show that can display your pictures
- Create an HTML photo catalog that you can add to your Web
  site
- Send a photo as an e-mail attachment

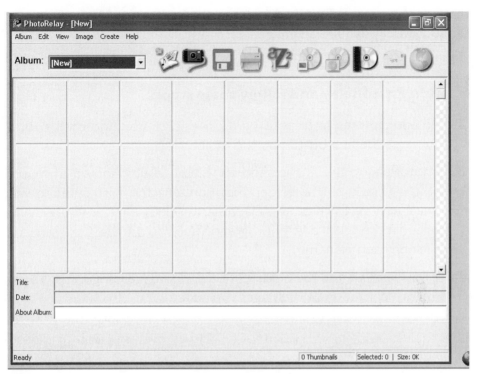

FIGURE 11.1 The main PhotoRelay window.

Creating a Thumbnail Album

Because the album is the starting point for everything in PhotoRelay, let's create a new album now. I'll add pictures from two sources: a folder of pictures that I've already downloaded from my digital camera and an image I'll acquire directly from my scanner.

tip To download (or, in the technospeak of imaging gurus everywhere, to *acquire*) a picture from a scanner or digital camera directly into PhotoRelay, both your hardware and the software it uses must support the TWAIN standard. TWAIN is my absolutely favorite computer acronym: It stands for Technology Without an Interesting Name! (Never let it be said that computer techno-types don't have a sense of humor.) Anyway, virtually all scanners and digital cameras are TWAIN-compatible these days, but you must make sure that your hardware's **TWAIN** drivers are correctly loaded before you can successfully acquire an image.

✔ **Run PhotoRelay and follow these steps:**

1. To add pictures from your hard drive, click the Add toolbar button—it's the first button on the toolbar.

2. PhotoRelay displays the Add to Album dialog shown in Figure 11.2; navigate to the folder that contains the first pictures you want to add. Click on the filename to select it (or, if you'd like to select more than one photograph, hold down the Ctrl key and click on each filename).

3. Click Open to add the pictures to the album file—Figure 11.3 illustrates a collection of 10 images I've added.

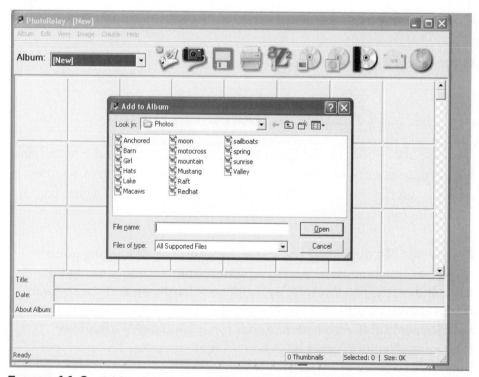

FIGURE 11.2 Adding images to an album from my hard drive.

FIGURE 11.3 I've added a number of images from my hard drive to the new album.

4. Next, let's acquire an image from the scanner: Click the Acquire Images button on the toolbar (it's the second button, which looks like an animated camera). PhotoRelay displays the Select Source dialog you see in Figure 11.4, which lists all of the active TWAIN hardware on your system; in this case, I'll click my scanner. Click Select to continue.

5. At this point, your hardware will display its own acquisition dialog, so what you see won't look exactly like Figure 11.5—however, most scanners are likely to have most of the same controls. (If you're not familiar with your hardware's TWAIN acquisition settings, check the manual for more information.) Begin the scan—in my case, that means clicking Start Scan—and watch as PhotoRelay adds the image thumbnail to your album.

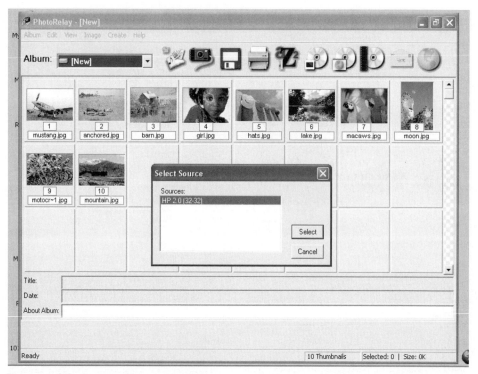

FIGURE 11.4 Specifying a TWAIN scanner as the source for new images.

6. Once you've added the photographs to your catalog, you can add a title, date, and description to any or all of the shots. Click on the desired thumbnail to highlight it, click in the desired field underneath the thumbnails, and type the corresponding text for the photo.

7. As a final step before saving the catalog, you can also sort the photographs in a number of different ways: Click the Album menu and choose the Sort menu item to display the Sort Album dialog you see in Figure 11.6. By default, PhotoRelay sorts the photographs in your catalog by their filenames; choose the desired sort order (note that you can enable the Reverse Order checkbox to switch between ascending and descending sort order), and click OK to rearrange your images.

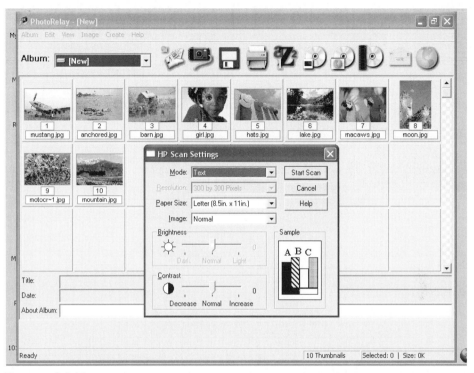

FIGURE 11.5 Configuring my scanner before acquiring an image.

8. Once you're satisfied with the contents, descriptions, and order of the photographs in your catalog, press Ctrl+S to save the album (or, if you're crazy about menus, click the Album menu and choose the Save Album item). PhotoRelay prompts you to name your new album, as illustrated in Figure 11.7 (note that the .PHB extension is automatically added); type the name, and click OK.

dvds & cds

FIGURE 11.6   You've got a choice when sorting your pictures in PhotoRelay.

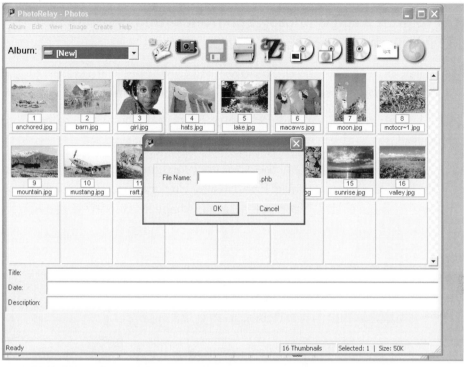

FIGURE 11.7   The final step: entering a filename and saving the album.

Printing Photographs

Although this chapter naturally focuses on recording your digital photographs, I'd like to take a moment to demonstrate how you can print a photograph from a PhotoRelay album. This program is wonderful for cataloging your images, and it's easy to print a photo directly from within an album—if you own a Hewlett-Packard photo-quality inkjet printer, for example, you can produce an image on glossy paper that looks as good as a print from a film camera!

dvds & cds

✔ **To print a single photograph from within PhotoRelay, follow these steps:**

1. Click on the Album drop-down list to display the names of the albums you've created, and click on the desired album.

2. Click on the thumbnail for the photograph you want to print to select it.

3. Click the Print icon on the toolbar (you guessed it, the icon that looks like a printer), and PhotoRelay displays the Print dialog you see in Figure 11.8. To print a single image that you've previously selected, click Print the current selected image.

FIGURE 11.8 Will that be one photograph or many?

4. The second Print dialog (shown in Figure 11.9) allows you to add a title or frame—you can optionally center your photo in the middle of the page or even create a 5x5 jewel case label for a CD case. (A nifty feature, indeed!) Click the desired checkboxes to enable or disable these features as necessary.

5. Next, drag the slider on the right side of the dialog to change the size of the photograph on the printed page; PhotoRelay displays the effects of the resizing in the preview window. You can also click and drag the image placeholder around on the page to move it wherever you like.

6. If you elected to add a title to the page, double-click in the title placeholder to type the text; PhotoRelay displays the Edit Text dialog you see in Figure 11.10. Note that you can also highlight the title text in the edit box and choose a new font for the title.

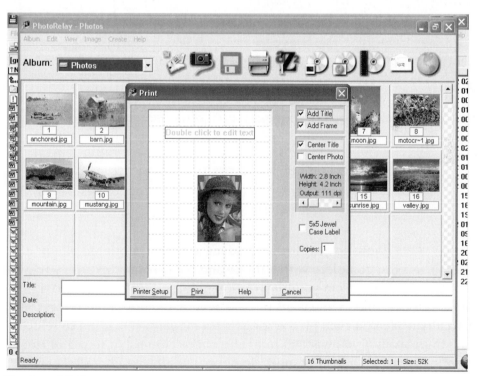

FIGURE 11.9 Setting options for our printed page.

dvds & cds

FIGURE 11.10 Changing the text for the page title.

7. By default, PhotoRelay prints a single copy of the photograph; to produce multiple copies of the picture, click in the Copies field and enter the desired number.

8. To print to your default Windows system printer, click Print—to choose another printer or to change printer options, such as DPI or image quality, click Printer Setup.

tip **PhotoRelay can also produce a very nice printed album of images, complete with a frame and background texture; you can also print text from your description fields, a title banner, and a custom footer line. If you want to print several pictures, hold down the Ctrl key while you click on the specific thumbnails. (No need to select any thumbnails if you want to print the entire album.) In step 3 of the printing process, click Print multiple photos or album—PhotoRelay will display a wizard that will lead you through the options. You can specify** all the pictures in the album, just those you've selected, or a numbered range of photos.

E-mailing Photographs

Besides printing images, PhotoRelay also works hand in hand with your e-mail software to send pictures from your albums across the Internet. By default, Windows XP uses Outlook Express for sending and receiving e-mail, so that's what I'll use in this section.

✔ **To send a single picture from within PhotoRelay using Outlook Express, follow these steps:**

1. Click on the Album drop-down list, and click on the desired album.

2. Click on the thumbnail for the photograph you want to send as an e-mail attachment to select it. (Note that you can select only one image when sending mail with PhotoRelay.)

tip **When selecting a picture to send, don't forget that most Internet e-mail servers place a limit on the size of an e-mail attachment—whenever possible, it's a good rule to keep your attachments below 1 MB in size.**

3. Click the SendMail icon on the toolbar—naturally, it looks like an envelope—and PhotoRelay automatically runs Outlook Express (or whatever e-mail program you've chosen in Windows) and prepares a new message, as shown in Figure 11.11. Note that the attachment has already been added; the size of the attached picture is also listed next to the filename, so you can keep an eye on the total file size for the message.

dvds & cds

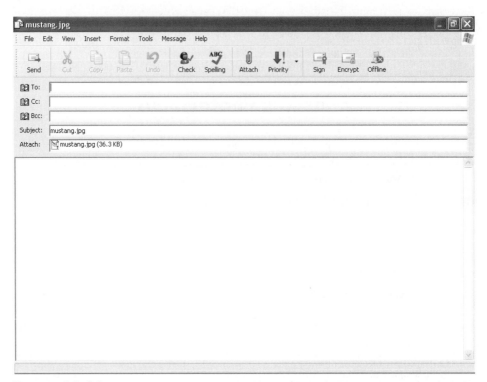

FIGURE 11.11 Sending an image in e-mail couldn't be much more convenient!

4. Type the recipient's e-mail address in the To: field (or click the To: button to add the recipients from your Address Book).

5. By default, PhotoRelay adds a subject using the name of the image, but you can click in the Subject: field and type a new subject if you like.

6. Click in the message edit box and type the text of your e-mail message.

7. When you're ready to "post" your e-mail message with the picture attached, click the Send button in the toolbar. Figure 11.12 illustrates a completed message, ready to send.

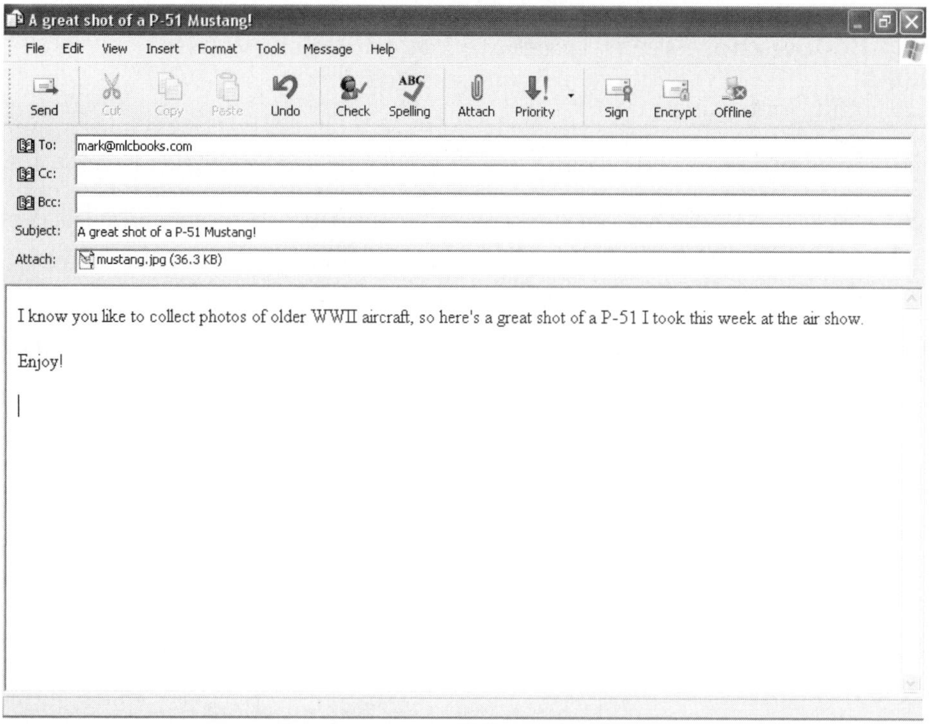

FIGURE 11.12 This message is ready to go.

Project: **Creating a Family Photo CD with PhotoRelay**

Ready to put your photographic memories in binary? Forget that old-fashioned slide projector…in this project, I'll show you how to create an impressive automated slide show using pictures from a photo album that you've already created. You'll be able to view the show on any PC running Windows 95 through Windows XP.

Requirements

- A PhotoRelay album of images
- A blank CD or CD-RW

dvds & cds

✔ **Follow these steps to create your slide show disc:**

1. Run PhotoRelay.

2. Select the desired album from the Album drop-down list to load it.

3. Click the Create a Slide Show button on the toolbar (which looks like a CD-ROM, overlaid with a traditional film slide). PhotoRelay displays the Select File dialog box (Figure 11.13).

4. Hold down the Ctrl key and click each photo you want to add to the slide show in the left list box, then click Add. Note that, as you add pictures, PhotoRelay displays the amount of space on the CD required to create the disc underneath the right list box. Once you're done selecting the photographs for the slide show, click Next to continue.

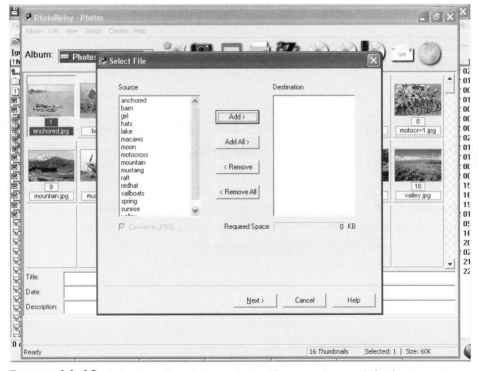

FIGURE 11.13 Selecting the pictures that will appear in our slide show.

tip **Do you want to add all of the photos from the entire album? Never mind clicking each photo name—to add all images in the album, just click Add All, then click Next to continue.**

5. From the Audio Options dialog (Figure 11.14), you can add a digital audio file in WAV or MP3 format to your show. The audio plays in the background while you're viewing your pictures. To use an audio file from your hard drive, click Play Single Audio File and click the Browse button to select the file, then click Open to load it. Click Next to continue to the next screen.

6. PhotoRelay displays the Select Destination dialog you see in Figure 11.15. Load a blank CD-R or CD-RW disc into your recorder. (Do not use a disc with an existing session; also, if you're using a CD-RW disc, make sure that it's completely formatted.)

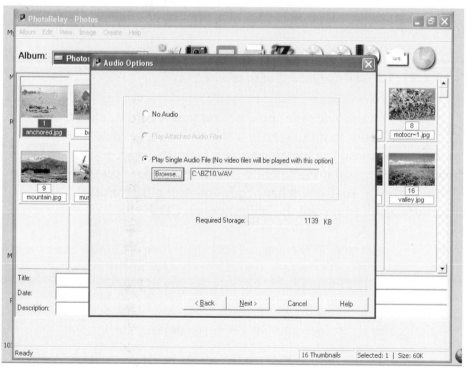

FIGURE 11.14 Adding a background audio track to your slide show.

dvds & cds

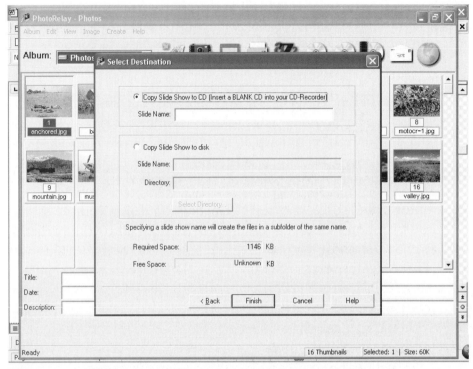

FIGURE 11.15 Will that be disc or hard drive?

tip **To test the slide show before you record it, click Copy Slide Show to disk. Specify a Slide Name and click Select Directory to choose the location for the files—this way, you can run the show from your hard drive to check things out before using a disc. (Note, however, that you'll have to follow this entire project procedure again to record the slide show on CD.)**

7. To create the slide show in a separate folder, click the Slide Name field and enter the name you want; however, I recommend that you leave the Slide Name field blank and create the slide show in the root (top level) of the disc; this way, others won't have to change to the folder manually before running the show.

8. Click Finish to start the recording—PhotoRelay will automatically load Easy CD Creator to handle the actual burn!

Once the recording has finished, it's easy to run your slide show: Load the disc into a computer CD-ROM drive. If you chose to record the files in the root directory of the CD, Windows will automatically recognize the disc and start the show!

 tip **To run the show manually, open the CD, locate the file SLIDE.EXE and double-click it.**

Project: **Creating a Video Postcard on CD**

Our second PhotoRelay project concerns digital video—along with the CD-based screen show you just produced, this surprising program can also create a professional-looking *video postcard* that you can send to others on a CD-R or CD-RW disc. (This is a neat way to share digital video with those of your family and friends who don't have a DVD player.) In fact, you can even capture the digital video from any device that's compatible with the Video for Windows AVI video format! The video postcard can be shown on any PC running Windows 95 through Windows XP.

Requirements

- A digital video source (or a digital video clip that's already been saved to your hard drive)
- A blank CD or CD-RW

Because I've already discussed digital video transfer and capture earlier in the book, we'll assume that you're using a digital video clip you've already saved to your hard drive.

✔ **Follow these steps to create the postcard:**

1. Run PhotoRelay.

dvds & cds

2. Click the Make Postcard icon on the toolbar (which looks like a CD-ROM, overlaid with a strip of movie film). PhotoRelay displays the Select Template dialog box you see in Figure 11.16. Choose the category for the postcard background and click one of the background thumbnails to select it—alternatively, you can click on From Image and click the Select Image to import your own picture into PhotoRelay as the background for the postcard.

3. Choose the size of the video clip—PhotoRelay adjusts the "window" within the background to match the dimensions you choose. As you might expect, a larger window of 320 ∞ 240 results in a much better postcard, but the larger video clip may not run smoothly for older PCs. Click Next to continue.

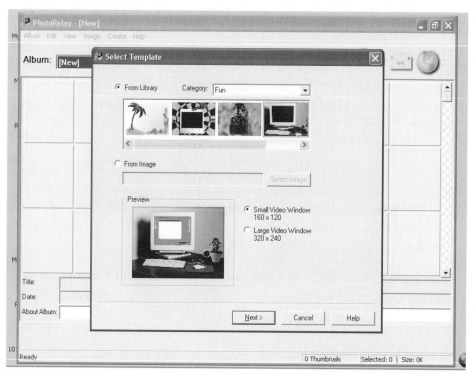

FIGURE 11.16 Choosing the background and clip size for our postcard.

4. PhotoRelay displays the Postcard Message dialog you see in Figure 11.17. Click Select Font to choose the font for your text, then type your message in the left side of the "virtual postcard." You can also enter your name and the name of the recipient by clicking in the To: and From: fields on the right side of the card. Click Next to continue.

5. Time to select the video clip: Click the Select Video button (Figure 11.18), navigate to the location, click on the clip, and click Open. (The program accepts digital video in .AVI, .MOV, and .MPG formats.) You'll notice that PhotoRelay displays the familiar VCR Play and Pause buttons next to the video clip filename; click on Play to preview how your clip will look.

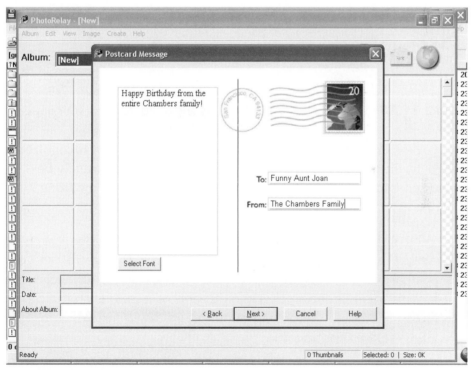

FIGURE 11.17 I guess a "virtual postcard" needs only 20 cents postage!

dvds & cds

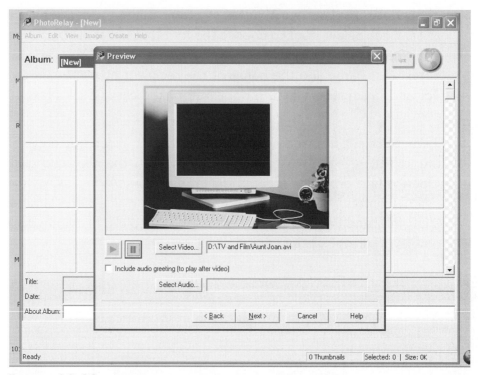

FIGURE 11.18 Selecting the digital video and audio clips to use in your postcard.

tip **If you're using another video format that's not recognized by PhotoRelay, don't despair—that video clip can usually be converted into one of the supported formats, using a video editing program such as Adobe Premiere or ArcSoft's ShowBiz.**

6. Why not personalize your video postcard with your voice, as well? (You can say hello to Grandma yourself!) If you'd like your postcard to play a digital audio clip after the video is done, click the Include audio greeting checkbox to enable it, and click the Select Audio button to choose an audio file in .WAV or .MP3 format. Click Next to continue.

7. The final PhotoRelay wizard dialog displays the Select Destination dialog shown in Figure 11.19. Load a blank CD-R or CD-RW disc into your recorder. (As with the slide show CD you created earlier, do not use a disc with an existing session; also, if you're using a CD-RW disc, make sure that it's completely formatted.)

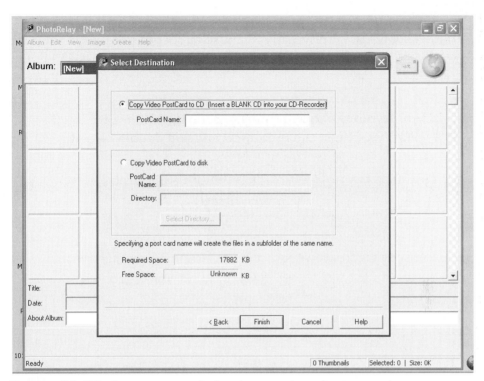

FIGURE 11.19 Setting options before burning the video postcard.

tip **Click Copy Slide Show to disk to try out the postcard before you record it. Click PostCard Name to choose a folder name for the files—PhotoRelay will create the postcard on your hard drive, so you can run it without recording a disc. (You'll have to follow this entire project procedure again in order to burn the postcard on a CD.)**

8. It's a good idea to leave the PostCard Name field blank and record the postcard in the root (top level) of the disc; this way, others won't have to manually change to the folder, and it should start automatically under Windows. However, if you want to place the postcard files in a separate folder, click the PostCard Name field and enter the desired name.

9. Click Finish to start the recording, and watch as PhotoRelay launches Easy CD Creator to record the disc.

dvds & cds

It couldn't be easier to run the postcard: Simply load the disc into a computer's CD-ROM drive. If you chose to record the files in the root directory of the CD, Windows should automatically recognize the disc and display the card!

 tip **To run the show manually, open the CD, locate the file VPLAYER.EXE in the root directory, and double-click it.**

Summary

This chapter focused on the multimedia program PhotoRelay and how you can use it to create spectacular self-running slide show CDs and video postcard CDs from your digital pictures and video.

chapter

12

Making Movies with ArcSoft ShowBiz

In This Chapter

- ✔ Opening and creating albums
- ✔ Adding elements to the storyboard
- ✔ Adding transitions
- ✔ Using the timeline
- ✔ Applying effects
- ✔ Adding text
- ✔ Previewing your movie
- ✔ Saving your movie to disk

In Chapter 6, "Recording a DVD with Existing Files," I discussed how you can create your own DVD video discs and cDVD discs using MyDVD; we used digital video files that you had already created and stored on your hard drive. Often, these video files are simply raw DV footage that you've copied directly to your computer from your DV camera or video that you've captured to your hard drive from an analog source.

But what if you want to create your own cinematic masterpieces? What if you want to edit that footage and add things such as special effects, still images, or even your own separate audio track? Now you're talking about a video editor: a program that's specifically designed to help you take the various "building blocks" of a movie and combine them to create an entirely new and original movie.

In this chapter, I'll show you how to use ArcSoft ShowBiz, the easy-to-use video editor that's bundled with many HP DVD-Writer drives. You'll discover how professionals use a storyboard and a timeline to "assemble" a movie, and you'll build your own original wedding video!

Introducing ShowBiz

The ShowBiz main window that you see in Figure 12.1 has four main parts:

1. **Player window.** This window can display your movie at any time while you're editing; it can be resized to several different dimensions.

2. **Media library.** The tabbed list at the upper right of the ShowBiz window allows you to choose elements from four different media libraries that you can add to your movie: video, still, and audio media; transitions between scenes; special effects; and text. You can also display miniature thumbnails of the items in your library: Click the Album view mode button at the upper right of the library list to toggle the display of the thumbnails on and off.

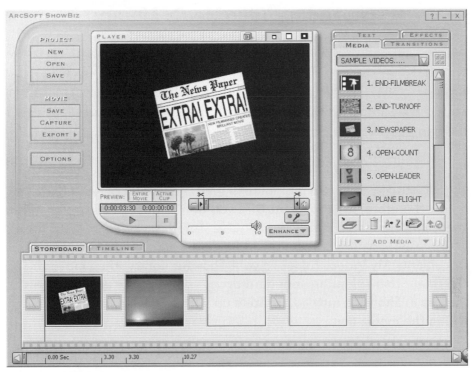

FIGURE 12.1 The ShowBiz main window.

3. **Storyboard strip.** This strip at the bottom of the window allows you to add elements to your movie from the media library.

4. **Timeline strip.** The timeline display usually hides behind the storyboard strip—click the Timeline tab, and you can alter the length of effects and transitions or edit your movie's audio track.

Although ShowBiz doesn't use a traditional menu system, common command buttons for opening and saving projects and movies are grouped at the upper left of the window. To display the program's help system, you can press F1 at any point.

> *tip* You can also learn more about ShowBiz by using the Showbiz Basics help system, which you can open by clicking on the child's "building block" that appears on the main window. You'll find that the Basics dialog will answer most of the common questions that a novice will ask about the program.

dvds & cds

Expanding Your Media Library

Before I get to the actual movie creation process, you should learn how to add your own video and still elements to the ShowBiz media library—otherwise, you'll be creating great movies, but you'll be limited to the sample elements that ArcSoft provides! (As you'd imagine, this can get pretty boring pretty quickly.)

tip **ShowBiz Media elements are stored in *albums*, which are actually collections of links to multimedia files on your hard drive—therefore, it's important that you don't add a video clip or still image to your media library until you've stored it where you want it on your system! To illustrate, if you add a digital video clip from your \My Documents\My Videos folder to your ShowBiz library, then move the clip to another folder on your hard drive, you won't be able to access the clip in ShowBiz; instead, it shows up with a red "unavailable" flag within the media library.**

✔ **To add your own video or still image elements from your hard drive, follow these steps:**

1. Click the Media tab within the media library, and click the Add button that appears under the list (it looks like a book with an arrow).

2. ShowBiz displays the standard Windows Open file dialog. Navigate to the location of the file you want to add, click on the filename to select it, and click Open.

3. The program displays the dialog you see in Figure 12.2, prompting you either to create a new album or to select an existing album that you've created. (You can't add media elements to the Sample albums.) To create a new album, click <New Album>; to select an existing album, click on the drop-down list, and select the destination.

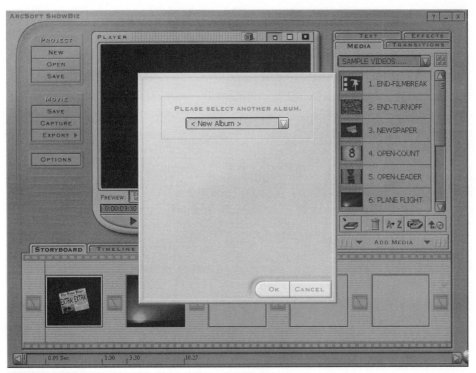

FIGURE 12.2 Creating a new media album.

4. Depending on the format of the element you've added, ShowBiz may prompt you for scene or image options; leave these options set to their default values, and click OK.

5. The new album (or the existing album) with the new element appears in the media library. If you've created a new album, you can rename it by clicking in the album name at the top of the list and typing a new name.

tip You can also download new media library elements from ArcSoft's Web site; click the Download new content button at the bottom of the media list (it looks like a globe with an arrow). Windows will open your Web browser, and you can download additional media files to your PC.

To acquire a still image from a TWAIN-compatible scanner or digital camera, click the Acquire button, and select the image source. You can also sort the elements in an album by clicking the Sort button, which displays the different sort criteria you see in Figure 12.3. Click the sorting option you want and click OK.

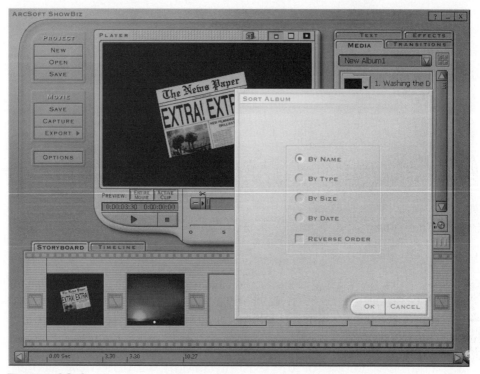

FIGURE 12.3   You can sort album elements by four different criteria.

Building a Movie from Media Elements

Creating a movie is easy within ShowBiz: You add the elements that you want to appear in linear order, moving from left to right. Usually, these media elements will be video clips and still images that you've added to your library, but they can also include text titles, *effects* (where a special look is applied to an image or a scene) and *transitions* (an animation or special effect that occurs between scenes and images).

✔ **To create a movie using the storyboard strip, follow these steps:**

1. If you've been working with ShowBiz on another project, click New under the Project menu—ShowBiz gives you the option of saving the existing project before closing it.

2. Decide what you want to appear first in your movie—either a video clip or a still image—and click on the Media tab in the media library to display the elements of that type. To switch to another album, click the drop-down list arrow next to the album name.

> *tip* **To view a media element before you decide to add it to the storyboard strip, right-click on the element in the list and choose Preview Media from the pop-up menu. ShowBiz displays the element in the Player window.**

3. ShowBiz offers two methods of adding the element: You can either click and drag the element from the media library to the storyboard, or you can click the element you want to add and click the Add button at the bottom of the media library display. Either way, it appears in the next open media square on the storyboard. Figure 12.4 illustrates a still image I've added as the first element in the storyboard display.

Once you've added a number of still images and video clips to your storyboard, you can click and drag elements from one media square to another to change their positions (great for those times when you discover that you've put your aunt on-screen before your mother). To delete an element from the storyboard, right-click the offending element and choose Delete. Note that you can also choose to delete all video clips and still images at once, in case you want to start over from scratch.

> *tip* **Need information about a clip or image that you've already added to the storyboard? Right-click on the element in the storyboard and choose Properties from the pop-up menu, and ShowBiz will display the relevant identifying information for that element.**

dvds & cds

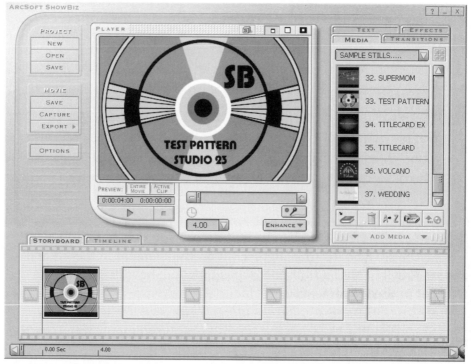

FIGURE 12.4 I'll use a still image to begin my movie.

Adding Transitions

No matter how visually interesting, any film can be enhanced by the use of animated, moving transitions between elements—personally, my favorite transitions are the old "twirling rainbow Bat symbols" you probably remember from the Batman TV series (and yes, you can set those up with a Spiral transition). Once you've added at least one still image or video clip to your storyboard, you can place a transition.

Note, however, that it's easy to add too many transitions to your project! Use restraint, and your viewers will appreciate it. Watch for transitions in your favorite TV shows and commercials, and you'll see that there's certainly no need for a transition at every scene change.

✔ **Follow these steps:**

1. Click the Transitions tab in the media library to display the list of transitions—remember, you can click on the album drop-down list to choose from different types of transitions. When you rest your mouse pointer on top of a transition for a second or two in the library list, the example image animates to show you how the transition will appear.

2. Click the entry in the media list for the transition you want to use.

3. Click Add Transition to copy the transition into the next open transition square on the storyboard; transition squares are smaller than media squares, and they carry a filmstrip icon with a diagonal cut.

tip **If you're pressed for time, but you'd still like to add a different transition between each element in a movie, right-click any media or transition square on the storyboard strip and choose Random Transition to All; this adds a transition that ShowBiz chooses at random between each video clip and still image. To duplicate the same transition throughout the entire movie, right-click the transition square that contains the transition you want to replicate, and choose Apply Transition to All.**

Editing with the Timeline

Once you've added the video clips, still images, and transitions to your film, you might think you're done and ready to review your work—but ShowBiz offers you the ability to add creative touches with the timeline strip display. The storyboard strip is a linear representation of the elements that make up your movie—the timeline strip allows you to add:

- Special effects
- Animated text
- Background audio

dvds & cds

You can also use the timeline to adjust the starting and ending points for these additions. To display the timeline, click the Timeline tab at the top of the strip; Figure 12.5 illustrates the timeline for a movie I'm working on. Note that you can still see the media elements from the storyboard; however, the transitions may be a little harder to pick out, because they are actually combined with the media elements in the timeline view. If you get confused and forget what's been added on the storyboard side, place your mouse pointer over a media element for a second or two, and ShowBiz will remind you of any transitions that you've added.

Note that four additional rows appear on the timeline strip: above the strip are the text and effects displays, and below you'll find two audio track displays. Again, these are linear controls—they help you "block" the location and duration of each type of edit you can make.

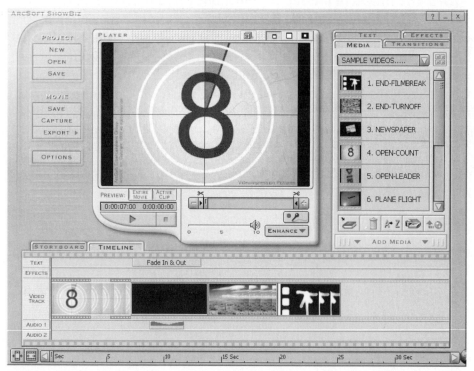

FIGURE 12.5   Preparing to add effects, text, and audio using the timeline strip.

tip When you're editing, remember that experts in the movie industry use only about 10% of the content they shoot! If you leave that camera running because you don't want to miss that special moment, you'll end up with a tape full of noncritical footage that you and your friends and family may not want to see. Keep your audience's attention span in mind while you're editing your video clips.

Creating a Different Look with Effects

Effects can add an entirely new dimension to all of your media elements—for example, one of my favorite effects, Film Grain, is perfect for turning that video clip you shot yesterday into "antique" 8-mm movie footage! Other filters you'll use often include vertical and horizontal hold "problems" (in the TV album), wacky frames that you can add around the borders of a clip (in the Fun Frames album), and the Blur and Ripple effects in the Filters album.

✔ **Follow these steps to add an effect to your movie:**

1. Add all of the stills and video clips you need for your movie, then click the Effects tab in the media library to display the list of effects. To switch effects albums, click on the album drop-down list box.

2. Click the entry in the media list for the effect you want to use.

3. Click Add Effect to copy the effect into the next open block on the Effects row—remember, the Effects row appears alongside the timeline strip; therefore, ShowBiz automatically switches to the timeline strip display (if necessary) as soon as you add an effect or a text title.

4. Drag the beginning and ending edges of the effect to specify where the desired effect will start and when it will finish during the movie—note that you can also click and drag the entire effect

dvds & cds

block along the row to wherever you like during the movie. You can have only one active effect at a time, but the effects can follow each other in sequence.

Adding Text to Your Movie

There are two ways to add a text title to your movies:

1. **Using a still image.** You can use an image editing program such as Photoshop or Paint Shop Pro to create a still image that has the title you want—you can then add the image to your media library, and add it to the proper media square so that it appears at the right time.

2. **Adding a text element.** ShowBiz includes a number of preset animated text effects that you can use to display your message during your movie.

As you can imagine, the Text elements inside ShowBiz are much easier to add than a still image—you don't have to open up another application or add a special image to your media library—and they're much more interesting from a visual standpoint.

✔   **Follow these steps to add text to your movie:**

1. Once you've finished adding stills and video clips to the storyboard strip, click the Text tab in the media library. Click on the album drop-down list box to select the type of text effects you want to use.

2. Click the entry in the media list for the type of text you want to add.

3. Click Add Text to copy the effect into the next open block on the Text row, which appears at the top of the timeline strip. ShowBiz opens the Text panel you see in Figure 12.6, where you can type the desired text, specify the number of seconds it remains on-screen, and set options such as the font, alignment, type size, color, and shadowing.

FIGURE 12.6 Specifying the text options for text that will fade in and out.

4. Once you've typed the text for the title and set the type options, click the Options button to return to the timeline.

5. As you did with the effects row, you can click and drag the beginning and ending edges of the text block to specify where it will appear.

Audio Tracks

If you like, you can add one or two audio tracks for your movie—for example, one track might include your narration of events in your video, and the other track could be background music. Note, however, that it isn't necessary to add audio (your video clips will likely carry their own audio, and the media clips and animation provided with ShowBiz also carry their own audio). You can insert audio tracks from the Media tab (choose the Sample Audio album)—both .MP3 and .WAV files can be added to your library.

In fact, there's a trick you can use to add more than two audio tracks to

dvds & cds

your movie: Just save the file and reopen it! For example, let's say you have three audio tracks you want to use. Add the first two audio tracks in the Showbiz timeline, then save the file as an MPEG2 video clip. Now you can add your new clip (which already contains the first two tracks) into your ShowBiz media library, and you can add your third audio track! (Note that when you save the file to a MPEG2 file or other video format, you can no longer change the edits you made previously.)

Previewing Your Work in ShowBiz

When you're ready to review your work by previewing your movie, ShowBiz can preview the project in the Player window in two ways:

1. **View a single clip.** Click a media square on the storyboard strip and click the Active Clip button (under the Player window) to view a still image, video clip, or transition. You can also use this setting to view effects and text or listen to audio tracks while you're using the timeline strip.

2. **View the entire film.** Click the Entire Movie button under the Player window to view the entire movie—typically, this will display the "Processing" progress bar that you see in Figure 12.7, which means that ShowBiz must *render* (or "build") the effects, transitions, and media elements into a single video stream. This process usually occurs each time you view the entire film if you've changed or edited anything in your movie: The longer the movie and the more effects and transitions you use, the longer the processing will take.

tip Make sure that you hit the Stop button after you view the entire movie to ensure that the cursor is placed at the beginning of the timeline.

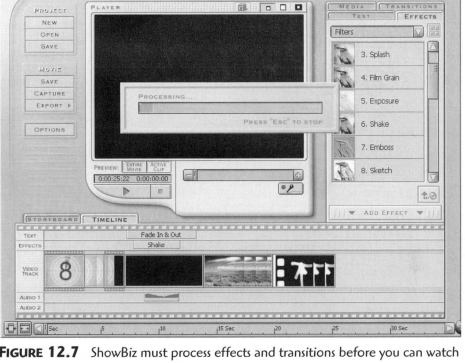

FIGURE 12.7 ShowBiz must process effects and transitions before you can watch your entire movie.

Once you've selected the proper preview mode (and any processing has completed), you're ready to watch: Click the green Play button underneath the Player window. Note that ShowBiz displays a moving vertical yellow line to indicate the current point in the storyboard or film strip; this can help you "debug" spots where an effect fades too fast or an audio clip doesn't play at the right time. Click the yellow square Stop button to stop the action at any time. To jump forward or backward, click and drag the moving slider underneath the Player window in the desired direction.

You can expand the ShowBiz Player window using the three buttons at the top right corner of the ShowBiz window; the default is the Normal view, but you can also switch to Large view (shown in Figure 12.8) and a full-screen display.

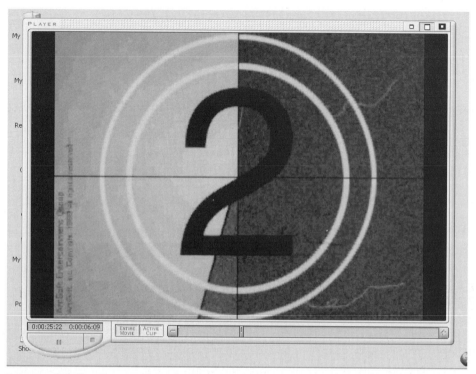

FIGURE 12.8 Expanding the Player window to a larger size helps when you're reviewing your project.

The first time counter above the Play and Stop buttons displays the total duration of the clip or movie, and the second displays the elapsed time.

Saving Your Classic to Disc

Ready to immortalize your cinematic work? ShowBiz gives you a wide range of possibilities for creating your final movie—note that this is different from simply saving the project to your hard drive (which you can do from the Project group at the top left corner of the ShowBiz window).

Final movie options include:

- **Saving your movie as a digital video file.** Click Save in the Movie group at the upper left of the ShowBiz window to display the dialog you see in Figure 12.9: From here, you can save your movie in MPEG1, MPEG2, QuickTime MOV, and Windows AVI formats. You can even save your movie as raw DV footage or in an executable format that you can send as an e-mail attachment. Type a filename and click Browse to select a location where the file will be stored, then click the Format drop-down list box to choose the format—click Settings to specify options such as the frame size and audio quality. When you're ready to save, click OK. If you're creating a DVD or cDVD, use MPEG2—for video that's destined for use in a VCD, choose MPEG1. It's important to remember that switching compression standards will cost you image quality and detail in your movie, so choose the right codec from the start (and always save your project so that you can open it and export it again in ShowBiz if necessary)!

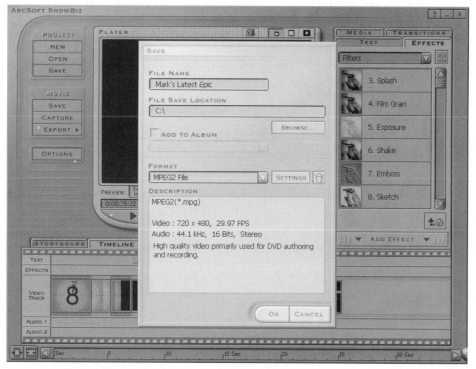

FIGURE 12.9 *Saving your movie as an MPEG2 file.*

dvds & cds

tip Need to send your movies overseas to someone using the PAL video standard? No problem: ShowBiz can also convert NTSC video to PAL or PAL to NTSC! Click the Options button and choose the desired standard when saving or exporting video.

tip To add your completed movie to the Media Library as a video clip for future projects, click the Add to Album checkbox to enable it, and click the Album drop-down list box to specify the album where the new clip will appear. (This is a great way to create a standard "title" sequence that you can use at the beginning of all your movies.)

- **Capturing your movie to other video hardware.** If your PC has video capture hardware or a FireWire connection, you can send the signal to an analog VCR, analog camcorder, or DV camcorder and record it. Click Capture in the Movie group to display the Capture dialog you see in Figure 12.10. Click the Video and Audio Device drop-down list boxes to select the output hardware, and use the Play, Record, and Stop buttons to control the playback of your ShowBiz movie. (The exact procedure you follow will depend on the type of capture connection you're using; refer to your capture hardware documentation and the ShowBiz Help system for specifics.)

- **Exporting your movie to CD, DVD, DV tape, or MyDVD.** ShowBiz makes use of MyDVD, the application that I cover in detail in Chapters 6 ("Recording a DVD with Existing Files") and 7 ("Direct-to-DVD Recording"), to copy your movie directly to several different types of digital media. Move your mouse pointer over the Export button in the Movie group and click on the desired output—you can even create a MyDVD project from your completed ShowBiz movie! Depending on the type of exporting you chose, ShowBiz will prompt you for the required settings; follow the on-screen instructions.

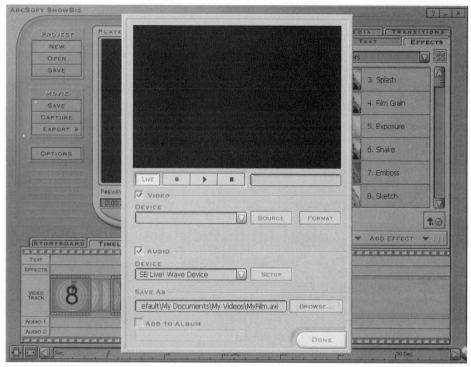

FIGURE 12.10 Capturing a ShowBiz movie to digital or analog video hardware.

Summary

In this chapter, I discussed ArcSoft's ShowBiz, and you learned the basics of movie editing in the digital world. We covered how to create your own movie using your digital video clips, still images, transitions, effects, and animated text, and I showed you how to save your movie to hard drive or import it to MyDVD.

dvds & cds

13

Troubleshooting Recorder Problems

In This Chapter

✔ Solving common hardware problems

✔ Solving common software problems

✔ Solving buffer underrun problems

The goal of this chapter is a simple one: to help you diagnose and solve both common hardware and software problems you may encounter with your recorder. Techno-types call this process troubleshooting—it's usually frustrating and often complex, but the good news is that you can successfully troubleshoot virtually all of the possible tribulations that are likely to crop up with your recorder.

dvds & cds

henever possible, I've provided cross-references to relevant chapters throughout the rest of the book.

Common Hardware Problems

In Chapter 2, "Installing Your DVD Recorder," I covered possible installation problems you might encounter. In this section, I'll discuss various hardware-related problems that can crop up with any type of recorder.

The recorder keeps telling me it's not ready (or it won't eject the disc)

This problem can be particularly irritating—and, if the disc doesn't eject at all, not just a little bit frightening, as well. Check these solutions:

- **Mounting delay.** Some recorders take longer than others to recognize a blank disc (or, if you're trying to read an existing audio CD, to extract tracks). Wait until the drive is ready before continuing—it's a good idea to watch the front panel light to see whether it's flashing (your recorder's documentation will have the specifics). Although it doesn't happen often, it's possible to load a disc off-center in the tray, which can cause circular scratches on the surface of the disc—make sure that you take a second when loading a CD to verify that it's setting in the center of the drive tray!

- **Lead-in/lead-out recording.** Your drive may still be recording the lead-in or lead-out portions of the disc; these delays occur at the beginning and at the end of a CD recording session. Unfortunately, many recording programs don't indicate that they're writing these areas, so it's easy to think that your computer is locked up. Give your recorder at least a couple of minutes to finish this processing.

- **Check your SCSI termination and device IDs.** If you're using a SCSI recorder and you've recently changed your SCSI settings or device chain, there's likely a problem with your computer's SCSI hardware. Run the diagnostic software supplied by your SCSI adapter card or drive's manufacturer to verify that you've correctly installed the drive.

- **Reinstall your recorder's drivers.** Have you recently been experiencing lockups, or has your computer been displaying error messages that you haven't seen before? Your drive's software drivers may have been corrupted or deleted because of a power failure or a misbehaving program. Reinstall the software drivers that you received with your drive, or download the updated drivers from the manufacturer's Web site and install them.

I can't read the discs I record on one particular CD-ROM/DVD-ROM drive

On the positive side, this particular problem indicates that there's nothing wrong with the discs you're recording—instead, look to the drive you're using to try to read the disc as the source of the trouble. Consider these possible culprits:

- **Drive is not a MultiRead model.** CD-ROM drives built before the days of the MultiRead specification can't read a CD-RW disc, so record the data on a standard CD-R, instead. DVD-ROM drives don't have this problem with recorded CDs, but don't forget that a DVD+RW drive may not be able to read a DVD-RW disc— the reverse is often true, as well.

- **Media incompatibilities.** You may have noticed that some CD-R discs use different combinations of dye color and reflective layers; recently, for instance, I've used discs with blue, gold, purple, green, and even pink dyes! Technically, this is *not* supposed to be a problem (any drive should be able to read these discs), but I have personally encountered drives that basically "don't like" a certain dye color. For example, a drive may be able to read a recorded CD that uses a blue dye layer and silver reflective layer, but it may not reliably read a recorded CD with a green dye layer and a gold reflective layer. Try reading a disc recorded with another combination of dye color and reflective layer.

dvds & cds

- **Alignment problems.** It's possible that the drive is incorrectly calibrated; if this is the case, it will probably have problems reading *any* discs you've recorded. If the drive returns errors with a commercially manufactured disc of the proper type—for example, if a CD-ROM drive can't read any audio CDs or a DVD-ROM drive can't read any DVD movies that you've bought, bring the drive to your local computer repair shop and ask the technician to check it.

Common Software Problems

Which is worse—hardware problems or software problems? That's a common question I hear all the time, and the answer is both! Windows, Mac OS, and Linux are difficult beasts to tame if a driver is corrupted or a software installation overwrites your recording application.

In this section, I'll describe a number of common problems due to software and how you can solve them.

My computer locks up when I try to record

Unfortunately, this error can be due to problems outside your recording application and its associated files—if Windows has become unstable because of some other problem, for example, the source of the trouble isn't your recording software. Try these tricks and solutions:

- **Reserve sufficient free space on your hard drive.** Remember, both Windows and your recording software need additional space for temporary files to record a disc successfully. I recommend that you reserve at least 200 or 300 MB of free space to avoid recording errors and lockups.
- **Read your log file.** Because your computer locks up, you're not likely to see an error message; this makes the job of troubleshooting even more difficult. Use the log file option if your recording software supports it—the log file may contain error messages that will help you in troubleshooting the problem.

- **Reinstall CD recorder drivers.** If your recorder doesn't work at all, your drive's software drivers have probably been corrupted or deleted. Reinstall the software drivers that you received with your drive or download the updated drivers from the manufacturer's Web site and install them.

My recording software reports that a blank disc isn't empty

This same problem may cause your computer to report that the disc doesn't have enough room or is incompatible with the format you're trying to use. Check these solutions:

- **Wrong disc type or overburning.** Older CD recorders aren't compatible with CD-RW discs, but these drives are museum-quality antiques in 2002! These days, this error message can be caused by attempting to overburn 80-minute "extended" discs in some recorders.
- **Previous session.** Check to make sure that you're not running out of room on the disc because of a previous session that you've recorded. Within Easy CD Creator, you can click CD and select the CD Information menu item to display the disc summary, which will show if that disc is really blank.
- **Bad media.** It's possible that the blank disc you're trying to use is bad; try recording with another disc from another manufacturer.
- **Reformat.** If you're writing a DVD+RW disc, DVD-RAM, or CD-RW disc, this error message often indicates either that the disc has not been formatted or that a previous formatting operation was interrupted before it could complete. Reformat your disc to refresh it.

I get a fixation error when I try to write a new session to a CD-R disc

In effect, your recording software is complaining that it can't close the last session on the disc. You may receive this message if the recording session is interrupted by a power failure or your computer locks up. Unfortunately, the disc may be unreadable; however, you can try using

dvds & cds

Session Selector to read data from the disc. (If it's a multisession disc, you should be able to read data from previous sessions this way.)

tip **If you're using Easy CD Creator, you may be able to recover some or all of the data, even if the fixation process didn't complete properly. Click CD and select the CD Information menu item to display the disc summary. If your recorder is able to recognize the data on the disc, use the Recover feature to attempt fixation again.**

I can't record MPEG, AVI, MOV, or ASF clips to a DVD or Video CD

These problems occur while you're using MyDVD (Chapter 6, "Recording a DVD with Existing Files") or VCD Creator (Chapter 10, "Recording Advanced Formats and Video CD Discs"). Possible solutions include:

- **Compression/codec problems.** Your recording software may not support the compression and codec used to record a particular video clip. If possible, use a video editing program to convert them to the standards supported by your recording software.
  - If you suspect that a video file you imported is using a codec you don't have, try to play it in the built-in Windows Media Player. If the file plays, then you have the codec in your system; otherwise, the program will automatically attempt to download the required codec. This often works, but it won't help if the video clip was recorded using a hard-to-find commercial codec.
- **Unsupported formats.** Both MyDVD and VCD Creator recognize AVI and MPEG, but there are numerous other, more exotic video formats that these programs can't handle. Again, use a video editing program to convert them, if possible, or use the application that created the clip to save the files in MPEG or AVI format.

Windows (or Mac OS) long filenames on my hard drive are truncated on discs I record

- **Long filenames not enabled.** If you're recording a disc for a Windows system, use Microsoft Joliet file format, which enables long filenames, instead of ISO 9660 file format. If you're writing a Mac disc, check the documentation for your recording software to determine where you can enable support within the program for long filenames. (Note that all of the software that ships with HP DVD-Writer drives defaults to long filenames.)

My recording software says I can't create a nested folder

This one's pretty easy: Use Microsoft Joliet (under Windows) or Apple Extended (under Mac OS). You're attempting to create a disc using the ISO 9660 file format, which won't allow more than eight levels of nested folders. Use Microsoft Joliet, if possible, or disable DOS/ISO 9660 conventions. You also have a limitation of 255 characters on your pathname under ISO 9660.

My DVD-ROM or CD-ROM drive doesn't recognize the disc I just recorded

There are several possible solutions to this problem—note that some of these problems apply only to CD recording.

- **Session remains open.** If you recorded a session on a CD-R or CD-RW and left it open, a standard CD-ROM drive will not be able to read it—you either have to close the session using Easy CD Creator or read the disc in your recorder. Programs such as MyDVD will close the disc automatically when writing to CD or DVD.
- **Unrecognized format.** Depending on the recording format you used, a disc created on the Macintosh may not be recognized by a PC. Consider recording cross-platform discs in true ISO 9660 format.
- **Dirty disc.** Dust, grease, and oil on the surface of a DVD or CD can prevent your drive from reading data—the section titled

"Cleaning Discs the Right Way" in Chapter 1 shows you how to care for discs.

- **Auto insert notification disabled.** If a program is supposed to run automatically when you load the disc, try using Windows Explorer to run the program from the disc—if you can, then Auto insert notification has been disabled within the Properties panel for the drive you're using.

- **Faulty recording.** You can use the verify feature within HP RecordNow or Easy CD Creator to make sure that the disc is readable (although rare, it is possible for a recording program to indicate that a disc has been recorded successfully when, in fact, something went wrong during the process).

I hear a click between every track of the audio CDs I record

This is a very common problem when recording audio CDs using MP3 files, but it usually appears only on some audio CD players—in fact, you may be able to listen to the disc on another player without any problem at all. You should be able to eliminate these clicks by recording your audio CDs using Disc-at-Once mode, which enables the laser to record the entire disc without shutting off between tracks—this area between the tracks is causing the clicks. If you're using the HP Record-Now program, digital audio is always written as DAO.

An MP3 track I recorded plays in mono instead of stereo (or it's "chopped off")

This problem isn't due to your recording hardware or software at all! Instead, you used a substandard MP3 file. Not every MP3 file you receive over services like Napster or LimeWire is recorded with CD quality—in fact, the original audio may have been recorded in mono. Also, it's a good idea to preview an entire MP3 track before you record it, because these files are often badly edited!

My Linux/UNIX system can't read the discs I've recorded

Again, beware of the cross-platform compatibility issue with Linux and UNIX computers. These tips should help:

- **Use ISO 9660.** Most older variants of these operating systems don't recognize Joliet or Mac HPFS file formats, so use ISO 9660 file format when recording for Linux/UNIX.
- **Watch your case-sensitivity.** Linux and UNIX are case-sensitive, which may cause problems when running programs or accessing data files directly from the disc.

I can play the audio tracks on a CD-Extra disc, but my computer can't read the data track

This problem turns a perfectly good CD-Extra disc into a plain audio CD. Check these potential fixes:

- **Unsupported format.** Your computer's older CD-ROM drive probably doesn't support the CD-Extra format—see whether you can read the data tracks on a late-model CD-ROM.
- **Disc incorrectly closed.** The data track may have been incorrectly saved. If you're using Easy CD Creator, you can click CD and select the CD Information menu item to display the disc summary, which will show whether that disc is really blank. If your recorder is able to recognize the data on the disc, use the Recover feature to attempt fixation again.

I can't read Kodak PhotoCDs on my computer

No secret on this one: Discs created for use on a Kodak PhotoCD player can't be accessed on a computer, and your recorder can't create Kodak PhotoCDs—they use a proprietary format.

Eliminating Buffer Underrun Errors

If your recorder doesn't support burn-proof recording, even the fastest computer may fall victim to the dreaded buffer underrun error; as you learned in earlier chapters, this error results when your computer can't transfer data to the recorder at the necessary rate to ensure a successful recording. The older and slower your computer, the more likely it is that a disc will be ruined. Try these solutions:

dvds & cds

- **Record from a disc image.** Rather than recording a number of smaller files "on-the-fly" (which is far less efficient), try creating a disc image, then record from the image—this is much more efficient and requires less overhead, because the image is a single file.

- **Record at a slower speed.** Although your system may not be able to support the highest speeds available with your recorder, you can always record at a slower speed—for example, if you can't record at 32x, try recording at 16x, instead.

- **Don't multitask while recording.** Dedicate the entire resources of your computer to recording by shutting down all unnecessary applications (including those running on the Windows taskbar).

- **Defragment before recording.** A defragmented drive transfers data significantly faster; I describe how to defragment a hard drive running Windows XP in the section titled "Defragmenting Your Hard Drive" in Chapter 3.

- **Use the fastest drive on your system.** Whenever possible, choose the fastest drive on your system as the location for source data and temporary files created by your recording software.

tip Even if you use all of these tricks, an older computer may still not be able to handle the data transfer speeds required by today's DVD recorders. Don't give up hope, however; you can still try to record that material! There is a way to make sure you don't lose a blank CD-R or DVD-R disc: Use your recording software's simulation or test mode first, before the actual recording begins. If the data can be successfully recorded in test mode, you can be certain that there will be little likelihood of errors during the recording process. For example, MyDVD allows you to record the image to the HD instead of disc. If that works, all the encoding has been done, so it will take less processing time (and will significantly lower the chance of an error) when you burn the image from the hard drive to the disc.

Summary

This chapter covered the common hardware and software problems that often occur while recording CDs and DVDs, as well as recommendations on how to troubleshoot and avoid them.

14

Adding an HTML Menu System

In This Chapter

✔ Determining whether your disc needs a menu

✔ Adding menus to a DVD

✔ Introducing HTML as a menu language

✔ Designing a menu system

✔ Comparing HTML creation software

✔ Project: Building an HTML Menu

In Chapter 9, you learned how to add labels and jewel case inserts to enhance the appearance of your discs—with a good labeling program such as CD Label Creator, you can produce a professional-looking CD-ROM that will impress your friends, co-workers, and customers.

To be honest, however, that's just the outside of your project! As the old adage goes, "You can't tell a book by its cover"—even the nicest-looking project disc can suffer from

dvds & cds

bad organization and a lack of those user-friendly convenience features that are common among software that's commercially produced. For example, if you're distributing MP3 music files, you might want a button on your disc that installs those music files to the computer's hard drive.

You can help prevent "data chaos" by using folders and the common-sense guidelines I covered in Chapter 3 (in the section titled "Organizing Files"), but what if the person who'll be using your disc has no computer experience at all? If you're a software developer, you'll probably design and write a custom menu system using Visual Basic, C, or REALbasic that will make the disc easy to use and navigate...but what if you have no programming skills? You may end up shaking your head and giving up entirely on adding any menu system to your discs.

Luckily, there is a solution to this problem that I've been using since the early 1990s! It requires no computer programming degree or expensive software, and it allows you to create an easy-to-use, fully featured menu system that will run on virtually any PC with Windows. What's my secret? It's HTML—the Hypertext Markup Language—that's used to create the billions of Web pages on the Internet.

In this chapter, I'll provide all the information you need to understand when and why you should add an HTML menu to your discs—as well as why you shouldn't use HTML with every disc you record. I'll discuss the guidelines you should consider while designing your menus. I'll provide you with a comparison of HTML page creation programs, then I'll demonstrate how you can use Netscape Composer to produce your menu system.

Do I Need a Menu?

First, let's consider when a disc needs a menu (and when it's best left as-is): I'll be honest, it takes time to create a good-looking and well-designed menu, and you won't want to take that time and effort with most of the data discs you record. Also, a menu system is unnecessary for some discs: Naturally, you won't need a menu system for a standard audio CD. In this section, I'll consider examples of recording projects that are suitable for an HTML menu system.

Multimedia Material

I always consider an HTML menu whenever I'm sending photos, digital video, or audio files to other people. Just like today's Web pages, your HTML menu can have built-in buttons or links that will display images and video or play sounds and music through the computer's speaker.

tip **Remember, other programs that I've talked about earlier in the book can also create discs that specialize in displaying images and video (such as PhotoRelay, which I cover in Chapter 11 ("Recording Digital Photographs on CD"), and ShowBiz, which I discuss in Chapter 12 ("Making Movies with ArcSoft ShowBiz"). Discs you create with these programs have menus and controls added automatically.**

Internet Content

Talk about a perfect fit! If you need to add Internet content to a project—such as links to your e-mail address, your Web page, or a file that resides on the Internet—any computer with an Internet connection can use these links within your HTML menu.

dvds & cds

Text-Based Material

Another type of content that's particularly well suited to HTML display is a long text file; in fact, the Web was originally conceived as a text-based search and retrieval system. For example, a number of commercial discs I have in my software collection use their own HTML-based menus to provide the complete text of historical documents and classic literature, such as Shakespeare's work. Your text can contain formatting, links to other documents, and complete search functionality.

tip **To use all of the formatting and search functions provided by your browser, you'll have to convert text files into documents in HTML format; most Web design programs will do this automatically when you copy text onto the page. You can also convert a document directly into a Web page from within Microsoft Word, which you can use as a submenu in your menu system: Click File and choose Save As, then click the Save As Type drop-down list box at the bottom of the dialog and choose Web Page.**

Off-Site Web Content

I've used this trick a number of times before: If you're recording your Web site to a disc so that you can carry it with you, an HTML menu can provide a front end with direct links to certain pages (which allows others to jump directly to important pages during a presentation without actually having to "click down" from the Web site main menu).

Programs to Download

Figure 14.1 illustrates the download page from my Web site (http://home.mlcbooks.com), where you can try out the shareware and freeware programs I feature in my books. Without an Internet connection, folks couldn't download these files...unless, of course, I create a data disc that contains the same files and an HTML menu system. (In fact, I've done just that.) If you need to provide a way to move programs from a disc to a person's hard drive, an HTML menu is a fast and easy solution.

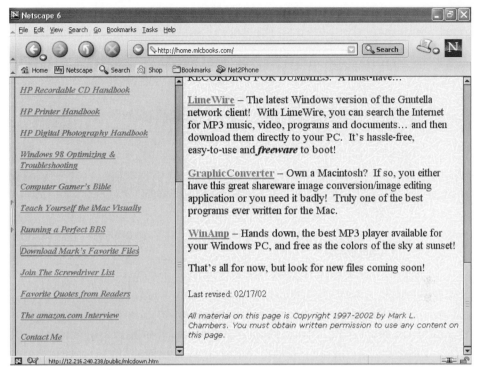

FIGURE 14.1   These download files from my Web site will work well with an HTML menu.

Discs You'll Give to Others

Finally, an HTML menu system is a worthwhile addition to any disc that you plan to distribute to others, because HTML is so compatible among different computer systems (and, if you're trying to create a professional impression, the animation and interactivity you can build into a custom menu will really appeal to the eye). As I mentioned earlier, an HTML menu system is easy for the novice to use, too—just put the index page in the root of the CD, and tell your friends, family, clients, or customers to double-click it. Convenience like that is hard to beat without some sort of programming!

Of course, there are different degrees of necessity here: Just because your project includes one or two digital photographs and a couple of longer text files doesn't automatically mean that you need to

dvds & cds

go to the trouble of preparing an HTML menu. Just keep the option in mind (and save the files for the menu systems that you do create, because they can be easily reused for other projects).

Adding Menus to a DVD

"Should I add a menu to a DVD?" If your project is a simple data DVD and it follows the guidelines I just outlined, it's probably a good candidate for an HTML menu. In fact, the sheer quantity of files that can be stored on a recorded DVD may make a menu practically a requirement; imagine a computer novice trying to locate a single file among thousands in a folder.

However, don't forget that many of the DVD discs you've learned about in earlier chapters already have a menu system when you record them. For example, if you've recorded a DVD movie disc using MyDVD or ShowBiz, there's no need to add an HTML menu system—these discs can be viewed on your computer already, using programs such as PowerDVD.

tip **An HTML menu system is also not a good idea for a rewriteable DVD+RW, DVD-RW, or DVD-RAM disc, because these discs are likely to be reused. There are exceptions to this rule, though—for example, if you rerecord a DVD+RW disc with the same structure and updated files to distribute to software beta testers, you can use the same HTML menu over and over with minor changes.**

Why Use HTML?

At this point, you may be wondering why I'm such a fan of HTML and why it has worked so successfully for me (and many of my readers) in the past. (After all, I'm also a programmer and a shareware developer, so I could write a menu system in REALbasic or Visual Basic almost as quickly.) You may be asking yourself, "Can I really write HTML code?

Although HTML is one of the easiest languages to learn on the planet, it's still a computer language, right?"

How about a little reassurance? Before I launch into a full-scale discussion of HTML, I'd like to discuss the details and explain why HTML is so compatible, easy to use, and easy to program.

Easy to Learn

Although it's technically a programming language, HTML is *very* easy to learn, compared with other languages—the Web wouldn't have experienced such phenomenal growth if HTML had been cryptic or hard to understand. In fact, today's sophisticated Web design tools— such as Netscape Composer, which I'll use in the project at the end of this chapter—make it a simple matter to create an attractive menu system with *no* programming work at all! You just run the Web design program, create the menu within that application, and save the result as an HTML page—the rest is done automatically.

Compatible with Most Computers

HTML is a universally recognized standard, so it really doesn't matter whether the person is using a Windows PC, an Apple Macintosh running Mac OS 9 or Mac OS X, or even more technical operating systems such as UNIX, Linux, Solaris, or BeOS. If your operating system has a Web browser, your menu will work.

Large Installed Base

That's a term that software developers often toss around; it means that the vast majority of computers running today already have a Web browser installed, so there's no preparation necessary to use your disc. A person can simply load the disc and double-click to go.

tip **If—through some cosmic chance—someone doesn't have Internet Explorer or Netscape Navigator installed on his or her PC or Macintosh computer, you can even include the distribution version of either browser on the disc for free!**

dvds & cds

Did I Mention It Was Free?

Not only are most Web browsers free: You can also find HTML editors and Web design programs included with today's operating systems! For example, a version of FrontPage is likely already installed on your Windows computer. Other HTML editors, such as Arachnophilia (which I'll discuss in a page or two) are free of charge or are very cheap shareware. In other words, you don't have to spend a fortune on development software just to create your own disc menu system.

Familiar Controls

Do you know how to use a Web browser? I'd be willing to bet the answer is yes—in fact, even if you don't know how to use a Web browser, it's simple just to click on a link! This friendly front-end to your disc will help reassure even the most nervous novice.

A Wide Range of Commands

As I've already mentioned, the basic commands of HTML will provide just about all of the functionality that your disc menu is likely to need, without any worry about such cryptic programming terms as *protected memory space* or *dynamic link libraries*. (Two of my favorite examples of the techno-speak that I try to avoid.) The computer's Web browser takes care of all that's necessary behind the scenes, leaving you free to concentrate on the look and feel of your menu.

More to Come

If you are willing to spend money—or you already have a commercial Web design tool— you can add even more functionality to your menu system. Think of all that you've seen on your last visit to the Web, such as Java applets (you can think of them as "miniature programs" that will run directly from your HTML menu), animation, interactive games, and high-quality graphics: With very few exceptions, the rule is that, if it works on a Web page on the Internet, it'll work on an HTML menu, too.

With every passing day, Web designers and software developers are producing more features and functions that you can add to an HTML page. I won't be covering any of these tools in this chapter—after all, this is a book about burning discs—but you can find help and tutorials at your local bookstore or on the Web.

For these reasons, I often say that HTML is "the code for the normal, nonprogramming person"—and that's why it works so well for building disc menus that will work on practically every computer.

As you might have already guessed, the actual process is very simple: After you create the HTML pages that make up your menu system, you add them to your data CD layout. You'll also include any graphics, video, sound, and support files that are required by the menu system; if you're using an HTML editor such as FrontPage, these are automatically saved in the folder you specify.

Designing Your Menus

Before you fire up your HTML editor or Web page design program, pause for a moment and consider what type of menu system you want to create. You should jot down the answers to these questions:

- **Is the appearance of the menu important?** Your menu system can pull out all the tricks of today's Web designers, with animated graphics, video, and sound, or you can choose the Spartan appearance of simple formatted text—which is naturally much easier to produce. As an example, consider a demo disc for a new software product on one hand (which is likely to use plenty of graphics and sound to impress potential customers) and compare that with a clip art disc for distribution to your co-workers (which is strictly utilitarian, as in "I want to download this graphic to my hard drive *right now*, without any eye candy." The demo disc is meant to be explored, whereas the clip art disc simply needs a method of retrieving files.

dvds & cds

- **What type of computer will use the disc?** Is your menu likely to be used on the latest hardware, or will it have to run on older computers that may not perform well when trying to display video or high-resolution graphics?

- **Will the contents of the disc be downloaded or viewed inside the browser?** This will determine whether you need any commands for downloading files to the hard drive; for example, a CD with text documents converted to HTML can be viewed directly within the browser.

- **Will you need any Internet connectivity?** If not, your disc menu can be totally self-contained.

> *tip* As a consultant, I have found through personal experience that it's still somewhat dangerous to assume that a connection with the Internet will be available! There's certainly nothing wrong with adding links to your e-mail address or Web page to your menu system; if an Internet connection isn't available, those links simply won't operate. However, if you don't take the extra step of including programs or files on your disc and instead provide a link to those files on your Web page, don't automatically assume that the person will be able to download them...red-faced embarrassment could follow.

- **Are submenus appropriate?** Like a typical Web site, your HTML menu system can provide anything from a simple, one-page interface to a complex hierarchy of submenus; typically, I like to keep things to either a single main menu or a main menu with a single level of submenus. Submenus come in handy when the contents of the disc fall into specific categories: for example, a disc that has company logos and artwork on one submenu page and press releases in Word format on another submenu.

Your next step is to write down each of the functions your menu must provide and where they should appear in your menu. A typical list for a software demo disc might look like this:

- Product features (text shown on the main menu).
- System requirements (text link shown in a submenu).

- Demo program download (download link on the main menu).
- Sales e-mail (e-mail link on the main menu).
- Company Web address (Web link on the main menu).
- Installation instructions and troubleshooting (text link in a sub-menu).

tip **Of course, it's impossible to cover Web design in this chapter—there are hundreds of books devoted entirely to the subject! However, there are three basic guidelines that graphic artists and Webmasters use to help steer clear of chaos and keep their menus attractive to the eye. First, if your menu system will use color and graphics, it's a good idea to stay consistent throughout your menu—perhaps your company logo and a single color. Second, remember that "the message is the thing"—your menu system shouldn't draw attention away from the subject, whether it be text, files, or multimedia. Finally, don't forget the "Two Clicks Rule": Make sure that the material you're presenting is no more than two links (or clicks) away from the main menu.**

Once you've got the basic design specification on paper—or in Word—it's time to create the menu pages!

HTML Editing vs. Web Design vs. Page Layout

"Hang on, Mark—I've never created a Web page before!" Don't panic, good reader: In this section, I'll discuss what's available and introduce Netscape Composer, which I'll use to create an example menu later in the chapter.

There are actually three types of programs commonly used today to create Web pages: the HTML editor; Web design programs, such as Microsoft FrontPage and Netscape Composer; and page layout/processing programs, such as Microsoft Word.

dvds & cds

The Basics: HTML Editing

Because HTML is completely text-based, any text editor can function as a basic *HTML editor*; for example, I often make quick changes to my Web sites using Windows Notepad. No visual "drag-and-drop" page creation here; like any other programming language, HTML is edited using the keyboard. The language uses commands called *tags*, each of which is a line in the file that instructs the Web browser on what to do (for example, which color to use for the background or what size the text should be). Within the editor, you're actually looking at the tags that make up the page; to see the page as it will appear in a Web browser, HTML editors either offer a "preview" mode or automatically launch your Web browser.

To be honest, I would recommend that most PC owners avoid an HTML editor! As you'll see later in the chapter, it's very easy to create a page using a Web design application, which takes a visual approach rather than text-based coding; you don't have to worry about typing a single HTML tag.

On the other hand, if you're already familiar with HTML programming and you'd like to work directly with the commands in an HTML editor, I can highly recommend Arachnophilia (Figure 14.2), a free "CareWare" application that includes professional features such as programming macros, table support, and a spell checker. You can download this great HTML editor at www.arachnoid.com/arachnophilia/index.html.

The Visual Approach: Web Design

Next, let's consider Web design applications such as Microsoft FrontPage and Netscape Composer: These programs offer a much easier-to-use "drag-and-drop" approach to page creation, so you won't have to edit any actual HTML code. Once you've added text, inserted graphics, and set up your links, the application automatically generates the HTML file for you. Definitely the way to go for most of us!

Because these applications are meant to help those with no design experience, a Web design application will likely have wizards to walk

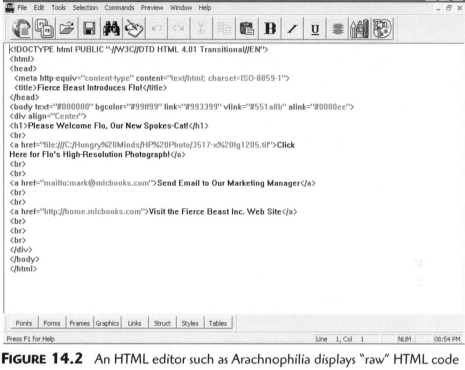

FIGURE 14.2 An HTML editor such as Arachnophilia displays "raw" HTML code in text format.

you through the page creation process, as well as a number of ready-made templates and designs that you can use or modify for your menu system. You won't need to know a single HTML command to use one of these programs, and once you're familiar with the way your Web design program works, you can produce a quality menu page for a disc project in a few minutes.

By the way, if you don't already have a Web design program (and you'd rather not spend any money on a shareware or commercial application right now), visit www.netscape.com and download the latest version of the Netscape Web browser—you'll also install a free copy of Netscape Composer, the company's easy-to-use Web design program.

The Alternative: Page Layout and Word Processing

Today's word processing and graphic page-layout programs have branched out into Web design, as well, including such workhorses as Microsoft Word and Adobe Pagemaker. Although these programs don't have the full range of specialized features and functions of a dedicated Web design application, they do have one big advantage: You're likely already familiar with them! For example, Figure 14.3 illustrates one of the ready-made Web page templates that come with Microsoft Word.

The HTML menu pages produced by these applications will vary quite a bit in functionality and appearance, but generally the result will be more than adequate for all but the most demanding multimedia menu system.

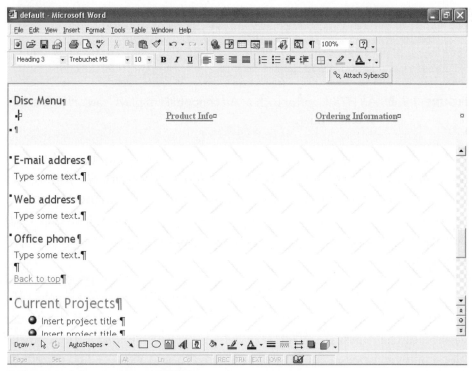

FIGURE 14.3   This simple HTML page was created in seconds, using Microsoft Word.

tip **If you're unsure whether your favorite page layout or word processing program can produce Web pages, check to see whether it can save (or export) documents in HTML format.**

Project: **Building an HTML Menu**

Let's create an example single-page menu for a fictitious cat food company, Fierce Beast Incorporated. The disc will contain a digital, high-resolution photograph of the company's new spokes-cat that can be displayed, as well as links to the company's Web site and an e-mail link to the company's marketing contact. I'll be using Netscape Composer under Windows XP.

Requirements

- An installed copy of Netscape Composer
- A digital photograph

✔ Follow these steps:

1. Click Start and choose All Programs | Netscape 6.2 | Netscape 6.2, which runs Netscape Navigator.

2. Within Navigator, click File, select New from the menu, and click Blank Page to Edit. The Composer screen you see in Figure 14.4 appears.

3. Let's begin by changing the rather plain white background and adding a little color. Click Format and choose Page Colors and Background, and Composer opens the dialog you see in Figure 14.5.

4. Click Use Custom Colors and click the Background button, then select a lighter color (which will keep our text easy to read) from the samples. Click OK to accept the color change.

Burn It! Creating Your Own Great DVDs and CDs

FIGURE 14.4 Netscape Composer, ready for duty.

FIGURE 14.5   Selecting a suitable color for our background.

5. Next, we need a title: I'll type *Please Welcome Flo, Our New Spokes-Cat!* Like a word processor, you can simply type text directly into Composer.

6. The program also allows you to edit using the familiar click and drag, so select the text, click the Paragraph Format drop-down list box, and choose Heading 1. Click Format, choose Align, and click Center on the pop-up menu to finish our title (Figure 14.6).

7. Our first link will be to the photograph FLOPIC.JPG, which will be included in the root directory of the CD. Press Enter twice and click the Link button on the toolbar; Composer displays the dialog box shown in Figure 14.7. Type the text that will appear on the menu in the first box.

dvds & cds

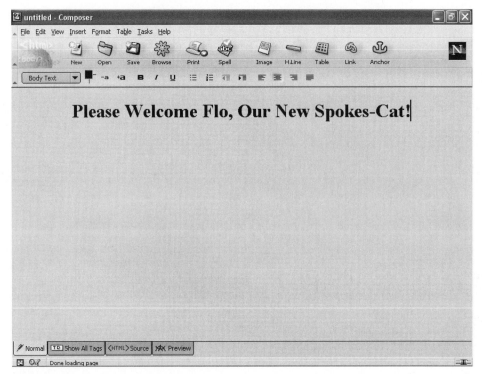

FIGURE 14.6   Our title is now in place.

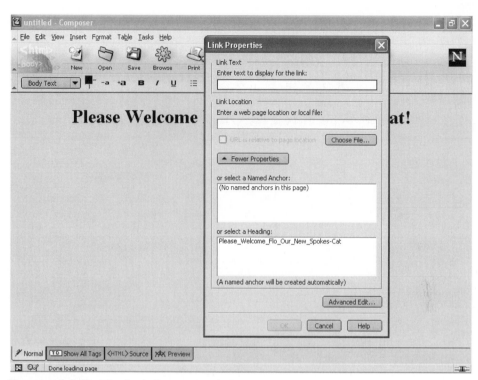

FIGURE 14.7 The Link Properties dialog.

8. Now we must "connect" the link to the file on the disc. Click the Choose File button to locate the file. Highlight the filename and click Open. Click OK to create your first link (Figure 14.8)!

tip **If your image doesn't show up in the Choose File dialog, Composer is looking for only HTML files; make sure that you choose the All Files view in the Files of Type drop-down list box.**

9. Because the image will actually be stored on CD (and not on the computer's hard drive), right-click the photo link and choose Link Properties. Click in the Link Location field, erase the current contents (which point to your hard drive), and type the name of the file—in our case, FLOPIC.JPG. Click OK, and the computer will now look for the file in the same location as the HTML file. (Remember, both of these files will be included in the root direc-

dvds & cds

FIGURE 14.8 You did it! That's a link to your photo.

tory of your data CD layout, so don't panic because the link doesn't work at this time.)

10. Next, add the e-mail link. Press Enter twice, click Insert, and choose HTML to display the dialog shown in Figure 14.9. Type this text into the box:

```
<A HREF ="mailto:mark@mlcbooks.com">Send Email to
Our Marketing Manager</A>
```

11. As you might have guessed, the line you just typed was an actual HTML tag—I wanted to give you a taste of what the language looks like. Change the e-mail address (the part immediately following the mailto: that appears within the quotes) to your e-mail address and click Insert, and the link appears (Figure 14.10).

FIGURE 14.9 Typing an HTML tag into Composer.

FIGURE 14.10 You've added an e-mail link to your menu.

12. Finally, we need to add a link to the company's Web site. Press Enter twice and click the Link button on the toolbar to display the Link Properties dialog again; type the text for the Web page link in the Link Text box.

13. To specify the Web address, click in the Link Location field, and enter the full address—for example, a link to my MLC Books Online site would be `http://home.mlcbooks.com` (note that the `http://` part is required). Click OK, and Figure 14.11 illustrates our completed menu!

14. Click File and choose Save As to save the page. Composer displays the dialog you see in Figure 14.12: Type the text that will appear in the browser's title line, and click OK.

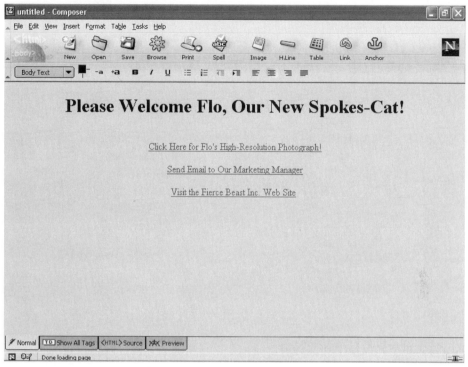

FIGURE 14.11 Our basic disc menu is ready to save.

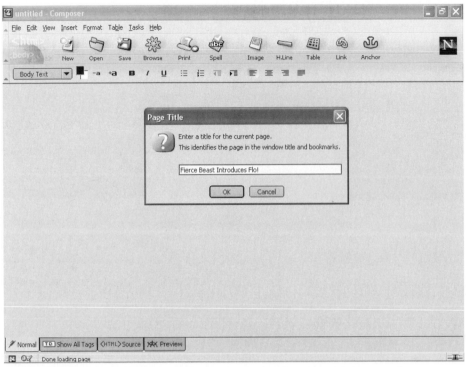

FIGURE 14.12 Entering a title for the completed page.

15. From the Save Page As dialog box, select the folder where the menu should be saved. Click in the File Name text box, enter a short name, such as MAIN.HTM, and click Save.

You're ready to burn a test disc! Open HP RecordNow or Easy CD Creator and create a disc layout that includes the menu files you created—in this case, MAIN.HTM—and any files that will be downloaded or displayed—in this case, FLOPIC.JPG—in the root directory of the disc. (This is very important, because recording these files in other locations—like folders *within* the root directory—will cause your links to fail.)

Once you've recorded your disc, you can test your menu. Load the disc and run your Web browser, then click File and choose Open (in Internet Explorer) or Open File (in Navigator). Locate and double-click on the MAIN.HTM file on the CD, and click on all the links to make

FIGURE 14.13 That's some cat!

sure they work. Figure 14.13 illustrates our completed menu (and Flo herself!), as displayed in Navigator.

Naturally, this project only scratched the surface of what's possible—we didn't add any graphics or sound, for example—but it also showed you just how easy it is to create a basic menu. As you become more familiar with your Web design software, you'll be able to enhance the look of your menus and expand the functionality of your disc projects.

dvds & cds

Summary

This chapter introduced you to HTML and demonstrated how an HTML menu can add an attractive appearance and the convenience of a point-and-click interface to your CD projects. I discussed which types of discs will benefit from a menu system, as well as the basic concepts of menu design and the HTML applications that you can use to create your pages.

15

Converting Albums and Cassettes to Audio CDs

In This Chapter

✔ **Connecting your stereo and computer**

✔ **Project: Transferring a Cassette to MP3 Files**

Are your rare and precious vinyl albums "dying a slow death" from scratches and warping? Are your home-recorded cassettes losing their range and quality? Or (and this shows my age), do you have 8-track tapes that are close to extermination?

If you're like me—an audiophile with several dozen albums and cassettes of irreplaceable music and vocals—you'd prefer to have that material on audio CDs, instead. But how can analog data be transferred to digital format and recorded for posterity?

dvds & cds

303

T his final chapter shows you how to use the Spin Doctor portion of Roxio's SoundStream—one of the programs included with Easy CD Creator 5—to make the jump from analog to digital. You'll learn about the equipment you'll need, and I'll demonstrate how to transfer the audio from an album to an audio CD.

A Word of Caution

Before you read any further, take note: *Transferring analog to digital should be done only for those recordings you can't already get on audio CD!* In other words, dear reader, it's just plain ridiculous to spend your valuable time and effort copying your old Beatles albums to an audio CD. Why? Those albums are almost certainly available already on audio CD, and no matter how good a job you do in transferring the music, it will always sound better when professionally mastered from the original recordings. (Plus, you're likely to get liner notes.)

With this in mind, consider an analog-to-digital transfer a last resort for the truly *irreplaceable* audio in your collection: tapes you've made of your family, for example, or your audio diary. Or that bootleg recording of Ella Fitzgerald and Frank Zappa jamming together live. (Come to think of it, send me a copy of that one, too.)

What Do I Need?

To transfer analog-to-digital, you'll need the following equipment (besides the SoundStream software):

- **A stereo system that can play the original media.** Your stereo's amplifier, preamp, or tuner needs standard Audio Out jacks that will allow it to connect to your computer.
- **Your computer's sound card.** Virtually all computer audio cards now have Audio In jacks, and any card should be able to record CD-quality music.

- **The proper cables.** Ah, here's the rub. Unfortunately, many computer sound cards on the market today have proprietary connectors—often called *dongles* (and usually with irritation)—that are required to connect standard audio cables.

Due to the wide range of stereo hardware and the equally wide range of computer sound card connections, I can't provide any specific instructions for connecting the cables; luckily, your sound card manual should include this information (as well as an explanation of which audio jacks you need to use).

Project: **Transferring a Cassette to Audio CD**

Without further ado, let's copy a cassette to separate MP3 files, then to an audio CD—in this case, a live performance of a local band that I captured from the DJ's sound board. (It's not likely that I'll encounter this band in a record store, because they split up over a decade ago without ever releasing anything except a handful of demo singles!)

Requirements

- Original audio media—for this project, a cassette tape
- An installed copy of Easy CD Creator 5, which includes Sound-Stream
- An installed copy of HP RecordNow (or other recording software)
- A stereo with a cassette deck and cables to connect to the computer's sound card
- A blank CD-R disc

dvds & cds

✔ **Once you've connected the cables between your computer and your stereo, follow these steps:**

1. Run SoundStream by clicking Start and choosing All Programs | Easy CD Creator 5 | Applications | SoundStream. The program's main menu appears, as shown in Figure 15.1.

2. Click on the Option Drawer button—the button at the bottom of the SoundStream window with the arrow) to open the drawer, and click Spin Doctor to display the dialog shown in Figure 15.2.

3. Choose Sound Cleaning, and click the Tape preset button to allow Spin Doctor to choose the best settings for Sound Cleaning and Pop/Click Removal.

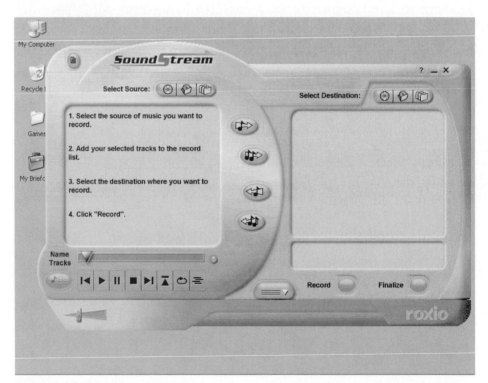

FIGURE 15.1 Roxio's SoundStream can transfer any analog audio signal to an audio CD.

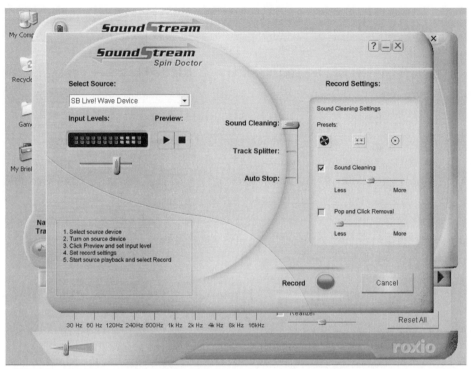

FIGURE 15.2 Configuring Spin Doctor before the recording.

tip If you have a single sound card in your PC, leave the Select Source drop-down list box set to the default—however, if you have more than one sound card or sound input device, you may have to use this option to choose the proper input/record source.

4. Choose Auto Stop, and choose either Manual Stop—where you have to stop the recording by hand—or Auto Stop after 3 to 4 seconds of silence. Personally, I use Manual Stop (I like to be in complete control), but as long as there are no songs with long periods of silence, Auto Stop should work fine.

5. OK, it's time to check the audio levels. Turn on the stereo and begin playing the cassette—it's typically a good idea to set the stereo amplifier volume about one-quarter to halfway.

dvds & cds

6. Click the Preview button, and click and drag to adjust the Input level slider until the loudest passage of music lights the entire green portion of the level meter. Note that you do not want the peak portion of the music to move the level meter into the red zone for more than a split second! When the level is properly set, click Stop.

7. Now you're ready to start the actual recording process. Click Record to display the dialog shown in Figure 15.3. I recommend recording the music in File format, which allows you to check the quality of the recording later, without potentially wasting a blank CD-R disc. (Plus, this also allows you to add the title, artist, and track names before you burn the disc.) Click File.

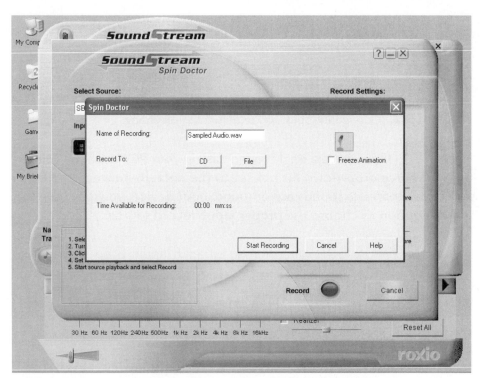

FIGURE 15.3 It's a good idea to record your tracks to MP3 first.

8. Click the Save As Type drop-down list box on the Save As dialog (Figure 15.4) to specify WAV or MP3 format, and select the folder where the tracks should be stored (or click New Folder to add a new folder on your hard drive). When you've navigated to the proper spot, click Select Folder.

9. Rewind the cassette and start it playing, then click on Start Recording. If you chose Auto Stop, Spin Doctor will create separate tracks in the folder you specified.

10. Once the last track on the cassette has finished, click Stop and click OK to return to Spin Doctor.

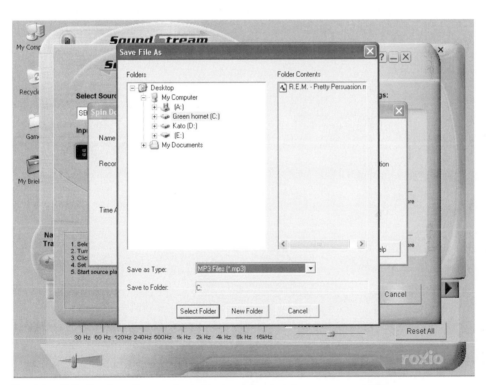

FIGURE 15.4 Specifying a location and format for your sound files.

Congratulations! That aging cassette has been transferred to clean, pure digital satisfaction. However, before you toss it into the closest trash can, you'll want to review each track using an MP3 player, such as Windows Media Player or WinAmp, to make sure that the recording went well. Once you're satisfied with all of the tracks, use HP RecordNow or Easy CD Creator to create a standard audio CD with the MP3 files you've recorded.

Summary

In this final chapter, I demonstrated how to use SoundStream to transfer audio from older media, such as albums and cassettes, to digital MP3 format, where they can be enjoyed and—optionally—recorded to an audio CD.

A

Hewlett-Packard Technical Support's Frequently Asked Questions

The questions and answers in this appendix were collected by the Hewlett-Packard technical support staff at Customer Care Centers around the world.

tip **Additional information is always available online at the Hewlett-Packard CD Writer home page (http://www.hpcdwriter.com/).**

How much can I fit on a 74-minute CD?

For audio, the answer is simple enough:

HP RecordNow

Using this software, you should be able to place 650 MB of data on the disc. You can store 74 minutes of audio on a 74-minute CD. To maximize the storage space on an audio disc, use DAO recording mode (Disc at Once), which removes the 2-second gaps between tracks.

dvds & cds

311

HP DLA

The capacity of an HP DLA disc depends on whether you are using a CD-R or CD-RW disc. CD-R, when formatted with DirectCD, usually will have between 550 and 600 MB left after formatting. A CD-RW disc will generally have between 500 and 550 MB left after formatting.

Why do my recorded audio CDs hiss and pop?

This is caused primarily by the source drive used to extract the audio tracks for burning. Many older CD-ROM drives were not designed to perform the audio extraction technique required by today's CD and DVD recorders at a fast enough speed. Errors normally not audible in the source content often surface during this process. To test and verify the issue, use your recorder as both the source and the destination drive for an audio CD burn. On the resulting disc, the audio quality should be corrected. If this resolves the issue, you may continue to use the recorder as your source drive, or you may wish to investigate a new CD-ROM for your computer, capable of faster audio extraction.

Why can't I read my recorded CDs on another computer?

There are a few different issues that can affect what we call *disc interchange*, or reading a burned CD on another computer system or CD device.

CD-R vs. CD-RW Media

CD-R discs are recommended for any CDs you wish to take to another computer system. CD-RW can be used, but some older CD-ROM readers will have problems accessing the information on these discs. If the CD-ROM reader has a MultiRead icon on the front plate, that drive will be able to read RW media.

Using Roxio's Easy CD Creator or CD Copier Deluxe

These two burning applications write to the CD in the standard track format, adding a table of contents to the end of the session. This method of writing is most widely recognized by other CD devices and will increase the chance for successful disc interchange.

Even with this method, however, the preceding information about CD-RW media still applies. Using Easy CD Creator or CD Copier Deluxe with RW media may still create difficulties reading the information, unless the reader device is MultiRead-capable. Using CD-R with this software, however, affords you the best chance of reading your created CDs on another computer and is the recommended method.

How do I clean my HP CD or DVD recorder?

HP CD-Writer and DVD-Writer drives require no maintenance or cleaning. If you simply keep your discs clean, you will prevent most problems.

Do not attempt to use the CD-ROM cleaning CDs that use a small brush to sweep dirt off the laser mechanism.

How do I create discs for other operating systems?

The process for setting up the software is simple. Using Easy CD Creator, click File on the menu, select CD Project Properties, then select ISO 9660 from the drop-down menu. This will set the software to burn the CD in the most universal format available. Even with the disc burned properly, there are some things to keep in mind:

- The naming structure of any files you will be burning must meet the 8.3-character naming convention set forth in DOS. Additionally, if you select an option other than MS-DOS 8.3-character naming, the software will allow you to use more types of characters (*&%$#), but this will make the CD less likely to be readable on another operating system.
- Remember that, even though you can create a disc that another system can read, the code within the files may not make sense to a given operating system. For example, if you create a CD for a Macintosh computer containing a program written for Win-

dvds & cds

dows, the Mac's CD-ROM drive will be able to see it, but the Mac will not be able to run the program.

Why are files that are copied from a DVD or CD to the hard drive assigned the Read Only attribute on the hard drive?

This will always be the case with optical media such as CD-R discs, because they are read-only media. This is actually one of the more important features of optical technology, in that data is virtually incorruptible once it's written to disc. It cannot be accidentally overwritten or erased when the disc has been closed. The most straightforward approach to resolving this problem is to change the attributes of the files after copying them to the hard drive. This procedure is accomplished by selecting the files individually or as a group, right-clicking the mouse button, and choosing Properties. The dialog box that appears enables you to remove the Read Only attribute.

I was formatting a disc with DirectCD and the process was interrupted . . . now I can't use the disc! Can I fix this?

If power is lost while a CD-RW disc is being formatted, the disc will become unusable in any application, and it will fail if another format is attempted.

To solve this problem, use the Easy CD Creator Erase feature to erase the disc fully, then try the format operation again.

Can I play an audio CD on either my internal HP recorder or my CD-ROM if my sound card has only one input?

Yes. Use an audio "Y" cable connector. Some of these connectors require that a small switch be installed in the system case. Toggling the switch will enable you to select either drive for playback. Some newer sound cards allow two devices to be connected, so check with your sound card manufacturer before buying a Y cable connector.

Some sound cards have more than one audio connector, but they're not suitable for connecting two devices—the extra connector is only to accommodate different styles of audio cables. Attaching more than one CD-ROM/CD-Writer to these types of sound cards is not recommended. Check with your sound card manufacturer before connecting more than one drive. For example, some versions of the Sound Blaster Live sound card have an SP/DIF digital input, which is not compatible with the output from a recorder.

B

Tips on Buying a Recorder

If you're like most readers of this book, you probably already have your DVD recorder: Either it came with your computer as standard equipment, or you've already bought it, and now you're ready to install it. (You'll find installation guidelines and procedures in Chapter 2, "Installing Your DVD Recorder.")

However, if you don't fit into one of these two categories and you haven't bought your recorder yet, you'll find this appendix a valuable list of features and tips that you can use while shopping for the right drive.

Picking the Features You Need

This section will help you determine which features you should look for when shopping for your drive.

Internal or External?

For most of us, an internal DVD recorder is likely the right choice. A number of reasons have made internal drives popular:

dvds & cds

- An internal drive doesn't require a separate power supply.
- It doesn't take any additional space on your desktop.
- An internal recorder is typically cheaper than an external model.

On the other hand, if you need these specific advantages, an external recorder may be right for you:

- External drives are much easier to install, because you don't have to open your computer's case.
- Some computers—such as a typical laptop or an "all-in-one" computer, such as the Apple iMac—may not have internal bays for expansion (or you may have internal drive bays, but they may be all used for other devices).
- An external drive can be carried with you on trips.
- External drives are easy to share between computers—for example, a small office with computers that aren't already hooked to a network.

To save money—and if you don't need to transport your drive or if your computer can't be expanded—I usually recommend an internal recorder.

Comparing Drive Speeds

In general, today's DVD recorders will record all of the common formats that I've discussed in the book: audio, data, mixed-mode, CD-Extra, Video CD, and UDF/packet-writing. However, how fast they can record a disc is a different matter! The more discs you record, the more that extra speed will save you time.

Drive reading and recording speeds are measured by something I call the *X factor*—for example, a drive advertised as 12x/10x/40x means the drive has a 12x recording speed, a 10x recording speed with rewriteable discs (which is a significantly slower process), and a 40x read-only speed. The faster the X factor, the better the drive's performance (and typically, the more expensive). CD-ROM and DVD-ROM read-only drives usually carry only one X number, which refers to the speed that a disc can be read.

So what does the X factor stand for, anyway? It's a multiplier of the original transfer rate for the first single-speed CD-ROM drives that appeared in 1980, which was 150 KB per second. To illustrate, a 40x CD-ROM can transfer data at a whopping 6,000 KB per second.

The Advantage of Burn-Proof Recording

I've mentioned burn-proof recording earlier in the book, but it's worth a reminder here: If at all possible, *make sure that your new drive has this feature*, because burn-proof recording will eliminate buffer underrun errors and prevent you from wasting blank discs. Additionally, a drive with burn-proof recording can be used while you're working on other tasks—for example, I've often recorded discs while working on book manuscripts in Microsoft Word, and because of this feature, I've never encountered a recording error (even when Word was making heavy use of the processor and hard drive when loading, saving, and virus checking documents).

Luckily, burn-proof recording is now a common feature on the latest drives, and you no longer have to pay a king's ransom and buy the most expensive drive to enjoy the benefits of burn-proof recording.

Choosing a Larger Data Buffer

Your recorder's data buffer (sometimes called a *cache* or *internal RAM*) is designed as a "storage area" for data that has already been read from your hard drive but isn't ready to be recorded to the disc yet. A buffer is necessary because today's hard drives can read and transfer data much faster than your recorder—therefore, the buffer helps ensure that the entire recording process is as efficient as possible by providing your recorder with a steady supply of ones and zeroes to write to the disc!

However, a closer inspection of the specifications for today's drives shows that many recorders offer far more data buffer space than others—the storage space can range anywhere from 512 KB of buffer memory on the low end to 1, 2, or even 4 MB on better drives. Just remember that the larger the buffer your drive has, the better will be

dvds & cds

your drive's performance—particularly at its maximum recording speeds or if you're using your computer for other tasks while you're recording.

Shopping for Audio Controls

If you're an audiophile and you've added a great-sounding expensive speaker system to your PC, I heartily recommend that you consider investing in a recorder that has a full set of audio CD drive controls (along with the ubiquitous volume control and headphone jack that appear on every drive). You'll find it much easier to use these buttons, rather than clicking on the buttons on your audio CD player program!

Audio CD drive controls usually include track-forward and track-reverse buttons, a pause button, and a play button, mirroring the controls on a standard audio CD player.

tip **If you're wondering where to find all of these features and specifications on the drives you're considering, visit each manufacturer's Web site—most drive manufacturers now provide a complete description and specification sheet on each model they make. Use the Google search engine at www.google.com to search the Web for specific drive models; you'll be amazed at the range of information you find, including various newsgroup messages and comments from other drive owners. You can also find details—and often, even compare drive features on one screen—on www.buy.com, www.pricewatch.com, or www.computershopper.com. Finally, don't forget that computer magazines will feature hardware comparisons, so check your favorite magazine's Web site for any reviews that cover the models you're considering.**

The Importance of Technical Support

It's a common mistake, and most computer owners shopping for new hardware have made it: neglecting to evaluate the technical support available for your new recorder (or any hardware device) before you buy it. (Believe me, this is a tough lesson to learn *after* the fact.) Certainly, most manufacturers appear to offer the same range of technical support services—usually including a Web site, telephone support, and updated drivers—but these services are definitely not "created equal."

For example, consider the questions you should be asking about the telephone tech support that's provided with the drive you're evaluating:

- Is telephone tech support available at all, or is all tech support handled by e-mail?
- Is a toll-free phone number available for voice support?
- Is voice support free, or will you be charged for it?
- Can you get support 24 hours/7 days a week, or will you have to wait for business hours during a weekday?

When you visit the company's Web site, check for the availability of updated drivers and firmware updates. Are they released regularly, or is the last driver listed with a date of 1999? Other Web criteria to check include:

- Does the manufacturer provide a "bulletin board" message area for owners to converse together online?
- Are there FAQ (short for *Frequently Asked Questions*) files you can read with common problems and solutions?
- Is there a knowledge base you can search for answers to your technical questions?
- Are specifications and user manuals provided for downloading?

Remember, it's just as important to "peek behind the curtain" when it comes to technical support as it is when comparing hardware features.

Tips for Buying Your Recorder Online

Most of us are familiar with the advantages of buying locally—immediate gratification and easier returns for defective hardware—but you're practically guaranteed to get a better price by buying your new drive online. I'll end this appendix with the top four tips I provide my readers when they ask about buying a drive online.

dvds & cds

- **Be cautious about buying refurbished hardware.** I know that refurbished—read that as "used and repaired"—hardware is very inexpensive, compared with the same hardware bought new, but make sure you check the return policy for a refurbished recorder, and buy refurbished components only from a reputable company. You have no idea what broke the first time, and you'll be taking a chance if you can't return a "lemon" that looked like a good deal.

- **Compare prices before you buy.** This sounds like a given, but many folks buy from the very first Web site they visit (or from a site with a name they recognize). Don't get me wrong—building an ongoing relationship with a Web store you trust is a good thing, and I have a number of favorite stores that I always visit— but would you buy something *locally* without checking other stores for their prices? The same holds true online; for example, I recently saved myself over $100 by doing 20 minutes of comparison pricing on a new computer. As a starting point, I heartily recommend www.pricewatch.com, where you can search for a specific drive and see at a glance the range of prices available from popular Web stores.

- **Don't buy online without a secure connection.** The chance of a hacker obtaining your credit card number and personal information is relatively slight, but it is certainly possible. Therefore, I buy only from stores that offer a secure, encrypted connection. When information is encrypted, a hacker has a much harder time intercepting your data as it's being transmitted to the Web site. Both Internet Explorer and Netscape Navigator tell you whether a site has an encrypted (or secure) connection: Check to make sure that your browser is displaying a closed padlock icon on the status bar at the bottom of the screen. If the connection isn't secure and you're being prompted for your credit card number or personal information, find another store!

- **Avoid high shipping costs.** Many online stores now default to hideously expensive next-day or overnight shipping for your drive—usually, you can save up to half of those shipping expenses if you wait a day or two more for your recorder and pick ground shipping! Pay close attention to what you're paying *before* you click the Buy button.

appendix

C

Using Musicmatch Jukebox

*Although most PC owners are familiar with MP3 files—
what they are and how to get them—there are a number of
folks I've met who have only listened to audio CDs on their
computers. If you've never played or extracted (or "ripped")
tracks from an existing audio CD in your collection, then
this appendix will guide you through both procedures in two
projects; we'll use Musicmatch Jukebox, my favorite MP3
player/utility/toolbox program!*

 tip You can get a free copy of the Basic version of Jukebox
by visiting the Web site at www.musicmatch.com.

Project: Extracting MP3 Files from Existing Audio CDs using Jukebox

Musicmatch Jukebox makes it easy to rip a track from an audio CD
using your DVD recorder; when the process has finished, you'll
have the track in MP3 format on your hard drive.

dvds & cds

caution   You can only extract tracks from audio CDs that you own—for example, to create a compilation CD of your favorite songs from a single artist. If you didn't buy an audio CD, you're violating copyright law by ripping tracks from it.

Requirements

- An installed copy of Jukebox
- An audio CD

✔ **Follow these steps to rip MP3 files:**

1. Run Jukebox (under Windows XP, click Start->All Programs-> Musicmatch->Musicmatch Jukebox) to display the program's main window, as shown in Figure C.1.

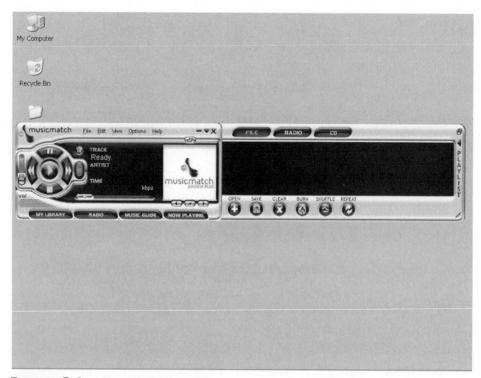

FIGURE C.1   The Jukebox window.

2. Load the audio CD into your DVD recorder, and Jukebox automatically displays the track names and begins playing the CD (Figure C.2). Since we don't want to listen to the disc right now, click the Stop button on the circular control panel to stop the playback (it has a square icon, just like an audio CD player).

3. Next, it's time to pick the proper settings for our MP3 recording—in this case, I want to rip Track 1, "Movin' In" (in my opinion, one of the best songs Chicago ever performed). Click the Options menu and choose Recorder->Settings to display the dialog you see in Figure C.3. Choose MP3 recording format, CD Quality (128 kbps) and make sure that the Recording Source is set to your DVD recorder. Click OK to save any changes that you've made.

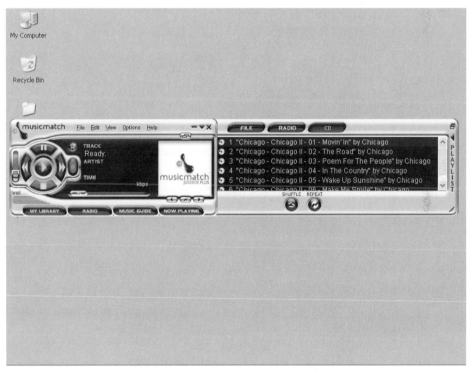

FIGURE C.2 Jukebox begins playing my Chicago II CD.

dvds & cds

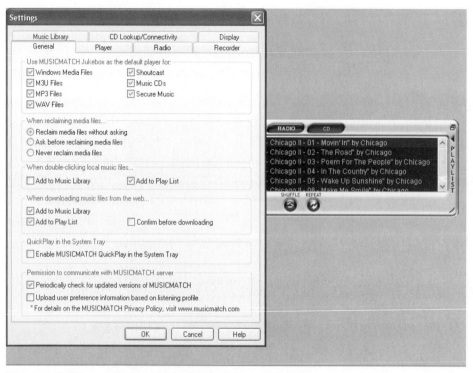

FIGURE C.3   Setting recording options for Jukebox.

4. Now it's time to start the actual extraction! Click the red Recording button on the circular control panel to display the Recorder
panel (Figure C.4). To mark a track for recording, leave it checked—
clear the checkbox next to each track you want to skip. In this case,
we want to make sure that only the first track is checked.

> *tip* By default, Jukebox marks all the tracks on the disc for
> recording—if you only want one or two tracks, however, you
> can click the None button to uncheck all of the tracks, and then click
> the checkboxes for just the tracks you want.

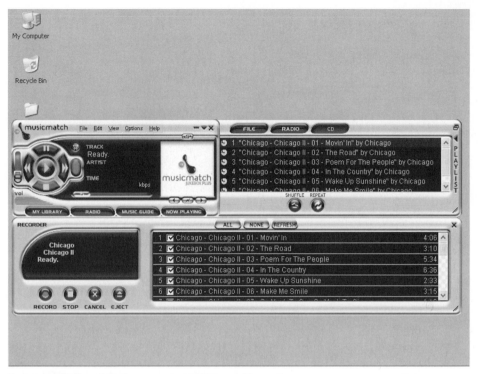

FIGURE C.4 Jukebox is now in "Record" mode.

5. Click the red Record button on the Recorder panel. (If this is the first time you've ripped tracks with Jukebox, the program performs a short test and calibration procedure, then continues.) You can watch the progress of the extraction—Jukebox displays a progress bar next to the track name (Figure C.5).

tip If you're using Windows Me or Windows XP, Jukebox stores the MP3 files you've downloaded in the My Music folder in the My Documents folder. A separate folder is automatically created with the artist and album name to keep things organized. Neat!

dvds & cds

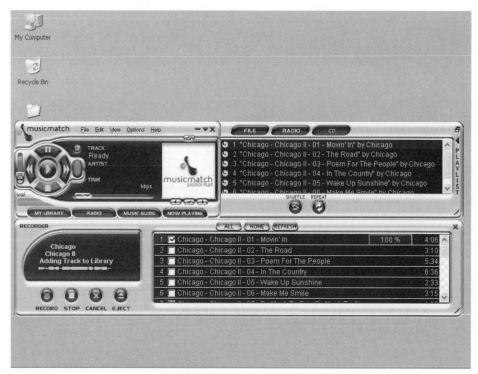

FIGURE C.5   The extraction progress bar lets you monitor the ripping process.

Project: **Extracting MP3 Files from Existing Audio CDs using Jukebox**

Now that I've demonstrated how to rip MP3 files, let's use Jukebox to listen to them.

> *tip* If you're using a PC running Windows Me or XP and you don't have Jukebox installed, you can also use Windows Media Player to listen to MP3s; just double-click on the file to launch Windows Media Player.

Requirements

- An installed copy of Jukebox
- MP3 files on your hard drive

✔ **Follow these steps to listen to MP3 files:**

1. Run Jukebox and open an Explorer window.

2. Drag the MP3 files you want to hear from the Explorer window and drop them in the Jukebox Playlist pane at the right, and they'll be automatically added. Although Jukebox will automatically begin playing the first song in the list, you can continue to add MP3s and they'll appear at the end of the Playlist.

3. Click and drag the Volume slider control to set the desired volume. You can also use the Previous, Next and Pause keys to move through the Playlist or pause the playback while you're away from your PC.

tip **Alternately, you can simply double-click on an MP3 file in Explorer, which automatically launches Jukebox and plays the song—however, use the procedure I've demonstrated to add multiple tracks and create a Playlist.**

dvds & cds

Glossary

A

Adapter card A plug-in computer circuit board that you install to add functionality, such as a FireWire port adapter card.

Audio cable All DVD and CD recorders have a connector for an audio cable that runs from the drive to your computer's sound card—this cable is used when you're playing an audio CD using your recorder.

B

Binary Computers use the binary language to store data (including the data on DVDs and CDs) and to communicate with each other. Binary data has only two values, zero and one.

Bootable CD A CD-ROM containing all of the operating system and support files necessary to boot a computer without a hard drive. Bootable CD-ROMs use the El Torito format.

Burn-proof recording A feature offered on most new recorders that allows the drive to pause during recording when the data transfer rate falls below an acceptable level—for example, when your computer is busy opening a large spreadsheet. A drive with burn-proof recording will not return "buffer underrun" errors.

Byte A single character of text stored by your computer (on a DVD, in RAM, or on your hard drive).

C

Case Your computer's metal cover—when you install additional hardware, you can remove the case by unscrewing it or opening a hinged door.

dvds & cds

CD-Extra A specialized mixed-mode disc that contains both audio tracks and a data track; unlike a standard mixed-mode disc, a CD-Extra disc can also be played in a regular audio CD player (the audio track is recorded first on the disc).

CD-R Short for *Compact Disc-Recordable*. The first CD-recording technology that was generally available to the public; a CD recorder can store computer data and digital audio on a CD-R by creating a pattern on a layer of dye with a laser beam. Unlike a reusable CD-RW disc, a CD-R disc can be recorded only once.

CD-ROM Short for *Compact Disc-Read-Only Memory*. A CD-ROM is a CD with computer data recorded for use on a computer.

CD-RW Short for *Compact Disc-Rewriteable*. A recordable CD technology that uses an amorphous crystalline layer—the crystalline layer can be changed over and over, so the disc can be erased and rewritten.

cDVD A specialized Video CD format supported by the MyDVD recording program. cDVDs can hold digital video and can be displayed on most computers running Windows.

Chapter DVD movie discs are usually separated into sections called *chapters* that allow the viewer to jump from one major section of the film to another.

Crystalline layer The layer of amorphous crystals in a CD-RW disc that darkens or discolors when struck by a recorder's laser beam. Unlike the CD-R disc's dye layer, the crystalline layer in a CD-RW disc can be "reset," and the disc can be used again.

D

Data buffer Internal memory (similar to your computer's RAM) used by your CD or DVD recorder to store data from your hard drive until it's ready to be recorded. Generally, the larger the data buffer, the fewer errors your drive will encounter while recording discs.

Defragmenting The process of optimizing your hard drive by reading the files it contains and rewriting them in contiguous form, one after another. Files written contiguously can be read faster and more efficiently—a good idea when burning files from your hard drive to a CD or DVD.

Digital audio extraction The process of copying tracks from an existing audio CD to your hard drive as WAV or MP3 digital audio files. Extraction is often referred to as *ripping*.

Disc-at-Once When recording in Disc-at-Once mode, your drive writes the entire disc at once without turning the recording laser off between tracks. Older CD recorders may not be able to record discs in Disc-at-Once mode.

Disc image A file stored on your hard drive that includes all of the information necessary to create a CD or DVD. You can burn copies of a disc directly from a disc image.

Digital video Full-motion video stored on your hard drive (usually in AVI, MPEG, or MOV format). Digital video can be recorded to CDs and DVDs and viewed on your computer or your DVD player.

DVD Short for *digital video disc*. A DVD disc can hold anywhere from 4.7 GB to 17 GB. DVD discs can hold computer data, digital audio, and movies in MPEG format.

DVD+R/DVD-R Standard DVD recording formats that typically store 4.7 GB on a single disc. DVD+R and DVD-R discs cannot be rewritten.

DVD-RAM A standard DVD recording format that can store up to 9.4 GB on a single disc. DVD-RAM discs are rewriteable.

DVD+RW/DVD-RW Standard DVD recording formats that typically store 4.7 GB on a single disc. DVD+RW and DVD-RW discs are rewriteable.

Dye layer CD recorders use a laser to discolor the dye layer in a CD-R, which allows it to scatter laser light in the same way as a pit on a commercially made CD-ROM.

E

EIDE Short for *Enhanced Integrated Drive Electronics*. The most popular interface standard for connecting internal hard drives and CD/DVD drives to your PC. A typical PC has both primary and secondary EIDE connectors; each connector can handle two EIDE devices (for a total of four drives).

El Torito format A format standard used to record bootable CD-ROM discs for use in PCs.

External drive A device such as a hard drive or DVD recorder that is placed next to your computer (instead of inside the case). External drives are connected to your computer by a cable and usually need their own power supplies.

F

FireWire A type of connection that allows external devices such as recorders, DV camcorders, and scanners to exchange data with your computer at a very fast rate. FireWire connections also allow you to control a DV camcorder from your computer.

dvds & cds

FireWire is the common name for the IEEE-1394 standard, which was originally developed by Apple.

Formatting The process of preparing a hard drive, floppy disk, CD-RW, DVD-RAM, or DVD+RW/DVD-RW disc to store data. UDF/packet-writing programs such as HP DLA and Adaptec's DirectCD also require you to format a disc before you can use it.

G

Gigabyte (GB) A unit of data equal to 1,024 MB (megabytes).

H

Hard drive An internal or external device that stores data and programs, allowing you to save, move, and delete files.

HTML Short for *Hypertext Markup Language*. The programming language used to create pages for the World Wide Web. HTML can also be used to create menus for CD and DVD discs.

HTML Editor A text-based program used to create or edit HTML pages.

I

Incremental multisession disc A multisession disc with data imported from a previous session. Incremental multisession discs allow you to update existing data on a disc that you've already recorded.

Interface A standard method of connecting a hardware device to your computer. For example, DVD and CD recorders typically use EIDE, FireWire, and USB interfaces.

Internal drive A hardware device that fits inside your computer's case—for example, a hard drive, floppy drive, or DVD recorder.

ISO 9660 The original CD-ROM file system standard that is supported by virtually all computer operating systems. ISO 9660 is a good choice when recording a CD-ROM that will be read on many different types of computers, but it doesn't support long filenames.

J

Jewel box A plastic storage case for a compact disc. Jewel boxes can contain a cover and back insert. DVDs should not be stored in a standard CD jewel box; always use a DVD storage box instead.

Joliet file system The CD-ROM file system developed by Microsoft for Windows 95. Joliet allows long filenames of up to 64 characters that can include multiple periods and spaces.

Jumper A small wire and plastic electrical crossover designed to connect two pins on a computer circuit board. Most EIDE drives use a jumper to set the drive's master/slave configuration during installation.

K

Kilobyte (KB) A unit of data equal to 1,024 bytes.

L

Land An area on the surface of a compact disc that reflects light. Recorded CDs and DVDs use a clear area within the dye or crystalline layer to act as a land.

M

Master A configuration setting used with EIDE drives to specify that the drive is the primary device on the EIDE cable. Your recorder should be set to "single drive, master unit" (if it's the only drive on the cable) or "multiple drive, master unit" (if it's the primary drive and there is another EIDE device on the same cable).

Megabyte (MB) A unit of data equal to 1,024 KB.

Mixed-mode disc A CD recording format that combines both digital audio tracks and a data track on one disc. Because the first track is recorded as computer data, a mixed-mode disc can't be played on an audio CD player.

Motherboard Your computer's main circuit board—it holds the processor and RAM chips, and most of the circuitry. You can expand your computer's features by plugging adapter cards into your motherboard.

dvds & cds

MP3 The most common and popular digital audio format for storing music on your hard drive (or as files on a CD or DVD). With a recorder, you can burn audio CDs with CD-quality stereo MP3 files.

MPEG Short for *Moving Pictures Expert Group*. The video format used on commercial DVD movie discs. MPEG video can also be recorded to Video CDs.

Multisession A multisession disc (sometimes called *CD-ROM XA*) can carry separate discrete recording sessions, each of which can be accessed one at a time. There are two different types of multisession discs: incremental (where only the last session is available) and multivolume (where each of the sessions can be read). Older CD-ROM drives may not be able to read multisession discs.

Multitasking Running more than one program or application on your computer at once.

Multivolume multisession disc A multisession format that stores data in separate volumes on a single disc, each of which can be accessed one at a time.

N

Network A connected group of computers that can share files, printers, recorders, and modems through a cable or wireless system. Recording over a network is usually not a good idea.

P

Packet-writing (Also called *UDF recording*) A method of recording data directly to a disc, without running special recording software. A program such as HP DLA allows you to copy files directly to the recorder, just as you would with a hard drive.

Pit An area on the surface of a compact disc that scatters light (without reflecting it). Recorded CDs and DVDs use an opaque area within the dye or crystalline layer to represent a pit.

R

RAM Short for *random access memory*. Your computer's RAM temporarily stores programs and data while your computer needs them; when the computer is turned off, the information stored in RAM is lost.

Red Book The common name for the international standard that specifies the recording layout of audio CDs. In order to be read by an audio CD player, an audio disc must conform to the Red Book standard.

S

Safe zone The viewable area of a digital video clip when it's displayed on a television set.

Screen printing A method of labeling CD and DVD discs involving the application of layers of different inks in stages through stencils; the end result is a single multicolored image.

Secure connection An encrypted connection to a Web site that protects your personal data from a hacker; never use an online Web store unless it offers a secure connection.

Slave A configuration setting used with EIDE drives to specify that the drive is the secondary device on the EIDE cable. A DVD recorder can be set to "multiple drive, slave unit" if it's the secondary drive and another EIDE device acts as the primary master device on the same cable.

Slideshow A display program that shows images and video on your computer's monitor.

Static electricity Residual electricity that can damage your computer's hardware. Because static electricity can be stored in the body, never touch your computer's motherboard or adapter cards without first touching the metal chassis of your computer.

T

Tag A separate line in an HTML file that determines the display or specifies the contents of the page.

Thumbnail A miniature representation of a much larger image—a display of thumbnail images makes it easy to search for a specific digital photograph on a disc or your hard drive.

Timeline A control used in video editing that allows you to "assemble" and synchronize the image, soundtrack, and any transitions or effects into a cohesive whole.

Track On an audio CD, a track is a single section of audio (typically, a single song) that you can immediately access—data CDs also store information in one or more tracks.

Track-at-once A disc recording mode where the laser writes each data or audio track individually. The laser is turned off between tracks.

dvds & cds

Transition An optical effect placed between two video clips to act as a segue; common effects include dissolves, fades, and wipes.

U

UDF Short for *Universal Disc Format* (also called *packet-writing*). A method of recording data directly to a disc, without running special recording software. A program such as HP DLA allows you to copy files directly to the recorder, just as you would with a hard drive.

UPC Short for *Universal Product Code*. A unique number assigned to every commercial audio CD. Most audio CD player programs and audio CD cataloging programs can use the UPC number to identify the disc and download the artist, title, and track information, if necessary.

USB Short for *Universal Serial Bus*. A connection for external devices such as hard drives, scanners, digital cameras, and CD/DVD recorders on both the PC and the Macintosh. USB devices can be plugged in and used without rebooting your computer.

V

Video CD A recording format that allows you to store MPEG digital video with a simple menu for viewing on a DVD player or video CD player.

Virtual memory An increase in the amount of RAM available to your computer, accomplished by your operating system temporarily using hard drive space to store additional data. With virtual memory, Windows can run applications that require more RAM than you physically have available in your computer.

W

WAV Microsoft's standard format for digital sound files. CD-quality WAV files can be recorded in Red Book audio CD format, using most CD recording software.

Index

dvds & cds

339

dvds & cds

dvds & cds

Indexes for
The Official
HP Guides

Index for
hp pavilion pcs
made easy

hp pavilion pcs

hp pavilion pcs

Index for

creating your own great

dvds & cds

 integrated

hp education training

it just works

®
invent

HP's world-class education and training offers hands on education solutions including:

- Linux
- HP-UX System and Network Administration
- Advanced HP-UX System Administration
- IT Service Management using advanced Internet technologies
- Microsoft Windows NT/2000
- Internet/Intranet
- MPE/iX
- Database Administration
- Software Development

HP's new IT Professional Certification program provides rigorous technical qualification for specific IT job roles including HP-UX System Administration, Network Management, Unix/NT Servers and Applications Management, and IT Service Management.

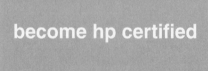 become hp certified

 http://education.hp.com

free subscription

in vent

Want to know about new products, services and solutions from Hewlett-Packard Company — as soon as they're invented?

Need information about new HP services to help you implement new or existing products?

Looking for HP's newest solution to a specific challenge in your business?

inview features the latest from HP!

inview

4 easy ways to subscribe, and it's FREE:

- **fax** complete and fax the form below to (651) 430-3388, or

- **online** sign up online at www.hp.com/go/inview, or

- **email** complete the information below and send to hporders@earthlink.net, or

- **mail** complete and mail the form below to:

Twin Cities Fulfillment Center
Hewlett-Packard Company
P.O. Box 408
Stillwater, MN 55082

reply now and don't miss an issue!

name	title
company	dept./mail stop
address	
city	state zip
email signature	date

please indicate your industry below:

☐ accounting	☐ healthcare/medical	☐ online services	☐ telecommunications
☐ education	☐ legal	☐ real estate	☐ transport and travel
☐ financial services	☐ manufacturing	☐ retail/wholesale distrib	☐ utilities
☐ government	☐ publishing/printing	☐ technical	☐ other:_____

LICENSE AGREEMENT AND LIMITED WARRANTY

READ THE FOLLOWING TERMS AND CONDITIONS CAREFULLY BEFORE OPENING THIS SOFTWARE PACKAGE. THIS LEGAL DOCUMENT IS AN AGREEMENT BETWEEN YOU AND PRENTICE-HALL, INC. (THE "COMPANY"). BY OPENING THIS SEALED SOFTWARE PACKAGE, YOU ARE AGREEING TO BE BOUND BY THESE TERMS AND CONDITIONS. IF YOU DO NOT AGREE WITH THESE TERMS AND CONDITIONS, DO NOT OPEN THE SOFTWARE PACKAGE. PROMPTLY RETURN THE UNOPENED SOFTWARE PACKAGE AND ALL ACCOMPANYING ITEMS TO THE PLACE YOU OBTAINED THEM FOR A FULL REFUND OF ANY SUMS YOU HAVE PAID.

1.　　　**GRANT OF LICENSE:** In consideration of your payment of the license fee, which is part of the price you paid for this product, and your agreement to abide by the terms and conditions of this Agreement, the Company grants to you a nonexclusive right to use and display the copy of the enclosed software program (hereinafter the "software") on a single computer (i.e., with a single CPU) at a single location so long as you comply with the terms of this Agreement. The Company reserves all rights not expressly granted to you under this Agreement.

2.　　　**OWNERSHIP OF SOFTWARE:** You own only the magnetic or physical media (the enclosed software) on which the software is recorded or fixed, but the Company retains all the rights, title, and ownership to the software recorded on the original software copy(ies) and all subsequent copies of the software, regardless of the form or media on which the original or other copies may exist. This license is not a sale of the original software or any copy to you.

3.　　　**COPY RESTRICTIONS:** This software and the accompanying printed materials and user manual (the "Documentation") are the subject of copyright. You may not copy the Documentation or the software, except that you may make a single copy of the software for backup or archival purposes only. You may be held legally responsible for any copying or copyright infringement which is caused or encouraged by your failure to abide by the terms of this restriction.

4.　　　**USE RESTRICTIONS:** You may not network the software or otherwise use it on more than one computer or computer terminal at the same time. You may physically transfer the software from one computer to another provided that the software is used on only one computer at a time. You may not distribute copies of the software or Documentation to others. You may not reverse engineer, disassemble, decompile, modify, adapt, translate, or create derivative works based on the software or the Documentation without the prior written consent of the Company.

5.　　　**TRANSFER RESTRICTIONS:** The enclosed software is licensed only to you and may not be transferred to any one else without the prior written consent of the Company. Any unauthorized transfer of the software shall result in the immediate termination of this Agreement.

6.　　　**TERMINATION:** This license is effective until terminated. This license will terminate automatically without notice from the Company and become null and void if you fail to comply with any provisions or limitations of this license. Upon termination, you shall destroy the Documentation and all copies of the software. All provisions of this Agreement as to warranties, limitation of liability, remedies or damages, and our ownership rights shall survive termination.

7.　　　**MISCELLANEOUS:** This Agreement shall be construed in accordance with the laws of the United States of America and the State of New York and shall benefit the Company, its affiliates, and assignees.

8.　　　**LIMITED WARRANTY AND DISCLAIMER OF WARRANTY:** The Company warrants that the software, when properly used in accordance with the Documentation, will operate in substantial conformity with the description of the software set forth in the Documentation. The Company does not warrant that the software will meet your requirements or that the operation of the software will be uninterrupted or error-free. The Company warrants that the media on which the software is delivered shall be free from defects in materials and workmanship under normal use for a period of thirty (30) days from the date of your purchase. Your only remedy and the Company's only obligation under these limited warranties is, at the Company's option, return of the warranted item for a refund of any amounts paid by you or replacement of the item. Any replacement of software or media under the warranties shall not extend the original warranty period. The limited warranty set forth above shall not apply to any software which the Company determines in good faith has been subject to misuse, neglect, improper installation, repair, alteration, or damage by you. EXCEPT FOR THE EXPRESSED WARRANTIES SET FORTH ABOVE, THE COMPANY DISCLAIMS ALL WARRANTIES, EXPRESS OR IMPLIED, INCLUDING WITHOUT LIMITATION, THE IMPLIED WARRANTIES OF MERCHANTABILITY AND FITNESS FOR A PARTICULAR PURPOSE. EXCEPT FOR THE EXPRESS WARRANTY SET FORTH ABOVE, THE COMPANY DOES NOT WARRANT, GUARANTEE, OR MAKE ANY REPRESENTATION REGARDING THE USE OR THE RESULTS OF THE USE OF THE SOFTWARE IN TERMS OF ITS CORRECTNESS, ACCURACY, RELIABILITY, CURRENTNESS, OR OTHERWISE.

IN NO EVENT, SHALL THE COMPANY OR ITS EMPLOYEES, AGENTS, SUPPLIERS, OR CONTRACTORS BE LIABLE FOR ANY INCIDENTAL, INDIRECT, SPECIAL, OR CONSEQUENTIAL DAMAGES ARISING OUT OF OR IN CONNECTION WITH THE LICENSE GRANTED UNDER THIS AGREEMENT, OR FOR LOSS OF USE, LOSS OF DATA, LOSS OF INCOME OR PROFIT, OR OTHER LOSSES, SUSTAINED AS A RESULT OF INJURY TO ANY PERSON, OR LOSS OF OR DAMAGE TO PROPERTY, OR CLAIMS OF THIRD PARTIES, EVEN IF THE COMPANY OR AN AUTHORIZED REPRESENTATIVE OF THE COMPANY HAS BEEN ADVISED OF THE POSSIBILITY OF SUCH DAMAGES. IN NO EVENT SHALL LIABILITY OF THE COMPANY FOR DAMAGES WITH RESPECT TO THE SOFTWARE EXCEED THE AMOUNTS ACTUALLY PAID BY YOU, IF ANY, FOR THE SOFTWARE.

SOME JURISDICTIONS DO NOT ALLOW THE LIMITATION OF IMPLIED WARRANTIES OR LIABILITY FOR INCIDENTAL, INDIRECT, SPECIAL, OR CONSEQUENTIAL DAMAGES, SO THE ABOVE LIMITATIONS MAY NOT ALWAYS APPLY. THE WARRANTIES IN THIS AGREEMENT GIVE YOU SPECIFIC LEGAL RIGHTS AND YOU MAY ALSO HAVE OTHER RIGHTS WHICH VARY IN ACCORDANCE WITH LOCAL LAW.

ACKNOWLEDGMENT

YOU ACKNOWLEDGE THAT YOU HAVE READ THIS AGREEMENT, UNDERSTAND IT, AND AGREE TO BE BOUND BY ITS TERMS AND CONDITIONS. YOU ALSO AGREE THAT THIS AGREEMENT IS THE COMPLETE AND EXCLUSIVE STATEMENT OF THE AGREEMENT BETWEEN YOU AND THE COMPANY AND SUPERSEDES ALL PROPOSALS OR PRIOR AGREEMENTS, ORAL, OR WRITTEN, AND ANY OTHER COMMUNICATIONS BETWEEN YOU AND THE COMPANY OR ANY REPRESENTATIVE OF THE COMPANY RELATING TO THE SUBJECT MATTER OF THIS AGREEMENT.

Should you have any questions concerning this Agreement or if you wish to contact the Company for any reason, please contact in writing at the address below.

Robin Short
Prentice Hall PTR
One Lake Street
Upper Saddle River, New Jersey 07458

About the CD

To install this software, place the CD into your CD-ROM drive. If you are using Windows, the Setup program should automatically start up (if it doesn't, just navigate to your CD drive under *My Computer* and double-click *Setup*). The Setup program will then guide you through the rest of the steps to install the software.

If you are using a Macintosh, just drag the *Printing Projects* folder onto your *Applications* folder on your hard drive.

In either case, you will need a minimum of 150 MB of free hard drive space to install all of these remarkable printing projects.

After you have installed the software, double-click the *Printing Projects* kitty icon (in Windows, a shortcut will be created on your desktop and a program group icon will appear under the Start/Programs menu) to run the program. *Please note: It may take a minute or two for the program to begin. Note, too, that the program runs off of your hard disk and you do not need the CD in your CD drive to run the program.*

The first time you run your *Printing Projects* program, it checks to see whether you already have Adobe Acrobat Reader installed. Acrobat Reader is needed to view and print all of the project files. If you don't already have it installed, your *Printing Projects* program will launch Adobe's (free) installer to allow you to install Acrobat Reader. If that is the case, you will need to re-launch *Printing Projects* after you finish installing Acrobat Reader, and the fun can then begin!

Using the program itself is very easy and intuitive. Just choose the project category you are interested in by clicking once on its icon. Submenus will appear to allow you to further refine your choice,

until you find just the project you are after. If you are confused at any step of the way, just look to the bottom of the screen where there will be a helpful hint to tell you what to do next. After you finally get a project open, you can print it by clicking on the Acrobat Reader printer icon (again, there is a hint in the program to show you how it looks). Some files have instructions included right in the project file. Some are more complex (such as iron-ons), and those will have separate (also printable) instructions. There are buttons for all such options along the top of the screen. One such button, the orange *Select a Project* button, opens a drop down menu that will allow you to select from different project variations or designs. Click on it to select a particular project.

Another button, the green *Helpful Products* button, suggests a few products that will help you create the project you are making. There's even a Web link there (in case you have Internet access) that takes you right to the Hewlett-Packard online store where you can shop for those products or other helpful printing products.

Also, there are *Back* and *Home* buttons that you can use to navigate back to a previous screen or to the home screen—just like a Web browser. Finally, use the *Exit* button to quit the program when you are finished.

It's all self explanatory, and LOTS of fun, so experiment, navigate, print, create, and have fun with *Printing Projects Made Fun & Easy*.

Technical Support: Prentice Hall does not offer technical support for this software. However, if there is a problem with the media, you may obtain a replacement copy by e-mailing us with your problem at: disc_exchange@prenhall.com.